LINES OF FLIGHT

POST-CONTEMPORARY INTERVENTIONS
SERIES EDITORS:
STANLEY FISH AND FREDRIC JAMESON

LINES OF FLIGHT

Discursive Time and Countercultural Desire

in the Work of Thomas Pynchon

Stefan Mattessich

Duke University Press   Durham and London 2002

© 2002 Duke University Press   All rights reserved

Typeset in Quadraat by Keystone Typesetting, Inc.
Library of Congress Cataloging-in-Publication Data
appear on the last printed page of this book.
An earlier version of chapter 1 first appeared in the journal
ELH 65 (1998), and an earlier version of chapter 2 first
appeared in Postmodern Culture 8, no. 2 (May 1998). Chapter 7
is a considerably reworked piece based on a review-essay
published in Postmodern Culture 8, no. 1 (September 1997).

To Thomas A. Vogler and Hayden White

CONTENTS

Introduction 1

1 Imperium, Misogyny, and Postmodern Parody in *V.* 23

2 Ekphrasis, Escape, and Countercultural Desire in
   The Crying of Lot 49 43

3 Turning Around the Origin in *Gravity's Rainbow*:
   Parody, Preterition, Paranoia, and Other Polymera 70

4 A Close Reading of Part 1, Episode 19, of *Gravity's Rainbow* 95

5 Docile Bodies and the Body without Organs:
   Gravity's *Gravity's Rainbow* 133

6 Totality and the Repetition of Difference: Rereading the 1960s
   in *Vineland* 207

7 A Vigilant Folly: Lines of Flight in *Mason & Dixon* 231

   Conclusion: Toward a Theory of the Counterculture 246

   Notes 255

   Works Cited 285

   Index 289

LINES OF FLIGHT

INTRODUCTION

Near the end of Thomas Pynchon's *Gravity's Rainbow*, set in the last year of World War II, the narrator recalls one of Tyrone Slothrop's first encounters with Seaman Pig Bodine. The text has by this point begun to fragment into random subsections, tarot card readings of various characters, and political rants on a techno-rational social order. In the encounter described by the narrator, Bodine sings a song he wrote about a nameless sailor "stuck in wartime San Diego" who expresses a desire to escape by "going north, to Humboldt County," California (740). This detail constitutes one of the many proleptic jumps that blur temporal continuity in the novel, since the line of flight it delineates resonates with another and historically later moment in American society: the counterculture's return to the land, to nature, and to a simpler and more communal way of life. Pynchon followed this proleptic impulse to "Vineland" literally in the early 1970s and then again textually in the late 1980s when he wrote *Vineland*. The repetition implied in this movement realizes a textual desire for escape and then textualizes the reality of that escape in a progression and recursion that catches one up in a strangely discursive time. This doubling back in Pynchon's corpus and career underscores how much the delirium that quite literally "strings out" *Gravity's Rainbow* by its end should be understood as a slide from the enounced utterance to the subject of enunciation, or rather to the time of writing itself, to the "present" of a textual recapitulation of history.

This book grew out of a desire to explore the relation between the double nature of writing and the "personal" dimension of the countercultural moment in recent American life—personal not only for Pynchon but for me as well, since my parents also "went north" (to Mendocino) in the early 1970s, catching me up in a movement of escape from the exigencies of modern urban and technocratic life. As a teenager, I started hearing about the famous writer who lived "somewhere up in Humboldt" and whose life echoed my own in this one respect. I ended up, not surprisingly, in graduate school at the University of California–Santa Cruz, writing a comparative dissertation on

Thomas Pynchon and another icon of my countercultural life, William Blake. But even though both the dissertation and this book have been more or less conscious attempts to understand the belief structure immanent to this movement of "escape" in which I have "come of age," it might be hard in the pages that follow to trace this intention with much assurance. Perhaps a certain fidelity to that movement underlies here a mode of digression that almost overwhelms its historical specificity in a welter of French theory. The line of flight on which the time of my own writing can be plotted in effect cancels itself out because self-cancellation is its properly delirious dynamic. The experience of recognizing in redwood trees and California beaches the textures and shapes of a Jean Dubuffet painting, or mingling a rhetoric of vision and prophecy with that of deconstruction or Deleuzian expression, has led me in this book to the principle of deviation, of elliptic or parabolic tangency, that informs the historical and cultural moment under consideration (centered, let us say, around the year 1968).

Pynchon inscribes this principle vividly in the structure of his most celebrated novel, both in the arc of the Rocket's flight and in the ambiguous overlay of "drift" and "submission" that Tyrone Slothrop comes to exemplify in his final "scattering." The novel's devolving and involving overlaid form frames Pynchon's analysis of the postwar period in which the counterculture emerges as one structural effect. The rise of the military-industrial complex, consumerism, bureaucratization and specialization in the workplace, standardization at all levels of social life, the growing influence of the mass media—these features of late capitalism point for Pynchon to a transformation in the cultural time-sense or duration governing identity and place in contemporary America. The trauma of a postwar period inaugurated by World War II, the Holocaust, and the dropping of atomic bombs over Hiroshima and Nagasaki happens, that is, to time itself (or to the schemata of cognitive, social, and political experience) and implicates the subject in a catastrophic history making change much harder to conceptualize or carry out. The "new kind of time" (*Gravity's Rainbow*, 472) that Pynchon expresses in fictional terms reveals itself only symptomatically, only through its own displacement, in what Pynchon might call a "preterite" language that elides and eludes. The concept of "preterition"—a Puritan term for those "passed over" by God's predestinarian grace, opposed to the "elect" members of the community by their intrinsic wretchedness and so linked to low culture, haplessness, failure, even depravity—signifies for the Pynchon of *Gravity's Rainbow* a kind of temporal tense, an ontic state incapable of finding for itself any difference between its own being and the being of language. For those bygone postwar preterites Pynchon writes about and for, the "real" presents itself as a pure formality, a text of enigmatic density in which the absence of context implied by their elliptical condition denotes a context of absence, an abstracted social space in which illusion becomes primary and reference unstable.

This is why the central descriptive category for the counterculture in *Gravity's Rainbow* might be "escape" (with its overtone of escapism) rather than "revolution," a word that implies more coherence than the various political and social movements of the 1960s (at least in the United States) were able to sustain. The failure of those movements to effect substantive change in the structures of power in America can be traced to an incoherence that seized the idea of the political itself. Theodore Roszak suggests the ground for this incoherence when he remarks that protest in the 1960s began paradoxically "not in the failure, but in the success of a high industrial economy. It arose not out of misery but out of plenty; its role was to explore a new range of issues raised by an unprecedented increase in the standard of living" (xii). Affluent society meant for its "disaffiliated" members that rebellion could only take the form of a complex *fulfillment* of that society's desire, could only repeat its plenitude in all the gestures of excess, satiation, or power with which we are familiar. Jimi Hendrix's guitar licks, the crowds at Woodstock, Berkeley love-ins, the Black Panthers armed with machine guns, Abbie Hoffman's guerrilla theater—no matter how outrageous, these actions expressed the deepest superfluous tendencies of the society they outraged, and the critical "exploration" Roszak claims for the counterculture could therefore only take place in a mode of coimplicated experimentation that implied an almost necessary failure, a necessary catching up of oneself in an overflowing time, or rather in an overflowing of time itself.

The principal political mode of the day, one could argue, was an "overstuffing" farce or folly, a satisfaction continually tried if not gotten, an escalation in culture of freedom, of pleasure, of innocence, of the "natural," indeed of any value at all so long as it ceased to be relative to its opposite, exposing in the social field an essentially arbitrary and differential semiotic logic. As Fredric Jameson argues in his influential essay "Periodizing the '60s," this logic entails a schizoid tendency toward pure equivalence, abstraction, or autonomy discernible at many levels of postwar life: in reification and fragmentation on the social and economic level, as local or molecular resistance to totalization on the political level, as artistic abstraction and solipsism on the cultural level, and as the disjunction between sign and referent on the semiotic level. In each case, what can be observed is a crisis of dimension, of the spatial and temporal coordinates for reality itself, which, like the referent, disappear behind "the mirage of some ultimate language of pure signifiers" (*Ideologies of Theory*, 2:202). Pynchon's world finds itself dominated by what Heidegger called "metalanguage," the overdetermination not just of politics, art, science, and philosophy but of everyday life by the drive to install rationality at the place of its (irrational) other, to make reflection unconscious, to make the planned, the organized, and the managed return in our dreams as the ground of being and history. An incorporation of the eye takes place in the individual and in the socius such that social experience becomes double, the scene of a spectacle, suffused by signs and virtualized by the apparatuses of their production and reproduction. Henri Lefebvre, writing in 1968, refers to this process as the institution of a grammatological terrorism that, in making all reference self-referential, commits one to a world of "make-believe" for which "the meaning of life is life without meaning" and "self-realization is a life without a history, total quotidianness, but unseen and evaded" (*Everyday Life*, 122). Everyday life for Lefebvre, unfolding at the heart of language, is, like language, "self-elusive," subtextual, disappearing, the singular point where meaning becomes nonmeaning (or vice versa), contradiction becomes aporia, and the subject confronts his or her own constitutive implication in discourse.

Social movements and cultural strategies of the 1960s understood to varying degrees that the crucial political problem consisted in finding ways to resist this project of a metalinguistic hegemony. Because reality is rational and idealized precisely in the act of fixing its limit, unearthing its artifice, and positing escape (freedom) in or as the nondiscursive element (the irrational, the instinctive, the sexual, the non-Western, the spontaneous, the autonomous, etc.), resistance had to be theorized in relation to a (hetero)logic of capture and complicity. The constraint of implication experienced by "counterhegemonic" groups such as the counterculture, the New Left, the women's movement, the civil rights movement, and the gay rights movement engendered an array of politico-discursive modes dedicated to transforming deep structures of belief, short-circuiting normative representations, and creating cultural spaces for silenced voices to be heard and respected. "Cultural" revolution meant projecting the political into a linguistic element, borrowing its powers of reversibility, its capacities for substitution and displacement, to transfigure the tropes of personhood, sexuality, the family, and community.

Politics as transfiguration—changing how one lived, dressed, thought, related to oneself or to others—implied a convergence in metalanguage, in the drive to actualize the (non)meaning of meaning in a "double" world it only managed to reflect. The price of change was its suspension in a virtual state, its "real" impossibility engendering the impossibility of the real. The counterculture therefore disclosed a "self-elusive" component; it became a symptom, a sign of the times, even exemplary of its time when its refusal of dominant social order, catching itself up in the terms of that order, in effect canceled itself out. This self-cancellation was not simple or uncritical. It signified a complicated and ambivalent engagement with a profoundly overdetermined "time," a reiteration of the symptom of the "pure signifier" and a symptomatic modality of cultural participation that the time in fact demanded.

Gravity's Rainbow sets out to ramify this symbolic dimension of the counterculture, the dreamlike empty form legible in the time's "mindless pleasures," its exacerbations of discourse, its overt travesties of sense and meaning. The novel's stake is always one of a political desire adequate to the immanent rationality of social life, and indeed it could be read as an allegory of this desire insofar as its desire seeks its own end in the metalinguistic systems regulating its appearance. In this book, I attempt to map the singular point of this desire in Pynchon's anarchic literary world, the tip of the Rocket that becomes in *Gravity's Rainbow* the implement of a writing that takes the real as its text. Pynchon's emphasis on the physics of the Rocket's flight underscores a preoccupation with escape that sutures his work to the countercultural withdrawal from dominant society; at the same time, it focuses a displacement in that withdrawal that makes it more than an imaginary escapism, and more than the state of childish "enchantment and playfulness" to which even its most sympathetic theorists (such as Theodore Roszak) allude. The counterculture's intelligence consisted in the projection of a cultural "reverie" that conserves the imaginative capacity to transform the representations on which social reality is based. According to the phenomenologist Gaston Bachelard, whose book *The Poetics of Reverie* was first translated into English in 1969 and stands as an exemplary articulation of its "spaced-out" cultural moment, reverie indeed designates the positivity and fullness of a creative imagination. It "assembles being" around itself in an "awareness without tension" that neutralizes a rationalized time and space (151). As such, it suggests for Bachelard the "confidence" or "easy certainty" of a "cogito" rather than the anxiety of a constitutively split subject, the calm "solidarity" of a poet who incorporates a "happy world" (163) within a space that "does not stop at any frontier" and unites "our being which dreams with the intimacy of the beings which we dream" (162). Reverie for Bachelard presupposes an "ontology of well-being [bien-etre]" in which "one discovers that being is a possession [bien]" (153), and this (good) possession of being (good) in turn conditions the "plasticity of man and his world" (167), their mutual implication in a seamless, undivided unity.

> Truly inhabiting the whole volume of his space, the man of reverie is from anywhere in his world, in an inside which has no outside. It is not without reason that people commonly say that the dreamer is plunged in his reverie. The world no longer poses any opposition to him. The I no longer opposes itself to the world. In reverie there is no more non-I. In reverie, the no no longer has any function: everything is welcome. (167)

The metaphoric connotations of Bachelard's language—reverie as easy, certain, confident, happy, without tension or conflict—are suggestive for an understanding of the "spacey" counterculture, in particular its attempts to stabilize communities of intention (the commune, the rock concert or rock band, Haight Ashbury, the love-in or be-in, the happening, the collective, etc.) that were in principle (if not in fact) inclusive and egalitarian. Indeed the principle of community at work here is clearly marked in the displacement of reverie: in opposing everything, the counterculture opposed opposition itself, argued against a motivated social and political space of extension (the "outside") that excluded a "world" given only in the nonopposability of subject and object, in an interiority stretched to the very horizon of the real. This was the stake in "dropping out": to expose the fundamental ideality of distinction itself (the function of no) and to conserve the "intimate space" in which an imagination of the world becomes possible through a specific type of awareness. One can infer this "cogito" in rhetoric such as the inimitable Abbie Hoffman uses, writing in *Woodstock Nation* before the conspiracy trials that followed the 1968 Democratic National Convention:

> When I appear in the Chicago courtroom, I want to be tried not because I support the National Liberation Front—which I do—but because I have long hair. Not because I support the Black Liberation Movement, but because I smoke dope. Not because I am against a capitalist system, but because I think property eats shit. Not because I'm against corporate liberalism, but because I think people should do whatever the fuck they want, and not because I am trying to organize the working class, but

because I think kids should kill their parents. Finally, I want to be tried for having a good time and not being serious.[1]

The irresponsible, even apolitical, nature of the counterculture comes through in the way Hoffman erodes the positionality implied in the word "against." Signifiers like "long hair," "smoking dope," "having a good time" and "not being serious," while they don't mean Hoffman withdraws his support for the National Liberation Front, for the Black Liberation Movement, or for organizing the working class, do suggest a type of resistance predicated on an antinomic slackening of a contradictory (or dialectic) tension. Politics become a matter of resisting the discursive categories that inhere in syntaxes of being, struggling (by not struggling) "against" the "outside" assumed in contradiction. This "outside" resists the imaginative production of the world insofar as its materiality forces on the subject a conceptual apparatus of representation. The "outside," in Bachelard's words, is "encumbered with solids—and solids have a reserve of pure hostility. They keep their forms and when a form appears, it is necessary to think, it is necessary to name" (168).

In the *poeisis* of reverie, one can feel the cogency of a countercultural critique of technocratic society's "hostility" to nature and its instrumental construction of the earth as a resource to be exploited in the name of an ideal, that of capital, or profit. Whether the counterspace set up to displace the subject-object duality implied by this society was construed in terms of a polymorphously perverse sexual freedom (calling into question the nature of subjective [Oedipal] organization), or more politically on a model of antinomian or anarchist sects (calling into question the technicizing constitution of things and people), what each had in common, one could say, was a conception of membership or inclusion extended to the limits of the real itself, so long as this real implied as its "true" form an "inside" that exists everywhere and without "frontier." Reverie for the counterculture specified a world-making capacity essential to any conception of social change, which, as theorists like sociologist Pierre Bourdieu can help us appreciate, must entail "changing the social world by changing the representation of this world which contributes to its reality or, more precisely, by counterposing a *paradoxical pre-vision*, a utopia, a project or programme, to the ordinary vision which apprehends the social world as a natural world: the *performative* utterance, the political pre-vision, is in itself a pre-diction which aims to bring about what it utters" (*Language and Symbolic Power*, 128). The counterculture illuminated the necessary link between reverie-like neutralizations of discourse and the performative utterance by playing out in the social field the utopian desire of a "paradoxical pre-vision" capable of challenging the doxa of an authoritative social form. As such, it constituted a historical intervention precisely in its displacement from and in history, its escapism becoming a kind of genuine escape in the limit it was able to produce as its own symptomaticity.

This is why the inadequacies of its utopian and prophetic investments in imagination are equally evident, for at the same time that the infinitude of reverie operates the countercultural critique, finitude returns in the form of a now internalized limit that mandates for every inclusion the structure of a co-optation. The "good" possession of "well-being" becomes a possession of "goods." The displacement of every "frontier" suggests not only a rhetoric of Manifest Destiny but a Puritan interweaving of "God's promise" (a spiritual legitimation) with a secular economic push toward empire that, as Sacvan Bercovitch has persuasively argued, underlies the laissez-faire creed of American economic life.[2] The counterculture's fetishistic denial of the lack-in-being that encodes social contradiction in the subject signifies less a concrete realization of a utopian vision than a utopian "text" disclosing the historical limits of a postwar epoch characterized by autonomy and abstraction. Jameson, in his essay "Utopia, Modernism, and Death," writes of a "Utopian vocation" that, analyzed historically, depends less on "eluding or outwitting the reality principle" than on a particular "failure" or finitude. The utopian text's "epistemological value lies in the walls it allows us to feel around our minds, the invisible limits it gives us to detect by sheerest induction the miring of our imaginations in the mode of production itself, the mud of the present age in which the winged Utopian shoes stick, imagining that to be the force of gravity itself. . . . the Utopian text really does hold out for us the vivid lesson of what we cannot imagine: only it does so not by imagining it concretely but rather by way of the holes in the text that are our own incapacity to see beyond the epoch and its ideological closures" (*The Seeds of Time*, 75). The vacuolized text of imagination in our time, one could say, stems both from the historical failure of the counterculture to realize its political visions and, more subtly, from the perception of a necessary failure or constitutive incapacity that the counterculture helps to make possible. This is one reason why *Gravity's Rainbow*, as a novel about the contemporary scene of its writing, shifts to Europe and World War II as the mode of its commentary on its own moment: it displaces itself to grasp its asynchronous period and to specify through its indirection (drift, ellipsis) the symptomatic participation that informs the counterculture to which, by not belonging, it belongs.

I return, then, to a notion of discursive time that is cyclical, englobing itself in a structure of return, rewriting, or writing over that crosses out, erases, or effaces itself. This is what I have tried to study here, in a textual "reverie" that doubles itself, that opens its own double nature as what in chapter 5 I call a *body without organs* that is also a *docile body*, "drifting [and] being led," as Pynchon will write of Tyrone Slothrop in his movement through (and dispersion into) the Zone of *Gravity's Rainbow*. Reverie, for Bachelard, signifies "the *materia prima* of a literary work" (160), an "oneiric matter" that "inflates" a text, invests it with a plenitude proper to its poetic essence. That Slothrop indeed becomes a kind of oneiric matter for the novel does not, however, imply for it the same "plenitude" or "poetic essence" in any conventional sense. Slothrop's malleability suggests a much more overdetermined "plasticity" governing the relation between "man and his world," a coimplication of the two that eviscerates the confidence of a "cogito" in delivering the "dreamer" to the "new kind of time" that is plastic in *all* the meanings of the word. Slothrop in *Gravity's Rainbow* conjures, rather, what Bachelard calls the "man without a subject" of the "night dream" (distinct from reverie), "the immobile, the anonymous man" for whom consciousness has ceased to be intentional (150). He becomes the catatonic body or the body "without an image" of which Deleuze and Guattari write in *Anti-Oedipus*, focusing a textual desire not only to be a symptom but to catch out its own symptomaticity and make it the object of discursive attention.

The first principle of this desire is its independence from economies of pleasure, identity or intention, and representation. This implies an immediate caveat: as a desire invested in the critical destabilization of these discursive economies, it can only be groundless, virtual, or "unreal," not *another* desire than the "Oedipal" type it disavows, but that type encased in a citational structure. This book builds the crystal of that structure on the model of a ground, origin, or unconscious that is coextensive with its own limit, its own negation, lived at a figural surface where mechanisms of social repression act directly on bodies (figures) and where bodies (figures) invest the social field in its entirety. Here the emphasis is placed not, as in the state of reverie, on an inside with no outside but conversely on an outside with no inside, a radical exteriority into which the subject disperses or becomes multiple (like Slothrop). Deleuze and Guattari make this "outside" (which they liken to a historical "delirium") a central component of their argument in *Anti-Oedipus*, seeing in its mirror image of social representation (as defined by Bachelard) a world-making capacity (*poeisis*) tied to the production of discourse. The world that an "anti-Oedipal" subject "assembles" is that of social representation;

only now it is understood to be an infinite set that cannot remain closed no matter how hegemonic it might be, hence its necessary relation to a symptomatic structure based on the principle of an articulating "break" and its own essential groundlessness. Such a subject makes the world in which the world-making capacity is unmade, becomes a subject only in the process of a dehumanizing spatialization, experiences itself only as the context of its own abstraction into language or text. This fractalizing and masochistic dynamic of "desiring-production" is the most profoundly political subtext of Slothrop's scattering, and the scattering structure of *Gravity's Rainbow* as a whole. In it one sees a preterite strategy at work: incorporation of that context of absence (exacerbating a state of wretchedness) in which the absence of context discloses a desire to render in discourse the asignifying limit of discourse itself. This nondiscursive limit is by definition other to all definition, but it only appears in the kind of discourse that inscribes the problem of reference in its own "body," playing out through its paradoxes the "real" it simultaneously virtualizes. In a sense, the world of the novel is "happy" insofar as this means rational or inside one's head—happy but nonetheless negative, parodic, or farcical, glimpsed in the double and inverse "turn" of reverie into a schizophrenia that it always already prefigures.

To say that the counterculture is also already schizophrenic is only to situate it more complexly in relation to a historical formation (late capitalism) for which, as Deleuze and Guattari put it, schizophrenia is the "characteristic malady" (*Anti-Oedipus*, 34). The advantage of the approach taken in this book—theoretically saturated close readings of Pynchon's major works seen as exemplars of a postwar schizophrenia—is that it allows me to read the countercultural matrix of my own discursive production for a simultaneous complicity in, and resistance to, a late capitalist social logic. But more interestingly, it allows me to broach the problematic of a necessary complicity that characterizes the epoch about which and in which I write. It allows me to highlight the necessity today of an implicated thought and practice that sees in the assumptions of resistance, identity, agency, and truth the action of social power that thought and practice are charged to unmask. This is why I have written the book in the way that I have: not to reproduce ahistorically the cultural reverie out of which it has been generated, but to specify the schizophrenia to which it also (but also necessarily) belongs. The goal is to exemplify a criticism receptive to what Michel Foucault in *The Order of Things* called "a mode of thought, hitherto unknown in our culture, that will make it possible to reflect at the same time, without discontinuity or contradiction, upon man's being and the being of language" (338). The first requirement of such a criticism is that it grasp the precise vibration between the two registers (being and the being of language) as the effect of an antinomic social logic.[3] But a second requirement (at least for a countercultural criticism of the counterculture, as this purports to be) is that it keep in its antinomies to the limit of thought where lived experience discloses its virtual nature, its material singularity in the discursive forms of its intelligibility. Singularity in this sense is the main theoretical stake of this book; it informs a critical desire conceptually indebted to the work of Deleuze, and Deleuze and Guattari, and here active at all levels of connotation and construction. My ambition is twofold: to grasp this desire in the imperative to write and read performatively, and to see clearly the ethical reasons for this performativity in the "double" light it is able to shed on the metalinguistic dynamic of our time. Desire in our time is not a predicative state of being, linked to signifieds in which it finds satisfaction. Encased in discourse, trivialized by consumerism, terrorized in everyday life, it recovers itself in the abyssal apprehension of its own disappearance.

This critical desire, grasping the singularity or virtual ground in textual, psychological, and socioeconomic forms, is predicated on the notion of a neutral and displaceable, nonreferential "energy" present in an experience of narcissism, yet at the same time not reducible to it. This energy expresses itself tautologically, through a mirroring (double and inverse) repetition that disarticulates, disorganizes, and destabilizes (again, at each formal register). Repetition hollows out much like a fractal divides into itself, and I will refer this effect in what follows to an "empty form" that Deleuze glosses as finitude, *time* itself. Repetition is experienced as an ontological trauma that engenders a primary sublimation into discourse. This is why I elaborate the force of repetition in terms of a linguistic turn already modeled in the chiasmic shift from reverie (an inside with no outside) to schizophrenia (an outside with no inside). Pynchon calls this sublimated state "preterition," and I argue that it is a principal characteristic of social and subjective being in the postwar period generally and for the (narcissistic?) counterculture of the late 1960s in particular. The time of the counterculture in Pynchon's work is precisely the presence in it of this empty form, this fractalizing desire that metonymically contains the world that contains it. Each reading given here, no matter how focused on the minutiae of the particular text in question, resonates with this countercultural temporality. At the most fundamental level, it constitutes the argument of this book.

A corollary interest is the immanence of this discursive time to the interpretive act. Accordingly, *Lines of Flight* has been organized as a series of readings that form an implicated structure working at once on two levels: (1) that of *content*, where implication itself is, in the most general sense, the object of thematization; and (2) that of form or, echoing the linguist Louis Helmslev, *expression*, where that implication is repeated or performed in the methodological choice to theorize with a vengeance. The dual structure of the book, rather than postulate the object of analysis as *given* (whether that object is Pynchon, his texts, or the time in which and of which he writes), emphasizes a *practice* of writing that conjures the object of its analysis through its own production and at the tension surface of an "endlessly present past."[4] Not to do so, the informed critic tells us, is already to presuppose in circular fashion what one sets out to establish about that object. This is especially true when one is interested in the postwar "period" of American cultural life, for its limits do not readily offer themselves to the autonomizing impulses of investigation and knowledge. Or if this is too extreme a statement for some, one may say instead that the *essence* of the postwar period defined as a *field* is its catastrophic inability to be a period, which forces its historian, its native informant and ethnographer, its sociologist, and its literary or art historical critic to understand their own belonging to it precisely in the moment it becomes an object of epistemological desire.

It is the "history" of this moment in which I am necessarily implicated that I attempt to honor here. The symptomatic outline of this history, however, is once again displaced, or rather *is its own displacement* in a fabulating or fabricating language. Time dissimulated in language (discursive time) is the subject of this book because it is a principal preoccupation in Pynchon's fiction (and, I might add, of such contemporaries as Ellison, Nabokov, Heller, Vonnegut, Gaddis, Gass, Barth, Burroughs, Kozinski, and others). It is as if what that fiction tells us about its own time is that time is a function of language, projected in a linguistic medium that becomes, in its time, singularly transparent, literal, and material.

The first chapter, "Imperium, Misogyny, and Postmodern Parody in *V.*," introduces this symptomatic modality of historical narrative in Pynchon's first novel. I focus on the deployments and effects of a parody pushed so far to the limits of pastiche that the novel becomes what I call a parody of parody, double parody or metaparody. Through its exacerbated iterations, the text engenders an infinitely regressing empty form that stands in as a metonymy for a postwar moment understood in its totality as an "open set" of decontextualizing ironies. The novel achieves this exemplary relation to its own time not by dominating it in an adequate representation or theme but by pushing its own referentiality to a point of breakdown under the pressure of a more fundamental asignifying semiosis. I call this self-sabotaging dynamic the "broken machine" of Pynchon's text and analyze it through the lens of Deleuze and Guattari's desiring-production, a process of subjective and social self-definition that thrives on the transgression of its own limit (the body without organs). V., by keeping to that limit and refusing its own stabilization in a single semantic identity, reflexively produces its own implication in a history of technological domination, imperialism, war, and sexual violence.

Chapter 2, "Ekphrasis, Escape, and Countercultural Desire in The Crying of Lot 49," extends this analysis of broken or implicate textual form. Here I attend to a structural incoherence in the novel that, notoriously, never yields to a consistent explanation (this is often read as a weakness, even, it could be inferred, by Pynchon himself in Slow Learner).[5] Oedipa Maas's search for the meaning of the Tristero and of the communication system known as WASTE is never far away from an impoverishment of sense that threatens to collapse the novel into a heap of ambiguous signs. What I attempt to demonstrate in this chapter is that the meaning of the novel lies in its formal incoherence. Its ambiguity functions to raise the question of the separability between content and form, the essential abstraction that such an opposition implies. By undermining its own narrative and analogical consistency, the novel dramatizes a social order that subsumes subjects in immaterial nexuses of discourse, communication systems, and information. The reader no less than Oedipa is caught in these nexuses and compelled to grasp the truth of the novel in its parodies of the interpretive act itself. The time of the novel englobes us in its metalinguistic immanence, in other words, and demands a performative theorizing to be understood.

To make the stake of this readerly implication clear, I focus in chapter 2 on Pynchon's ekphrastic quotation early in the novel of a painting by the late Spanish surrealist Remedios Varo, "Bordando el Manto Terrestre." By identifying in this part the whole of the novel's structural investment in a self-reflexive artistic or literary practice, I can go on to specify in the text the same type of "broken machine" outlined in the reading of V. The principal modality of this machine is a vertiginous repetition that engenders the entropic anomie of a late capitalist consumer culture. The possibility of "escape" from a totalized social world referred to throughout the chapter depends not on a represented temporality in which "freedom" would entail a linear movement in extension; on the contrary, it depends precisely on the immanence of a time (*The Crying of Lot 49* was first published in 1966) that displaces its own represented form and makes "freedom" a discursive transformation in the symptomatic sense described earlier. The *Crying of Lot 49* belongs to its time by denying its readers the stable perspective (on consumption and spectacle in postwar America, for instance) that, if achieved, would effectively repress the historically vertiginous character of that time. In particular, what would be repressed is a textual or symbolic preterition that Oedipa comes to signify in her hermeneutic failure to find in WASTE (and waste, excess, consumption itself) a genuine redemption of her empty social life. The argument of chapter 2 is that only in this failure, this subsumption in a simulacral time, does the possibility of that social world actually emerge (and less for Oedipa than for the reader), a possibility predicated not on foreclosing one's preterite nature in a gesture of exemption or election but on ever finer realizations of the text-worlds to which one belongs. I end by linking the various dynamics explored in Pynchon's novel to the countercultural desire it manifests. The form of this desire is masochistic, predicated on a self-shattering sexuality that conditions the theoretical apprehension of a metalinguistic social order founded on the extension of power into the bodies and minds of subjects. The counterculture, I argue, was a name for this necessarily self-implicating apprehension.

The next three chapters assemble the concepts elaborated up to this point—implication, metaparody, texts as broken machines, repetition, preterition, and escape—and form out of them a theoretical matrix for the readings of *Gravity's Rainbow*. The novel is an attempt to widen the parameters of historical emplotment that make Pynchon's corpus a meditation on postwar society and its own countercultural desire. Set nominally in Europe in 1945, but moving back and forth through twentieth-century time, the novel draws together an encyclopedic array of referential detail—from the history of science, engineering, business, political history, modernist and popular culture—to tell the story of the emergent system of late capitalism. To do this, it has to account for a discursive and temporal shift in the notion of production, with its ancillary concepts: causality, origin, agency, control, freedom. To tell the story of that system is to evoke the loss of an intelligible world in which one's choices and preferences, actions and desires, carry with them a sense of consequence and value. With the coalescence of consumption as a primary interpellative fact of social life, enmeshing the subject within the spectral structures of global markets and the ideological "freedom" of commerce, new narrative forms and conceptual tools are needed to grasp the "event" that this development presupposes. *Gravity's Rainbow* can be understood as an attempt to meet this new cultural imperative by dramatizing an experience of disorientation in the basic teleological and dialectic space of the "book." The central story of Tyrone Slothrop's massively overdetermined manipulation by ambitious middle-class parents, corporate millionaires, behavioral psychologists, and military scientists is not simply about the vitiation of the subject as producer in a paranoid world; it also performs that vitiation in an iterative strategy that inscribes the crisis of a new global economic dispensation at primary conceptual levels where, for instance, subjects, things, and texts assume a categorical stability.

As such, *Gravity's Rainbow* has to be read for its iterative strategy and at the levels where this crisis appears. The goal of the closely interlinked readings presented in chapters 3, 4, and 5 is to unfold the discursive dimension of the novel's complex system, the reasons behind its chaotic (uniquely countercultural) subversions of realist convention. The central thematic and formal constant of the novel, in my account, is a *gravity* that functions as the absolute limit and ground of all endeavor, all sense of location, place, and movement. Chapter 3 begins by setting out the structural principle at work in the novel's gravitational field, which I take to be that double and inverse repetition of the (grammatic) subject in the predicate given as the form of a Heideggerian "turn." I establish through this form a model for the infolding of mind and matter, inside and outside, "world" and "earth" (or culture and nature), which governs the novel's preoccupation with the question of origin. An archaeological problematic is laid out at theoretical registers introduced in earlier chapters and linked, once again, to production and freedom. The fortunes of a textualized subject in a "political economy of the sign" are tracked through a reading of Jean Baudrillard, specifically his "seductive" strategy of paratactic contiguity in response to the hegemonic social and conceptual forms of late capitalism. I argue for an analogy between this and Pynchon's use of parody in *Gravity's Rainbow* because both are directed at the deepest assumptions of a humanist ideology functioning to mask those forms. The remainder of chapter 3 is devoted to an analysis of the novel's reflexive "movement" of self-objectification in which this parody becomes legible. By drawing attention to its materiality as language and flattening the illusion of depth into its textual surfaces, the novel reiterates a metalinguistic abstraction at the same time that it indicates a deconstructive possibility heard in the difference made by parody. The theme of implication returns in the internal or inclusive nature of this difference between the parodied object and its citation, and I go on through various examples to demonstrate how this constitutive paradox in *Gravity's Rainbow* makes even its own parodic strategy an "object," thus indicating a metaparody that situates the production of the novel within the crisis of production it evokes.

Chapter 4 zeroes in on the structure implied in this metaparodic mode of historical self-location by reading in detail episode 19 of part 1, the story of Franz and Leni Pökler. I look to the narrative elements of that story for how they allegorize the practice of writing and reading. The breakup of the Pöklers' marriage and the different destinies set forth for Franz, who becomes the rocket scientist responsible for making the "Schwarzgerat" (a modification in the nose of the 00000 V-2 rocket assembled by Captain Blicero, designed to accommodate his young lover Hans Gottfried when Blicero shoots him into the sky), and Leni, who ends up a concentration camp victim, are read as inscriptions of a failed desire for resemblance, analogy, "coming together." Pynchon in this manner narrates the principle of disconnection that governs the episodic series of which the Pöklers' story forms a part. He also raises the stakes of a complicity in the very real historical violence that underpins this disconnection by thematizing in Franz's obsession with the rocket a susceptibility to exploitation and an erotic identification with power. Masochism is the dynamic of that complicity for Franz and, in a different way, for Leni as well, and in this chapter I analyze how this masochism works through a reading of Freud's *Beyond the Pleasure Principle* and Deleuze's essay on Freud and Sacher-Masoch, "Coldness and Cruelty." I argue that in masochism as it is narrated in the episode, a kind of textual escape from the schizoid situation it describes becomes legible. It does not consist in a particular content articulated by either Franz or Leni but in a formal deployment of humor and fantasy indexing the text's masochism where it vitiates the analogic structures of meaning proper. A displacement toward an intertextual and fabulating language thus produces the allegory of writing as a mandate to transgress the rules of order and truth in narrative, to exacerbate the disjunctions of signification, and to hone the aleph of implication to as singular a point as possible.

Chapter 5 lays out in detail the theory of countercultural desire that grounds this mandate in a textual form characterized by paratactic contiguity and metonymy. I present a reading of Deleuze and Guattari's *Anti-Oedipus* that specifies in the performative dimension of that text a strategic inversion of a dialectical and biunivocal discursive paradigm. What this inversion allows them to do is to construct an abyssal system constitutively invested in its own ungrounding. Desire, as the dynamic of this antisystem, constitutes for Deleuze and Guattari a metadiscursive apprehension of its own theoretical determination, a desire *of* desire that implies a withdrawal from ontic fields and foregrounds its own virtuality as a limit or potentiality of being. This means that desire for Deleuze and Guattari is uniquely a function of its expression, isomorphic with how one writes or reads, and *Anti-Oedipus* plays out this ethic of cultural production by deploying a peculiarly hologrammic logic of parts that includes the whole and intensive fields predicated on the parodic citation of their own foundational self-assurance. I argue that this logic yields as the structure of their text an open totality or infinite set that resists closure. As such, it exemplifies the social logic of the countercultural moment in which it was produced.

Like *Anti-Oedipus*, *Gravity's Rainbow* is a virtual book in this respect, organized around the fourth-dimensional vector of a desire to narrate the deeply implicate orders of discourse in late capitalism. Chapter 5 sets out to gauge the force and direction of this vector in the novel, to trace the line of flight it opens within the complicities, the symptomatic repetitions, and the preterite accommodations to power that Pynchon so excessively depicts. My reading, after establishing its theoretical bearings in the discourse of *Anti-Oedipus*, unfolds in five parts. The first is an account of the Franz Pökler subplot, in particular his relation to his daughter Ilse, as it develops in part 3 of the novel. The decoding of the family structure by technological, bureaucratic, and military forces recounted in this story allegorizes a violence of dehumanization and reification. But as part of the implied analysis of that violence, the text also identifies in the substances decoded (father, mother, child) a prior "axiomatic" of social control that complicates the allegory. Taking Deleuze and Guattari's critique of a triangulated Oedipal desire as a starting point, I explore how the narrative overlays the story about the family's destruction with another story about the implication of the family structure in the discourses underlying and legitimating that violence. The family and the subjects generated in its crucible are seen to index that violence prior to its event, and this abyssal priority becomes the "experience" that the text attempts to represent. My reading works simultaneously at the level of content (where characters attempt to grasp their own implication in discourse, unsuccessfully, since to do so is already to presume that implication) and at the level of expression (where a travesty of discourse could be said to operate), but it does so only to exhibit the slide from content to expression that governs the novel at both levels. What Pynchon narrates is a tropological turn in which the text produces its own discursive precariousness (along lines previously analyzed in chapters 3 and 4) and hence the textual vertigo on which its "escape" depends.

The second part centers on the theme of "innocence" raised by Pynchon's characterization of Ilse Pökler, who takes her place in a long series of innocents brutally sacrificed to technological power. Innocence is not, as one might expect, innocent of the complicities narrated by the text. Rather, it signifies a radical alterity that is always elusive, always disappearing, and never the "property" of any one character. As such, innocence is a privileged state of preterition in the novel, the site of a desire for escape, fantasy, or drift that generates its intricately interconnected structure. Pynchon sees in the eyes of his innocents not a repressed prelinguistic substance but what he calls the "Double Light" of an implication in the novel's schizoid tendency toward increasing complexity and autonomy. They instantiate, within the metalinguistic movement Pynchon stages, an internal difference that marks the limit of its abstraction, a semiotic motility that erodes the self-identity of a system even as it attempts to repress it (and in fact to make that repression the very ground of its self-identity).

The third and fourth parts focus more directly on the novel's metalinguistic movement or tendency. The *Anubis* episode, narrating the journey of the "jackal-headed" ship into the "white desolation" of the Baltic Sea, is read as an example of the novel's reflexive style. The sybarite exploits of the fascist revelers on the *Anubis* compound innocence and abstraction, the fetishization of innocence and its almost ritualistic violation, to make the vector of textual desire as involuted as possible. The *Anubis* becomes a figure for the novel's collapse of opposites, of analogic correspondence, and of dialectic contradiction in tautological (or uroboric) forms that evoke a spectral mode of production emerging at the end of World War II. The novel plays out in this episode its own symptomatic status in the postwar period; at the same time, it specifies the repetition that makes its critical "edge" a function not of detachment or perspective but of immersion in the social power travestied. The *Anubis*, as much as it signifies the reprehensible nature of the "white" drive for purity, vacuum, and sameness, also indexes a kind of symptomal imagination derived from the very nondistinction the *Anubis* exemplifies. The circularity of the desire it demarcates—grounded on metalanguage and so on its own displacement in a virtual space "like," but also singularly unlike, a rationalized social field—crystallizes the stake of the novel in implication at the levels both of content and of form. In the fourth part, I track this stake, first in the figure of Captain Blicero as the most vivid exemplar of a white logocentric desire, and then in a reading of Tyrone Slothrop's scattering. Slothrop's journey through the Zone and his eventual disappearance make more explicit how the line of flight staged in and as *Gravity's Rainbow* specifies a retreat to the zero degree of discourse. Slothrop conjures an absolute limit that renders his entropic slide into equivalence and solipsism a performative "meaning" of the text. To read Slothrop as a sign of the text's desire, and that desire as the decoded code of its broken allegorical machine, one has to sustain that inertial slide in the act of interpretation; one has to grasp entropy not as a force to be resisted but as the actuating principle of resistance to a discursive time that totalizes the world of the novel and the world in which the novel is written and read. *Gravity's Rainbow* in this way enacts the story of its own symptomatic relation to a postwar period inaugurated, not coincidentally, on August 6, 1945, the day both of Slothrop's final disappearance and of the atomic destruction of Hiroshima. This relation, analyzed throughout as hologrammic in nature, yields the peculiar part-as-whole structure of the novel that makes it a catastrophic and heterological representation of its time.

The fifth part analyzes the controlling metaphors of the previous readings: gravity, entropy, and singularity. It raises the question of Pynchon's tropological appropriations of science as a narrative tactic, exploring to what extent metaphors such as these function in their status as physical laws either to naturalize a cultural space or to relativize an objective reality. I argue that *Gravity's Rainbow*, principally in the trope of the Rocket, expresses a perspectivist critique of the technological paradigm at the heart of scientific institutions and methods. This paradigm is metalinguistic because it links social power to global systems of communication and information that satellitize social life. As Heidegger put it in 1959: "*Metasprache* and Sputnik . . . are the same" (*On the Way to Language*, 58). The Rocket in *Gravity's Rainbow*, figuratively the instrument of a writing that produces the singular point of analogic and dialectic collapse at work in the novel, becomes for Pynchon the signifier of an objective irony predicated on implication and germane to a cultural desire that keeps alive the differences so relentlessly elided in a rationalized society.

Chapter 6 begins by suturing the iterative dynamics of *Gravity's Rainbow* to its countercultural moment. I link the time's preterite character—displaced from the text of the novel because of its essential displacement—to a sublimating desire proper to the late 1960s. Critical in nature, this desire has been a subtext of my own theoretical digressions throughout *Lines of Flight*. To contextualize Pynchon's 1990 rereading of the counterculture in *Vineland*, I discuss the contemporary debate around the value of poststructuralist theory in intellectual circles. I take Fredric Jameson's self-conscious position in a Marxist dialecticism as one exemplary tactic of a general retreat from more overtly antidialectic hermeneutic methods. Jameson's critique of these methods as symptoms of social contradictions embedded in the late capitalist mode of production misses the complexity of their symptomaticity, the *repetition* that drives them to crystallize discourses of singularity and implication similar to those informing Pynchon's fiction from the 1960s. An understanding of that decade as autonomous and synchronic (at a number of social, political, and cultural levels) underwrites a perceived necessity in the 1980s and 1990s for a return to diachronic narratives and methods. *Vineland* is then read as an exhibit of this historical moment insofar as it stages a retreat from Pynchon's earlier ambitions to reorganize discourse. The novel is an anomaly in his corpus for this reason. Its rereading of the 1960s is flawed insofar as it projects into the 1960s (and the earlier work) an ahistorical hermeticism without adequately grasping the empty form at its heart. I gloss this form along with its refusing desire once again in terms of repetition and argue for a practice of reading that abjures the sacrificial construction of "theory" or a theoretical "time" as the enabling condition for a particular political narrative of social unity. At the most basic level, the problem here turns around the catastrophic character of that time, the continuing legacies of events such as World War II, the Holocaust, Hiroshima, neocolonialist police actions, consumerism, and the globalization of markets. If these are understood as coherent events rather than events that fracture the structures of time and space (hence their traumatic nature), then the risk paradoxically becomes a historical amnesia that cannot generate genuine political commitments or the sense of "utopian vocation" mentioned by Jameson.

Mason & Dixon resumes the metadiscursive project legible in Pynchon's pre-*Vineland* work, and in chapter 7 I argue for the political and historical relevance of the untimely displacements of its parodic strategies. Unlike *Vineland*, where those strategies are divested of their virtual character as virtuality becomes a theme of the now periodized 1960s, *Mason & Dixon* remains constitutively tied to a mode of iteration, doubling, and ghostly haunting that evokes its discursive time precisely in its digression to the eighteenth century and the beginnings of a modern era. In this final chapter, I analyze the central narrated act of inscribing the earth (as text, numen, or ground) in terms of the fundamental rationalizations of modernity. Specifically, I examine a historical sensibility rooted in the nonthetic dimensions of discourse that is committed to disclosing the depthless depth and (im)material force of metalinguistic domination in the present. Mason and Dixon's "Line" of flight into the American continent runs through a concept of space that I elaborate by reference first to Merleau-Ponty's preobjective "anthropological space" and second to Michel de Certeau's notion of space as a function of discursive practice. I then link this textual and textural space to the problematic of implication at work in the text. *Mason & Dixon* dramatizes a Newtonian determination of the real to highlight an ethical necessity to write and read for the complexly abyssal situations of everyday life in the late-twentieth-century world. The novel expands the symptomatic or epochal sensibility that *Lines of Flight* explores in Pynchon's corpus as a whole, and as a result it captures in its elliptical fabulations that strange immediacy with which discourse today is lived.

1
IMPERIUM, MISOGYNY, AND POSTMODERN PARODY IN *V.*

Broken lives, broken strings,
Broken threads, broken springs,
Broken bottles, broken heads
People sleeping in broken beds.
Ain't no use jivin'
Ain't no use jokin'
Everything is broken.
—Bob Dylan

No one who reads Pynchon can deny the force and inventiveness of his prose. His prolix imagination verges on the uncanny, and his mastery of various discourses has awed all who have experienced it. But if Pynchon is an exuberant writer, he is so only by virtue of a counterforce acting on that forcefulness, interrupting its flows in particular ways—cutting into a dramatic sequence with an absurd song, modulating from a clipped comic diction and tone to epic sentences a page long, mingling tragedy with pornography, melodrama with slapstick. The diffraction of modes and genres through the disjointed narratives of Pynchon's first novel, *V.* (1960), reflects a highly organized, crystalline structure that is nonetheless anarchic, patterned and intricate yet loose-jointed, expansive, at the same time. A subversion of expenditure takes place within the mutations of narrative form, undermining the illusions of continuity and depth, frustrating the possibilities of coherence and closure. A peculiar emptying out of content attends this subversion in *V.*, marking in the language a lightness and strange insubstantiality that is often difficult to gauge.

This quality in Pynchon's prose corresponds to what Baudrillard calls a logic of simulation, in which, through successive orders of abstraction, the "real" withdraws into a permanent elsewhere, and systems of meaning (signs, images, discourses) no longer bear any relation to a stable referent but instead float in the medium of their own "divine irreference," a hyperreal that "envelops the whole edifice of representation" (*Simulations*, 11). This breakdown of meaning is variously described by Baudrillard as a process of "satellitization" (10), as a proliferation of signs incapable of dissimulating their own hollowness, as an implosion or a "non-distinction of active and passive" opposites (58), as a neutralization or "annihilation of stakes" in the political and social spheres (60). In the postmodern world Baudrillard describes,

> All events are to be read in reverse, where one perceives . . . that all . . . things arrive too late, with an overdue history, a lagging spiral, that they have exhausted their meaning long in advance and only survive as an artificial effervescence of signs, that all these events follow on illogically from one another, with a total equanimity toward the greatest inconsistencies . . . thus the whole newsreel of the "present" gives the sinister impression of kitsch, retro and porno all at the same time. (71–72)

Although Baudrillard is here speaking about the effect of the news media on contemporary culture, it could be said that V. exemplifies this exhaustion, this artificial effervescence of signs exactly. Pynchon's novel enacts a search for meaning or substance behind the initial "V.," which stands for a whole range of possible signifiers, partial objects, fetishes, puzzles, secret codes, and for the novel itself, V. as the signifier of the desire for "real" or authentic writing. But in what critics Alec McHoul and David Wills call V.'s "eternal condemnation to the signifier" (*Writing Pynchon*, 168), the necessary failure of this voicing becomes an obsession of the text, and in this sense V. can be seen as a simulacrum in the particular "phase" Baudrillard singles out as modern—that is, in which "strategies of the real" or "a panic-stricken production of the real and the referential" become a predominant feature (*Simulations*, 13).

All of this may seem an overly elaborate introduction to a discussion of parody and the parodic in Pynchon's first novel, but it is necessary to broach the issue of how to read, or how to hear, that peculiar displaced tonality so original to it. Parody. *Para-ode*. Beside, beyond, or past another text; an echoing, and also a damping out of sound, an effect of distance, an entropic repetition, a doubling that in its attenuation becomes increasingly aware of an emptiness it cannot revoke, a speech that reveals in its midst a growing silence. It is here that the uncanny character of Pynchon's prose finds its dramatic voice, but not before transgressing as many rules of dramatic order and serious discourse as it can. Whether in the more obvious scandal of transposing the rituals of psychoanalysis into Eigenvalue's psychodontia, or in the brutal rape and suicide of an African slave described from the perspective of her Afrikaner assailant in the context of a two-month-long "Siege Party" limned with an almost comic-book flatness, a determined antiseriousness prevails in the novel at almost every level and becomes its point. The question of how to take seriously a nonserious discourse has implications for postmodernism in general. The usual criticisms leveled at its practitioners—that they reduce historical phenomena to language games, that they leave no way of talking about value, truth, or morality, that they collude in the "annihilation of stakes" Baudrillard describes—have their source, I believe, in a cultural confusion over how to read a particular kind of parodic refusal to mean within norms of cultural intelligibility. There is no common syntax capable of teaching how to read with a full awareness of the essentially generic nature of norms, and "parody" in its more contemporary form forces this issue directly. Pynchon's *V.*, as an early example of this contemporary form, encapsulates these problems, and it is with this in mind that I would like to proceed with a discussion of tone and voice in the novel.

The historical is one register at which reference and the real are thematized in *V.* It is across history, and in particular a history of European imperialism in the early twentieth century, that Stencil "hunts" the elusive figure of the woman V. The mystery of her identity and historical function is incarnated in a series of scenarios that provide the novel with one of its two central narrative axes. These scenarios are fictional or "Stencilized" elaborations of historical fields only partially recovered in the form of evidence or fact. The only thread tying them together is the recurrence in Stencil's "archive" of the initial, which may or may not be a particular woman, or a woman at all. As a "remarkably scattered concept" (389), one of whose attributes is "disguise" (388), V.'s very indeterminacy is an invitation. "She" draws into being Stencil's successive impersonations of historical characters and re-creations of historical scenes. "She" compels, by being absent, his imaginative distortions of the past and underwrites a strategy of "soul-transvestism," the effect of which is to fracture the narrative into subchapters, and the narrative voice into a host of different identifications.

Stencil thus becomes for Pynchon a means of calling into question the nature of historical objectivity. This problematic, taken up again in Fausto Maijstral's confessions near the end of the novel (included as a sort of chronicle of events at Malta during World War II, in which V. figures), injects an ambiguity into the process of constituting a past, collective or individual, an ambiguity that is figured as expressly "feminine." "Memory," says Fausto, "is a traitor: gilding, altering . . . based as it is on the false assumption that identity is single, soul continuous" (307). Rather than accept the gilded representation of a unitary past apprehensible as such, Fausto and Stencil fracture identity in a succession of "identities taken on and rejected ... as a function of linear time [and] treated as separate characters" (306). But this strategy of fracture is itself a gilding and an altering of an already gilded, already altered, unitary text. That is, their "ungilding" of that normative, unitary structure (of identity, of the past) is itself a (parodic) gilding, literally a masquerade, a series of disguises they take on. To gild is to "give (to someone) an attractive but deceptive outward appearance," to embellish, brighten, or excessively ornament. It's a word Shakespearean in its overtones and active within a male discourse on women and on the artist. The novel's critique of objectivity is couched in this discourse, as is the writing strategy (of polyvocal subversions of the single and continuous) that Stencil, Fausto, and Pynchon exemplify.

In this light, it is something of an equivocation either to suggest (as Pynchon does through Stencil) that V. isn't necessarily a woman or to rely on that suggestion as even his best critics (McHoul and Wills) do, by way of countering a feminist critique. V. functions as an example of Virginia Woolf's "looking glass ... possessing the magic and delicious power of reflecting the figure of man at twice his natural size" (A Room of One's Own, 35), and it is easy to miss the extent to which readerly complicity is a preoccupation of this text. Stencil and Fausto serve Pynchon as vehicles for a parody of that male discourse on women (and on the artist). As parodies of writers and writing, the novel in which they function becomes a parody of its own production within that discourse. As Fausto says, "Writing itself even constitutes another rejection [of identity], another character added to the past" (306). Pynchon's narration, then, as one "character" among others in the text, deserves to be looked at as an example of a writing always already caught up in its determinations, aware of itself as a constituted object, attempting to think (or write) itself into its own "objectness." V. belongs to a literature drawn to questions of technology, tools, and instrumentalities in their relation to humanist discourses, and as such it features its own inanimateness to an unprecedented degree. This particular self-consciousness produces semantic and syntagmatic encounters with the inhuman as an inner as well as an outer limit of the human. The interpretive armamentarium of personalities and character analysis feels distinctly out of place in this context as a result.

Perhaps the most conspicuous characteristic of Pynchon's narrative style is that he almost never writes in any other than the third person. When the narrative shifts into a Stencilized chapter, the voice does not change, except to limit its omniscience to particular characters. Where Pynchon does violate this general rule, in Fausto's confessions, Fausto explicitly refers to himself in the third person, a characteristic he shares with Stencil as well:

> Herbert Stencil, like small children at a certain stage and Henry Adams in the *Education*, as well as assorted autocrats since time out of mind, always referred to himself in the third person. This helped "Stencil" appear to himself as only one among a repertoire of identities. "Forcible dislocation of personality" was what he called the general technique, which is not exactly the same as "seeing the other fellow's point of view"; for it involved, say, wearing clothes that Stencil wouldn't be caught dead in, eating foods that would have made Stencil gag, living in unfamiliar digs, frequenting bars and cafes of a most non-Stencilian character; all this for weeks on end; and why? To keep Stencil in his place: that is, in the third person. (62)

"Forcible dislocation of personality" aptly describes the techniques used in *V.* insofar as it highlights a qualitative difference between "seeing the other fellow's point of view" and the impersonations that undergird that third-person omniscience. The latter involve a systematic defamiliarization of the self to the point where its resolution into a series of disguises in effect displaces its priority, as the narrative voice is invaded from within by its own multiple personalities.

This is seen, for example, in the sequence relating the Afrikaner Foppl's experience with the African woman in the chapter "Mondaugen's Story." Foppl's reminiscence of the events in Southwest Africa following the Great Rebellion of 1904, in which Hereros and Hottentots fought unsuccessfully against the German occupying army led by Lothar von Trotha, comes as part of a narrative Stencil hears from Mondaugen and reworks into the textual form it takes as chapter 9 of the novel. Four temporal moments are invoked: the time of the writing (by Stencil and/or Pynchon), the time of Mondaugen's telling, the time of Foppl's reminiscence, and the time he remembers. Each moment is laid over one another in a palimpsestic effect that comes increasingly to distort and fragment the narrative. Foppl's siege party (the time of the reminiscence) becomes a disjointed sequence of events (mysterious seductions, voyeuristic overhearings, dreams, potential conspiracies) while the language of the text modulates through a range of tonal variations and generic forms (historical fact, low comedy, melodrama, and epic story). Foppl's reminiscence, which starts out plainly enough as a dialogue with Mondaugen, is slowly taken over by the omniscient narrator and is interwoven with the text in the form of a limited omniscient narration not signaled by any markers (breaks or ellipses). The narrative voice takes over Foppl's story, but Foppl also to some extent invades the narrator, with the effect that the voice must be heard through a quadruple mediation: Pynchon impersonating Stencil, who impersonates Mondaugen, who impersonates Foppl, who impersonates his younger self. Each tonality and each tense is given a parodic resonance, and this is true even in the description of the woman's rape and eventual suicide. The following extended passage recapitulates the interlocking themes of time, nostalgic reflection, and colonial violence in a clear parody of a Conrad-like diction.

> If a season like the Great Rebellion ever came to him again, he feared, it could never be in that same personal, random array of picaresque acts he was to recall and celebrate in later years at best furious and nostalgic; but rather with a logic that chilled the comfortable perversity of the heart, that substituted capability for character, deliberate scheme for political epiphany (so incomparably African); and for Sarah, the sjambok, the dances of death between Warmbad and Keetmanshoop, the taut haunches of Firelily, the black corpse impaled on a thorn tree in a river swollen with sudden rain, for these the dearest canvases in his soul's gallery, it was to substitute the bleak, abstracted and for him rather meaningless hanging on which he now turned his back, but which was to backdrop his retreat until he reached the Other Wall, the engineering design for a world he knew with numb leeriness nothing could now keep from becoming reality, a world whose full despair he, at the vantage of eighteen years later, couldn't even find adequate parables for, but a design whose first fumbling sketches he thought must have been done . . . on that terrible coast, where the beach . . . was actually littered each morning with a score of identical female corpses, an agglomeration no more substantial-looking than seaweed against the unhealthy yellow sand; where the soul's passage was no more a mass migration across that choppy fetch of Atlantic the wind never left alone, from an island of low cloud, like an anchored prison ship, to simple integration with the unimaginable mass of their continent; where the single line of track still edged toward a Keetmanshoop that could in no conceivable iconology be any part of the Kingdom of Death; where, finally, humanity was reduced, out of a necessity which in his loonier moments he could almost believe was only Deutsch-Sudwestafrika's (actually he knew better), out of a confrontation the young of one's contemporaries, God help them, had yet to make,

humanity was reduced to a nervous, disquieted, forever inadequate but indissoluble Popular Front against deceptively unpolitical and apparently minor enemies, enemies that would be with him to the grave: a sun with no shape, a beach alien as the moon's antarctic, restless concubines in barbed wire, salt mists, alkaline earth, the Benguela Current that would never cease bringing sand to raise the harbor floor, the inertia of rock, the frailty of flesh, the structural unreliability of thorns; the unheard whimper of a dying woman; the frightening but necessary cry of the strand wolf in the fog. (273–74)

I take the liberty of quoting at length to show how complicated Pynchon's style can be. This single sentence, a long stringing together of subordinate clauses and enthymematic reflections, presents itself as a kind of literary tour de force in the way it builds toward a dramatic and moral climax. Its rhetorical bravado, reminiscent of the excesses so typical of Conrad, signals a mode of consciousness or of meaning production heavily invested in its own associativeness and rhythmic flows. The accumulation of words works to draw attention to itself as such and in fact threatens to overwhelm itself in that accumulation. It is thus possible to read this sentence as a species of elaborate nonsense, in which its mode of production displaces its content. Henri Michaux once observed this phenomenon in a "freakish" table that had been constructed by a schizophrenic carpenter. "As it stood, it was a table of additions, much like certain schizophrenics' drawings, described as 'overstuffed,' and if finished it was only in so far as there was no way of adding anything more to it, the table having become more and more an accumulation, less and less a table" (*Major Ordeals of the Mind*, 125–27). The erosion of the table's functionality, its use value, is precisely the point of this sort of production. Pynchon's rhetoric in a similar fashion erodes its own use value, heaping words on words by way of exhausting signification itself. Hence phrases like "the comfortable perversity of the heart" or "these the dearest canvasses in his soul's gallery" function to echo a signifying practice based on a nostalgic and melancholy conjuring of the past. The parodic undertones, a sense in the diction of anachronistic exaggeration (anachronistic in two ways, as an outmoded realist language written in a modern time, and as a modern language infecting its older counterpart: "in his loonier moments," for instance, jars with the overall tone of the passage's "full despair"), break up rhythmic continuities and neutralize metaphoric effects.

It is significant that the displaced content of the passage relates explicitly to an African context. Its associativeness—both in the language parodied and in the parody itself—can be seen to mirror Foppl's nostalgia for the "random array of picaresque acts" of the good old days of epiphanic imperialism. The limited omniscient stance the narrator takes suggests a degree of complicity with, if not Foppl's explicit racism, then the implicit racism of the parodied style. The thematic of an indifferent or hostile nature, "frightening but necessary," figured as "the unheard whimper of a dying woman," recurs throughout the novel in different permutations. Nature is the African woman Foppl rapes and drives to suicide, and which threatens to dwarf his meanings within an insubstantial landscape, "a sun with no shape, a beach alien as the moon's antarctic . . . the inertia of rock, the frailty of flesh." The metaphoric presence of "sketches," "canvasses," and "galleries" points to a focus on artistic production and its relation to the African landscape. Within the displacements of parody, in a range inaudible to "human" ears, a meditation on writing and history unfolds, asking questions about how language and how narrative means in the context of European imperialism, or at the limit where desire encounters its other.

At issue is how well parody as a formal response answers these questions. It could be argued that V.'s third-person narration, in spite of the narrator's multiple personalities and parodic subversions of a realist discourse, retains a structural similarity to that discourse. Roland Barthes, in his essay "The Discourse of History," notices this similarity when he characterizes the historian's objectivity in terms of the psychotic's refusal of the negative. "The historical fact is linguistically associated with a privileged ontological status: we account what has been, not what has not been, or what has been uncertain. . . . historical discourse is not acquainted with negation" (14). He goes on to characterize this discourse in terms of the psychotic's identical incapacity to countenance the negative utterance.

> "Objective" discourse (as in the case of positivist history) shares the situation of schizophrenic discourse. In both cases, there is a radical censorship of the act of uttering (which has to be experienced for a negative transformation to take place), a massive flowing back of discourse in the direction of the utterance and even in the direction of the referent: no one is there to take responsibility for the utterance. (14)

The utterance, or the signifying surface of a text, becomes the scene of the utterer's displacement; its positivities mask the speaker or writer in order to avoid "responsibility" for the text spoken.

In some respects, V.'s displacements of narrative voice mirror the situation

Barthes describes. A similar "radical censorship" of the act of uttering attends Stencil's third-person perspective, a purging of the utterer from the utterance that catalyzes a "massive flowing back of discourse" to the latter. The writer of parody, like the positivist historian, absolves himself of any responsibility for his discourse by disappearing from it. The difference is that Pynchon draws attention to the signifiers of his discourse by that censorship, whereas the historian, in Barthes's account, refers to the signifieds of his, or the referents that "speak for themselves." The parodist's game is of a different order, centered on the question of responsibility rather than avoiding it, but in such a manner that what it means to be responsible admits of no easy answer, no easy resolution.

Benny Profane, a young man whose desultory "yo-yoing" along the eastern seaboard during the winter and spring of 1956 constitutes the novel's second main axis, also yo-yos through the novel as a figure of hapless inexperience and immaturity.

> He has a problem with the world of objects: He made his way to the washroom of Our Home, tripping over two empty mattresses on route. Cut himself shaving, had trouble extracting the blade and gashed a finger. He took a shower to get rid of the blood. The handles wouldn't turn. When he finally found a shower that worked, the water came out hot and cold in random patterns. He danced around, yowling and shivering, slipped on a bar of soap and nearly broke his neck. Drying off, he ripped a frayed towel in half, rendering it useless. He put on his skivvy shirt backwards, took ten minutes getting his fly zipped and another fifteen minutes repairing a shoelace which had broken as he was tying it. . . . It wasn't that he was tired or even notably uncoordinated. Only something that, being a schlemihl, he'd known for years: inanimate objects and he could not live in peace. (37)

This litany of near disastrous encounters with various man-made tools underscores the relation between inanimate and animate, tools and their users, that the novel is constantly troping. For Profane, that relation is complicated by desire for the inanimate and desire as the inanimate in us. This is why the novel abounds with characters who are in love with machines (Rachel Owlglass with her MG, Pig Bodine with his Harley Davidson), and why, more disturbingly, characters reveal themselves to be machines, rigged with switches or constructed out of synthetic plastic. Sexual desire, Profane observes, reduces people to the level of objects, inserts them within a machine of imaginary projections and partial objects made to bear the weight and function of an irretrievably lost and full presence. His strategy in the face of this is to refuse the sexual as best he can, to hide in a sort of celibate withdrawal and watch how desire is articulated into the inanimate.

The novel itself is structured in terms of this celibate observation of the sexual and, by extension, the psychoanalytic. The chapter entitled "V. in Love," another of Stencil's scenarios, maps the trajectory of (male) desire through a lesbian love affair between Victoria Wren ("V.") and a young actress, Melanie, who functions for V. as a mirror or screen to reflect her own desire.

> Melanie had hurried off to change into her Su Feng costume. Lacing on her slippers she looked up and saw the woman, leaning in the doorway.
> "You are not real."
> "I . . ." Hands resting dead on her thighs.
> "Do you know what a fetish is? Something of a woman which gives pleasure but is not a woman. A shoe, a locket . . . une jarretiere. You are the same, not real but an object of pleasure."
> Melanie could not speak.
> "What are you like unclothed? A chaos of flesh. But as Su Feng, lit by hydrogen, oxygen, a cylinder of lime, moving doll-like in the confines of your costume . . . You will drive Paris mad. Women and men alike." (404)

Melanie's role as Orientalist stereotype Su Feng (in a play entitled "The Rape of the Chinese Virgins") does not render her "doll-like" so much as emphasize the degree to which she is already inanimate, "lit by hydrogen, oxygen, a cylinder of lime." The costume only highlights a materiality "flesh" has by itself, "confining" or shaping the body in a parody of that materiality. And it is the parody that functions as a fetish.

V. the fetishizer also stands in as the fetish that exercises her various male fetishizers (Stencil, Godolphin, Father Fairing, Fausto) and that thus organizes or constitutes their desire. Melanie therefore is a fetish of a fetish, an object of an object, trapped within this double determination. And it is literally pinned to the wall of this object world that she dies during a performance in which she is accidentally impaled on a long pole after neglecting to wear a self-protective "metal device." Within the context of a dehumanizing representation expressly tied to the exigencies of art, Melanie becomes another of the novel's female (and colonized) victims whose victimage the reader can code only through a parodic displacement. How can one avoid the feeling that it's all an elaborate (and perhaps a bad) joke? Parody as a form of representation, as this novel's form, is not exempt from the critique embedded in Melanie's story. Artistic production is implicated throughout in a history of Oedipalized desire, imperialism, and misogyny, as the search for V. (as transcendental signifier, as lost object, as essence or telos) becomes a critique of art, and by extension a self-critique of the novel's motivations. Parody is the mode of that self-critique and the object of its interrogation as well; as such it takes on a specifically contemporary form and function, more simulated and overdetermined than ever.

Teresa de Lauretis argues that discourses of structuralist semiology and psychoanalysis rest on, or are conditioned by, "a performance of the absence of woman," her production as text and pure representation. The effect of this discourse is a double negation of women as subjects, the occlusion of a material history of oppression that takes the form of a "definition" of women as "vehicles of men's communication—signs of their language, carriers of their children" (*Alice Doesn't*, 20), a double reduction to symbolic "woman" and a biological "machine." By referring to a text from *Invisible Cities* by Italo Calvino that exemplifies this dynamic, de Lauretis extends her argument to discourse in general, and to postmodern discourse in particular. The renewed focus on the "signifier effect" in poststructuralist writing runs the risk for her of transmitting in toto this "double negation" of women, unless it takes into account modes of production, material praxis, and historical determinations involved in the constitution of subjects—an accounting that brushes against the grain of the poststructuralist move toward symbolic surfaces and synchronic functions.

McHoul and Wills devote an entire chapter of *Writing Pynchon* to V.'s susceptibility to this kind of critique. Although they concede that the novel's gender politics are "by the standards of *any* feminism one might care to name . . . dubious" (197), they set out to defend the novel by characterizing a debate within feminism whose positions are represented by Alice Jardine and Teresa de Lauretis. Jardine's method of "gynesis," focused on the representations, metaphorizations, and "increasing fictionalization" of women, is contrasted with de Lauretis's reversion "to an arbitrarily separate category of 'real historical women'" (191). Where both are "clearly dissatisfied with the women produced in phallocentric representations, [de Lauretis] would seek to 'correct that representation of woman by reference to women as they (somehow) *are* in spite of such representations, while [Jardine] would 'redefine' woman by reference to a series of radical recent attempts to recast

33

representation itself" (192). Jardine, because of her interest in postmodern fiction, is then seen by them as exemplifying the branch of feminism most likely to read *V.* sympathetically.

I suggest that McHoul and Wills's version of the conflict too starkly polarizes their respective positions, and that recasting "*representation itself*" must not imply a simple capitulation to symbolic structure, to representation itself, which the withdrawal of the referent behind the play of signifiers always threatens to become. Such a move travesties the more disturbing insight that withdrawal can give to the material stakes of a restriction of meaning to the fixed orders of the symbolic. De Lauretis understands this when she says that "in the psychoanalytic view of signification, subject processes are essentially phallic; that is to say, they are *subject* processes *insofar* as they are instituted in a fixed order of language—the symbolic—by the function of castration" (*Alice Doesn't*, 25–26). The minute any attempt to recast representation itself accedes to the linguistic or discursive symbolic as descriptive of everything, says de Lauretis, it also accedes to the function of castration in the construction of subjects and the displacement of desire into an imaginary and intrinsically male equivalent.

> Concepts such as voyeurism, fetishism, or the imaginary signifier . . . are directly implicated in a discourse which circumscribes woman in the sexual, binds her (in) sexuality, makes her the absolute representation, the phallic scenario. It is then the case that the ideological effects produced in and by those concepts, that discourse, perform . . . a political function in the service of cultural domination including, but not limited to, the sexual exploitation of women and the repression or containment of female sexuality. (25–26)

The complicity of the psychoanalytic machine in maintaining the phallocentric disjunction between symbolic desire and material history must be addressed in any critique of representation for it to be itself critically incisive.

In this sense, Pynchon's use of parody in *V.* is closer to de Lauretis than McHoul and Wills allow, since Pynchon too is focused on the way machines (and not just psychoanalytic machines) literally invade and transform bodies. If the reader cannot experience Melanie's death at the end of "V. in Love" in a fully affective (i.e., Oedipalized) way, it is because, properly speaking, she is only an element in a representation of a representation (the "Rape of the Chinese Virgins"), an actor in Pynchon's staging of a psychoanalytic scene that determines her fate from the outset. Fetishism (V.'s of Melanie, Stencil's of V., the reader's of V.) becomes a prop in a larger, parodic theater of discourse itself. If female sexuality is once again, to use de Lauretis's words, "negated, assimilated into the male's," it is done so in a parody of that negation. In fact, the parody is all that keeps the scene from being read as the uncritical reproduction of "concepts" already implicated in the support of a phallocentric order. An uncanny affective response to the juxtaposition of imperialism and misogyny with comedy is possible, I think, but only when the role of discourse in the violence of imperialism and misogyny is clearly understood.

But if psychoanalysis unfolds within a masculinist order, and Pynchon refuses psychoanalysis, does he necessarily refuse the masculinist order? The question of complicity returns at every level, and even parody may be fetishized, may even be the supreme fetish, the fetish of the fetish (like Melanie). For Pynchon, as for de Lauretis, one's options do not extend to refusing discourse. One must take a stand on or within discourses to see how they subjugate, inscribe, and define bodies as subjects.[1]

It is the process of subject construction that Pynchon, most notably through Benny Profane, watches in *V*. The line between animate and inanimate, nature and culture, human and machine, which is crossed so often throughout, delineates a space in which Pynchon's characters apprehend themselves in (or as) the mutual determinations of each. At one point Profane has a dream that is glossed by the narrator in the following passage:

> Somehow it was all tied up with a story he'd heard once, about a boy born with a golden screw where his navel should have been. For twenty years he consults doctors and specialists all over the world, trying to get rid of this screw, and having no success. Finally, in Haiti, he runs into a voodoo doctor who gives him a foul-smelling potion. He drinks it, goes to sleep and has a dream. In this dream he finds himself on a street, lit by green lamps. Following the witch-man's instructions, he takes two rights and a left from his point of origin, finds a tree growing by the seventh street light, hung all over with colored balloons. On the fourth limb from the top there is a red balloon, he breaks it and inside is a screwdriver with a yellow plastic handle. With the screwdriver he removes the screw from his stomach, and as soon as this happens he wakes from the dream. It is morning. He looks down toward his navel, the screw is gone. That twenty years's curse is lifted at last. Delirious with joy, he leaps up out of bed, and his ass falls off. (39–40)

Aside from being an almost perfect encapsulation of the whole novel, with its detours through "doctors and specialists" and through the Third World, its overdetermination as dream, its obsession with machines, and its sheer comic splendor, this anecdotal story underscores the mutuality of animate and inanimate forces in the construction of subjectivity. To love a machine, to be a machine, is always treated with a marked ambivalence in V. The golden screw holds together upper and lower portions of the body, the dreaming mind and the shitting anus. What performs this function is something manufactured, literally machined, requiring for its construction a whole industrial apparatus. And that is what the dreamer can't abide in himself, the "malady" of culture he looks to doctors to cure, that drives his movement through discourses (medical, psychoanalytic, mythic) to find a "natural" alternative, an innocently "human" body (the unscrewed navel) that is freed from its machinic being. Experienced as a kind of domination that is nonetheless "golden," the dreamer's desire for escape runs up against his need for the connective work the screw performs for him. He is at work in that connection at the same time he desires not to be, struck with the intuition that the screw is somehow necessary.

Deleuze and Guattari designate what I here call a limit-space between animate and inanimate the "body without organs." Conceived as a "recording or inscribing surface," a numen, a place of inclusive and nonpersonal energy flows, it is the "unproductive, sterile, unengendered and unconsumable" site where "process[es] of production of desire" are recorded, a site of pure resistance to the depredations of "desiring-machines" that attach to it in the process of constructing desiring subjects. The body without organs "is not the proof of an original nothingness, nor is it what remains of a lost totality. Above all it is not a projection; it has nothing to do with the body itself, or with the image of the body. It is the body without an image" (Anti-Oedipus, 8). This automaton-like, static, negative place is nonetheless also produced "as the identity of producing and the product" (8), an identity that makes it clear how "anti-production" becomes an element in desiring-production. This resistant surface is where a desiring-machine (for Deleuze and Guattari, psychoanalytic desire conceived in terms of a constitutive lack and fantasmatic projections, a "trap" set by a social formation [capitalism] into which desire falls and by which it comes to invest that social formation, to want its own regulation within it) writes itself as real, establishing its limit as the body without organs, which then defines that desire by being what it is not. This relation that the limit "stencilizes" comes to figure in an analysis of how desire invests the apparatus of its own repression, an apparatus that codes into itself necessary ruptures, necessary resistances or "transgressions" of its laws. In this way, desiring-machines are always broken machines; they "work only when they break down, and by continually breaking down" (8), in a process of controlled deterritorialization for the purpose of reterritorializing the body without organs. This is why Deleuze and Guattari can say that the schizophrenic, whose domain is the body without organs, come to be capitalism's (or the capitalist machine's) limit, and schizophrenia the "characteristic malady" of our era (34).

What's at stake in this weird language of energy flows and desiring-machines, for its authors, is the possibility of a revolutionary politics (distinct from transgression and the regime of prohibitions it presupposes) that comprehends the way discourses (as simulations of desire) conceal their own material bases and thereby persuade their subject interlocutors to an active acceptance of a social hierarchy (by telling them not only what they want but that they don't know what they want as well).[2] Profane's dreamer wants to unscrew his navel, and the dream tells him how to go about doing it; but once he does it, he's left with himself as a broken machine. His desire both locks him in a twenty-year activity of plugging into machines that can't help him and leads him to discover himself in a condition of being always already caught up in a process of production that is, precisely, himself as product (Profane, that is, produces himself as producing). If the anecdote's punch line can be read as disclosing his unconscious wish, it isn't only to be a machine (i.e., to desire his own repression) but also, more obscurely perhaps, to gain control over the machine that he is, to master his own machinic being. What the dreamer discovers, in Deleuze and Guattari's words, is a relationship between the body without organs and a desiring-machine that has been "miraculated" or naturalized; that is, the relationship has been subsumed into the provenance of a first cause or source that covers over the process of desiring-production, which is always one of engineering and manufacturing subjects.[3]

This glimpse into the workings of desire afforded to Profane by the unhinging of his ass gives to his inveterate nomadism a new critical urgency, a dimension of mature apprehension that (contrary to the bildungsroman structure he parodies) pushes him more and more toward a nomadic existence and a refusal of forms. In Deleuze and Guattari's terms, Profane "falls back on" the body without organs in a schizoid recoil from the miraculating process. But because he is that process at the same time, what he does is *break down*, or rather, he remains at the place of dysfunction, at the deterritorialized rupture (on the body without organs), refusing to be reterritorialized in turn.

This can be seen most clearly in Profane's consistent refusal to be sexual in spite of his own inclinations and in spite of the various female characters Pynchon throws in his way as available temptations: Paola, Fina, Rachel, all of whom incarnate aspects of virgin-whore and mother figure stereotypes, figments of a male imaginary Profane interrogates in his own bumbling way. Each asks him to give up his "pedestrian" lifestyle; each demands that he get a grip on the world of objects they symbolize for him: "Women had always happened to Profane the schlemihl like accidents: broken shoelaces, dropped dishes, pins in new shirts" (134). His inability or unwillingness to meet that demand and commit himself to another has a doubled valence in the text: at one level, it denotes his immaturity; at another, his intuition that the discourse of love represents a kind of territorialization by an Oedipalized social machine. It's a double bind Profane represents, and one, moreover, that lies at the heart of V. and its parodic mode. Profane is also a parody, a staging of desire for the purpose of highlighting a constructive process intrinsic to writing. Parody is a "schizo" strategy of perpetual self-revelation, a masking and unmasking of the self (as text) according to a principle of subject "states" through which one passes rather than a fixed identity one assumes. Deleuze and Guattari call the agent of such a movement a "celibate machine" that overlays the process of repulsion and attraction alluded to earlier (a "paranoiac machine" becoming a "miraculating machine").

> By means of the paranoiac machine and the miraculating machine, the proportions of attraction and repulsion on the body without organs produce, starting from zero, a series of states in the celibate machines; and the subject is born of each state in the series, is continually reborn of the following state that determines him at a given moment. (20)

This principle of states bears as well on Stencil with his "repertoire of identities." If, as I want to maintain here, V. is a broken machine that refuses to fix itself, then its very form and style, its very mastery, will register this rupture, this awkwardness. Stencil's search for the meaning and identity of V. also proceeds in fits and starts, ass-backwards, as Pynchon might say. In the following quotation, Stencil is likened to a spy who lacks a professional sense of calling.

> But somehow in [Stencil's] hands the traditional tools and attitudes were always employed toward mean ends: cloak for a laundry sack, dagger to peel potatoes; dossiers to fill up dead Sunday afternoons; worst of all, disguise itself not out of any professional necessity but only

as a trick, simply to involve him less in the chase, to put off some part of the pain of dilemma on various "impersonations." (62)

This anxiety and even boredom driving Stencil's undercover activities, his displacement into the third person, engenders a misapplication of traditional tools. Instruments intended for particular uses are used for "mean ends"—used wrongly, that is, in misalliance with established rules or "professional necessity." Disguise and impersonation are "tricks," evasions of responsibility to a "field" of spying and for a "dilemma" he cannot resolve.

And what is that dilemma? Is it V., or the endless search for V., or is it the embarrassment of the search, the nagging suspicion that it's all absurd, a trick, a trap—a machine, finally, V. as imagined by Stencil near the end of the novel, "an inanimate object of desire . . . skin radiant with the bloom of some new plastic, both eyes glass but now containing photoelectric cells, connected by silver electrodes to optic nerves of purest copper wire and leading to a brain exquisitely wrought as a diode matrix could ever be"? (411). V. is the machine heart of V., what drives the novel but also what the novel turns on, what it attempts to deconstruct. Stencil's and Profane's narrative axes converge (like a V) by the end, I think, because they share this basic "lack of competence," this depression that catalyzes anoedipal intuitions of their machinic hearts. It establishes a distance from (beside, beyond, or past) that core, a peripheral perspective from which to observe its mechanisms. "This [schizo] subject," says Deleuze and Guattari, "itself is not at the center, which is occupied by the machine, but on the periphery, with no fixed identity, forever decentered, *defined* by the states through which it passes" (20).

Profane and Stencil are, of course, quite literally "states," since they're only characters in a novel, impersonations fabricated by Pynchon. And in a strict sense, V. is a parody of a parody, a double or metaparody. That is the nature of its own lack of competence, that it catches itself up in a seemingly infinite regress of ironic decontextualizations. Even the peripheral, deconstructive moment that parody tries to stage passes within the centralized normative structure it deconstructs. The discontinuous temporality of that moment always threatens to fall back to a linear mode, even as it threatens to explode that mode. It is this tension that gives Pynchon's prose in *V.* its force. The novel invests the forms it parodies even as it disavows them, and makes that fetishizing activity itself the object of a parody. Perhaps this is not even parody anymore, but rather what Fredric Jameson calls pastiche, a "neutral practice" of parodic mimicry "without any of parody's ulterior motives, amputated of the satiric impulse, devoid of laughter and of any conviction that alongside the abnormal tongue you have momentarily borrowed, some healthy linguistic normality still exists" (Postmodernism, 17). At what point it becomes a mere game, a trick without meaning, a helical displacement upward (like the waterspout at V.'s end) of all referents, depends on how one reads responsibility in the novel. Pynchon's 1990 novel, Vineland, suggests there is a limit to this satellitized kind of thinking (and writing), and that his novels can be historicized in relation to a discrete period, the 1960s, and discrete social and political imperatives. But it's also true that his kind of fiction opens the door to a complex engagement with referents, bodies, modes of production, and determinate histories. Deleuze and Guattari see this response to a socioeconomic reality exemplified in the schizophrenic artist (Proust, Artaud, Beckett) and in Nietzsche:

> There is not Nietzsche-the-self, professor of philology, who suddenly loses his mind and supposedly identifies with all sorts of strange people; rather, there is the Nietzschean subject who passes through a series of states, and who identifies these states with the names of history: "*every name in history is I. . . .*" The subject spreads itself out along the entire circumference of the circle, the center of which has been abandoned by the ego. . . . It is not a matter of identifying with various historical personages, but rather identifying the names of history with zones of intensity on the body without organs; and each time Nietzsche-as-subject exclaims: "They're me! They're me!" No one has ever been as deeply involved in history as the schizo. (21)

If the trajectory of the postmodern kind of parody here explored in V. runs through these "states," then an analysis of its historicity must assess the extent to which this statement rings true, and how it does. Pynchon's nomadisms do yield a theory of history capable of grasping its relation to the past without marooning itself in simulated orders of abstraction. This can be seen both in his novel's persistent preoccupation with the inanimate (as discourse, as technology) and in its structural affinity for peripheral and asubjective historical "Situations" (the Dutch colonization of Southwest Africa, intrigue on Malta during World War II, the theft in Florence by Argentinean gauchos of Botticelli's *Birth of Venus*, and so on). As Stencil puts it near the end of the novel, each of these "Situation[s] take shape from events much lower than the merely human" (483), and as such they "involve" subjects at the most immediate levels of being in the implicate order of a twentieth century understood as a moment of traumatic fracture in symbolic modes of representation. In this light, the novel's episodic form, its fantastic distortions of historical record, its fabulating departures from realist conventions of narrative, all signify not a "hothouse" abstraction from the determinate and material concerns of history but a much more constitutive encounter with that fracture. Or rather, to be more precise within the overall argument of this book, the novel *does* signify that hothouse, but in the symptomatic mode of a necessary complicity. This mode is always self-implicating, always invested in undermining the analogic mechanisms at work in the manufacture of truth. It is the element of shock in Pynchon's prose that gives it its uncanny quality and links it to a modern antitradition at least as old as Baudelaire, who famously redefines the artist's task in a decontextualized social space as the willful destruction of meaning, value, and continuity with the past.[4]

Pynchon provides a telling commentary on the vigilance about claims to truth that this self-implication requires of the cultural producer. Near the end of *V.*, a minor character, Brenda Wigglesworth, reads a "phony college-girl poem" she wrote to Benny Profane, who listens abstractly by "star[ing] at the pattern in the rug." Entitled "I am the twentieth century," the poem reads like a self-parody of the novel's fundamental concerns. It could also be read as a proleptic parody of the Deleuze and Guattari quoted earlier.

> I am the ragtime and the tango; sans-serif, clean geometry. I am the virgin's-hair whip and the cunningly detailed shackles of decadent passion. I am every lonely railway station in every capital of Europe. I am the Street, the fanciless buildings of government; the cafe-dansant, the clockwork figure, the jazz saxophone; the tourist-lady's hairpiece, the fairy's rubber breasts, the traveling clock which always tells the wrong time and chimes in different keys. I am the dead palm tree, the Negro's dancing pumps, the dried fountain after tourist season. I am all the appurtenances of night. (454)

The metonymy at the heart of this bad schoolgirl poem (the "I" contains the world in which she moves, with all of its historical sedimentations) sums up the schizophrenic logic I have been analyzing through the novel and does so in an explicitly trivializing (peripheral or incidental, supplemental) context. It is this triviality in the claim that the metonymy constitutes a kind of truth for the novel that makes "true" its singular historical claim. If the hermeneutic circle implied in this type of reasoning too strongly suggests the relativism of pastiche, it does so with the conviction that only through its iterations can works of art connect to the legacies and tensions of the modern epoch. In particular, it underscores the relation of Pynchon's first novel to its own postwar time, wherein culture begins to feel the imperative to push the limits of representation to the point of an unprecedented implication in the social and economic forms of late capitalism.

2
EKPHRASIS, ESCAPE, AND COUNTERCULTURAL DESIRE IN *THE CRYING OF LOT 49*

The schizophrenic is someone who's found out what's going on.
—William Burroughs

The reflexive parodic mode examined in my reading of Pynchon's first novel enacts a necessary implication in the social, cultural, and industrial production of subjectivity. To be a "person" is to experience complicity in a world that effectively depersonalizes, reduces to caricature, to outline, to silhouette. What this means is that the subject in its activities, processes, or consciousness can experience its difference only as generality, or only in a certain theoretical apprehension of the ways by which singularity comes to be the reflection of a dehumanizing mode of production. This displacement of the subject (character, author, and reader) to the negative spaces around what "is," to the molded (usually plastic) stencil of being, is what Pynchon attempts to represent in his fiction—a loss of substance, of affect, of reality. Difference returns—if it returns—not in the externalization of the inhuman world but in a perception of the externalized and intrinsically discursive character of subjectivity. The strategic value of a parody that takes itself as an object lies in its ability to highlight the mediated structure of that perception, its nonseparability from the "thing" it focuses.

Pynchon's metaparodic interest connects his work clearly to the cultural crucible of the late 1950s and early 1960s, in particular to the embrace of mass culture that emerges fully blown in pop art. Like Jasper John's targets and flags, Robert Rauschenberg's combines, and Andy Warhol's various photogrammic deployments of seriality and citation, Pynchon's "broken" textual machines present the reader with a curiously empty repetition of a social order based more and more on mechanical reproduction, an economic logic of sign value exchange, and a juridical zeal for categorization. What gets repeated is oneself and one's products *as symptoms of that order*, caught up in it precisely when one feels oneself *not* to be caught up in it (that is, in those moments of leisure, privacy, fantasy, or escape that only express the desublimating logic of the commodity form). The mode of production produces its own symptom, in other words, its own internal difference, the ghostly contour of its own otherness. This putting to work of difference, uniqueness, and originality indexes a general reduction of all social relations to economic ones, the interpellation of desire within market structures, and the dominance of a consumption that invests objects with the power of signification (as status symbols) and signs with the properties of objects.[1] The artist ceases to function as the exemplar of aesthetic freedom at the same time that aesthetic freedom becomes the ideology of the market itself. The only possible artistic response to this situation is to perform the impossibility of art, to place at the center of artistic production a machine on whose periphery precise displacements of an anoedipal kind can be registered.

Indeed, such displacements are a conspicuous feature of many cultural artifacts from this period. Humbert Humbert's recognition in Nabokov's *Lolita* (1955) that his aestheticizing and objectifying desire is a metonymy for consumerism parallels the discovery of his implication in Quilty's more inclusive aesthetic plot. When Yossarian, near the end of Joseph Heller's *Catch-22* (1960), announces that "I don't want the things I want," he voices not only the double and inverse logic of the novel but that dislocation of the subject in a system geared to control through incitement, to capture desire at the moment of its fullest extension. Perhaps the most vivid contemporary rendering of this catch-22 is John Frankenheimer's brilliant paranoid movie *Seconds* (1965), where a prosperous but disenchanted middle-aged banker is caught in the meshes of a shadowy "Company" whose business is to realize the agentive fantasies of its clients, with darkly apocalyptic results.

In cases such as these, what finds expression is an emptiness at the heart of a co-opted cultural desire that each text is able to dramatize only by highlighting its own immanence and finitude with respect to a late capitalist social form. *The Crying of Lot 49* is exemplary in this regard: impenetrably ironic, fabulously inconclusive, it inscribes in its form the double bind of a generalized market culture without offering redemption, transcendence, critical distance, or even a simple way out. Or rather, as I will argue, the way out it does offer depends on reading the novel as a kind of farce that exhausts its redemptive energies in an accumulative repetition. The point of this strategy is to exhibit the novel's metonymic relation to an asynchronous time of crisis in basic metaphysical categories, to be a symptom of that time by way of underscoring a possibility for "escape" in an implicated writing and reading. This possibility, simultaneously performed and thematized in Oedipa Maas's encounter with the virtual communication system WASTE, is evident in the text's peculiar hologram-like structure, its status as a part that contains the whole of a late modern world characterized by social entropy and metalinguistic abstraction.

This chapter analyzes the part-whole relation at the heart of the novel's signifying system in an example of *ekphrasis*, in Oedipa herself, and in the novel proper. The concern here is once again with the notion of implication, although an attempt is made to multiply its theoretical registers across a dense field of metaphors founded on the notion of an "infinite substance" in Spinoza's sense. This substance, central to what Deleuze and Guattari mean by a body without organs, names the "pure continuity that any sort of matter ideally possesses" (*Anti-Oedipus*, 36), the "unformed, unorganized, nonstratified or destratified body in all its flows: subatomic and submolecular particles, pure intensities, prevital and prephysical free singularities" (*A Thousand Plateaus*, 43). Taking "matter" in both a physical and a semantic sense, I invest the figures of my reading with the immaterial support of this "subtle" body to apprehend the emancipatory possibility held out in the novel. These figures include *desiring-machines* that internalize their own form and so displace a categorical self-identity; the *production of production* insofar as this indicates a conflation of an open-ended process and a fixed result, production and product; the virtual contour or *abstract line* of the structure implied in the previous two concepts (and applied to Pynchon's novel); a *collective assemblage of enunciation* mandating for the producer (of oneself as product) an inclusive relation to a fundamentally discursive ground; the *nomadic* dynamic of that assemblage as a cyclical or repetitious movement within uniform spaces; and finally masochism, along with its main psychoanalytic mechanism, *incorporation*. The use of these theoretical constructs allows me to highlight in The Crying of Lot 49 an anoedipal dislocation of desire from its socially constituted double—a "broken" machine, once again, working, as in V., on a principle of internal fracture and retreat to a limit-space or body without organs. In this case, the asignifying limit appears in the functions of ambiguity, that zero degree of meaning where the novel, verging on incoherence, thereby produces itself as an escape.

With this thematic and formal focus on escape, The Crying of Lot 49 also participates in the counterculture it came to exemplify for many during the late 1960s (its iconic power was comparable to such works as Norman O. Brown's Love's Body, Tom Wolfe's Electric Kool-Aid Acid Test, or the film Easy Rider). A goal of this chapter is to exemplify at a hermeneutic level a tactical use of "reverie" evident in the counterculture's disruptions of discursive norms. What made these disruptions effective was a destabilizing of representation itself. The basic dichotomies that structure and legitimate a systemic regime of power (like subject and object, inside and outside, human and machine, male and female) collapsed in an enacted imaginative state that worked precisely through the reference to a "subtle" substratum where the organized character of social reality became intolerable—and indeed no longer desired. Thus the novel is exemplary not for its timely allusions to LSD, rock music, and popular culture, nor even for its critical attitudes toward mainstream society that, while resonant for so many readers, may not have been quite so resonant as they seemed. In fact, it may be the novel's untimely character that makes it countercultural, its allusion to the reverie-like ground of a genuinely transformative desire that makes it an avatar of its time.

Embroidering the Mantle of the Earth

Near the beginning of the novel, Oedipa Maas recalls a trip to Mexico City with the recently deceased real estate mogul Pierce Inverarity, and in particular an art exhibition she saw there by the Spanish surrealist Remedios Varo (fig. 1). The text, in a moment of *ekphrastic* digression, describes one painting in detail:

> In the central painting of a triptych, titled "Bordando el Manto Terrestre," were a number of frail girls with heart-shaped faces, huge eyes, spun-gold hair, prisoners in the top room of a circular tower, embroidering a kind of tapestry which spilled out the slit windows into a void, seeking hopelessly to fill the void: for all the other buildings and creatures, all the waves, ships and forests of the earth were contained in this tapestry, and the tapestry was the world. (20–21)

This room in Varo's tower assumes for Oedipa the fatal and enigmatic attraction of a destiny from which there is no escape, a point of departure and arrival that exposes the illusion of movement between a here and a there, between life "among the pines and salt fogs of Kinnaret," California, and the imagined or imaginative freedom of Mexico (20). Time as both a causal sequence and a signifying chain suffers its catastrophic involution, turns in on itself, immobilizes or suspends the presumption of an animate nature, a substantial self, and an autonomous desire. The experience precipitates in Oedipa an immediate paranoia:

> Oedipa, perverse, had stood in front of the painting and cried. . . . She had looked down at her feet and known, then, because of a painting, that

what she stood on had only been woven together a couple thousand miles away in her own tower, was only by accident known as Mexico, and so Pierce had taken her away from nothing, there'd been no escape. What did she so desire escape from? Such a captive maiden, having plenty of time to think, soon realizes that her tower, its height and architecture, are like her ego only incidental: that what really keeps her where she is is magic, anonymous and malignant, visited on her from outside and for no reason at all. (21)

If Oedipa's tower is "only incidental," however, it is also omnipresent: she finds it everywhere. It is a human condition, the human condition *as* incidental, as nonessential subordination, remainder, residue, or WASTE, the spectral system of exchange and community that Oedipa encounters in the novel. Pynchon's metaphors here signify a paratactic displacement beside one's self that characterizes the feeling of subjection to a fundamentally irrational exteriority. Oedipa is an incident person, a projection, a hologram whose point of origin, that which "keeps her where she is," suggests a terrifying complicity between "anonymous" gravitational force and "malignant" social power, between ineluctable physical law and fantasmatic structures actively vitiating (to borrow a Marxian locution) the social field in which self-recognition (as a subject, as a citizen) is possible.[2] Oedipa's imprisonment in the tower, at least on one level of implication, cannot be understood apart from her reified fabrication of the external world that "keeps her" in her place. To be "incidental" is therefore to experience alienation in the form of a fantasm installed at the center of being, a fantasm that destabilizes any clear sense of the human or the real.[3] The novel specifies this experience a little later on in the figure of Metzger, who relates to Oedipa his dual career as an actor-lawyer in the following terms:

"But our beauty lies," explained Metzger, "in this extended capacity for convolution. A lawyer in a courtroom, in front of any jury, becomes an actor, right? Raymond Burr is an actor, impersonating a lawyer, who in front of a jury becomes an actor. Me, I'm a former actor who became a lawyer. They've done a pilot film of a TV series, in fact, based loosely on my career, starring my friend Manny Di Presso, a one-time lawyer who quit his firm to become an actor. Who in this pilot plays me, an actor become a lawyer reverting periodically to being an actor. The film is in an air-conditioned vault at one of the Hollywood studios, light can't fatigue it, it can be repeated endlessly." (33)

1. Remedios Varo, "Embroidering the Mantle of the Earth," 1961. ©2000 Artists Rights Society (ARS), New York/VEGAP, Madrid. Reproduced by permission.

With this permutative logic, Pynchon weaves a profound textual likeness of life in a world of signs, images, filmic doubles, digitized desires, a world effectively transformed into a simulacrum, suspended in the etherous medium of an endless repetition. If Oedipa is one of the women in Varo's tower "embroidering the mantle of the earth," her peculiar capacity or labor power is limited by this spectrality, incapable of transcending its own determination from without and so condemned to wallow in a postmodern America generated as if by "magic." Of course it is actually generated not by magic but by Oedipa herself in her tower, and the virtuality that Oedipa represents rests on a simultaneous abstraction from, and reduction to, material forms of existence that are no less real for the unreality in which they are lived. This is why Oedipa is essentially a machine, a kind of information-processing computer that organizes or links the elements of the textual world through which "she" seeks answers to the mystery of the Tristero and WASTE, much in the same way that Maxwell's Demon "sorts" molecules and "connects the world of thermodynamics to the world of information flow" (106) and communication for another character in the novel, John Nefastis. In and around Oedipa, a bewildering conspiracy of *physis* and *technē* manifests itself, deploys its secret as secret, as the blank and impervious surface of an impossible matter, a matter that does not mean even as it conditions the possibility for signification. Submission to gravity, to entropy, to a repetition "automatic as the body itself" (120), to a sign that is pure or unmotivated, constitutes the destiny that Oedipa sees figured in Varo's tower, a destiny so totalizing that no escape is possible; indeed, the desire for escape only apotheosizes the law it seeks to transgress by perfecting the illusion of freedom that supports it.

Deleuze and Guattari make a distinction in *Anti-Oedipus* between "technical machines" that are defined extrinsically in terms of their functional use value or in proportion to how well they work, and "desiring-machines" that work only by always breaking down. This latter type of machine denotes a system characterized by an intrinsic boundary or invaginated contour that gives it an indeterminate locus. A desiring-machine can only oppose its own determination; this is why it always malfunctions, and why its proper mode is catastrophic or singular, tending toward its own disappearance. Pynchon's preoccupation in *The Crying of Lot 49* with the process of entropy closely parallels this malfunctioning modality of desiring machines and suggests a fundamental structural principle of the novel. Oedipa's attempt at escape through her search for the Tristero (a figure, finally, for freedom) multiplies possible meanings to a point of saturation so total that her quest becomes meaningless, an "endless, convoluted incest" of semiotic as well as social waste (14). But the deliberate manner in which this strategy of excess unfolds through the novel suggests that it cannot be read as a simple neutralization of her desire. If this were the case, then *The Crying of Lot 49* would only be a technical machine to which the reader/worker is subjected, and not a broken machine that works by metabolizing itself, by becoming a residual supplement within an underground economy of WASTE. To see how the novel posits its machinic essence in the process of revealing a possibility for escape, one must acknowledge that Oedipa never ceases being that machine, never escapes the quotation marks that underscore "her" intrinsic virtuality, "her" status not as a "real" character but as a representation in a universe of signs. The solidity and force of the paranoid moment in Pynchon's novel is such that it never yields to any reaffirmation of a lived concrete existence apart from its textual condition of possibility. Quite categorically, I would say, no alternative to the late capitalist social form implied in Oedipa's predicament can be thought outside that moment of paranoid apprehension. In a sense, the novel too is woven inside Varo's tower, a proposition that suggests in turn that Varo's tower stands in metonymically for the entire text, its description of the painting taking on a function of ekphrasis with respect to its own artistic production. If this is so, and if it is not enough simply to assert a thoroughgoing pessimism (or full-blown paranoia) that the novel only sustains, then the stake of freedom, agency, or public space that it raises will be found as well in that ekphrasis, encrypted in the painting that figures the peculiar destiny of making a world or constructing the ground on which a world can be formed, weaving as well a "mantle" in the sense of a covering, an enveloping skin, a cortical interface between inside and outside that is the place of form or the limit where forms appear, where the "coral-like" genesis of structure occurs.[4]

Toward the Tower

"Embroidering the Mantle of the Earth" forms the central panel of an autobiographical triptych, and though Pynchon mentions this fact, he never expands the allusion or explicitly elaborates on the context it suggests.[5] The triptych lies dormant in the text not so much in a mode of figurative connotation as in one of simple displaced absence. It functions as a supplement without (apparent) necessity to the text, as the negative space of a reference that needs no other support than itself but nonetheless conjures a double dimension, an unconscious of that unconscious formed by the act of reference and accessible only through an intertextual (and cross-generic) digression from the novel proper. What one finds in this double unconscious, in this "other" dimension of reference, is a set of parallel themes centered on the chance at escape. The first panel, entitled "Toward the Tower" (fig. 2), introduces the "frail girls with heart-shaped faces, huge eyes, [and] spun-gold hair" of Pynchon's description emerging from a building of narrow gables set against an umber-colored sky (the same as that identified by Pynchon in the second panel as a "void"). The visual effect of the gables is to suggest a honeycomb, a fragment of latticework, or more generally a process of algorithmic or polymeric duplication. This effect recurs in the faces of the young girls, who appear as replicas of each other, a group of identically dressed figures with identically spellbound expressions. Varo's interest in the triptych lies clearly with an automaton-like sameness: the "replicant" girls leave a "replicant" building in a movement toward the tower and the compulsion it represents continually to remake their own oppression. But because the gables also indicate a plurality of towers as the girls' point of origin, this movement is qualified by an implication of tautology—further suggested by the fact that all the girls are riding bicycles and so evoke in the very act of "cycling" a static immobility.

2. Remedios Varo, "Toward the Tower," 1961. ©2000 Artists Rights Society (ARS), New York/VEGAP, Madrid. Reproduced by permission.

The condition of arrested motion seems universal in the first two panels and clearly expresses the girls' lack of freedom, their subordination to sinister overseers (the man carrying a bag full of crows, the woman in a nun's habit, the figure in the tower holding an open book over an hourglass-shaped container from which the filaments of thread used by the girls to embroider the earth's mantle are taken), and their palpable alienation in the work they perform. Conjoined with the visual motif of repetition is a focus on forced labor, on an activity of production subsumed under a bureaucratic management extending even into the bodies and minds of the producers. But if the story Varo tells here is about the artist constrained by a uniform and mechanical production, what she means by artistic (or productive) freedom cannot be understood as a simple opposition to that constraint. The theme of escape is introduced in the first panel by a small detail: one of the girls glances to her left out of the painting and back at the viewer in a scarcely perceptible deviation from the almost catatonic norm of the others. What is significant about this deviation is its slightness, the fact that it manifests itself in a mode of diminution or subtle variation, not as a constituted difference from the rote repetitiousness of work, but as a difference in repetition or repetition *with* a difference that becomes the essentially tautological movement of an emancipatory desire. In this light, Varo's triptych is more than a representation of an unfree dissimulation characteristic of her spectral social world; it is also itself dissimulatory, inherently catatonic, invested in its own (machinic) repetitiousness as the ground for any escape it makes possible.

To put this another way, escape for Varo will be the making of the triptych and the triptych itself; it will be this glance out of the world of the painting that makes the painting material. But to create oneself as the creator (of oneself) involves a double production through which one discovers in that labor a groundlessness that sweeps away the orienting markers of place and time. The materiality of the paintings thus consists in fantasmatic elements, deliberate ambiguities that give them a curious otherworldliness. The triptych dramatizes art as escape only by disrupting the semiotic claim to signify a "real" world that can be felt in meaning itself, in the attribution of truth to a particular event, situation, or identity (even the artist's).

It is this complicity between signification and the real, between truth and self-identity or self-presence, that the triptych disrupts in its emphasis on a schizophrenic subjectivity shifting ambiguously between "she" and "they." The girls are all the same girl, existing only in terms of each other. They constitute holograms repeating the whole in each part, making each part a totality as such, a complete part or complete incompletion enclosing a process and a result, a processive result, a product that changes or that indexes in itself a motion predicated on the immobilizing passage within its own object-nature or objectification. The triptych treats the artist's relation to a reified and alienated context from within the latter's own deepest tendencies, and this inclusiveness informs a production bearing on the world itself, producing the real *as* a simulacrum and *in* its fundamental artifice.

For this "convoluted" reading to be persuasive, the possibility of escape

3. Detail from Remedios Varo, "Embroidering the Mantle of the Earth."

held out by Varo will have to pass through the world made by the artist or within the woven mantle that serves both as the world's ground (an interior layer of the earth) and as its peripheral limit (a covering or skin). The central panel of the triptych rejoins the thematic of minimal variation or difference in repetition by once again skewing the eyes of the girl farthest to the left of the tower. Her expression, more cunning than her predecessor's, here registers a consciousness of her overseer and the impassive suppression of guilt. What has she done? In what Varo herself, commenting on the triptych, describes as the girl's "trick" (fig. 3), one fold of the mantle flowing out from the slit window just underneath her station discloses two tiny upside-down figures within the enlacing branches of bare trees, "woven" together in a posture of embrace.[6] These two eminently textual and textural lovers become the central figures of the third panel, entitled appropriately enough "The Escape" (fig. 4), which shows them standing in a vehicle of indeterminate type (it resembles in inverted form the umbrella-like rudder controlled by the woman but also suggests in its hairy texture some kind of vegetal or animal matter) as it conveys them upward toward mountain peaks and a clearing sky of yellow light.[7] This line of flight drawn through the three paintings does not go by way of a simple transcendence any more than it indicates a "real" freedom

4. Remedios Varo, "The Escape," 1961. ©2000 Artists Rights Society (ARS), New York/VEGAP, Madrid. Reproduced by permission.

from a simulacral labor, from repetition or from fantasy. It delineates an "abstract line" generated at the point where tension between form and matter, figure and ground, surface and depth, center and periphery, relaxes and gives way to a generalized nondistinction, to a formal, figural, or structural difference that is internal to itself and so not determinable in an empirical sense.[8] For the girl who makes her escape, for the artist who makes her escape, and for the triptych that constitutes their collective escape, this internal *difference* works to undermine the self-identity of escape itself, to open it/her/them to an exteriority from which no escape is possible except through this opening, this singular experience in life, in art, in structure, in meaning, of a fundamental displacement rendering what is real virtual.[9]

To account for Varo's triptych in its repetitions, its multiplicities, its automatons, its production of the real or the ground of the real, one must therefore rely on a differential and negative, essentially *fictive* model of being itself. Deleuze and Guattari provide one version of this model with what they call a "collective assemblage of enunciation" that subsumes within its form variables or "flows" of a semiotic, material, and social kind. Subjectivity becomes for them this collective assemblage producing a world (in speech, in acts, in art, in writing), which does not differ from that production (i.e., of the world where "you" exist), or rather from a production of production itself that appears in a "free" indirect discourse without agency or authorship.[10] The "outside," according to Deleuze and Guattari, "has no image, no signification, no subjectivity" (A Thousand Plateaus, 23), only a machinic coimplication or lived displacement in discourse. To be a collective assemblage is to claim this singular existential dimension as one's own, and to sustain it reflexively in the act of decision and creation. It implies for the subject a mode of radical becoming, the *movement of a free difference* or a *nun* that is always other than itself, but that also is this otherness in its strangely positive potentiality. This catastrophic ontology (or this catastrophe for ontology) serves as a clear subtext for Varo's triptych insofar as it relates the making of a world to a virtual contour or intensive trait, and insofar as it implies in its multiplicities an inclusive relation to the world that one becomes. "Becoming everybody/everything [tout le monde]," write Deleuze and Guattari, "is to world [faire monde], to make a world [faire un monde]. By process of elimination, one is no longer anything more than an abstract line, or a piece in a puzzle that is itself abstract" (280). To make *a* world is therefore to make *the* world become, to make it "imperceptible" precisely in its perceptibility, abstract in its very concreteness.

To understand movement in this way, however, implies a simultaneous stasis to which Varo's triptych alludes in the vehicular nature of the escape it constructs. The formal movement is akin to what Deleuze and Guattari call nomadism. "The nomad," they write, "is . . . *he who does not move*," or rather, "the nomad moves, but while seated, and he is only seated while moving. . . . Immobility and speed, catatonia and rush, a 'stationary' process, station as process—these traits . . . are eminently those of the nomad" (381). Such an arrested movement also expresses a discursive time or the time of a writing that is flush with the real, that materially writes, that writes the real in a book that is an "assemblage with the outside" rather than a representation or "image of the world."[11] The dynamics of Varo's triptych—static movement, the girl at her station weaving (writing) a mantle or a *flow* that is the earth— raise as a central issue the relation between art and the world, in particular as it is focused in the book held up by the man (if it is a man) in the tower. This book, it can be inferred, functions as a kind of instructional manual or plan for the process of embroidering the earth's mantle, and the "man" appears in this light as a priest interpreting the book by whose representations the world will be formed. The condition of oppression from which the girl desires to escape is coded in terms of a specific model of discourse, a mimesis of the book or labor according to bookish rules. That the paintings disrupt those rules through their "nomadisms," and that their stake is nothing less than a production of the real, indicate a transformation in the world of the book, its rewriting in terms that include the outside as an internal difference or in its textual and textural singularity.

At stake, in other words, is not a real or living present opposable to representation any more than it is a representation opposed to the present, but an art or a book in whose temporal dimension a "becoming everybody/everything" is played out.[12] As a result, the first index of any escape afforded by the book as an assemblage will be its indistinguishability from its condition of servitude. To escape will be to pass through the world without distinction, to project one's own separate individuality against an existential ground that envelops and penetrates it.[13] The nature of escape for Varo (and for Pynchon, as I will shortly argue) hinges on this desubjectification of art, of the book. Escape happens for both of them through a complicity that registers an experience of nondistinction or nomadic spatiality, an in-different freedom in difference itself, an almost masochistic incorporation of the world.

Oedipa's Night Journey: Repetition, Language, and Desire

This kind of theoretical insight informs a quite different reading of *The Crying of Lot 49* than that which would start from a condition of alienation Oedipa attempts to overcome (even if she does not succeed, and even if it is only the reader who experiences "escape" in the form of a catharsis). The novel must first be situated within this machinic logic of the assemblage, of an internal difference between the living present and its spectral analagon, of a discursive time disclosing in its dimension the abstract lines or intensive traits of a drama about making worlds or about producing the real. Only in this machinic light can the investments of the novel in its own convolutions and impenetrable enigmas be seen for the peculiar desire and freedom they evoke. The point, the moral resonance, of Oedipa's story is felt less in moments of recognition that lay bare the simulacra that separate her from a genuine relation to the world than in parodies of that recognition, fabulating ironies that impede communication or ambiguate meanings. Only in this reflux back toward its own textuality does the novel uncover the "human" condition that can be shared by characters and readers alike.

This, then, is the central premise I would like to substantiate for *The Crying of Lot 49*: that the basis for any escape from Oedipa's tower, for any freedom from the malignancy of social power in late capitalist America, or for any implied redemption of agency, is precisely the novel's refusal to mean, its attempt to write its world in a language that undermines its own referential coherence. Such an attempt governs the ambivalent tension that quite literally holds Pynchon's words in place. It can be felt in statements such as the following by Dr. Hilarius, a renegade psychoanalyst turned psycho who Oedipa had hoped would "talk [her] out of [the] fantasy" of the Tristero. Barricaded in his house, shooting at the media bystanders who film the spectacle for the local news, he advises Oedipa: "Cherish it [her fantasy]! . . . What else do any of you have? Hold it tightly by its little tentacle; don't let the Freudians coax it away or the pharmacists poison it out of you. Whatever it is, hold it dear, for when you lose it you go over by that much to the others. You begin to cease to be" (138).

Dr. Hilarius can hardly be a less reliable voice in the novel than he is at this point (he has just hinted at his sinister role as a psychiatric intern in Nazi death camps), but at the same time, his admonition cannot be dismissed as yet another symptom of anomie. The novel acknowledges the power of his contention that fantasy is necessary for being by encasing it in a fantasm of its own, and by deliberately modulating its tone into a farcical register. The value Dr. Hilarius places on fantasy becomes for Oedipa another clue that, far from simplifying her situation or clarifying its mystery, only exacerbates the paralysis that she feels slowly overtaking her ("trapped," as the text will put it, "at the centre of some intricate crystal" [92]). This means that fantasy works to retard signification in a double sense: as a symptom but also as a breakdown of the symptom, as Pynchon's diagnosis of a mystified America and as a refusal of the objectivity assumed in diagnosis itself (even his own). The subtext of Dr. Hilarius's insanity erodes the truth claims made by the master (analyst or doctor, author or critic) who is presumed to know. This is why the text so emphatically highlights its own absurdity at this juncture: not only does it represent the absurdity of its culture, but it also enacts that absurdity from within. The novel *is* Dr. Hilarius in this passage, reacting in the modes of violent scandal to the alienation a tabloid and TV-dominated society provokes.

In other words, the novel, reacting to its own alienation, compounds it in the same fantasmatic or virtual gesture by which it cogently indicates its escape. The function of paranoia (Hilarius's, Oedipa's, or Pynchon's) is to ground this double valence in an immanent relation to the world the novel describes. This gives to that paranoia the distinctly schizophrenic dynamic of becoming the world (or, like Mucho Maas on LSD, "a whole roomful of people"). The text cites the external (or exclusive) difference that denies its own internal (or inclusive) implication. It therefore denies itself, submits itself to the "rising" ground of a figure that turns in an abyssal space of paraleptic meanings. *The Crying of Lot 49* calls this figure the Tristero, but the displaced and elliptical context it signifies appears with the post horn drawn on latrine walls, doodled on Yoyodyne stationery, inset on rings, printed on stamps, recycled in dreams, scrawled in a San Francisco bus, or tattooed on a sailor's hand. As Oedipa presses on in her quest, she unveils a world where nothing is hidden and subtexts exist at a strangely textual surface, where what she doesn't know becomes precisely what she does know: consciousness transparent with what it represses to constitute itself. This transparency is the deepest "meaning" behind Oedipa's aestheticizing hermeneutic desire: she "pursues strange words in Jacobean texts" because they lead her to the inherently fictive nature of her life (104). Language is the medium of the power that keeps her in her place, that determines her as a person and as an object in the world. As such it constitutes the true aim of her quest and the real key to her freedom.

Deleuze gives us a model for Oedipa's desire in a death instinct that, not material or grounded in an inertial return to inanimate states (as Freud would have it in *Beyond the Pleasure Principle*), exists on the contrary as a "subjective and differential experience" of the limit death constitutes for the living. Deleuze counterposes to a "repetition of the same" (Freud also grasps the death instinct as a conservative drive toward stasis) that works through the material model a "repetition of difference" that is the subject's experience of its own finitude or *time* as an "empty form."[14] The latter repetition etherealizes the substance of the self and evokes an immaterial substrate of being itself. It drives a desire to catch (or "trick") oneself out in the symbolic orders governing the constitution of the mental schemata that organize sensible and intelligible events. The "malignant, deliberate replication" (124) of post horn symbols in the novel anchors a world of signs that does not stand over and against the real, but in which the real becomes legible as a text.

There is nothing outside the text in *The Crying of Lot 49*, and no place in it from which to guarantee an immunity from its mediations or its fantasms. But at the same time that the real is textual, the textual is also real; it signifies a condition of "real" virtuality that every character in the novel shares. They are all *triste*, all "wretched" and "depraved" (the etymology is given in these terms on page 102), all expressed in the system of simulacra known as the Tristero, so that what Oedipa (and the novel she structures) seeks is finally her (its) own implication in the underground that may not exist, in the world that she (it) projects and that claims her (it) precisely in its uncertainty. The object of this textual desire focused in Oedipa is Oedipa herself (the novel itself) in her (its) otherness or non-self-identity; it is therefore strangely anoedipal in nature, grasped in its approach to a limit where meanings and bodies break down, where words and things lose the stability of their difference and begin to flow together. Pynchon writes this flow in the long hallucinogenic episode of Oedipa's night journey through San Francisco, which in the following excerpt becomes a musical "score."

> At some indefinite passage in night's sonorous score, it . . . came to her that she would be safe, that something, perhaps only her linearly fading drunkenness, would protect her. The city was hers, as, made up and sleeked so with customary words and images (cosmopolitan, culture, cable cars) it had not been before: she had safe-passage tonight to its far blood's branchings, be they capillaries too small for more than peering into, or vessels mashed together in shameless municipal hickeys, out on the skin for all but the tourists to see. (117–18)

The city described here belongs to Oedipa; it is "hers," her city, the city *of* Oedipa. The consequent sense of "safe-passage" she feels at large in it conditions its transformation into a vast organism, a living thing "made up" of "words and images," a text-body that is strangely abstract, without affect or impersonal, breathing and pumping blood yet chimerical, as empty and unreal as Oedipa herself (or the novel itself). The text goes on:

> Nothing of the night's could touch her; nothing did. The repetition of [post horn] symbols was to be enough, without trauma as well perhaps to attenuate it or even jar it altogether loose from her memory. *She was*

meant to remember. She faced that possibility as she might the toy street from a high balcony, roller-coaster ride, feeding time among the beasts in a zoo—any death-wish that can be consummated by some minimum gesture. She touched the edge of its voluptuous field, knowing it would be lovely beyond dreams simply to submit to it; that not gravity's pull, laws of ballistics, feral ravening, promised more delight. (118)

Oedipa's fuguelike passage within the text-city or within the text-body of herself *as* city begins with a lack of "touch," of the skin's or the hand's abstraction from the sensuous capacities that indicate an animate nature. The city and Oedipa in it become an inanimate "repetition of symbols" that is posed not as the extinction of desire but as the ground for a pleasure that is indifferent yet "lovely beyond dreams." In this way Pynchon describes the allure of an interpretive labor that, as an end in itself, is also immaculate, a *pulchritudo vaga* sealing Oedipa in an almost psychotic autonomy. If Oedipa "means" an ability to remember or recognize, then that very ability evanesces in the peculiar lightness of a world transformed into the "toy streets" she sees from the detachment of a "high balcony," or with the conditioned appetite of animals in a zoo. Oedipa's desire is caught in "roller coaster" cycles of a culture geared to incite and satisfy a "death-wish" in its subjects, to direct desire toward objects that empty its "consummation" of any substance. To "submit" to the destiny of a remembering that nonetheless cannot remember, or that is infinitely attenuated, implies a movement as ineluctable as gravity, an orbitalized desire that immobilizes not only Oedipa but the novel with its own repetition of symbols and its own fascination with the Tristero.

There is no escape from that repetition, and indeed for Oedipa and for *The Crying of Lot 49*, it will have "to be enough." What follows from this is that one must understand the nature and function of repetition more clearly. What the post horns repeat, what Oedipa repeats, what the text repeats, is the empty form desire takes in a postmodern culture. But as this repetition approaches the relative limit of a death wish that must always reconstitute itself (to want again), Pynchon's text discloses what could be called an absolute or asignifying limit at which grammatical and semantic structure loses its edge or begins to blur.[15] A zero degree can be felt in the language in the same way that the executrix Oedipa, on first encountering Inverarity's complex legacy, notices a "sense of buffering, insulation, an absence of intensity, as if watching a movie just perceptibly out of focus, that the projectionist had refused to fix" (20). *The Crying of Lot 49* is also just perceptibly out of focus, slightly approximate in its diction—a feature evident in the earlier quoted passage's occasionally lapsed article or ambiguously deployed pronoun. Language begins to erode its own content as it plays out its submission to the "voluptuous field" of its repetitions, and in the process the text becomes a travesty of its own truth claims, the warp and woof of potentially empty meanings or of an impenetrably parodic "matter" that is the static condition for change itself, a textual *hylè* that bears its determination inside itself, or that appears in an "indifferentiated" form.

Like Oedipa, the novel presents a curious detachment and levity (implied even in her name) that complicates the desire it dramatizes in the Oedipal search for a truth that is triste, depraved, low, looked for in undergrounds or in (unconscious) depths that are flat, brought to the surface of a transparent consciousness "meant to remember" the secrets with which it is coextensive. This immanent reading of the object (i.e., language itself, iterative, abstract but isomorphic with the real) taken by desire in the novel suggests even as an imperative that one read escape or freedom from Oedipa's tower not in contradiction with an alienated socius but as the socius encased within a form of expression that (re)doubles its alienation, citing or incorporating its orbitalized effects to the point that they metabolize, become residual or excremental signs in an economy of WASTE. Language (or writing) is strung through the body in the process of becoming the alternative or "shadow" system that Oedipa witnesses only in an exacerbated degradation on the streets of San Francisco:

> So it went. Oedipa played the voyeur and listener. Among her other encounters were a facially-deformed welder, who cherished his ugliness; a child roaming the night who missed the death before birth as certain outcasts do the dear lulling blankness of the community; a Negro woman with intricately-marbled scar along the baby-fat of one cheek who kept going through rituals of miscarriage each for a different reason, dedicated not to continuity but to some kind of interregnum; an aging night watchman, nibbling at a bar of Ivory Soap, who had trained his virtuoso stomach to accept also lotions, air-fresheners, fabrics, tobaccoes and waxes in a hopeless attempt to assimilate it all, all the promise, productivity, betrayal, ulcers, before it was too late; and even another voyeur, who hung outside one of the city's still-lighted windows, searching for who knew what specific image. (123)

What Oedipa is looking and listening for in this series of encounters is her own belonging to the system of WASTE it implies—not its reality or real support for which she cannot find adequate assurances (but which is really there behind the appearances) so much as the perverse or denatured "interregnum" that it constitutes for time itself, the discontinuous space or gap in structure that renders it paratactic, double, and virtual. Oedipa takes her place within this series precisely by displacing herself, by loving the repetition of symbols, by desiring texts, and by failing to find any unmediated connection in a common ground or shared public space. What she seeks is not this common ground but the secret of disconnection that nonetheless communicates, the broken machine that links only by unlinking, that posits as the basis for community a reversal of communal values or the "assimilation" of an outside that is absolute and originary. In this light, the welder who "cherishes" his ugliness, the child who "misses" a "death before birth," the Negro woman "dedicated" to "rituals of miscarriage," the night watchman swallowing commodities, and the two voyeurs looking for their "specific images" together indicate a desire that, far from being trapped in passive cycles of consumption, actively seeks to undo the structure of repression in which it is caught, indeed from which it is not different. The "death-wish" implicit in each "species of withdrawal" (123) that Pynchon enumerates on Oedipa's Walpurgisnacht evokes a repetition that abrogates the natural and human functions of sociality, reproduction and digestion; it marks in the text-body a breakdown of its own organic constitution and categorical stability. But it accomplishes this break not through a process of externalization so much as by incorporating, like the night watchman, the products of a world that reduces desire to its most material (and empty) form. Desire for the inanimate (or as the inanimate) in Pynchon's novel has to be seen in a double light to contract two death instincts, two repetitions, two limits, since only in this doubleness can the desire of the text appear in its excessive expenditures, in its masochistic transgressions of its own realism and truth.

Oedipa's and the novel's desire is double, it repeats itself, it repeats itself repeating, it repeats repetition. This nomadic movement in place designates the central ekphrastic dynamic of the text, the precise way it feels itself into the world of forever deferred revelation it describes. Freedom from Oedipa's tower occurs only through this movement, never against it, never in reaction to it, for to do so would be to destroy the implicate and broken structure of the novel that is its critique of contemporary America. Repetition for its own sake, repetition as an end in itself, repetition at the surface of the text in all its slightness, all its insubstantiality, but also all its brutality, expresses a force at the heart of desire that seeks an end to desire itself (understood as captured within a logic of consumption). In tending toward its own nondistinction from the world in which it dies, this desire precipitates its own death, but as the "empty form" in Oedipa's heart that makes her so representative a figure of her "time." One senses its presence in the "great digital computer" through which Oedipa walks at the novel's end, sorting her world into ones and zeros:

> For it was now like walking among matrices of a great digital computer, the zeroes and ones twinned above, hanging like balanced mobiles right and left, ahead, thick, maybe endless. Behind the hieroglyphic streets there would either be a transcendent meaning, or only the earth. . . . Either Oedipa in the orbiting ecstasy of a true paranoia, or a real Tristero. For there either was some Tristero beyond the appearance of the legacy America, or there was just America and if there was just America then it seemed the only way she could be relevant to it was as an alien, unfurrowed, assumed full circle into some paranoia. (181–82)

The indecision Oedipa suffers between "transcendent meanings" and "just America" does not entail a choice between the world as computer or the world as human space. There is no option between paranoia and something else, since paranoia already figures the ground or frame for choice itself, for any formulation of agency one might attach to her example. The machinic nature of the human precedes any determination of its spontaneity and freedom, and as a result Oedipa's desire for escape cannot be thought outside her encasement in a machine of generalized communication. On the contrary, this encasement must be seen as the condition for that desire and in two senses: as the cause of her alienation and as the medium for her escape, as the stimulus for an escape *from* the nexus of power relations that constitutes social repression and an escape *in* that nexus (from which, again, she is not different). The possibility of freedom held out by the novel hinges on the precise function of this preposition *in*, or rather on the coimplicate or coincident structure exemplified by the novel itself where it achieves its peculiar effect of orbitalized meanings.

The Crying of Lot 49 does not choose one or the other of the possibilities confronted by Oedipa at the "crying of lot 49"; it chooses the impasse as such, it presents the tautological circle of that double bind as the vehicle for its escape. This elliptical and repetitious textual ambivalence signals a desire that includes the world and that refuses its own exemption or election in it, a "preterite" desire that takes the world as its object in all its "promise, productivity, betrayal." By weaving or inscribing in its very texture the empty form of a "wasteful" signification, the novel discloses the incorporating link between desire and a masochism that governs the underground or unconscious of the Tristero. This masochistic desire in turn links Oedipa to her world and makes her one of those outsiders who communicate via WASTE. The impingement of nonmeaning in the text therefore assumes a new urgency in the allegiance it suggests to an experience that is residual, left over, or paratactically displaced.

To grasp the linkages, the empathic connections, the asymptotic convergences, the calculus of simultaneity that can be observed in Pynchon's novel is thus to center analysis on its disjunctive nature, to underscore the lack of "touch" on which it everywhere insists as the condition for any "coming together." It is also to resist recuperative readings that define desire (Oedipa's and the text's) as a search for meaning, for identity, or for the recovery of a dispossessed communal space. Oedipa is not a "heroine" in this sense, not the locus of a potential agency capable of wresting her culture from its late capitalist catastrophe.[16] Or rather, she is this heroine in a parody, and one can only emphasize the heroic aspect of her character in the context of its parodic quotation, for otherwise one misses the very political point about the nature of dispossessed communities and the bonds (bindings, *Bindungen*) on which they are based. *The Crying of Lot 49* discloses a highly original mode of engagement with the schizophrenia of its time, one which understands critical distance to consist of immersion in the temporal element of discourse itself. Pynchon attempts to write the displacement of the difference between the real and the simulacral, and as such to imagine the America that follows from that displacement both in its vitiating effects and in its desiring modes. Only through this attempt does the "community" of "people" who "communicate" through WASTE come into being.

The Crying of Lot 49 as a Countercultural Text

It may be difficult for many to recognize in such an unavowable community the counterculture to which *The Crying of Lot 49* belongs, since rarely has its failure as a movement with genuine political and social consequences been understood as its condition of possibility, the deepest cogency of its emancipatory promise. The counterculture did not represent a public space that either betrayed itself through its excesses or succumbed to forces of social repression. It was the discovery that *there was no public space*, and this became what had to be repressed. The narcissism of its reveries, its pulverization into either mindless pleasure or micropolitics, discloses a political desire dying in two senses: dying out and incorporating the death (or virtual context) that actuates it. The constitutive failure at the heart of Oedipa's inconclusive quest is the dynamic of this double desire. The *negativity* of her story is what makes it so compelling a sign of its time.[17]

Of course the counterculture was a heterogeneous phenomenon and not easily reducible to one exemplary figure or meaning. There were many factions within it that had little to do with one another, and that even differed quite radically over matters of principle, practice, and taste. The back-to-the-land movement grew up alongside California free love (with its north and south, Haight Ashbury and Sunset Strip, variants), but the anarcho-politics of the Yippies or the Weathermen had in the end very different stakes. The New Left only partially overlapped with the counterculture, and according to participants like Todd Gitlin, it struggled to define itself in opposition to the latter's undisciplined excesses.[18] The relentlessly reflexive avant-gardism of the New York art scene had, in certain quarters and phases anyway, little in common with either West Coast idealism or radical politics.[19] The most salient characteristic of the counterculture may therefore have been its fractures, its loose confederation of subgroups or undergrounds actuated not by the goal of social unity but by the darker drive toward disintegration.

Pynchon's novel dramatizes this drive at the register of a temporality that is both subjective and social. I have attempted to rehearse some of its features in the foregoing reading: masochistic incorporation of consumption's superfluity and waste; rejection of organicism in favor of the "machinic" virtuality of the body without organs; a "preterite" subsumption in the displaced contexts of discourses that govern subjectivity, experience, and identity. The "death wish" active at each level of signification gives *The Crying of Lot 49* an almost diabolical power to confound the discursive orders of its late modern society, and as such it continues to trouble its readers, not least because of the risk it takes by upsetting even those concepts used to understand *progressive* political life: sovereignty, actualization, choice, communication, solidarity, representation, citizenship, democracy itself. *The Crying of Lot 49*, more than simply telling the story of civil society's sacrifice to the economic requirements of late capitalism, evokes the function of that civil society as the limit on whose transgression the capitalist machine depends in order to exist at all. This is the reason why that society has no substance, and why the attempt to revitalize it through the 1960s in the forms of counterculture fell hoisted on the petard of its own virtuality. What the counterculture bodied forth was the *empty form* of its time grasped as itself double: without substance in all the ways anomie may be felt today, and immaterial in the manner of an infinite substance that supports the counterculture's negative and differential imagination of the social body.

Herein lies its originality and even value as a historical moment: through an imaginative short circuit (or reverie), it opened out temporality in the form of a chiasmic inversion of end and origin, failure and promise, that allowed for new insight into the mode of production governing it. At stake in the "new kind of time" announced by artifacts like *The Crying of Lot 49*, beyond a clear perception of the ways we are disenfranchised in a rationalized capitalist society, is a countercultural desire that stays true to the *possibility* of genuine self-determination and social freedom. It does so by remaining in a state of indeterminacy (like Varo's artist, like Oedipa in her quest), indexing in its own heterological drive what Deleuze (reading Freud on narcissism) calls a reflux of libido on the self that forms a "desexualized, neutral and displaceable energy" (*Difference and Repetition*, 112). This energy works a collapse at the level of content that is experienced only formally or at the level of expression, in the failures to adequately define, represent, or narrate one's self-identity.

In a similar vein, literary and psychoanalytic critic Leo Bersani posits a "non-referential use of libidinal energy" that informs a constitutive masochism in the subject (*The Freudian Body*, 52).[20] The function of this energy is to expose in the need for psychic and semantic coherence the tautological presence of non-sense. He links this asignifying force to a self-shattering "sexuality" that disorients the binary oppositions grounding consciousness in a body fixed on both temporal and spatial coordinates: subject and object, theory and practice, imagination and reality, individual and civilization. The inimical relation of sexuality to the structured self leads to a paradox: the negative energy turns against itself, and in this reflexive torsion sexuality *disappears* or, rather, detaches from its objects or its contents to become a floating and "atemporal" substrate of the sexually organized person.[21] The alienated form it thus takes opens the body to an "ontologically traumatic fantasy" (43) that catches up its excitements in the infinite regress of its own representations: the body floats in a medium of language and loses its "reality." For Bersani, *the thought of desire is the desire of thought*, and in this double, inverse relation between subject and predicate, he sees a repetition exposing in the subject's representations a virtual or apocryphal "nature."

The counterculture became a theater for exploring this "sexual" dimension of social experience precisely in the fatalism of its inconclusive ends. Its more anarchic elements—dropping out, drugs and music, the pranks of the Yippies, occultism, and so forth—were only the more obvious signs of a broad social encounter with a negativity that required broken machines, willful short circuits of representation and action, fractiousness, and finally disillusionment. This negativity appeared as well in the counterhegemonic character of movements, single-issue identity politics predicated on localized tactics aimed at transforming discursive orders in which racial, sexual, and class discrimination becomes legitimate. The failure of the counterculture to achieve the consistency and stamina of a populist mass culture cannot be explained in terms of an inadequate commitment (by individuals or groups) to the principles of democracy. The social unity grounding a dialectical movement from necessity to freedom misses the line of flight that runs through its eschatological patterns like a moire. What this means is that those principles no longer actuate a desire capable of responding to the system of domination that appears with later phases of capitalist accumulation. This system, as thinkers such as Foucault have taught us, is *carceral* in nature; it extends into the consciousness of the individual, making the individual the agent of its reproduction. In it the relationship between subjectivity and power becomes an unmediated one. How the subject grasps its implication in the system, or let me say with Deleuze and Guattari the *assemblage*, of its spatiotemporal organization becomes a crucial political and ethical question from the moment this unmediated relationship is experienced in all its immanence. The counterculture, with greater or lesser degrees of self-consciousness, began to ask—and live—this question on a social scale.

The Crying of Lot 49 echoes its time precisely in its desubjectifications, in Oedipa as a caricature whose form wavers and whose essence is not fixed, and in a writing that undermines its own analogical coherence. Oedipa does not seek the meaning of the Tristero—the meaning of her countercultural desire—by moving through a space (*chora* or *topos*) that contains her as a centered subject; rather, that space becomes a function of her movement understood as a "pure becoming" that refracts her mobile subjectivity through the decentering prism of a schizophrenic multiplicity. Deleuze and Guattari call this type of movement an "involution" and refer it to the dissolution of fundamental metaphysical categories: being and appearing, resemblance and mimetic correspondence, filiation and production (A Thousand Plateaus, 238). To "involve" is to experience the field of intensive flows that one is even as the self, by its own (masochistic) nature, denies this condition of its possibility to project a distinct identity. Pynchon's novel attempts to dramatize this intensive and virtual experience or, what amounts to the same thing, nonexperience of the subject in a late modern context. At stake in this drama, beyond its representation of a carceral world, is an anomalous duration or temporality that, while not "true," remains nonetheless "in the true" as far as the biopolitical production of social order is concerned. Here the time of the counterculture takes on its greatest significance. Whether the issue was civil rights (for African Americans, women, or gay people), the Vietnam War, ecology, or sexual liberation, what mattered most fundamentally was the ability to understand "what's going on," the case of what is, beyond the technologies of mental and bodily control, in a complicity that was strangely inescapable. This entailed for the reveries of counterculture that they *perform* their own limitations, their own implications in the abstracting social contexts they symptomatized. In some senses, the counterculture was most radical at its most schizophrenic, because it thereby produced an "edge" (or line) where the necessity of the symptom took on its deepest experiential resonance.

But to articulate a countercultural desire of this anomalous type involves one's discourse in an evident double bind: one cannot express what one means without reiterating the structures of meaning that this desire attempts to shatter. Expression becomes the scene of the very repetition isolated as the subject matter of discourse.[22] Abstraction and complexity become symptomatic of a displacement upward that conditions the self-negating knowledge one needs to understand the world today. Indeed, for Bersani, sexuality is "coextensive" with a process of sublimation (45); the latter does not repress, but extends and elaborates, the sexual drives, which, in the inverted time they assume as a result, appear only in the light of a theoretical artifice.

This may be the best explanation for the unreal narrative worlds Pynchon constructs, and why maintaining them intact in our readings assumes an ethical urgency. Perhaps the most conspicuous characteristic of 1960s culture was the emergence of theory in aesthetic practices. To an unprecedented degree, artists pushed conceptual, narrative, and also social limits to a point of aggressive abstraction, where the subject's essential "sublimation" comes into view. If the excesses of such work (be it Le Weekend or John Cage's "Streets of Laredo," a Claes Oldenburg cheeseburger or Deleuze and Guattari's *Anti-Oedipus*) are viewed retrospectively as proof of a self-indulgence and narcissism since outgrown, such diagnoses miss in the symptom this material forms the *body* it recovers amid the terror of carceral life—the body in what Pierre Bourdieu calls its "habitus," the space of intersecting and overlapping social forces that suture it to the fields of its aims and objects. "The body is in the social world," Bourdieu writes, "but the social world is in the body. . . .

The very structures of the world are present in the structures (or, to put it better, the cognitive schemes) that agents implement in order to understand it" (Pascalian Meditations, 152). The subject on this account—containing what contains it—is not a figure against a ground grasped in perspective, seen from outside as an object among other objects (and capable of taking itself as an object), but the space that cannot be put into perspective by consciousness. Absorbed in its implicated or implicate order, this subject experiences itself as a "movement of world" through existential (text)ures that condition both its domination and its freedom—the difference between them being once again internal to that movement and felt in the instance of a subjective vertigo.

It is from the plane of immanence on which this reeling of the self transpires that the element of force proper to the system of late capitalism appears. Michael Hardt and Antonio Negri, elaborating a critical analysis of that system in their book Empire, refer to a virtuality in its dynamics that derives most fundamentally from a dematerialization of labor in networks of communication, information, and exchange.[23] The postindustrial metamorphosis of work signals an autonomization of the life-world (or what Marx called our species-life) in increasingly symbolic and discursive regimes. The linguistic production of social reality underwrites a biopolitical control that is for them without measure, placeless and nonlocatable, mixed and coextensive. The schizophrenia of the subject is a metonymy (or hologram) for the schizophrenia of the system. But it is also in this metonymy that the subject discovers its iterative and symptomatic possibilities of resistance to power; it is in the registration of its nonseparable discursive relation to the world that it reclaims its dignity as a person and as a citizen.[24]

The strange necessity of displacement and substitution, dream and theoretical fiction, language itself in the reflexes of counterculture would continue to concern Pynchon in his next and grandest novel, where he pushes the dynamics of desire present in the earlier work to a point of seemingly infinite density. Gravity's Rainbow seeks to situate its countercultural moment in a broader historical context than was possible in The Crying of Lot 49. To do so, he takes us back through the swerve of discourse to Europe and the origins of postwar America. Ironically it is this (a)historical detour that brings the time of the novel into sharpest relief—its exacerbated abstractions, precipitating a kind of delirium, that nest its own production in its distinctive context. In the following three chapters, I set out to track the principal features of the novel's time through the range of its chiasmic, iterative, and self-implicating effects.

3
TURNING AROUND THE ORIGIN IN
GRAVITY'S RAINBOW: PARODY, PRETERITION,
PARANOIA, AND OTHER POLYMERA

My life closed twice before its close—
It yet remains to see
If immortality unveil
A third event to me
—Emily Dickinson

Hydrogen fluoride . . . can form a type of aggregate which has been termed an "association polymer," by hydrogen-bonding. This may be due to resonance between the two structures, of equivalent energy content, differing only in the distribution of their valency electrons. Resonance between I and II would lead to a structure largely ionic in character . . . which we may write as III, each hydrogen atom being shared by two fluorines:
  (I) H—F H—F H—F H—F H—F
  (II) H F-H F-H F-H F-H F
  (III) H—F—H—F—H—F—H—F
—*A Chemistry of Plastics and High Polymers*

"Can you do Addition?" the White Queen asked. "What's one and one and one and one and one and one and one and one and one?" —Lewis Carroll, *Through the Looking Glass*

In *Gravity's Rainbow* Pynchon treats the force of gravity to a literary working over unprecedented, at least in directness and scope, in the history of the novel. But despite the fascinating changes in humanity's conception of gravity since Einstein first published the General Theory of Relativity, one suspects its principal metaphoric attraction for Pynchon is its very (Newtonian) self-evidence in our lives, its exertion there in the spaces of ordinary experience where we understand our freedom at its most basic level and in its most basic limitations. Gravity is a sign for that freedom and its limitations, a mode for Pynchon of understanding the paradoxical nature of a desire called into being by its limits or by its own negation. What this means is that gravity signifies for Pynchon not simply a constraint, the weighing down of an oppression, or the strange vertigo of a desire for unconsciousness, but rather the ground of a powerful facility for movement, for poise of thought and feeling, for what Pynchon might call "synthesis" and "control."

One medium for this facility is writing itself, the intense fashioning of sentences in which a kind of gravity confers on them a resonance with profoundly physical energies, a density that gives them the mass and texture almost of things. Heidegger refers to a similar substantiality for the work of art with what he calls man's "setting up of the world" and "setting forth of the earth," two essential features of the work or of its "work-being" ("Origin of the Work of Art," 47). The "repose of the work that rests in itself" is a "happening" for Heidegger, a movement or "at any rate not an opposite that excludes motion from itself, but rather includes it. . . . Where rest includes motion, there can exist a repose which is an inner concentration of motion, hence a highest state of agitation, assuming that the mode of motion requires a rest" (48). This paradox of motion in immobility governs the "opposition of world and earth" that the work of art instigates, the tension of a "self-opening" that "cannot endure anything closed" and a "self-enclosing" that "tends always to draw the world into itself and keep it there" (49). Only in this "struggle" does either world or earth manifest itself, the first as that discursive medium in which the second appears precisely in its "concealed" or displaced character. Thus the paradox of an "unfolding" repose in the work, indeed of a work that contains within itself the articulations of time, underlies an encounter between culture and nature where each conditions the other in the establishment of an origin whose "truth" derives from the fact that it is a source with a history, made as much as it makes possible.

The gravitational attraction of this source insists throughout Pynchon's most ambitious novel at all levels of implication. It opens a "Zone" of differential diachrony where the "earth" reveals a singularly semiotic appurtenance. *Gravity's Rainbow* dramatizes the *fiction* of origin, the arbitrary act of self-assertion that projects its own cause and grounds its self-presence only at the end of a subjectivizing process. This "turn" to fable and language is for Pynchon expressly political, for it charges writing with the an-archy of production, the fundamental violence of beginning, the negativity of change itself. The novel, fictionalizing the fiction of origin, redoubles that charge to grasp the death drive at work in its own textual body. This Thanatos-like "gravity" not only conditions intentionality but reveals its essential groundlessness. Deleuze and Guattari suggest a similar function for literature in their book on Kafka. They deploy another "nomadic" paradox to grasp the time of writing as a dimension proper to the subject of enunciation, whose immobility (in a room, writing) "gives the subject of the statement an apparent movement, an unreal movement" that underwrites a resistance to the real, a parodic dismantling in particular of the Oedipal law (*Kafka*, 31). For them, writing precedes that law—and the constitution of the subject it implies—not vice versa, and it is this ontologically prior status of writing that they want to isolate in Kafka by way of precipitating in his supposed dysfunctionality the capacities of "desiring-production." Writing is a sort of "immobile voyage" (35) that engages forces of a specifically historical, social, economic, and cultural kind, conducting these forces along lines that invert the world and expose its origin as a production of production itself.[1]

For Pynchon, writing is conceived in terms of its gravitational fields, negative spaces that hold language in a compressed form, in a stratified, almost geological, historical materiality. *Gravity's Rainbow*, one could say, stages the "struggle" of world and earth to actualize the capacity that derives precisely from the influence of gravity (as a limit, a negation, a death drive). That the act of writing is a recapitulation of history for Pynchon can be seen in the way the Rocket—its obsessional attraction, its construction, its firing, its detonation—becomes emblematic of that act, the assemblage that overdetermines writing so thoroughly it might seem difficult, if not impossible, to actualize in it any "capacity" not implicated in its sheer destructiveness and dehumanization. Gravity in the novel clearly colludes with that destructiveness as Pynchon represents it, since the significations that cluster around the Rocket, while they include the sense of an imaginary escape from gravity, also (and more pertinently) emphasize the contrary sense, that the Rocket apotheosizes or even fetishizes gravity as a symbol of death, as that against which one struggles to define one's self, but also that which perfects the struggle for definition itself. As a consequence, however, the only way to conceive of this death drive as gravity is to universalize it, and it follows from this that any resistance or counterforce can only be another imaginary escape, unless it too claims that death drive for its own life-affirming purposes. At one level, indeed, this political problem of how to resist the Rocket and its destructive capacity leaves Pynchon in a double bind, which is one reason why his depiction of the Counterforce in *Gravity's Rainbow* is such an unforgiving parody of political action. Certainly the Counterforce produces no coherent program for undoing the structures of death that menace civilization in the novel. This might not be the point. Where the life-affirming dimension of Pynchon's novel appears is rather in the parody itself, as a mode that makes visible the function of gravity as a ground or principle of creative production with respect to the "double" production of an origin as the foundation of truth. *Gravity's Rainbow*, one could say, is a "broken machine" that thrives on a certain entropy, a breaking down or burning out (a dying) that conditions its appearance (the best physical model for this would be the sun).

The "truth" of the novel must be grasped, then, in the movement of a counterharmony or discord that agitates against the fluid restitution of meaning to the text. One example of the difficult necessity for reading Pynchon in this fashion can be inferred from the following origin myth presented in the novel:

> What you felt stirring across the land . . . it was the equinox . . . green spring equal nights . . . canyons are opening up, at the bottom are steaming fumaroles, steaming the tropical life there like greens in a pot, rank, dope-perfumed, a hood of smell . . . human consciousness, that poor cripple, that deformed and doomed thing, is about to be born. This is the World just before men. Too violently pitched alive in constant flow ever to be seen by men directly. They are meant only to look at it dead, in still strata, transputrefied to oil or coal. Alive, it was a threat: it was Titans, was an overspeaking of life so clangorous and mad, such a green corona about Earth's body that some spoiler *had* to be brought in before it blew the Creation apart. So we, the crippled keepers, were sent out to multiply, to have dominion. God's spoilers. Us. Counter-revolutionaries. *It is our mission to promote death.* (720)

At its most explicit, this passage, even taken out of context (it occurs in a late episode with Tchitcherine and Geli Tripping), presents a coherent story with some legitimate metonymic claims on the narrative as a whole. "Human consciousness" is "crippled," "deformed," and "doomed," an agent of death whose appearance marks a taming and a rationalizing of the world as pure convulsive flow. A "Counter-revolutionary," man suppresses Eros to hold the Creation together, and in this role a constructive Apollonian drive can be detected, except that man's "promotion of death" has now come to threaten Creation itself, and counterrevolutionary consciousness has gone mad. The myth could be read as calling for either a reproportioning of the death drive to a more useful, sublimating function or its elimination in favor of revolutionary and Dionysian energy. Or it could be read in the spirit of quotation it exemplifies, in its double-voiced reference to other texts (particularly Norman O. Brown's *Life against Death*). Finally, it could be read in the full context of the novel as a complex parody of the form-matter structure that regulates the appearance of things, at least for philosophical discourse.[2] This parody refers the text to the question of humanity's relationship to the earth, to its informing of things, tools, and works as an activity taking its own manipulation of material to be the model of being for things in general. That is to say, all things become technology, or appear to the world in the guise of their availability for use. The subtext for the passage, as with all of *Gravity's Rainbow*, thus turns on the exploitive act that Pynchon highlights through the novel's intertextuality. The text's discordance would then arise from this acting out of other discourses to make its point, sustaining in itself the violence of a technicized and instrumentalized culture. This is what parody does for Pynchon: raise the issue of this violence through its double articulation, its effect of neutralizing sense, of modulating the text tonally toward the frequency of an incorporating masochism that can be heard in the "doomed" nature of human consciousness and in the extremity of "our" death-promoting "mission," a mission that involves, for example, the extraction of oil and coal from the earth and the synthetic replication of molecular elements taken from coal tar to make plastics. Indeed, it is when death is associated with gravity in Pynchon's novel that human self-destructiveness becomes so extreme as to seem like a law of nature, and Pynchon can be read as confirming the inevitability of the nihilative forces that threaten to destroy us. His critique of these forces begins with the question of form, which in the quoted passage is broached by the "transputrefied" remains of the earth's titanic flows, flows that human beings are only "meant to look at" in their dead state. Destruction of the earth is determined by this necessity, this centripetal pull toward dead flows, toward matter, toward energy. Nostalgia for flow, for the time before humanity, for that which "cannot be seen directly," underwrites the violence against flow and against the origin that is not properly an origin at all, not perceptible as such except by virtue of a domination and a forgetting. Titanic earth is as much a construction supporting violence as it is the object of that violence, and this constructedness, this corpselike transputrefaction of the energy source as metaphor for what the world does to the earth but also for how the earth undoes the world, is what Pynchon attempts to open out in the formal space of his novel.

In this sense, *Gravity's Rainbow* shares many of the same concerns explored in *V.* and *The Crying of Lot 49*, massively extending their experiments with "broken" textual form.³ Several narrative links indeed connect *Gravity's Rainbow* to *V.*, the most conspicuous of which is the presence in both novels of the character Weissmann, aka Captain Blicero, whose sexual love for the African Herero Enzian Oberst and the young German soldier Hans Gottfried establishes one of *Gravity's Rainbow*'s many complex networks of meaning: whiteness as a form of death but also a denial of death, Weissmann the "white man" and his imperialist relation to the nonwhite world, Blicero's "bliss" and Gottfried's "God's peace" at the heart of a desire that perfects itself in the figure of the V-2 rocket at Brenschluss, the height of its trajectory, and the pure moment of a deliverance to and from the laws of gravity.[4] As with V. in relation to its semantic constellations, *Gravity's Rainbow* is focused on its own overdetermined production within networks of meaning like this one, its structural complicity as a work of art in a Western culture, a metaphysics, intimately bound up with a history of violent ethnocentrism, genocide, and war. The place of technology in this history is the novel's central preoccupation, signaled not only by its metaphorizations of the machine but by its attentiveness to its own machinic textual being. *Gravity's Rainbow* is language as technē, the deployment of metaphor, analogy, repetition, and narrativity to tell the story of a culture's rationalization and objectification by thought. But it is also in some sense a broken language, the text of a resemblance gone mad, incited to a proliferation of meanings that overpowers itself in what Jean Baudrillard calls an "exponential strategy" (*Fatal Strategies*, 34), "arbitrary metamorphosis," a "dizzying over-multiplication of formal qualities" (9), a redoubling spiral that desiccates or "abuses" reference. "Ecstasy," writes Baudrillard, "is the quality proper to any body that spins until all sense is lost, and then shines forth in its pure and empty form" (9). *Gravity's Rainbow* spins like this. It performs a "passion for intensifying, for escalation, for an increase in power, for ecstasy—for any quality at all, provided that, ceasing to be relative to its opposite (the true to the false, the beautiful to the ugly, the real to the imaginary), it becomes superlative, positively sublime, as if it had absorbed all the energy of its opposite" (9). This absorption of opposite energies as the ruin of definition, judgment, substance, truth itself, gives to the networks of meaning Pynchon reticulates through the novel a feeling of superfluousness or overinflation, as though they were too obvious somehow to be the point. Nevertheless, the point has to do precisely with that obviousness, that *display* of meaning effects, of language in its materiality peeking through its representations, presenting itself as such, apart from its technicization in a world that understands itself no other way.

Clearly something disastrous has happened to language in Pynchon's universe, only what the nature of that event is, in what temporal dimension it takes place, cannot be grasped by the altered language itself. His novel is disastrous as much as it is *about* disaster. If *Gravity's Rainbow* is a challenge, if it strikes a tone similar to Baudrillard's provocative interpretations of late capitalist culture, it also registers confusion, ambivalence, a kind of mourning without an object, a sense of itself as the instrument of its own desecration. This "mourning" could be specified in Baudrillard's work as well, for instance where he analyzes the social logic of fashion as a sign system divorced from the discourse of use value, establishing its meanings (the "beautiful" and the "ugly") in the arbitrary and empty mode of pure equivalence.[5] Fashion, in other words, is also "ecstatic"; it exemplifies the autonomizing tendency of a capitalist system grown so abstract and free-floating that humanity no longer recognizes itself in its activities. An affirmative *symbolic exchange* devolves for Baudrillard into a reified *sign value exchange* that only reproduces a profound social fragmentation.[6] Because the capitalist sign system generates needs rather than bases itself on them, economic man, Baudrillard argues, cannot be understood in relation to an origin determined as "Mana, vital force, instincts, needs, choices, preferences, utilities, motivations . . . the same magical copula, the equal sign in 'A = A' " (*For a Critique of the Political Economy of Sign*, 71). Capitalism engineers *mana*; it "needs our needs" (84), encodes them precisely within a "doubling" or tautological operation capable of masking or miraculating itself as its own ground and legitimation. This sets up a curious bivalence in Baudrillard's discourse, constraining the critique of social order in terms of old socioeconomic theories incapable of penetrating the simulatory logic of the sign, and pushing it in the direction of an apparent embrace (and exacerbation) of the abstractions the sign ratifies.

This embrace is not an endorsement. If fashion, capitalism, and Baudrillard's writing can be linked to one another structurally, Baudrillard does not cease by this fact to be a critic of capitalism (sometimes even a moralizing one). He explores the nature of a spectral social form in which desire, the individual subject, the social body, and the body politic are bound up and determined to repeat the schizoid symptom of a metalinguistic domination. If the difference between sign value exchange and symbolic exchange in Baudrillard's work is to have any explanatory value at all, it is therefore not as a distinction in the usual sense. He cannot make the tautology a dialectic. Sign value exchange and symbolic exchange are at one level homologous, even if they are utterly different at another level, indeed, radically opposed and antagonistic. But the form this antagonism takes can be glimpsed only in a redoubling strategy that focuses the subject-object dualism of Western metaphysics in a "glare of parody" (24). To take another example, the distinction Baudrillard makes in *Fatal Strategies* between "obscenity" and "seduction" depends on a similar equivocation of opposite energies, their simultaneous dislocation from, and collapse back into, one another. "Seduction" is rebellion against a capitalist order, the "obscenity" of which consists in its "transpolitical" drive for total transparency, pure visibility or positivity, the exhibited trait, the exposed secret.[7] Seduction is a taking up of the artificial sign, of the illusion, of the "falser than false" that achieves once again a kind of truth, against the ideology of the real that lies at the heart of the capitalist system. It works by turning the elements of the obscene against it. Thus "if the false can be transparent with all the power of the true—such is the sublime form of illusion and seduction—the true, too, can be transparent with all the power of the false—and this is the form of obscenity" (54).

This double and inverse sentence is also a rhetorical model for Baudrillard's discourse and for the social logic he would like to analyze. Both can be understood as parodied tautologies, iterative strategies that foreclose the possibility of conceptual perspective. This is, as well, what makes Pynchon's similar project in *Gravity's Rainbow* so representative of a postwar sensibility predicated on decoding capitalist society through effects of implication. The counterculture, as I have argued, gives us in its reveries, its nonsense, its delirious excesses, one example of this sensibility at work, particularly in its positive relation to the very social and symbolic orders it opposes. In this and the next three chapters, I seek to specify the decoding functions in Pynchon's most famous novel, but I do so in the light of the counterculture's symptomatic time, importing into my readings discussions of a theoretical nature that echo its excesses in their willful abstractions. I juxtapose accounts of Deleuze's book on masochism (first published in France in 1967) and Deleuze and Guattari's *Anti-Oedipus* (1973) with those of Pynchon's novel in the context of an inquiry into juxtaposition itself, reading texts through other texts or "beside" other texts, a gesture central to Pynchon's work and to parody in general. Such a displaced and overdetermined writing enacts within itself interstitial encounters that are also pure events in an "involuted" time, what Baudrillard calls "catastrophe in the literal sense: the inflection or curve that has its origin and end coincide in one, that makes the end return to the origin and annul it, yielding to an event without precedent and without consequences—pure event" (*Fatal Strategies*, 17). The event conceived as a rupture of causality or rational occurrence affords in Baudrillard's view the possibility of a "pure contiguity" (151), connection without "contact" (146), reference, or logical succession. This aleatoric or oblique temporality is what the media, for example, packages and presents every day, but it is also a decoding of meaning structures perceived as inseparable from the violent history of Western culture. The disappearance of history (as "precedent") and of the sense that things matter (i.e., have "consequences") also enables a "seductive" strategy of response that does not reestablish "history" or a sense that things matter so much as parody them, double them, and transpose them into a "fatal" or "reversible" time.

Parody could be said to act out a seductive or fatal strategy of critical response to a late capitalist socius deploying itself on two fronts: the utilitarian, where it reduces everything to a use value it purports to find extant in the world; and the affective or consummative, where the exemplar for the useful object becomes the commodity that sustains in itself a more fundamental uselessness, an arbitrary and differential semiosis of value exposing the useful, the real, the real object (the earth) as a simulacrum. The desire that determines the earth this way, useful and useless at the same time, energy and waste, the site of a desecration that proceeds as much by abstraction as by concretion, appears in parody as its object, that the structure of which parody can illuminate for a culture caught in its inner workings. The desire of parody, then, must not be confused with its parodied object, except that this desire does not *lack* its object either, and the difference between the parody and what it cites can be understood only across a boundary inclusive to desire in general, a desire that divulges its origin in a "struggle" of the Heideggerian kind.

Pynchon critics McHoul and Wills argue the limitations of a hermeneutic approach focusing on parody in *Gravity's Rainbow*. Although examples of parody, along with satire, farce, travesty, parable, hyperbole, and ellipsis, abound in the novel, McHoul and Wills maintain that such conventional figures presuppose a dualistic and analogic integrity that the novel undercuts or rewrites (*Writing Pynchon*, 57). Even when the concept of parody is pushed to self-parody (or what I am calling metaparody), readings of this type tend to extol the virtues of an indeterminacy and interpretive autonomy, which, they suggest, too naively reinscribes a "bourgeois individualist ideology" of social constructionism in literary criticism.[8] The decision here to conserve parody as a register of critique—albeit one that shades into what Jameson (negatively) calls pastiche or McHoul and Wills (affirmatively) call "post-rhetorical" deconstructions of analogic duality—stems from the conviction that whatever rewriting of the semantic field takes place in Pynchon's novel does not amount to another modality so much as a "solicitation" (I will return to this Derridean term) of existing modalities (like parody) that exposes in itself the implicate order of its postwar (and countercultural) moment. McHoul and Wills rightly point out the dialectic or "transcending" dynamic of rhetorical operations that fail to account for the structure of analogy itself; by understanding the object of Pynchon's parody to be that structure in its relation to production, I am able to symptomatize a historical context predicated on a discontinuous temporality.⁹ *Gravity's Rainbow* highlights this discontinuity most explicitly through its narrative displacement from America in the late 1960s and early 1970s to Europe in 1945. This displacement is also reversed as Pynchon freights the text with more and more explicit reference to the present moment of its writing, intertextually sabotaging the unities of time, place, and action. In this manner, he calls attention to the reversibility of origins at the center of the novel's paratactic structure, a double inversion that becomes a figure for the autonomizing and reifying history of America from its inception in Puritan utopia to its apogee in a postwar society dominated by consumerist spectacle, bureaucratic and technological penetration into new and more intimate regions of the life-world, decoded sociopolitical structures from the state to the family, and a highly speculative exchange on global money markets. Pynchon thematizes each of these features (and many more) in his novel, but his critique works most profoundly at a nonthetic level where the abstraction of his time reveals its specific ground and principle of reproduction in a practice of writing.

The time of *Gravity's Rainbow*, one might say, is similar to that of Emily Dickinson's poem quoted at the beginning of this chapter: the present tense of a kind of lived or living death, poised between a life figured as double, two events, two closures, and the deferred revelation of a third event that may or may not confer a transcendental meaning on that double figuration, making it part of a (temporal) series that redeems it from the implication of meaninglessness. *Gravity's Rainbow*, like the poem, will forever remain in this peculiar suspension between life and death, in a present buried in the past and stretched toward the future, ironically aware of itself as caught in a breakdown signaled by a *repetition without sense*. How (or if) the two events of the speaker's life relate to each other is a question that needs another (God's eye) perspective for its answer. But in the absence of this perspective—an absence that is fundamentally constitutive of the speaker's subjectivity—that absence itself becomes the point, the essence, the strategy of the poem. It enacts or is the fracture of time, submerged in the element of a profound schizophrenia, turning (repetitively) around itself, attempting to grasp the peculiar positivity of its own fracture. *Gravity's Rainbow* makes this precession of the representationalist desire for meaning around the axis of its own schizophrenic nature more explicit, and I would like to focus on this movement here for how it evokes, through its detour into Europe and its own origins, the symptomatic contour (or abstract line) of a contemporary American experience.

The Time of Parody and the Parody of Time

Just after Tyrone Slothrop, haphazardly searching the white confines of the northward-driving ship *Anubis* for the lost child Bianca, is pitched abruptly into the "whipped white desolation" (491) of the Baltic Sea and retrieved by the smuggler Frau Gnahb (which backward spells "bhang," a Hindu word for marijuana,[10] and thus for Slothrop one more hallucinogenic deviation from the story of his will, or one more wrinkle in the superimposed story of his devolition), he learns from the good Frau's son Otto (spelled the same backward), about one of her principal talents.

"Ach, she's fantastic. She knows by instinct—*exactly how* to insult *anybody*. Doesn't matter, animal, vegetable—I even saw her insult a *rock* once."

"Aw, now—"

"Really! Ja. A gigantic clummmp of felsitic debris, last year, off the coast of Denmark, she criticized its," just about to fall into one those mirthless laughs we edge away from, "its *crystalline structure*, for twenty minutes. Incredible." (496–97)

If that mirthless laugh (even withheld) sounds familiar to readers of *Gravity's Rainbow*, it is not only because Pynchon shares with Frau Gnahb the unerring instinct to insult. Something about her particular talent (with its particular application here) could be said to exemplify, at a number of levels, an effect of discomfort Pynchon regularly induces in us. Indeed, detractors might even point to this passage as one egregious example of the novel's mannered style, its habit of straining credulity for the sake of the punch line, the pleasure it takes in its techno-scientific virtuosity, finally the not-so-sneaking suspicion that the joke itself just isn't that funny. Perhaps what most goads mature sensibility here is the implied attribution of consciousness to a rock that Frau Gnahb's prodigious need for a victim wreaks on her readers. And not only are we to believe that she *knows* what will hurt a rock's feelings, but we are expected to consider that for twenty minutes she *elaborates* on that knowledge.

How is one to read the provoking tone of this deliberately bad joke? How is one to assess what I suspect is its fatefully metonymic relation to *Gravity's Rainbow* as a whole, its juxtaposition with the *Anubis* episode, its status as interlude or aside, its displaced time in a narrative overwhelmed by such displacements? Through the embarrassment of the joke that Frau Gnahb even insults rocks, the claim of a certain seriousness can be felt, only we seem to lack adequate rules for its reception. To associate feeling with the inanimate, to enter within its "crystalline structure" to disturb realist expectations linked to subjectivity, is to involve us in meanings that always threaten to become absurd. If we are *not* to feel for or along with the rock in this case, then the joke is either on us as readers forced to consider such a trivial possibility, or it's on Pynchon, whose joke simply founders on its own irrelevance and exposes in his poetics a radical reduction of meaning and an almost masochistic mode of self-parody.

Pynchon, that is, might very well be making fun of himself here, and this "insult" turning back on itself may be what constitutes the joke's proper relation to the novel as a whole. *Gravity's Rainbow* knows it's "bad," and the recursive form this knowledge takes turns around a desubjectivized feeling for the nonhuman world, indeed a penetration into the inanimate expressed by a certain objectification of language. McHoul and Wills refer to a "material equivalence between . . . signifiers" (53) in *Gravity's Rainbow* that neutralizes distinctions or "relations of difference" (48). What they call "material typonymy" reduces rhetorical figures, the signs of classical semiology, the metaphorical/analogical work of meaning in the novel, to the strange salience of its textual existence, language in its bare objecthood apart from the sublating tensions set off between binominal terms such as animate/inanimate, elect/preterite, us/them, or reality/fantasy. The figures at work in the novel, on their account, don't so much inhabit one or another side of such dualisms, and moreover don't instantiate a synthesis at a higher semantic level or maintain themselves in an ambivalent "middle way"; instead, figuration works to "flatten" meanings and establish paratactic relations between signifying bits of text (53). The figure they use for this flattening effect is a Möbius strip: opposite terms come to occupy a "single dimension" that is simultaneously linguistic and existential, and in which, at the fold of collapsing differences, "the idea of subject separation" disappears.[11] *Gravity's Rainbow* becomes for them the site of a critique of "consciousness as transcendent" that proceeds by way of leveling characterological and temporal categories onto the disorienting surface of intertextual discourse.

Within the terms of my argument, this surface constitutes an implicate order that holds the registers of language and being together in a single complicity. Pynchon does this precisely through a movement into the inanimate governed by the gravitational pressure of return to an origin understood across an impressive range of referents: the "earth," the text, the commodity, the machine, the object of a Thanatos-like desire, objective or aim itself, the

81

structure of intentionality, the subject as universal causality. Each of these senses of that movement can be said to animate or organize Pynchon's prose in *Gravity's Rainbow*. They work within its massive orchestration of language to breach its form and violate the "self-enclosedness" of the object. This movement is discernible everywhere in the novel; it is, one might say, its rhetorical style, its imaginative genius:

> They have begun to move. They pass in line, out of the main station, out of downtown, and begin pushing into older and more desolate parts of the city. Is this the way out? Faces turn to the windows, but no one dares ask, not out loud. Rain comes down. No, this is not a disentanglement from, but a progressive *knotting into*—they go in under archways, secret entrances of rotted concrete that only looked like loops of an underpass ... certain trestles of blackened wood have moved slowly by overhead, and the smells begun of coal from days far to the past, smells of naphtha winters, of Sundays when no traffic came through, of the coral-like and mysteriously vital growth, around the blind curves and out the lonely spurs, a sour smell of rolling-stock absence, of maturing rust, developing through those emptying days brilliant and deep, especially at dawn, with blue shadows to seal its passage, to try to bring events to Absolute Zero ... (3)

This "train passage," taken from Pirate Prentice's inaugural dream on the first page of the novel, is celebrated for its characterization of *Gravity's Rainbow* (of itself) as a "progressive *knotting into*" that looks like or desires to be a "disentanglement from" the complexities of Western culture at the conclusion of World War II and the beginning of the Cold War—the beginning, at any rate, of the world of *Gravity's Rainbow*. The train's centrifugal line of flight from the center to the periphery, across the industrialized city as scene of overlapping intentions, destinations, transports (the archways, the underpass, the trestles), and as scene also of a primary dislocation of purpose itself, mirrors the movement of the prose, its chaining together of subordinate clauses, its successive gerunds, its elliptical cadences, its brokenness and drift. Language moves through or across the grid of culture constituted as a temporal wasteland, and thus its time is strangely determined as a kind of static motion, an involuted progress, finally as a "coral-like" growth that comes to envelop not only the people on the train or the train itself but the landscape as a whole. The narrative has, as it were, passed within the "coral" of itself to circulate in its own objecthood, its own givenness as material, as language, as technology. It is this apprehension of textuality, this production of itself as product, that is catalyzed by a nostalgic reactivation of the city's past: a world "of Sundays where no traffic came through," a bygone innocence (albeit carefully figured as already industrialized) before the catastrophe of this particular language.

Much has been written about Pynchon's humanism, about whether he takes in his work a radical postmodern position that verges on nihilism (through its totalizing representations of a paranoid and entropic social order) or affirms the possibilities of care, love, responsibility, and community.[12] I would like to suggest that the "problem" of Pynchon's humanism is to some extent a false one; "nostalgia" in the novel can be read as the catalyst for this gravitational movement into its own quiddity, its own produced and producing nature. I define this movement (this line of flight) as a condensation of motion and immobility, of time as progressive (or causal) and another, one might say geological, or geo-linguistic, timelessness. Thus it is nostalgia for the past that is "developing through the emptying days" of the quoted passage. The "coral-like" growth (of language, of the city, of the world) is literally though by implication "smelled" by the text, sensuously conjured along with "naphtha winters," "rolling-stock absence," and "maturing rust," caught up in the same movement "to bring events to Absolute Zero." This approach to a zero degree enhances the time of dawn where a "sealing" of passage takes place. The desire implied by this "sealing" tends toward organic life (the halcyon time before technology got out of hand, the living coral), but also organic death (thinglike stasis, coral's simulation of rock). Moreover, it seeks a transcendence that admits in its perfection no motion and so negates itself. There is in the text both a natural cycle *and* a rupture or arrest of that cycle: traducements of nature, convention, or verisimilitude that envelop the binarisms that determine them.

Nostalgia in *Gravity's Rainbow* must therefore be understood within a "nomadic" economy of desire based on a repetition compulsion that inscribes its own source, ground, or "real" unconscious limit in its figural surface. The movement I am interested in tracing along this surface is less that of the *hysteron proteron*, with its theological overtones, and less a fascination with origins or the return to origins. Instead I attend to a fascination with the fascination with origins, its encasement or citation within the mode of a parodic doubling. To invoke the Derridean notion of the "trace" in this regard, it is clear that only via the operation of such a doubling can the abyssal or supplemental structure of writing be grasped so that the irreducibility of the trace is preserved against its metaphysical reduction in the "Living Present" of transcendental experience. The trace as "pure movement which produces difference" in discourse *before* "all determination of content" (*Of Grammatology*, 62) can be thought only if the transcendental problematic is first "worked through" and "seriously exhausted" (50). "The idea of the sign . . . must be deconstructed through a meditation upon writing which would merge, as it must, with the undoing [*sollicitation*] of onto-theology, faithfully repeating it in its *totality* and *making* it *insecure* in its most assured evidences" (73). The onto-theological *arche* (origin) reveals itself as a fiction (or a trace) on the condition that this repetition be "faithful."

> The value of the transcendental arche must make its necessity felt before letting itself be erased. The concept of arche-trace must comply with both that necessity and that erasure. . . . The trace is not only the disappearance of origin—within the discourse that we sustain and according to the path that we follow it means that the origin did not even disappear, that it was never constituted except reciprocally by a non-origin, the trace, which thus becomes the origin of the origin. (61)

It is within this concept of the arche-trace, and within a meditation on the origin of this idea of origins, that I would like to situate Pynchon's text and read the inscriptive marks of a coimplication with the "object" world. If the arche-trace in essence "destroys its name," canceling itself as the origin that is not an origin ("there is above all no originary trace," writes Derrida [61]) and establishing at the origin a structurally infinite regress, it remains the case that the "origin effect" must be duplicated as a moment of the discourse.

Gravity's Rainbow is focused, at a molecular level, on the nature of this duplication. As a "meditation upon writing," it strains its own functions till they turn back on themselves, become self-parody or metaparody in patterns of cellular or algorithmic replication.[13] The novel parodies its own algorithmic desires, not only with its numerous ghosts, double agents, printer's daughters, movie stars, shivering PFCs, and second-story men; nor only with its uroboric figures, polarized currents, double integrals, or modulated frequencies; but also with all the parodied voices, from Milton to the Rolling Stones, that populate its figurative dimensions. What can be specified in this replicative obsession is a kind of Heideggerian turn (*Kehre*) along the lines of its perhaps most celebrated formulation: "The essence of truth is the truth of essence," where the simultaneous repetition and inversion in the predicate triggers a "remembrance" of the "way truth essentially unfolds through the history of Being."¹⁴ This "turn" is the novel's "ass backwards" structure, as cat burglar and dope fiend Saure Bummer intuits it: "Why do you speak of certain reversals—machinery connected wrong, for instance, as being 'ass backwards'? I can't understand that. Ass usually is backwards, right? You ought to be saying 'ass forwards,' if backwards is what you mean" (683). This mystery of American slang, consisting in the verbal infelicity of saying backwards twice, confounds Saure's European sensibilities so much he prompts an explanation a page later.

> " 'Ass' is an intensifier," Seaman Bodine now offers, "as in 'mean ass,' 'stupid ass'—well, when something is very backwards, by analogy you'd say 'backwards ass.' "
> "But 'ass backwards' is 'backwards ass' backwards," Saure objects.
> "But gee that don't make it mean forwards," blinks Bodine. (684)

Even though to hear in this exchange the high ponderousness of Heideggerian discourse is hardly the point, it does signal at the heart of *Gravity's Rainbow* a more general rhetorical intent to engage or quote European and modernist discourses on the nature of truth.¹⁵ The novel's American language unfolds only in its encounter with Europe and indeed constitutes itself in the space of that origin, which is actually the nonoriginary space of the Zone, a textual dimension in which the reciprocal relation of the designations American and European crystallize. Thus as Saure, the smart European, in a sense becomes stupid in the quoted passage (his own literal-mindedness confounds him into the same tortuous repetitions he detects in American slang), Bodine, the stupid American, in a sense becomes smart at the same time (he gives a precise account of the figurative nature of the phrase).

This is one way to hear the novel's preoccupation with the idea of origins, how it stages a return to an archaeological moment to transform *original desire* into a parody of itself. Pynchon makes this aim of his narrative explicit when he traces Slothrop's American heritage backward to a Puritan mess cook on the *Arbella* and then literalizes this movement in a reversal of the fleet's passage across the Atlantic.

> —there go that *Arbella* and its whole fleet, sailing backward in formation, the wind sucking them east again, the creatures leaning from the margins of the unknown sucking in their cheeks, growing crosseyed with the effort, in to deep black hollows at the mercy of teeth no longer the milky molars of cherubs, as the old ships zoom out of Boston Harbor, back across the Atlantic whose currents and swells go flowing and heaving in

85

> reverse . . . a redemption of every mess cook who ever slipped and fell when the deck made an unexpected move, the night's stew collecting itself up out of the planks and off the indignant shoes of the more elect, slithering in a fountain back into the pewter kettle as the servant himself staggers upright again and the vomit he slipped on goes gushing back into the mouth that spilled it. . . . Presto change-o! Tyrone Slothrop's English again! (204)

The figure of reversal here highlights an identification with the mess cook against his more elect brethren that underlies the passage's subversion of the American myth. The parody it indicates is "preterite," bygone in its adhesiveness to old languages and old stories, political in its deployment insofar as it links the problematic of the origin to a hierarchized duality it seeks to invert. But as a name for what transpires at the level of expression, this parody also displaces that duality onto the "typonymic" plane of the text, collapsing the opposed terms until the distinction between them loses its stability. One can hear this in the way that the reversal "redeems" the mess cook, suggesting for the text a desire to transcend its own degraded station (as "low," fleshly, sinful, "passed over" in the more literal sense of damned or condemned). Preterition is in its lines of flight a tendency to seek (identity with) election (in forms of autonomous utopia or transcendence, be they social or textual), a state in turn defined by *not* being preterite. In this paradox, one in fact recognizes the figure of *praeteritio*, a conspicuous omission or constitutive substitution (a figurative "passing over") that indicates an ontological modality of exception both for the preterites in the novel and for the preterite novel. The paradox, in other words, opens in *Gravity's Rainbow* the abyss or groundless ground of its own figural nature.[16] In the temporal dimension of the parody, preterition not only occurs within the nexus of hierarchical values that organize social space; it causes or conditions that space. It names the enveloping framework or limit-horizon within which it appears but also passes away, and as such it premises a possible deconstruction.[17]

Of course, even as this allegiance to the preterite is established as a kind of textual politics, the passage at once calls itself back into question. It does this by being, as well, a first-rate reading of the Puritan ethos and its rhetorical ambiguities. Sacvan Bercovitch expertly articulates the modalities of the Puritan sermons in terms of a parodic time limned from Melville's *Pierre, or The Ambiguities*. The contradicting emphases in the sermons of John Winthrop, John Cotton, Samuel Danforth, Thomas Hooker, and others on (1) a cyclical or typological notion of history, and (2) the errand as a progressive realization of God's Promise, are together observed by Bercovitch to have an economic or productive function. The secularization of the errand and the sacralization of "the Law of Necessity and Utility" (*The American Jeremiad*, 22) that characterized the Puritan's laissez-faire creed suggests an underlying "denial of the contradiction between history and rhetoric," its translation into "a discrepancy between appearance and promise that nourished the imagination, inspired ever grander flights of self-justification, and so continued to provide a source of social cohesion and continuity" (17). Bercovitch's argument gains its strength from a reading of a particular rhetorical strategy that one can hear in Bercovitch's prose: "All of Cotton's examples, from nature and the Bible, are geared toward sanctifying an errand of entrepreneurs whose aim is religion, or, *mutatis mutandis*, legalizing an errand of saints whose aim is entrepreneurial" (22). Bercovitch credits Melville for first dramatizing this "turn" in American life. *Pierre*, Bercovitch argues, opens with a nod to the "American Way," then "proceeds to unveil ambiguity after ambiguity, until it ends in a solipsistic void, like a movie reel of the Puritan ritual run backward at top speed. The very reversal of movement suggests the continuity of the errand, even a madcap inevitability to it all" (28). *Pierre*, a satire of a "rhetoric turned relentlessly upon itself" (28), Bercovitch says, reveals in its ambiguation of the Puritan "synthesis of man's time and God's" a peculiarly cyclical mode of production that informs an American capitalist ethos (29).

It is this kind of insight that underwrites Pynchon's rhetoric, metabolizing its various reversals and inversions into progressively ironic figures. *Gravity's Rainbow* turns upon itself, or turns into itself, doubles its own (Puritan) desire to fuse the sacred with the profane, watches itself produce the effect of this desire in order to apprehend its contextualization in "orders beyond the visible." By doing so, the novel acts on a Puritan "instinct," apprehending the world as an infinite regress much like Pierre in the grip of his incipient paranoia. Man's time (causality) and God's time (cyclical, recursive) become accomplices in another enveloping continuity, a sort of overcoding (or, rather, to anticipate a discussion of Deleuze and Guattari, an axiomatizing) that implicates the text itself in the invisible or displaced functions of a capitalist order.[18] This paranoia in *Gravity's Rainbow* can be seen in Pirate Prentice's dream at the beginning of the novel (previously quoted). Where "they go in under archways, secret entrances of rotted concrete that only looked like loops of an underpass," the text in effect reads the industrial landscape as a pure or unmotivated sign, its ostensible function (the underpass as element in a system of transportation, or distribution) only an alibi for other as yet hidden equivalents. That alibi is the causality of industrial means and ends, and its dislocation (as a result of the war) allows its status as baffle or double to appear. This is the time of the Zone in *Gravity's Rainbow*, and the time of parody, which is always a parody of time. The paranoid perception of the world as a pure sign actuates an inversion of means and ends. Destruction of the city, rather than the end or aim of the war, becomes the means to something else, the dissimulating sign of a different condition with a nonlinear time frame. This is what Enzian Oberst, more clearly perhaps than any other character in the novel, can see in the war-torn landscape of the Zone.

> There doesn't exactly dawn, no but there *breaks*, as that light you're afraid will break some night at too deep an hour to explain away—there floods on Enzian what seems to him an extraordinary understanding. This serpentine slag-heap he is just about to ride into now, this ex-refinery, Jamf Ölfabriken Werke AG, is *not a ruin at all*. It is in *perfect working order*, only waiting for the right connections to be set up, to be switched on . . . modified, precisely, *deliberately* by bombing that was never hostile, but part of a plan both sides—"sides"?—had always agreed on . . . (520)

Enzian here reads the "text" of the Zone for a latent meaning that contradicts its manifest content. The war is a metaphor for a secret conspiracy that reduces it to the status of a diversion not from another event but from the actual event it is. The war is encased, co-opted, "neoterritorialized," taken and made to function differently within a larger theater of ends.[19] The "event" of this knowledge (the way it "breaks" on Enzian) takes the form of a turn: quasi-tautological, a resemblance is perceived through an inverse doubling to conceal a difference, and this difference, apparent yet invisible, changes the text Enzian thought he was riding through.

> But, if I'm riding through it, the Real Text, right now, if this is it. . . . if what the IG built on this site were not at all the final shape of it, but only an arrangement of fetishes, come-ons to call down special tools in the form of 8th AF bombers yes the "Allied" planes all would have been, ultimately, IG-built, by way of Director Krupp, through his English interlocks—the bombing was the exact industrial process of conversion, each release of energy placed exactly in space and time, each shockwave plotted in advance to bring *precisely tonight's wreck* into being thus decoding the Text, thus coding, recoding, redecoding the holy Text . . . (521)

This overdetermination of the Zone becomes "Real" to Enzian from the moment the historicity of the war loses its ostensible content and becomes imaginary, "an arrangement of fetishes, come-ons," an ideological smoke screen for an even more ghastly historical transformation. Enzian's reinterpretation of causality displaces the bombing of German infrastructure into another form of production "dictated by the needs of technology . . . by a conspiracy between human beings and techniques, by something that needed the energy burst of war" to fulfill its schizo-utilitarian purpose (521).

But the irony is that in the instant the Zone becomes a "Real Text," *another* form of causality instantiates itself on the old; Enzian leaves the temporality of his insight and, as Pynchon tells us down the page (in what amounts to a mediated dialogue between Enzian and the narrator), "capitalize[s] the T on technology." The decoded Real Text becomes itself a code, a conspiracy theory, a "decoded code" or code coded as decoded, which, the text implies, gets Enzian exactly nowhere. The inverse (or mirroring) repetition of his insight reinverts itself (looks back at him) and fixes Enzian in another more dangerous truth about the relation between technology (textuality) and being.[20]

Here the darker undertones of Pynchon's language come to be more palpably felt. The nature of historical time preoccupies *Gravity's Rainbow* to the point of obsession, particularly where its supplementary structure envelops the critique of technology and capitalism in a complicity inclusive of the novel itself. Thus the quest undertaken by Enzian and his band of Zone-Hereros, or Schwarzkommandos, to find in the decoded Zone of Western culture an answer to the problem of their profound dislocation, runs up against its own implication in the structures of racism and imperialism it seeks to decipher. This implication *is* racism and imperialism, rather, as becomes clear from the Schwarzkommandos' idolatrous fixation on the Rocket.

> —all right, say we *are* supposed to be the Kabbalists out here, say that's our real Destiny, to be the scholar-magicians of the Zone, with somewhere in it a Text, to be picked to pieces, annotated, explicated and masturbated till it's all squeezed limp of its last drop . . . well we assumed—naturlich!—that this holy Text had to be the Rocket. . . . our Torah. What else? Its symmetries, its latencies, the *cuteness* of it enchanted and seduced us while the real Text persisted, somewhere else, in its darkness, our darkness . . . even this far from Sudwest we are not to be spared the ancient tragedy of lost messages, a curse that will never leave us. (520)

The Hereros' interpretive desire for the Zone invests the Rocket with the symbolic truth they seek; but as the passage suggests, this investment in effect marginalizes their desire, ensures its perpetual dissatisfaction and, more disturbingly, its lack of true substance or authenticity. To annotate and explicate in this way is to masturbate the world, to empty the Text, to abstract oneself from the real Text persisting "somewhere else," in an elsewhere that nonetheless *belongs* to the interpreter ("its darkness, *our* darkness").

Desire for transcendence, for truth, for an end to the "ancient tragedy of lost messages" (the fact ultimately of "missing information," or entropy, a physical law that cannot be contravened) becomes the inscription of violence that Enzian begins to read in himself—a "white" desire, a "white" need for the Rocket as real Text grounding an essentially auto-affective epistomophilia. Three things are apparent here: (1) being in the Zone is textualized and interpretive; (2) insofar as this being is centered on the Rocket, it is a form of servitude or oppression; and (3) there is no freedom apart from a textualized being. What "breaks" on Enzian is the social logic of the sign, a differential and arbitrary dualism that abstracts him from a genuinely "symbolic" understanding of the world and, in the same movement of abstraction, engenders a nostalgic desire for an impossible truth or substance (the Rocket).

Gravity's Rainbow as a whole will likewise discover itself to be enmeshed in this logic of the sign, in particular where it implies reciprocity between victim and victimizer, preterite and elect, a "preterite" parody and the parodied object. "Go ahead," says the text to Enzian, "capitalize the T on technology, deify it if it'll make you feel less responsible—but it puts you in with the neutered, brother, in with the eunuchs keeping the harem of our stolen Earth for the numb and joyless hardons of human sultans, human elite with no right at all to be where they are—" (521). If the parody at issue here is a kind of preterition, linked to its "elect" opposite in a dual system of significations, then *Gravity's Rainbow* as a parody must learn what Enzian learns about German infrastructure. It must become a self-parody or metaparody in order to apprehend its actual relation to the evolving Western (industrialized, capitalist) society it depicts. Slothrop's Puritan ancestor, writing a tract on behalf of his Preterite brethren, began, Pynchon tells us, from the principle that "Everything in Creation has its equal and opposite counterpart" (555). This forerunner of an Emersonian compensation mandates the equalitarian embrace of both Jesus and Judas:

> Could he [Slothrop's ancestor] have been the fork in the road America never took, the singular point she jumped the wrong way from? Suppose the Slothropite heresy had had the time to consolidate and prosper? Might there have been fewer crimes in the name of Jesus, and more mercy in the name of Judas Iscariot? It seems to Tyrone Slothrop that

there might be a route back—maybe that anarchist he met in Zurich was right, maybe for a little while all the fences are down, one road as good as another, the whole space of the Zone cleared, depolarized, and somewhere inside the waste of it a single set of coordinates from which to proceed, without elect, without preterite, without even nationality to fuck it up. (556)

The preterite heresy, transposed forward to the depolarized Zone, dissolves the distinction on which it is based, but this dissolution, this *interpretation* of the Zone (both the anarchist's and Slothrop's), contains even from its inception the counterinvestments that undermine its own possibilities for change: compensation implies the structural permanence of duality; Slothrop's desire for a world without either elect or preterite expresses itself as a nostalgic "route back"; and the hope of a "single set of coordinates" cannot but carry a totalizing overtone.

And yet it seems clear that Slothrop's undermined and paradoxical preterite desire is a human condition in *Gravity's Rainbow*, and that this condition has the shape of a simultaneous progress and recursion, as Pynchon makes clear in the lines following the foregoing quote, where the narrator wonders if the Slothrop who remembers his ancestor's heresy is "drifting, or being led?" The ambiguities of an emotion that cannot tell the difference between these two states (drift and submission) should resonate back through what has been said here so far, underscoring the novel's formal concern with a social power deploying itself at the most intimate levels of decision and feeling. *Gravity's Rainbow* attempts to produce an objective limit in its discourse, to make discourse real through a textual "break" not unlike Enzian's, who is able to glimpse the mediated or conditioned inner workings of his desire *because* he catches himself up in the circularity of discourse, in that echo or involution gathering language into itself as it questions its own relation to a past it tries in vain to master. This is why the reader cannot experience Enzian except as a caricature, stripped of a genuinely tragic substance, rendered in a deliberately flat language that draws attention to textual surfaces and the discursive temporal dimension of writing and reading itself.

The parody of time enacted by the novel envelops both its production and its reproduction. It disrupts the analogic assumptions of meaning brought to bear on interpretation and involves us in its strange parodic time. This is the effect of the metatextual movement I have tried to analyze here as nomadic, double, a production of production, an articulation in the fragmentary text of a world made crazy by its reifications. To further underscore this involuted movement in Pynchon's work, let me end here with another example, an instance of ekphrasis, where the complex intention to render the catastrophe of late modern life in the novel can be read. The following passage, taken from part 1, is a description of the building called, with Pynchon's usual aptness, "The White Visitation," an old insane asylum and headquarters of the catchall wartime agency known as PISCES (Psychological Intelligence Schemes for Expediting Surrender). Under its auspices, several other projects are administered, including Operation Black Wing, an American-funded program aimed at developing strategies to exploit in German citizens any racial fear they might have of the Herero soldiers reported in their midst; Ned Pointsman's exploration of Pavlovian science; and the spiritualist researches of "Psi section." When Pointsman discovers Slothrop's mysterious sexual connection to the V-2 rockets falling regularly from the skies over London in late 1944, "The White Visitation" becomes a key nodal point through which the disparate elements of the novel's intricate plot are linked to one another, and indeed symbolic of that very intricacy.

> Overhead, on the molded plaster ceiling, Methodist versions of Christ's kingdom swarm: lions cuddle with lambs, fruit spills lushly and without pause into the arms and about the feet of gentlemen and ladies, swains and milkmaids. No one's expression is quite right. The wee creatures leer, the fiercer beasts have a drugged or sedated look, and none of the humans have any eye contact at all. . . . The rooms are triangular, spherical, walled up into mazes. Portraits, studies in genetic curiosity, gape and smirk at you from every vantage. The W.C.s contain frescoes of Clive and his elephants stomping the French at Plassy, fountains that depict Salome with the head of John (water gushing out ears, nose, and mouth), floor mosaics in which are tessellated together different versions of Homo Monstrosus, an interesting preoccupation of the time—cyclops, humanoid giraffe, centaur repeated in all directions. . . . Balconies give out at unlikely places, overhung with gargoyles whose fangs have fetched not a few newcomers nasty cuts on the head. Even in the worst rains, the monsters only just manage to drool—the rainpipes feeding them are centuries out of repair, running crazed over slates and beneath eaves . . . —from a distance no two observers, no matter how close they stand, see quite the same building in that orgy of self-expression, added to by each succeeding owner, until the present war's requisitioning. (82–83)

The first thing to notice about this (abbreviated) description of the "orgy of self-expression" inscribed in "The White Visitation" is that it is itself an orgy of self-expression. Pynchon's diction strives, as it were, to *be* what it represents, to close the distance separating word and referent even if the referent in this case is a *representamen*, delineating within itself the arbitrariness of reference, the regress of the "thing itself" before the very desire to capture it. Pynchon applies a representationalist desire to the "truth" of antirepresentationalism, and perhaps little more need be said about the catachrestic nature of his work. The building here characterized is the scene of a classical space gone mad, of a history become disjointed and discontinuous, of a functionalism pushed to such an extreme that it ceases to function except in the schizophrenic mode of pure addition. Time proceeds without any principle of connection or succession in this palimpsest. In the breakdown of meaning it discloses, "lions cuddle with lambs," experience and innocence collapse into each other, sexuality is polymorphously perverse, and the boundaries between the human, the animal, and the inanimate dissolve. Man is *Homo monstrosus*, "endlessly repeated" versions of a man-animal "tessellated together" in the mosaics of language.

Or are they mosaics of thought, of reflection, of the Enlightenment mind as a mirror representing the world in its infinite regress? "The White Visitation" seems to contain both possibilities. The labyrinthine complexity of the building clearly echoes the complexity of Pynchon's language and of *Gravity's Rainbow* as a whole. But it is also clear that history, and in particular the history of science in collusion with war (parodied by the various bureaucracies at "The White Visitation"), is also schizophrenic; that is, it works itself out through or within the same dehumanizing (or antihuman) discourses as *Gravity's Rainbow* itself. This paradox looms through the novel from beginning to end, structuring its principal thematic of responsibility for the (rationalized) energies it unleashes and care for those caught up in them. It matters to this text that "none of the humans have any eye contact at all" and that "no one's expression is quite right." If an alienation (of the body, of desire, of truth) at the most basic levels of human society has indeed occurred in the world of *Gravity's Rainbow*, what tactic will best precipitate this event of alienation in a language inextricably bound up with it? To push ("exponentially," as Baudrillard might say) the depersonalizations and schizophrenizing subversions of the human to their limit is to discover this as the deepest tendency of that alienating process. Instead of a "mad" alternative to the analytic excesses of rationality, madness becomes the intrinsic modality of those excesses. "The White Visitation" condenses in one figure both rational and irrational elements marshaled by the bureaucracies of war, bureaucracies that now function schizophrenically to perfect their own functionalism beyond any determinate end. This is why "the present war's requisitioning" of "The White Visitation" comes merely as another "addition" in a discontinuous temporal series.

The ironies of this peculiar "perfection" sustain themselves at every level of signification in *Gravity's Rainbow* and become unstable where even the novel itself is included in their networks. That "from a distance no two observers, no matter how close they stand, see quite the same building in that orgy of self-expression" indicates how much *Gravity's Rainbow* is itself a "white visitation," and how much its multiplicitous nature at one level colludes in the atomization of the social it also reflects. This is why the scientist in the novel (notably Franz Pökler) can be seen as a privileged metaphor for the writer. But at another level, the novel understands this about itself, and if still there can be no stable ironies, nonetheless that self-implicating dynamic of Pynchon's prose is able to focus the incommensurabilities at work in language (the singularities of each "White Visitation") and so point through them to a negative and critical textual desire of the type examined in previous chapters.

In what follows, I seek to draw out this desire of the text as it dramatizes the desire of a textual existence proper to the postwar period. The fluctuating movement from language to social reality and back constitutes a displacing energy or "nonreferential libido" that symptomatically reiterates a certain abstraction in order to grasp the immanence of its discursive time. This drive at the heart of Pynchon's language has the effect of stripping substance at the level of content; the reader no longer identifies with characters in a realist space so much as caricatures in an oscillating text-world that is dazzlingly complex, mixed and unlocatable, nonlinear and differential. The novel thus becomes a metonymy for its time, exploring the linguistic medium in which it appears with all the force of its strange fatality.

4

A CLOSE READING OF PART 1, EPISODE 19, OF *GRAVITY'S RAINBOW*

The people who are in control and in power and the class system and the whole bullshit bourgeois scene is exactly same, except that there are a lot of middle-class kids with long hair walking around... in trendy clothes. Nothing happened except that we dressed up. The same bastards are in control, the same people are running everything, it's exactly the same. —John Lennon, 1970

One consequence of the palimpsestic and implicated character of *Gravity's Rainbow* is that it resists any easy comprehension of its structure, as though its formal totality were only graspable in its parts, in an apprehension of fragments, in a kind of fetishizing activity that the novel both thematizes and induces in its readers as it goes. This peculiar hologrammic reduction of whole to part is a result of the novel's rhizomatic conjunctions of different semantic and generic registers, an oscillation between dimensions of discourse that generates a kind of vertigo in which the space-time of language reveals its own abyssal nature.

The novel's preoccupation with this vertigo can be seen in its construction of the Psi section seance in episode 18 of part 1, immediately preceding the section I would like to look at in detail here. It begins with an account of psychic Carroll Eventyr's "freak talent," his "splendid weakness," his gift of "surrender" to the irrational "Other Side" of the spirit world (145). His ability to communicate with the dead is figured in terms of a process of transformation from the animate to the inanimate, a "change to interface, to horn, and no feeling, and silence" (148). Eventyr is a pure medium, that is, a sort of relay at the interface, and as such he disappears from the dead voices that speak through him. This self-effacing talent of "receiv[ing] emanations, impressions... the cry inside the stone" is exploited by the eccentric scientists and bureaucrats at the White Visitation as a source of information, and since Eventyr remembers nothing of what transpires at a sitting, they monitor (and anatomize) his "sensitivity" with the latest psychometric means (recording his brain waves with EEGs) (150). When bombadier Basher St. Blaise sees an angel, "miles beyond designating" (151), rise over Lübeck on Palm Sunday (during the raid that first prompts Hitler in 1944 to order retaliatory attacks on London, using the V rockets), a probe is initiated at Psi section. Eventyr, surrounded by his superiors and compatriot "freaks," attempts, through his "control" on the other side, Peter Sachsa, to contact St. Blaise's deceased wingman, Terence Overbaby; but what he finds (or what Psi section finds through him) is a flow of information so saturating it renders all signification unstable. The "inputs" are confusing, "many versions of the Angel . . . might apply," and "there are problems with levels, and with Judgment, in the Tarot sense" (151–52). This indeterminacy produces an anxiety on "both sides of Death" and plunges Peter Sachsa (dead since a 1930 street demonstration in Berlin) uncharacteristically and by way of compensation "into nostalgia for life, the old peace, the Weimar decadence that kept him fed and moving" (151).

What is vertiginous here is Pynchon's technique of wacky association. The admixture of historical fact and blatant fantasy, the playful inventiveness of the names he gives to his characters, the ligature connecting the angel over Lübeck to the V-2 rocket (and the Psi section subplot to the novel's central obsessions), the weaving together of military and scientific terminology ("designating" targets, "inputs"), discourses of the occult and Christian symbolism—all combine to form an impression of intricate pastiche, a sort of verbal "folly" that, at the level of language, exemplifies the subversion of meaning that the novel also narrativizes. There is in *Gravity's Rainbow* an alternation between content and expression, theme and structure, at times so rapid they appear indistinguishable from one another, simultaneous, and it is this effect of simultaneity that conditions the strange tonality proper to Pynchon's style. It accounts for the levity or theatricality that everywhere marks his prose (or mars his prose, if you're a critic), the reflexivity or doubleness that effectively blocks any "serious" interpretation.

In an attempt to approximate in *Gravity's Rainbow* the range of its peculiar harmonics, I would like in what follows to read episode 19 of part 1, the beginning of the Franz and Leni Pökler subplot, for its mode of "standing in" for or performing (in the mode of a fetish) the novel's structure as a whole. In some ways this story is the most dramatically unified in all of *Gravity's Rainbow*, but the interior distortions of that unity are nonetheless deliberate and indeed pervasive. Franz and Leni are still parodies of characters, not "real," and it is this irreality that they explore within the illusion of their realism (as content), while at the same time that irreality formally envelops and displaces their story just as the novel does with its successive episodes, accumulating subplots, and paratactic strategies of analogy and association.

The story of Franz and Leni Pökler, actually, is not a subplot at all so much as a sub-subplot, since it literally constitutes the *deviation* Sachsa makes in response to the indeterminacy of meaning prompted by the appearance of the Lübeck angel. His anxiety deflects his attention (and Eventyr's, and Psi section's, and the narrative's) to Weimar Germany in the late 1920s, in particular to a seance he conducted for luminaries of the industrial cartel IG Farben and officers of the Nazi party. It is this seance that Eventyr's superiors (quickly adapting to the first shift) are most interested in, so when Sachsa's "obsessive love" for Leni Pökler displaces that sitting, or at least reverses the order of its priority in the narrative, focusing on the breakdown of her marriage first and only at the end returning to the seance, another deviation in effect occurs, rendering the incidental story of the Pöklers central to the narrative. What can be specified is a principle of deviation motivated by anxiety and obsession, a dreamlike displacement that governs the narrative itinerary. The oblique associations relaying the movement from the White Visitation, 1944, and Carroll Eventyr, through an intemporal "control" to Berlin in the late 1920s and the drama of the Pöklers, suggest the discontinuity, or rather the elliptical "drift," that both structures and is structured by the novel. Episode 19, set off not only by the usual sprockets from the previous episode but by an *ellipsis* that concludes the latter, could be said to exemplify the temporal strategies of *Gravity's Rainbow* in its analeptic return to the past, its elevation of the incidental and the elliptical (i.e., the preterite, that which is "passed over," "damned to hell," or dynamically repressed), its tenuous causality, and its suspension between states of life and death (Sachsa narrates from the Other Side, so the story in episode 19 is dead not only as memory but as the memory of a dead man, thus doubly dead, twice dead).

But the episode is exemplary in another sense as well, since Sachsa is not the narrator of what we read. Episode 19 is given as a version of transcripts made from Eventyr's seance, intended for review by higher-ups in the PISCES bureaucracy. The narrator, as it were, takes over these transcripts, retranscribes them as the third-person narration of a failing marriage, a failing "connection" that once again mirrors the novel's episodic or serial modalities. By thus framing the episode, Pynchon suggests that to some degree what we read (albeit altered in the retranscription) *is being read* as well by the people at Psi section. The act of reading is thus implicated in a set of meanings centered on the word *use*, to use, to be used by, to be used up. Retranscription, or writing, moreover, is similarly implicated as one more version of, one more supplement to, the obsessional desire (be it Sachsa's or Psi section's) that underpins that schizo-functionalist reading. At the level of how the episodes in *Gravity's Rainbow* relate to one another, of what kind of series (causal or schizophrenic, i.e., additive) the narrative makes, a question about the nature of relation is being worked out at a number of different registers: that of the connection between husband and wife; that between "medium" and "control," and thus between the living and the dead; that between the artistic (the "sensitive") and the bureaucratic; that between the reader and the text; and that between the writer and the text.[1]

The compression or layering of dimensions like these is what accounts for the density of Pynchon's prose, the temporal involutions that confer on it a dynamic turned upon itself, producing the paradoxical impression of movement and arrest explored in the last chapter. The writing itself participates in the supplemental logic specified at the level of the narrative, and any series, even the schizophrenic, Pynchon implies, can be used, can be turned into a form of abuse. The text of *Gravity's Rainbow* thus includes itself within its own meanings, colludes in the operation of mastery, or at least asks the question of its collusion.

It is this possibility (of collusion) that organizes the language and structure of the novel, producing as an imperative the distortions of narrative time and generic propriety, the circularity of discourse, and the necessary opacity of the structure. *Gravity's Rainbow* sets itself up even (perhaps especially) in its parodic subversions of power and mastery as subject to its own critique (subject, that is, to its desires for power and mastery), and it is the tactics of this "setup"—reducing the whole to a part, giving to writing the (fetishistic) function of an element within its own fiction, thus rendering it doubly fictive, twice determined, a virtual or hologrammic text—that interest me here. In particular, what I want to establish is a stake in preserving that virtuality, above and beyond its mirror relation to a painful and oppressive social situation, for in its specific neutralization of the "real," one can trace the trajectory of a certain escape.

Episode 19 begins, not surprisingly, with a feeling of suspense and suspension in a Berlin dormitory, where Leni comes with her daughter Ilse after leaving her husband, "for good this time."

> They are shivering and hungry. In the Studentenheim there's no heat, not much light, millions of roaches. A smell of cabbage, old second Reich, grandmother's cabbage, of lard smoke that has found, over the years, some *détente* with the air that seeks to break it down, smells of long illness and terminal occupation stir off the crumbling walls.... Leni sits

on the floor with four or five others, passing a dark chunk of bread. In a damp nest of Die Faust Hoch, back issues no one will read, her daughter Ilse sleeps, breathing so shallow it can hardly be seen. Her eyelashes make enormous shadows on the upper curves of her cheeks. (154)

The poverty and transience of the room in which Leni finds herself mirror the future she has chosen by abandoning her marriage. They also refer to a particular Berlin subculture, bohemian, political, and alienated in the bourgeois fervor of the Weimar Republic. A state of arrest obtains both for Leni and her friends, a powerlessness, a self-consciousness, an overdetermination that leaves them all subtly paralyzed in the present moment. The narration marks this paralysis by assuming Leni's perspective:

Rudi, Vanya, Rebecca, here we are a slice of Berlin life, another Ufa masterpiece, token La Bohème Student, token Slav, token Jewess, look at us: the Revolution. Of course there is no Revolution, not even in the Kinos, no German October, not under this "Republic." The Revolution died—though Leni was only a young girl and not political—with Rosa Luxemburg. The best there is to believe in right now is a Revolution-in-exile-in-residence, a continuity, surviving at the bleak edge over these Weimar years, awaiting its moment and its reincarnated Luxemburg. (155)

Leni's (and the narrative's) ability to observe herself (itself) as if she (it) were just "another Ufa masterpiece," a movie in which each person becomes an impersonal "token," a shifter in a predetermined narrative pattern, both conditions the "Revolution-in-exile-in-residence" that the characters together constitute and dilutes the continuity they hope for to the point where its actuality (as a political movement, anyway) evanesces in a state of passive waiting and ironic reflexiveness.

This evanescence of the actual or the real operates at the level even of the sentence for Pynchon. "A smell of old cabbage, old second Reich, grandmothers' cabbage," he writes, "of lard smoke that has found, over the years, some détente with the air that seeks to break it down, smells of long illness and terminal occupation stir off the crumbling walls." The smell of grandmothers' cabbage casts a retrospective penumbra over the words (the smells) that follow and the Studentenheim room they describe, invoking the past as "long illness" and "terminal occupation," as lives lived in the mode of an approach to death that is also dead as memory. Time is implicitly construed as an attenuated death, the body of the past gradually decomposing the present, which is thus already a corpse, or at least *always dying*, always becoming past. In this circular movement from dead memory to a moribund present, Pynchon's characters can only take up a fragile existence, "shivering" in the cold or "breathing" like Ilse, asleep "in a damp nest of *Die Faust Hoch*, back issues no one will read." These vibrations in the midst of a literally textualized space (*Die Faust Hoch* is a fictional reference to expressionist magazines of the time) strive to maintain a kind of equilibrium before the decomposing forces that surround them. Likewise the sentence's accumulation of subordinate clauses and its repetition of "smell," "old," and "cabbage" achieve a kind of détente with the grammatical forces seeking to break it down, stabilizing it in a form that, while not exactly proper, is also not exactly awkward. Do all the subordinate clauses form the subject that predicates the verb *stir*, or does the last constitute a clause in and of itself, thus rendering the sentence incomplete, more like a list or catalog? The way it is written produces a hesitation between these two readings, since the plural form of *stir* seems to agree with the noun *smells*. The sentence seems to flicker here, to hover on the edge of a syntactic entropy, or at least maintain at that edge its own peculiar equilibrium.

Pynchon's language could thus be said to vibrate (shiver or breathe) along with (or beside) the characters in the Studentenheim, pitching itself at a frequency "so shallow it can hardly be seen." The obsession with seriality and replication is here internal to his discourse and registers an identification with the characters and their situation so thoroughgoing that it verges on the physiological. It becomes in a sense so real or close to life that it ends up being more real than real, or, so to speak, hyperreal. In this way the language becomes another character, enveloped in its own constructions, intrinsically simulatory or theatrical. This is the secret of its lightness or "shallowness," for the process of identification the text undergoes is more on the order of impersonation and parodic masquerade than of a realist conjuring or empathic reconstruction. The allusions to 1920s German culture—the magazine *Die Faust Hoch* (again, a fictional reference) or the chiaroscuro shadows on Ilse's face suggestive of expressionist cinema—are not intended to describe a moment in history so much as parody description itself. Nor is the flashback meant, for example, to historicize or account for the rise of Nazism in Germany or the beginnings of World War II, except insofar as history itself is called into question and made to confront its own textual nature. Pynchon's Berlin is a sketch, a "slice of life," a scene in which the "real" scarcely disturbs the fictional surface. The text suspends itself in a process of literal and figurative biodegradation, you might say, a complex state construed as both a breaking down and a structuration of elements, or rather the structuration of a breaking-down process, a structured breakdown, in other words, a dual dynamic of decay and conservation that could be said to constitute, beyond what is manifest or implied in the text, an encrypted dimension of connotation in *Gravity's Rainbow*.

This dual dynamic informs the entire novel, conditioning its reflexivity, the way it seems to know all its own moves in advance (even as it moves so elliptically through the various subplots), preempting itself as it goes, constructing the effect of its own belatedness. The novel, you might say, sees itself seeing itself, an effect referred to in the following excerpt from episode 19, the beginning of a conversation in the Studentenheim:

> "It's true," Vanya now, "look at the forms of capitalist expression. Pornographies: pornographies of love, erotic love, Christian love, boy-and-his-dog, pornographies of sunsets, pornographies of killing, and pornographies of deduction—*ahh*, that sigh when we guess the murderer—all these novels, these films and songs they lull us with, they're approaches, more comfortable and less so, to that Absolute Comfort." A pause to allow Rudi a quick and sour grin. "The self-induced orgasm."
> (155)

The question of how to read this passage is not, I would like to suggest, as simple as it might appear. At the surface level of signification, everything denoted in Vanya's speech is colored by its callow tone. The paragraph recapitulates the narrative structure Vanya analyzes, accumulating phrases, attenuating the sense of suspense, and building to a climax by way of undermining its own ironic content. Beyond the evidence of a clear parody, however, a self-parody can also be discerned at a second level of signification: Vanya's rhetorical bravado mirrors Pynchon's own in its "listing" cadences, and his self-consciousness reads like a small travesty of the novel's manifest pretentions. Yet this does not keep us from registering in the argument presented a certain cogency more penetrating than either significative level can absorb (or neutralize). Vanya's Brechtian sentiments do not fall under the aspersion of immaturity cast on him by the text, and we are able to read them "straight," or at least in a manner that does not impair any deeper irony that might still be at work. The idea that narrative is pornographic functions (like the other references to the Weimar era) as an element in the parodic construction of a "sketched" or fictionalized history, but it also plays a part in the history of (modernist) narrative and culture to which *Gravity's Rainbow* belongs. At this level, the novel seems to ratify the critique of "forms of capitalist expression" implied in Vanya's speech. Its own displacements of the pornographic payoff in conventional narrative owe a debt to this idea (to the Epic Theater generally) and parody "all these novels, these films and songs they lull us with" as so many examples of a nonsubversive art.

Gravity's Rainbow, that is, does not want to be merely a good commodity, a prop in the theater of an autoerotic consumption. The approach to "Absolute Comfort" here echoes all the approaches offered up by the novel to a Zero figured as pure and empty transcendence, an escape from history that simultaneously delivers one to it. To recall once again the terminology of Jean Baudrillard, a genuinely symbolic exchange is reified in the purely differential and arbitrary equivalent of a sign system. The novel (or narrative in general) becomes a "sign-object" that, "instead of abolishing itself in the [symbolic] relation that it establishes . . . becomes autonomous, intransitive, opaque, and so begins to signify the abolition of the relationship (*For a Critique of the Political Economy of the Sign*, 64). The "self-induced orgasm" triggered by the consumption of narrative inscribes a lack of relation in the body of the text that is here clearly the object of a critique. Gravity's Rainbow parodies this lack of relation, and this parody is signaled, paradoxically, only in a serious reading of the foregoing excerpt. The text must appear at one level as a nonironic narrative to be read as this parody. A problem arises, however, from the moment it becomes clear that the passage is also making fun of itself *as a parody*. At the point where the parody reveals its parodied target (lack of relation, commodification, sign value exchange), another parody is taking place, complicating the narrative even where it understands itself in a capitalist context. Or rather, what it understands about that context is that in it, narrative is commodifiable even when it subverts itself (that is, parody is still a form of narrative, and thus—if you take the Brechtian critique *seriously enough*—still nonsubversive). This kind of insight moves the text in the direction of a double parody or self-parody (conceived as a sort of oscillation between the levels of signification), since it is only in this mode that it can truly grasp the reduction in culture of social relation to sign value exchange. Only by recognizing itself as a sign system, objectified and objectifying, can Gravity's Rainbow begin to participate in (or perhaps I should say add to) the history of narrative, even if the role slotted for it is to be one of its final terms. In the quoted passage, the approach to that "Absolute Comfort" can be read as a movement of objectification, a becoming-object that the text undergoes as well as undermines. This movement gathers into itself a number of different senses—nostalgia, transcendence, auto-affection and abstraction, fetishism, Eros but also Thanatos—all of which share the same vector or the same valence, with the result that they cannot easily be differentiated from one another, or understood in the moral terms we (as readers) are likely to bring to them. Pynchon displaces the value judgment implied in the quoted passage (that narrative is pornographic under capitalism) not by negating it or contradicting it but by encasing it in the becoming-object of the novel, making it impossible to read without at the same time experiencing the vertigo of a crystalline, "latticed," or multileveled parody of parody.[2]

This is not to say such judgments aren't made and endorsed, or that in *Gravity's Rainbow* a profoundly moral substrate can't be discovered, only that each rhetorical effect (of this or any other kind) produced in the text must be read through the displacements that shape its predominant narrative strategy. The novel pays attention to the fact that it is a commodity, that it is consumed in being read, and as such it must question itself even as parody. As episode 19 progresses, in fact, it becomes clear that a meditation on the novel's own commodified status is working itself out through that strategy, as seen in the following response to Vanya's speech:

> " 'Absolute'?" Rebecca coming forward on her bare knees to hand him the bread, damp, melting from the touch of her wet mouth, "Two people are—"
>
> "Two people are what you are told," Rudi does not quite smirk. Through her attention, sadly and not for the first time around here, there passes the phrase *male supremacy* . . . why do they cherish their masturbating so? "but in nature it is almost unknown. Most of it's solitary. You know that."
>
> "I know there's coming together," is all she says. (155)

Rebecca's dissent extends the field of association in which the theme of connection is articulated to include a specifically sexual politics. Rudi's and Vanya's investment in the critique of sexual love they voice is problematized by the suggestion that it is "their masturbating," *their* critique, that somehow it belongs to them and they "cherish" it, and that to some extent they are performing precisely what they critique by speaking as they do. Their self-consciousness is figured as a form of *male supremacy* based on a denial of the body, linked to a dry abstraction by the contrast it makes to Rebecca's sensuality. The imputation of dishonesty to what the text calls on the next page "intellectual code" in the male discourse of critique raises as an issue or a stake the destiny of the body in the discourse of *Gravity's Rainbow*.

But it does not do this at the level of the manifest or "enounced" utterance. The dualism of mind and body (with its concomitant binary pairs, masturbation and "coming together," male and female, or, more disturbingly, Christian and Jew) quickly outstrips the characters who bear its symbolism, peeking baldly through the story and sabotaging the illusion of its dramatic unity.[3] The abstractions are what interest Pynchon here, although not simply as abstractions, either (which would be to ratify the male discourse he parodies in Vanya and Rudi). Their presence in the text points to the operation of another parody directed at meaning itself, at the binary systems, the sign systems, that make up the novel. As such, the meanings so abstractly present in the episode become, in the parodic reduction to which they are submitted, virtually meaningless. The reader cannot take the argument between Rudi/Vanya and Rebecca seriously because of a displacement upward that overwhelms the plot and refocuses the reader's attention on duality itself, especially as it is implicated in or as narrative. The parody of duality that, it becomes clear, we are actually reading cannot register this implication, however, without simultaneously implicating itself as well. The movement of transcendence in which the mind/body binary appears as a parodied text in effect passes within that which it parodies, discovers in its desire for transcendence the very thing it would transcend. This is the way to understand how Pynchon invests the story he constructs in episode 19, how the text "cares" for (or identifies with) its caricatured characters and opens the possibility for a serious reading of its antiserious strategies. The text inscribes itself in the dualistic grid it also deconstructs, or put another way, it caricatures itself, becomes another caricatured character, depersonalized, "biodegraded," disembodied, caught within the vertices of representation by the same agency as the other characters—that is, by itself, in the operation of a self-perpetuating victimage.

It is this state of victimage that episode 19 sets out to explore in the trauma of Leni's separation from her husband. Franz, "swimming his seas of fantasy, death-wish, rocket-mysticism" (154), presents another version of the abstract man, the scientist who sees "not persons but forms of energy" (161), lost or "at sea" in the obsessions that draw him away from his body, away from the exigencies of the social and the political, away from the possibility of a "coming together." Franz is not, however, identical in his function to Rudi and Vanya, since his obsessions entail an analytic ability to manipulate the physical world, produce energy, do work; and so his rationality, unlike their self-consciousness, has an economic value and can be used in an industrial and military society. As Leni (cum narrator) says to herself, "Franz is just the type they want. They know how to use *that* [i.e., his abstraction]. They know how to use nearly everybody. What will happen to the ones they can't use?" (155).

The difference between Franz and his counterparts in the Studentenheim (male and female) is the same that separates those who can be used from those who are of no use, and this sets up a different dynamic, raising the stakes of Pynchon's discourse to a new level of historical implication.

Franz's "death-wish," his desire for escape from the "real" world, has been determined more explicitly in its relation to power, the way it conditions an attitude of acquiescence to, and complicity in, the "real" world, the way it lends itself to a process of reification. Franz is passive, apolitical, a dreaming man without a moral sense capable of resistance or protest. His peculiar talents only thrive in a kind of dehistoricized vacuum, a steady state sheltered from time. The irony is that as a scientist, he also adheres strictly to a "cause-and-effect" philosophy: he stands on the side of causality as long as it is so sheltered from time. His empiricism contains within it the paradox of a simultaneous avowal and disavowal of the real, and it is this paradox that renders him so eminently pliant to those in power, the "military and the cartels" whose representatives use him for the development of the rocket (163).

It is clear that the shifter "Franz Pökler" demarcates at least in part a place or moment of self-critique in the novel. His particular moral incapacity could be said to focus the problem of a language that exposes its own referential function only to find this exposure at the core (quite literally) of its own being as a sign-object. This implication can in one sense be grasped as a parody of the language of capitalism, thus demonstrating that the text undermines the reduction to its own signifieds implied by the reifying mutation into a "sign-object" precisely by adhering to its signifiers. But there is nonetheless a sense in the novel that this parody exists as well in the form of a quotation, cited within another discourse that plunges back into itself, ceaselessly reopening the wound of its transcendence.

That Franz can be read as a figure for this "forgetting" in the novel becomes more evident as Pynchon links him to the V rocket. If any history is being told in the analepsis of episode 19, it is that of the rocket as the obsession of the novel. When Franz, wandering at night in an industrial suburb of Munich (years before Leni's departure), inadvertently witnesses one of the first "static tests" for the rocket, he has what amounts to a mystical or "out-of-body" experience:

> The sound began to change, to break now and then. It didn't sound ominous to Franz in his wonder, only different. But the light grew brighter, and the watching figures suddenly started dropping for cover

as the rocket now gave a sputtering roar, a long burst, voices screaming *get down* and he hit the dirt just as the silver thing blew apart, a terrific blast, metal whining through the air where he'd stood, Franz hugging the ground, ears ringing, no feeling even for the cold, no way for the moment of knowing if he was still inside his body . . . (161)

The rocket in this passage precipitates for Franz a disappearance of the body and a mode of being that is purely empty or negative. The event that precedes this precipitation so immediately it seems rather to accompany it ("he hit the dirt *just as* the silver thing blew apart") is a falling to and "hugging" of the ground. To touch the ground for Franz is to leave his body. In the negative space "where he'd stood," the rocket bursts apart, breaks, "metal whining in the air." Where "Franz" had been, now a metallic blast obtains, literally a broken machine, since the test, it turns out, is a failure: "it failed, Leni," he says on the next page, "but they talked only of success. Twenty kilograms of thrust and only a few seconds, but *no one's ever done it before*" (162). That the rocket fails does not detract from its success; indeed, that failure constitutes the singularity of the event. Franz merges with this successful failure, or rather it merges with him, takes his place, contracts in him the obsession with the rocket that will carry him all the way through its creation and eventual deployment, and all the way through the novel as well. The rocket, in fact, could be seen here as a figure for *Gravity's Rainbow* as a whole insofar as it too is a "broken machine" that precipitates a "fall to the ground" and a disappearance of the body, a transcendence that is "metallic," a sublime text that strips itself of its own "ominous" qualities and insists to be read only on a strange "difference."[4] The apprehension of this difference is the "wonder" Franz feels in the face of a technological quantum leap, an absence of fear that carries with it a concomitant absence of moral insight. In this way, the ominous returns in the very lack of ominousness the rocket inspires, encrypted there, remote from its own (lack of) affect: "no feeling even for the cold."

But if the rocket in this passage *is Gravity's Rainbow*, it is also an element *of Gravity's Rainbow* as well. The rocket is the object to which obsession attaches, the fetish the novel fetishizes, but as a figure for the novel, this fetish is also the activity of fetishizing, so that in essence the novel fetishizes fetishization itself. The circularity of this operation verges on auto-affection, and in this respect the novel is like Franz, like but also unlike, a whole reduced to a part that nonetheless cannot bear the weight of any adequate similitude. In condensations such as these, you begin to glimpse the novel exploring itself as text, as metaphoricity, as object and as work—a crystal, a coral, a cyborg, a machine. Each term in this series has a different sense: the crystal is a natural object; the coral is a half-animate, half-inanimate organism; the cyborg is part human, part machine (and also part animal); the machine is a mechanical tool. The novel plays within and on these metaphors, warping them into a single movement of desire that encompasses the text itself, or rather metaphoricity itself. This desire appears even in Franz's first encounter with the rocket, a machine the trajectory of which runs straight at him, turning him into a cyborg, driving him toward an inanimate ground and out of an animate body. In that instant, you could say the rocket "chooses" Franz, or rather is "meant" for him, and that what he experiences is a kind of *coup de foudre* or love at first sight. This is why Franz *finds* the rocket, chances upon it quite passively, carried along, the narrator tells us, by a "wind" of fate, a sort of compulsion woven into the order of things. And this is why, in his ignorance of what he witnesses (there being no such thing as rockets up till then), he can see it only as "the silver thing." The rocket presents itself to him as prior to or outside any attribution, a thing in itself, standing for a rupture in language at the same time that it is made to bear the weight of pure meaning. The rocket becomes all metaphoricity by foreclosing all metaphoricity.

In this, one sees exemplified a principal narrative tactic of the novel. Pynchon is interested (or obsessed) with the structure of addiction (Franz's encounter could also be conceptualized as a "rush" or a "hit") and builds his novel according to principles of doubling, replication, recurrence, pattern, and plot to reflect a historical moment for which addiction has become a general condition. The "coral-like growth" of *Gravity's Rainbow* situates this moment at the level of language and its redundancies, thus within or as itself. The novel is a symptom of that moment as well as a reaction to it, and it registers this historical specificity by returning to the question of its own complicity (as an obsessed or addicted text). For this reason, the relation between Franz and the rocket that begins in episode 19 can be read as one clue to the labyrinth of the novel's structure, and in a quite literal sense. Major Weissmann exploits Franz's passivity at Peenemunde so that at the appropriate time (the fruition of another obsession) he will build the plastic fairing in which Weissmann, as Blicero, houses Hans Gottfried in the nose of the 00000 V-2 rocket and blasts him into space. This fairing is made of Imipolex-G, the quasi-organic plastic that intervenes so fatefully in Slothrop's early life as the stimulus in a Pavlovian experiment conducted on him by Dr. Laszlo Jamf (Franz's professor for a polymer theory course in college). The fairing is the Schwarzgerat, Holy Grail of Slothrop's quest for his own identity. Franz's rearticulation through the novel's predominant narrative networks (further complexified by his relations to Greta Erdmann, the movie *Alpdrucken*, and his daughter Ilse, discussed in more detail in the next chapter) confers on him a tangential conspicuousness that is perhaps the most representative state of everything in the novel, an incidence it renders formally significant, a preterition it suffers and explores.

Pynchon adds another layer of perspective and complication to his text in the figure of Leni, whose resistance to her husband's "rocket-mysticism" presents what appears to be a cogent alternative. The separation she has already initiated at the beginning of episode 19 formalizes the feeling of dislocation that pervaded their marriage. Franz's "absent presence" drives her to the Studentenheim and the possibility of a more genuine exchange, a more genuine touching or "coming together."

> Leni, from inside her wasted time with Franz, knows enough about coming alone. At first his passivity kept her from coming at all. Then she understood that she could make up anything at all to fill the freedom he allowed her. It got more comfortable: she could dream such tendernesses between them (presently she was also dreaming of other men), but it became more solitary. (155–56)

The loneliness Leni feels within the sexual relation, while she rejects it in rejecting Franz, nevertheless deepens her understanding past the sexual politics she witnesses in the Studentenheim. Like Franz in relation to Rudi and Vanya, Leni is not symbolically synonymous with Rebecca's sensuality.[5] She greets the possibility of "coming together" with a skepticism of her own, striking a more thoughtful note in the narrative progression. She too "dreams," she too experiences in the "wasted time with Franz" a kind of fantasmatic freedom that can be for her either mere escapism or a politicized "flight" ("Real flight and dreams of flight go together," she says on page 159), in itself a potential act of refusal. When she leaves Franz, she does not simply acquiesce to a discourse of the liberatory body (a "coming" together); she fantasizes the frank desire for escape, alleviation from the pain of a life figured as a "street" in which one always "impersonates," always dissimulates and hides, always feels oneself to be a criminal before the (despotic) law. To escape from impersonation is what Leni wants and can "least allow herself" as a now single mother, so her sole recourse is fantasy, and if her desire yields a reductive escapism ("dream[s] of gentleness, light, her criminal heart redeemed, no more need to run, to struggle, a man arriving tranquil as she and strong, the street becoming a distant memory" [156]), it also turns upon or seizes a political content. The text narrates one of her fantasies as follows:

> On a multi-leveled early evening of balconies, terraces, audiences grouped at different levels, all looking downward, in toward a common center, galleries of young women with green leaves at their waists, tall evergreen trees, lawns, flowing water and national solemnity, the President, in the middle of asking the Bundestag, with his familiar clogged and nasal voice, for a giant war appropriation, breaks down suddenly: "Oh, fuck it . . ." *Fickt es!* "I'm sending all the soldiers home. We'll close down the weapon factories, we'll dump all the weapons in the sea. I'm sick of war. I'm sick of waking up every morning afraid I'm going to die." It is suddenly impossible to hate him any more: he's as human, as mortal now, as any of the people. There will be new elections. The Left will run a woman whose name is never given, but everyone understands it is Rosa Luxemburg. The other candidates will be chosen so inept or colorless that no one will vote for them. There will be a chance for the Revolution. The President has promised. (158)

The multileveled structure of this scene, with its centripetal pull "in toward a common center," its comical blend of pastoral imagery and Bundestag, its transformation of President von Hindenburg into political savior, all combine to form a kind of dream precise in its historical references.[6] Both reductive and progressive forms of fantasy are present here, condensed in a single movement toward a center that explodes into the margin, making possible "a chance for the Revolution." That this is only a form of patently wishful thinking does not, for Leni, detract from an efficacy that dream has for social change. It functions as a kind of leaven for the moment of collective action or decision, a catalyst for the transformation of time into the dreamlike equivalent of the protest. This is why the problem of her marriage with Franz hinges on the theme of time.

> She tried to explain to him about the level you reach, with both feet in, when you lose your fear, you lose it all, you've penetrated the moment, slipping perfectly into its grooves, metal-gray but soft as latex, and now the figures are dancing, each pre-choreographed exactly where it is, the flash of knees under pearl-colored frock as the girl in the babushka stoops to pick up a cobble, the man in the black suitcoat and brown sleeveless sweater grabbed by policemen one on either arm, trying to

keep his head up, showing his teeth, the older liberal in the dirty beige overcoat, stepping back to avoid a careening demonstrator, looking back across his lapel how-dare-you or look-out-not-me, his eyeglasses filled with the glare of the winter sky. There is the moment, and its possibilities. (158)

Leni's "penetration" of the moment counterposes itself to Franz's epiphany with the rocket. Both are metamorphoses in the sense of duration that alleviate fear and confer agency (for Franz, the rocket opens up a whole career or project to which he devotes himself). And both, moreover, involve a (sexualized) process of entering within or becoming machinic: Leni's moment is "grooved" and "pre-choreographed," "metal-gray but soft as latex," metallic and plastic at once, as though it were prosthetic in relation to the human body living through it (but also inside it), artificial and supplemental.[7] Into this experience of simultaneity, a mechanism is introduced, or rather a causality is reintroduced, even if the experience is also a purely performative dance. What the text is describing, once again, is a kind of cyborg existence, only here it transgresses and rebels, marking a refusal and not a complicity, or a refusal in spite of complicity, a "symbolic" body that breaches the boundaries of the "human," collapsing the programmatic and utilitarian realism of cause and effect (which Franz symbolizes) into the "parallel" time of language: "It all goes along together," says Leni to her husband. "Parallel, not series. Metaphor. Signs and symptoms. Mapping on to different coordinate systems" (159).

But if Pynchon voices through Leni a powerful and persuasive "symbolic" critique, he does not hold it out as a mode of redemption (or of a redemptive reading), and indeed the text undermines its own persuasiveness at the same time in ways already apparent from the foregoing (see note 4). Although now the slide from the narrative to language (or from the enounced to the enunciated utterance) is included in the manifest content of the episode, Pynchon in effect displaces the displacement. He strips away the illusion of transparency masking language wherever a serious or nonironic interpretation might articulate itself, and he calls attention to the levels of meaning that always stratify the text. The two versions of time presented by Leni and Franz constitute, albeit in a more complex form than the previously parodied mind/body split, another dualistic system, and the method of double displacement Pynchon uses will consist in rendering this dualism obvious and pulling the binary terms down into a single complicity. Those terms can be laid out in the following schematic way:

Leni	Franz
radical	liberal
delta t	function taken to limit
metaphor/sign/symptom	cause and effect
fantasy (flight)	fantasy (production)
(symbolic exchange)	(sign value exchange)

Although the difference between Leni and Franz is clear and indeed incommensurable, Pynchon carefully builds into this episode a dimension of reciprocity between them. Both are middle-class in origin, for example, and detest the narrow, "strangulating" sameness and neutrality of this common background (162). Franz's obsession with the rocket and Leni's revolutionary fervor are both characterized as escapes from a repetitiveness without meaning: for Leni this is symbolized by the "twin spires of the Dom" rising over the city of Lübeck, where she grew up, and for Franz by a "Destiny" that "will betray you, crush your ideals, deliver you to the same detestable Burgerlichkeit as your father" (162). The difference between them lies not between acceptance and refusal but between kinds of escape. Leni can see how Franz's dread of "Destiny" ends in mere escapism (i.e., the very thing he dreads) and, indeed, can see her own "dread" as regressive in an identical way. Their marriage fails, finally, because Leni represents for Franz an escape from the past, but Franz represents for Leni only a capitulation to that past (even if she finds herself tempted by it). But both of them nonetheless still exist in the medium of fantasy, and though Leni is not subject to the same obsessional psychology as Franz (indeed, she is perhaps the least obsessed character in the entire novel), she is in fantasy essentially isolated or solipsistic. Her account of "parallel" time as "delta t approaching zero, eternally approaching, the slices of time growing thinner and thinner, a succession of rooms each with walls more silver, transparent, as the pure light of zero comes nearer" (159), echoes not only Franz's experience with the rocket (a "silver thing") but the various other approaches to zero discussed earlier, and indeed it folds into the same fetishizing or objectifying movement at work in (and as) the novel.[8] This does not entail a collapse of the binary pairs so much as their exaggerated display, their overt foregrounding in the narrative. Franz is used by the military and the cartels, and Leni is useless to them (or almost), hence her destiny in the novel will be the concentration camp Dora. Franz's complicity cannot be designated Leni's in this respect, which is why his destiny will be Nordhausen, the rocket factory, located (with Pynchon's usual irony) right next to the camp. In the world of *Gravity's Rainbow*, the domination of an industrial and capitalist system verges on total, and this condition compels Pynchon to bracket the constituted differences Franz and Leni represent, for it is only by acknowledging the saturation of all things, all material (language, or narrative, in this case), by a technicized rationality that enables him to perceive or expose the exercise of power in the deployment of binary systems, of meaning itself.

In at least one sense, then, Leni and Franz are alike: they are victims of this deployment, not "real" but caricatures, denuded of substance. They are not victims of the same order, nor with the same degree of complicity, but both suffer in the transparency of their own domination. Leni experiences Franz's rocket-mysticism, his peculiar epiphanic time, as alienating, the opposite of the solidarity she wants from human society; Franz, on the other hand, experiences Leni's parallel time in similarly alienating fashion. "Franz was never much in the street. Always some excuse. Worried about security, being caught on a stray frame by one of the leather-coated photographers, who will always be at the fringes of the action" (158). Franz's concern for security is also a fear of getting caught in a form of mechanical reproduction (the photograph), a kind of incipient paranoia based on a horror of the reifying effects of the "street." In the following passage, taken from a later episode, Franz remembers another demonstration similar to the one Leni describes:

> He found the street full of tan and green uniforms, truncheons, leather, placards fluttering unstable in all modes but longitudinal, scores of panicked civilians. A policeman aimed a blow at him, but Pökler dodged, and it hit an old man instead, some bearded old unreconstructed geezer of a Trotskyite ... he saw the strands of steel cable under a black rubber skin, a finicky smile on the policeman's face as he swung, his free hand grasping his opposite lapel in some feminine way ... and his eyes flinching at the last possible moment, as if the truncheon shared his nerves and might get hurt against the old man's skull. Pökler made it to the doorway, sick with fear. (399)

Franz sees the truncheon as an extension of the policeman's arm, a coimplication of man and weapon that terrifies him but that also blinds him to another coimplication, that of Franz and the unreconstructed geezer. The experience of naked power prevents him from recognizing his solidarity with the protesters, and in fact he turns against them in a strangely reflexive or automatic identification with the policeman and the truncheon he wields. Franz sees the policeman's "finicky smile" and "feminine" manner as signs of a capitulation that will become his own from the moment he lets his fear dominate him. Indeed, fear has already altered his perception by inverting qualities such as hard/soft and feminine/masculine: the inanimate becomes sensitive in this passage, and the animate becomes hard. This almost hallucinatory inversion is a central motif in *Gravity's Rainbow*.

The point is that both Franz and Leni experience the deployment of power as a form of interpellation (regardless of how well they resist it), suspending them in fantasy where investments of the machinic object can only be overdetermined. They are what Pynchon in a later comic song calls "Victims in a Vacuum," masochists "alone with those fantasies that don't look like they'll ever come true" (414). This masochism is a principal underlying thematic of episode 19, signaled most explicitly in the sentence that recurs twice in the course of the narrative: "AN ARMY OF LOVERS CAN BE BEATEN." Presented as a slogan scrawled on Berlin walls and "without author or painter," Pynchon calls it a "text, revealed in order to be thought about, expanded on, translated into action by the people" (155). What kind of interpretation this text demands, and what kind of action it is meant to elicit, is never made clear, however, and the note it strikes resonates ambiguously through the whole episode. At one level, it is an expression of the arrested or suspended atmosphere that Pynchon is so careful to suggest, and thus the feeling of helplessness that grips each character. The historical inevitability of Nazism in Germany is also implied in the passive construction of the sentence, although such a reading may miss the always displaced functions of historical detail in the novel. How this sentence assumes the oneiric mantle of a Pynchonesque text depends on how one conserves its oblique and middle-voiced stress in the reading it provokes.

Masochism

As with the implicit reference to Brecht and the Epic Theater, the thematic presence of "masochism" in the text functions to recall a modernist moment, only this time in its psychoanalytic incarnation. *Gravity's Rainbow* is firmly rooted in the realm of the drives, the ego instincts and the sexual instincts, the death drive and the pleasure principle, the strange itineraries (the "vicissitudes") linking aims to objects that constitute the panoply of perversions elaborated by Freud and others. What I have been calling a gravitational movement of self-objectification in the novel expresses this perverse location within an economy of pleasure and unpleasure as Freud outlines it, for instance, in *Beyond the Pleasure Principle*. The manner in which the novel takes itself as its own object in fact echoes the "point of departure" for all psychoanalytic thought, in Freud's words "the impression, derived from examining unconscious processes, that consciousness may be, not the most universal attribute of mental processes, but only a particular function of them" (*Beyond the Pleasure Principle*, 26). Consciousness undergoes with this insight a decentering and metonymic displacement, disclosing in its peripheral status a liminal form and function. The system Cs., site of perceptions and feelings (external and internal excitations respectively), is said by Freud to originate not in the interior depths of an organism but at the skin, at the surface (the cerebral cortex), the "borderline between outside and inside" (27). At this interface, consciousness has the dual function of *receiving* and *protecting against* the always excessive influx of stimuli. It becomes a "shield" against the external world literally by dying and by hardening: the "outermost surface ceases to have the structure proper to living matter, becomes to some degree inorganic and thenceforward functions as a special envelop or membrane resistant to stimuli" (30). This dead part of the living organism cannot, however, turn its shield toward the inside, and the inability to screen unpleasurable feelings as it would stimuli leads to a "tendency," writes Freud, "to treat [feelings] as though they were acting, not from the inside, but from the outside, so that it may be possible to bring the shield against stimuli into operation as a means of defence against them" (33). The transformation of feeling into stimulus, the projection of the inside on the outside, is one method by which consciousness becomes experiential, and the pleasure principle, as the law of this experience, proves its hegemony over psychic life.[9]

Consciousness, generated at the surface where excitations are organized into sensible and intelligible forms, grasps itself on this account only through the attempt to master a vertiginous implication in its world, which is to say only by catching itself up in a paradox: as a *part* of the *whole* it strives to totalize and cannot (being peripheral), consciousness intuits the nontotalizable whole it always already is in its partiality. Consciousness is the virtual boundary of this gestalt, an infinite set that cannot remain closed and thus an opening, a breach, a margin enveloping itself, an outline internal to the being it limns. *Gravity's Rainbow* traces out this nontotalizable whole in its metonymic structure, at the levels of content and expression, indeed most indelibly in the slide from content to expression that everywhere marks its "preterite" and paranoid textual strategies. In this section, I would like to explore the relation between a slide toward language, toward the discursive articulation of being, and the "story" of consciousness that Freud tells, in particular his concern with the virtual nature of the drives and of desire, their constitutive relation to the modes in which they are narrated.

For Freud, that story of consciousness is agonistic in nature: to breach the inorganic shield from without, or to flood it from within, amounts to an "invasion" of the mental apparatus against which it marshals as much cathectic energy (or libido) as it can to close the breach, "bind" the invading excitation, and render it "quiescent" once again (34). This is how Freud describes pleasure or discharge of instinctual energy in general. But when the excitation is so extreme as to render discharge impossible, constituting the event as a trauma, Freud detects a disturbance in the normal functioning of the pleasure principle. Traumatic neurosis, he says, occurs when the degree of shock is such that it paralyzes the anxiety of the trauma in a repression, compelling as a symptom the repetition of the painful event (in dreams) by way of "master[ing] the stimulus retrospectively" and reexperiencing the omitted anxiety (37). In this repetition Freud uncovers what seems to be an exception to his rule that all dreams are fulfillments of wishes and, more significantly, that the pleasure principle is the most dominant force in psychic life.

The compulsion to repeat observed in trauma turns out for Freud to be an attribute general to all instincts, which he defines as "urge[s] . . . to restore an earlier state of things" or "expression[s] of the inertia inherent in organic life" (43). In tension with the notion that the instincts are self-preservative, Freud ascribes to them a conservative nature, a death wish, a retrogressive insistence toward an inanimate state that is self-canceling and self-identical (that is, the urge to return to a more primitive state expresses itself as both a desire to die and a desire to stay the same, identical, changeless). The sexual instincts arise as more and more complicated detours in the progress of life toward death, brought on under the pressure of contingent external influences (i.e., excitations).[10] "The organism," writes Freud, "wishes to die only in its own fashion" (47), and as the detours (over time) grow more complex and circuitous, the death instinct comes strangely to guarantee the itineraries that trace out its desire, indelibly underwriting the life instincts in spite of the fact that life and death appear to oppose one another absolutely. This does not mean that the pleasure principle has ceased to operate, only that the "vacillating rhythm" (49) between ego instincts and sexual instincts, between Thanatos and Eros, so complicates the relation between pleasure and pain that the latter may constitute not only a stage in the progress toward satisfaction but even an aim proper to it. The compulsion to repeat, that is, turns out not to disturb the principle (except in extreme cases) so much as confirm it at the deepest levels of its economy.

This, at least, is one starting point for Deleuze's reading of Freud with respect to the ensemble of symptoms, or the formal structure or *genre*, called masochism in his essay "Coldness and Cruelty." Neither writer questions the determining role of the pleasure principle, and Deleuze underscores the extent to which Freud's interest in a "beyond" in *Beyond the Pleasure Principle* entails less a focus on exceptions to the principle than an inquiry into its grounds, its foundations, that which necessarily escapes it by virtue of conditioning its appearance, its systematic presence in psychic life (*Masochism*, 113). This transcendental ground is repetition itself, the "binding action of Eros" on the excitations that mark the emergence of life from its inanimate sleep.[11] Freud's inquiry attempts to stabilize his concept of the death instinct and so establish the pleasure principle on firmer ground, but it also acknowledges a difficulty, since the concept implies a destabilizing dynamic that works against his own objectivist desire, within the text he writes and also on that text. Deleuze seizes on this implication of the writer in the theory he propounds to identify an ambivalence in the concept. Instead of a death instinct realizing itself in an experience of pleasure (through however indirect a circuit), Deleuze speaks of a "double" repetition that refers desire to the process of its own constitution, and hence to a reflexive apprehension of its own theoretical attribution. "How indeed could excitation be bound and thereby discharged except by this double action of repetition," Deleuze writes, "which on the one hand binds the excitation and on the other tends to eliminate it? Beyond Eros we encounter Thanatos; beyond the ground, the abyss of the groundless; beyond the repetition that links, the repetition that destroys" (114). Deleuze's argument with Freud hinges on a reading of Thanatos that sees it not simply as the grounded groundlessness (a "secondary negation") that drives and ultimately guarantees a psychoanalytic theory of the subject but as a groundless ground (a "primary negation") that destabilizes and contests its referential claims. Two death instincts are implied here, and two theories of desire. But more importantly, two theories of *theory* are in evidence: one that understands desire in terms of a regressive urge toward primitive states, cathexes of undifferentiated (and as such threatening) excitations, and the ultimate primacy of the pleasure principle; and one that understands desire to invest the first theory with its more purely annihilative energy (Thanatos) and undermine its (but also its own) coherence. The death instinct underwriting Eros signifies a content of (or in) the first theory, but in the second theory, the death instinct dissolves that content and focuses the form of the first theory in its self-negating or virtual light.

The problem for Freud in a text like *Beyond the Pleasure Principle*, given that pleasure is the ultimate aim of all the instincts, consists in accounting for the "defusion" or desexualization of libido or Eros energy generally observable in the formation of the self, the lapse of pleasure into unpleasure that induces "traumatic" or perverse repetitions, irruptions of Thanatos, the groundless, into the ground of Eros.[12] As Deleuze is careful to point out, the death instinct as primary negation cannot be given in experience. It is not a self-identical drive in a competing theory but a metatheoretical reflection on its own postulation as a secondary negation in psychoanalysis. It signifies a repetition that functions to highlight the transformation in the death instinct this entails, the method by which its foundational priority is inverted and it becomes an *effect* of the theory it generates. Deleuze reinverts this inversion in Freud's text, analyzing how repetition, even in cases of perversion, goes from being an "unconditioned condition" of the pleasure principle to a subordinated experience of previous pleasures. Deleuze sees in masochism a desire that indexes a primary negation, and Freud's reading seeks to foreclose this desire by denying it the power to unsettle his conceptual apparatus. Masochism is in this sense not an exception but a limit to his theory, an intelligent neutralization of its deepest assumptions about the subject, the body, sociality, and the real itself.

Masochism, like all perversions, involves on Freud's account a defusion or desexualization of the instincts, such that pleasure becomes impossible. But unlike sublimation or neurosis (where displeasure is eventually resolved through a cathexis), this desexualization becomes in perversion the object of a sexualization, and this development engenders the seemingly paradoxical phenomena of pleasure in pain, sexuality in coldness, love in hate, that characterize both sadism and masochism. Freud defined such phenomena as failures (of whatever degree) to integrate the components of the self—specifically the ego and the superego—in a normative, fully Oedipalized manner. For Deleuze, however, the structural split between ego and superego merely characterizes one set of techniques for negotiating the complexities of experience, not a failure of negotiation. In adverting to the form of the masochist *genre* in this way, Deleuze both identifies and enacts the restoration of a prior and independent repetition, inverting Freud's priorities. "Instead of repetition being experienced as a form of behavior related to a pleasure already obtained or anticipated," he writes, "instead of repetition being governed by the idea of experiencing pleasure, repetition runs wild and becomes independent of all previous pleasure. It has become an idea or ideal. Pleasure is now a form of behavior related to repetition, accompanying and following repetition, which has itself become an awesome, independent force" (120). Repetition, in other words, assumes a categorical existence here: instead of pleasure providing repetition with its source material, repetition becomes exactly the suprasensible source of pleasure as an ideal (of pure negation) for being.

Deleuze's reading of Freud takes its cue from this kind of move to invert a temporal sequence and by so doing expose the violence intrinsic to interpretation (or diagnosis) when it bases itself on what he calls a dialectical synthesis of opposites (*Masochism*, 14).[13] Deleuze sees an example of this in Freud's postulation of a "sadomasochistic entity" or single energetic substance that undergoes transformations or reversals from one pole of the binary to the other, depending on the direction of its flow. This "transformist" argument can only explain masochism as an aggressive-sadistic impulse "turned around upon the self" in a deflection from its original object, the father, prompted either by a resultant "fear of loss of love" or, more centrally, by a feeling of guilt connected to the development of the superego (103–4). The pivotal role played by the father image in this case presupposes the single aggressive substance, or rather, they reinforce each other in the Oedipal drama to which Freud reduces the complex symptomatology of the masochist. Even though in the masochist genre (exemplified for Deleuze in the novels of Leopold von Sacher-Masoch) it is the mother who plays the primary role (as torturer), Freud relates the masochist's aims to a rivalry with the father, which produces a series of identifications and projections to account for the subject's choice of "being beaten" (106). In this theory, the father is always disguised within the figure of the "bad" mother and thus carries out in indirect fashion the punishment the subject feels himself to deserve.

For Deleuze, no derivation of masochism from sadism is possible, since each represents a distinct and incommensurable "syndrome." One must, he argues, attend to the mark or the "gap" that resolves them into separate formal structures rather than posit a single unifying substance for both. Only in this way can the specificity of masochism appear in an analysis of it, and Deleuze's argument exposes this limitation in Freud by systematically inverting his explanations wherever they obscure masochism's "particular kind of formalism" (109). Thus the emphases on the bad mother and on the motivating power of guilt miss the theatrical or humorous parody that is the principal generic characteristic of masochism. Deleuze:

> The theme of the bad mother does indeed appear in masochism, but only as a marginal phenomenon, the central position being occupied by the good mother; it is the good mother who possesses the phallus, who

beats and humiliates the subject or even prostitutes herself. . . . The existence of the good mother . . . implies the existence of a gap or blank which stands for the abolition of the father in the symbolic order. Again, while the sense of guilt has great importance in masochism, it acts only as a *cover*, as the *humorous outcome* of a guilt that has *already been subverted*; it is no longer the guilt of the child toward the father, but that of the father himself, and of his likeness in the child. (108, italics mine)

For the masochist, the bad mother is idealized and "transferred" onto the good "oral" mother, who stands in an intermediate relationship between the "uterine, hetaeric," on the one hand, and the "Oedipal," on the other (62–63). This tripartite division of the functions of the mother establishes the matrix of a symbolic order conceived as "intermaternal," and the tension or resonance between them (produced in the oral mother) has as its consequence the expulsion of the father from the symbolic.[14] In the masochist genre, the father does not hide in the mother; rather, mother and child contract in alliance against the father's resemblance in the child: the father is not beating the child; he is being beaten in the child by the mother and with the child's consent. It is the "humiliated father," Deleuze maintains, that provides masochism with its basic formula.

What the psychoanalytic account misses is the singular dimension of the masochist's "intermaternal" symbolism, its manner of signifying a particular "mythic" time, a particular parodic displacement of its own content. How the sense of guilt, for instance, can function as a "cover" for, and "humorous outcome" of, an "already subverted" equivalent has everything to do with a certain fantasmatic quality intrinsic to the masochistic situation, its status as a travesty of real time that the psychoanalytic privileging of the father can only rupture and destroy. In fact, masochistic fantasy is engendered against the possibility of the father's aggressive and hallucinatory return from the side of the real, which, when it happens, promptly negates the fantasy. Deleuze calls this resistance a form of disavowal, an "operation that consists neither in negating or even destroying, but rather in radically contesting the validity of that which is: it suspends belief in and neutralizes the given in such a way that a new horizon opens up beyond the given and in place of it" (31). This "new horizon" demarcates the fantasmatic place of a "suspension" of the real not, however, for the purpose of idealizing it but, more subtly, "in order to secure an ideal which is itself suspended in fantasy" (32–33).

One example Freud gives of disavowal is fetishism, a process of double negation by which, in Deleuze's words, "we deny that the woman lacks a penis" (31). The fetish enables the subject to insist on the existence of the female phallus by functioning as its stand-in—less a symbol of that imaginary power lost through experience than a "frozen, arrested, two-dimensional image, a photograph to which one returns repeatedly to exorcise the dangerous consequences of movement, the harmful discoveries that result from exploration" (31). As such, the fetish image underpins the peculiar atmosphere of the masochist milieu: arrested, suspended, cold, frozen, that milieu is condensed in the figure of the woman torturer, who appears icy, glacial, hard as stone or marble, a statue (53). The fetishist and the masochist share a common cause in their disavowal of the sensual, the warm, the animate; they sexualize the inanimate, the moment before life, the repetitive urge to "restore an earlier state of things," or in other words the death instinct, Thanatos, that which cannot be "given" in experience except as an idea or ideal, which is thus what "hangs" in the dense medium of fantasy for the masochist. This is not to say that the disavowal of sensuality is also a negation of feeling, but it is to say that the masochist seeks to transcend sexual love (understood as given over to pleasure, bound to an object, cathected) in a movement of impersonal or asexual rebirth, a parthenogenesis that transforms him into a "new sexless man," a realized ideal (52). Masochism, then, in its generic features is an imaginary and dialectical apprehension of the death instinct, according to Deleuze, and its temporal form is given as a kind of frozen progression or "pure state of waiting" for a pleasure that is always late, always postponed.[15]

At this point in Deleuze's argument, its logical rigor exhausts or exasperates itself, and he appeals to the "profound mystery" of repetition, likening perversion to mysticism, "a 'black' theology where pleasure ceases to motivate the will and is abjured . . . the better to be recovered as a reward or consequence" (120). The pleasure that attends the resexualization of Thanatos must be seen as empirical, an actual satisfaction, to rescue the masochist from the diagnosis of dysfunction, says Deleuze, but it nonetheless seems clear that resexualization in this case implies pleasure only in a special sense that, on Freud's terms, precludes satisfaction.[16] The "pleasure" taken in the transcendental "beyond" of the unconditioned condition, the groundless ground, pure negation, is what interests Deleuze in the experience of masochism as well as sadism. Both are methods for acting out what cannot be acted out in experience except in the mode of an asymptotic approach, which is why repetition plays such a conspicuous role. For the sadist, whose objective is "thinking out the Death Instinct . . . in a demonstrative form" (31), repetition functions as a "pure delirium of reason" (28), a negation of what Sade calls secondary nature (the "given") that "would necessarily reverberate and reproduce itself *ad infinitum* in primary nature" (28). This deductive drive in an inductive world, this ideal of pure negation that must settle for partial processes of destruction, yields a strategy of overmultiplication or acceleration, an exorcism of all sensuality or secondary pleasure done "in cold blood," without any "pornographic" enthusiasm. The art of Sadean "pornology" seeks a perfect apathy as the negative of all inspiration or impulse; it sexualizes thought and in so doing, for Deleuze, betrays its affinity not with the narcissistic ego but with the superego (this is another reversal of Freud's theory).

In contrast to the speculative and analytic character of sadism, with its emphasis on negation, the masochist uses the imagination and fantasy to disavow secondary nature. Repetition here works as a form of suspense, of pure waiting; it is, according to philosopher Pierre Klossowski, quoted by Deleuze, "Life reiterating itself in order to recover itself in its fall, as if holding its breath in an instantaneous apprehension of its origin." Here one glimpses the desire that Deleuze wants to see as an inner dynamic of masochism, a desire geared to apprehend itself in the processes of its own determination. As such, Deleuze can observe this desire only as a function of writing (and reading), since only by implicating himself in the categorical construction of masochism can construction itself appear as the object this desire invests in the moment of its own generation (and fall). Masochism signifies for Deleuze a textual performativity reflexively grasping its own content in the expression that gives it form, against a writing that assumes an objectivist privilege over its objects of analysis.

Part 1, Episode 19: A Close Reading, Continued

Many of Pynchon's critics have sensed the importance of repetition in *Gravity's Rainbow*, most notably Hanjo Berressem in his book *Pynchon's Poetics*. He analyzes a "belatedness" (*Nachtraglichkeit*) in the novel's structure associated with the "retroactive staging of an impossible event" in a mode of repetition compulsion (48). He theorizes his concept with respect to a "return of the inanimate" that nonetheless inscribes a subject in language; it thus situates a fundamentally absent or unconscious "real" in the interstices of a text as an internal figural limit. Belatedness names a death instinct in Pynchon's novel predicated on the impossible attempt to close the gap *between* language and reality that always takes place *in* language. To become inanimate displaces the subject into the materiality not of things but of words, and the result is to separate desire from the real and consign it to a longing for closure (or unity) it can never fulfill. While the reading given here, following Deleuze, of a "primary negation" in masochism that grasps its own discursive production parallels this inscription of the subject, it relies less on a rhetoric that defines the real in terms of this separation. The movement from the expression of a content to the content of expression engenders a "realized ideal" that catches out the ideality of a "real" defined in terms of its own displacement and as the ground of the symbolic order that then becomes its only scene. Masochism undermines the transcendental signification that guarantees the imaginary distortion of desire itself.[17]

What I would like to explore now is how much Pynchon's relationship to a psychoanalytic discourse in *Gravity's Rainbow* resembles that which Deleuze establishes with Freud's account of masochism. The novel stages the psychoanalytic reading to expose its blindness (and its anathema) to another temporal dimension of resistance to the real. The question is what formal principles underpin this scene of writing. My exposition up to this point has emphasized the way in which the novel reflexively turns upon itself in a repetitiousness that holds as much in common with Sade as with Sacher-Masoch. Within the space I am constructing here, the novel could be read either way or even in a third way, as obsessionally neurotic, without appreciable contradiction.[18] The relationship of episode 19, in which masochism is explicitly thematized, to the novel as a whole can only be seen within its limitations as a fragment. That said, however, it remains the case that all interpretation (my own included), suspended as it is in the abyss of repetition (what Harold Bloom has called the "predicament of misreading" [*Kabbalah and Criticism*, 91]), commits its totalizing errors repetitively, and at least for Pynchon no simple exception to this condition exists. What, then, is the scene of writing in *Gravity's Rainbow*?

That episode 19 constitutes, at all levels of signification, one version of this scene can be inferred from its conclusion in another seance, Sachsa's attempt to contact the dead industrialist and innovator of the cartelized state, Walter Rathenau, for a select group of "corporate Nazis" in his Berlin flat, where Leni goes after the Studentenheim. The return to a thematic of communicating with the dead recenters the narrative's preoccupation with media, with mediation, thus with the frame, the principle, or the condition necessary for its own appearance (as a manifest content but also as a structure). To touch across the various boundaries drawn by Pynchon—animate/inanimate, female/male, wife/husband, symbol/image, or symbol/sign—is to transmit or receive messages, to shape reality according to formal or temporal modes that interfere to such an extent that the activity of touching seems to warp back in on itself, to evanesce within its own desire. The metaphoric power of the psychic resides, for Pynchon, in the way the psychic effaces himself from that which he conducts or mediates, dissolving, as it were, into the interstice of an exchange of information, the content of which always escapes him. Unfortunately, this self-effacement makes Sachsa vulnerable to manipulation by the corporate Nazis. When Leni, just arrived, asks him, "What's going on?" Sachsa "snorts, meaning *they haven't told me*. They are using him—have been, various they's, for ten years. But he never knows how, except by rare accident, an allusion, an interception of smiles. A distorted and forever clouded mirror, the smiles of clients" (164). This "clouded mirror" signifies a displacement of meaning into the realm of pure connotation, and thus the space of being shared not only by Sachsa and his clients but by Sachsa and Leni as well. A fundamental discursive ambiguity governs the episode; no one is completely sure about the meanings they receive or even transmit. Sachsa's situation at the border between life and death exemplifies a state to which even writing is subject: that of the indeterminate meaning, of contact without touch, of the whole as fragment, "a net of information that no one can escape" and that deterritorializes (and then neoterritorializes) language itself (165).[19]

It is to this state or frame encompassing everyone in the narrative that Rathenau points in his tour de force speech from "beyond" the zero. Episode 19, itself a "cry inside the stone," itself inanimate, dramatizes or duplicates another cry inside the stone, Rathenau's voice speaking from, and perhaps on behalf of, the death instinct, inside the stone of *Gravity's Rainbow*, articulating a transhistorical movement that renders humanity's history, its time, virtually obsolete.

> "The path is clear," a voice moving Sachsa's lips and rigid white throat. "You are constrained, over there, to follow it in time, one step after another. But here it's possible to see the whole shape at once—not for me, I'm not that far along—but many know it as a clear presence . . . 'shape' isn't really the right word. . . . Let me be honest with you. I'm finding it harder to put myself in your shoes. Problems you may be having, even those of global implication, seem to many of us here only trivial side-trips. You are off on a winding and difficult road, which you conceive to be wide and straight, an Autobahn you can travel at your

ease. Is it any use for me to tell you that all you believe real is illusion? I don't know whether you'll listen, or ignore it. You only want to know about your path, your Autobahn." (165)

From Rathenau's cosmic perspective—itself only partial, the "clear presence" of absolute simultaneity denied him as a neophyte spirit—the Autobahn of human time appears a crude version of the "winding and difficult road" down which humanity is actually traveling. The confidence of industrial capitalism in its ability to extract energy and produce power, while it underwrites a planetary hegemony, also prevents the capitalist from understanding the actual scope or possibility of the events he puts in motion. For Rathenau, the inability of his auditors to see through their own causal idea of the real, to displace or "trivialize" their own obsession with the Autobahn (to make it a side street, as it were, rather than the main drag), only manifests a resistance to their own hegemonic project, and he goes on to illustrate this inertia with the historical example of coal tar, which, as a residue of the process whereby coal is extracted and refined to make steel, turned out in the nineteenth century to be so molecule rich that it spawned, among others, the chemical, pharmaceutical, and synthetic dye industries.

> Consider coal and steel. There is a place where they meet. The interface between coal and steel is coal-tar. Imagine coal, down in the earth, dead black, no light, the very substance of death. Death ancient, prehistoric, species *we will never see again*. Growing older, blacker, deeper, in layers of perpetual night. Above ground, the steel rolls out fiery, bright. But to make steel, the coal-tars, darker and heavier, must be taken from the original coal. Earth's excrement, purged out for the ennoblement of shining steel. Passed over. (166)

Here the text recapitulates a symbolic field stretched between the binarisms of dark and light, death and life, low and high, preterite and elect. Coal tar is an interface not only for coal and steel but for all the elements of industrial capitalism that intersect in it. Coal tar, that is, forms the central link or nodal point of an international conspiracy among those who control natural resources, means of production, and technological skill. This conspiracy renders all nationalist conflict (even world war) archaic, or rather it recontextualizes that conflict and, by so doing, effectively transforms its uses and functions, indeed its very nature or essence as an intelligible event. For Rathenau, capitalism could not initially perceive value in the "preterite" coal tar because of its negative inscription within the symbolic field *preterite/elect* (i.e., it was seen only as a useless residue without value or potential). Value itself has to undergo a change or an inversion to catalyze the historical transformation necessary to the development of a "Kartellized" world.[20] The generative power of coal tar, a "substance of death" distilled and compressed by gravity, had to be realized or put to work; the "preterite" had to be used, positivized, just as the corporate Nazis sitting at (the preterite) Sachsa's table have to positivize their own resistance, prime themselves for a quantum leap that even Rathenau does not see with complete clarity.

What this positivization entails is an abandonment of the belief in cause and effect, Rathenau's "secular history" (167), time construed as a "resurrection," rebirth, or progress. "The real movement is not from death to any rebirth," he argues. "It is from death to death transfigured. The best you can do is to polymerize a few dead molecules. But polymerizing is not resurrection" (166). Time is here not the "beautiful death" of the dialectic; rather, it transpires within a medium of death symbolized by the reduplicated patterns of the polymerized molecule. Polymerization, according to the New World International Dictionary "a chemical reaction where two or more small molecules combine to form larger molecules that contain repeating structural units of the original molecules," is the process whereby plastics are made, and thus literally as well as figuratively the arrest of a natural cycle, a neutralization both of life as an organic development and death as its decomposition. A temporal movement is suspended, locked in a repetitiousness that vitiates the real, a "synthetic" travesty of synthesis in all its senses.

> "You think you'd rather hear about what you call 'life': the growing, organic Kartell. But it's only another illusion. A very clever robot. The more dynamic it seems to you, the more deep and dead, in reality, it grows. Look at the smokestacks, how they proliferate, fanning the wastes of original waste over greater masses of city. Structurally, they are strongest in compression. A smokestack can survive any explosion—even the shock waves from one of the new cosmic bombs"—a bit of a murmur around the table at this—"as you all must know. The persistence, then, of structures favoring death. Death converted into more death. Perfecting its reign, just as the buried coal grows denser, and overlaid with more strata—epoch on top of epoch, city on top of ruined city. This is the sign of Death the impersonator." (167)

Rathenau's speech, especially when taken in the full context of the narrative, has to it a manifestly uncanny quality. It is uncanny because the novel's own structure, "strongest in compression," is so clearly articulated and exemplified in it. What Rathenau describes is not only industrial capitalism but *Gravity's Rainbow* itself, its own unnaturalness, its own delusive naturalness, its own "gravitational" persistence toward death, its own preterition. The novel is like a smokestack "fanning wastes of original waste over greater masses of the [humanist] city," secreting a second or "double" waste as a kind of fuel for its polymeric narrative progressions. As Rathenau exposes the illusion of the "growing, organic Kartell," so Pynchon exposes the growing, organic narrative as a "robot," more "deep and dead" the more dynamic it becomes. This antidynamic expresses itself in the techniques of caricature, impersonation, and palimpsestic displacement that crystallize language as the novel's proper subject (or the object toward which it aims). *Gravity's Rainbow* is "machinic" insofar as it presents its own representations as instruments or tools, in a materiality the structure of which—repetitive, "favoring death"—yields a desire intrinsically linked to the inanimate, to the earth as a preterite source for its catchrestic energy.

The question then becomes how to read the privilege granted Rathenau's character, and by extension the corporate mysticism he espouses, to name the "winding" and entropic structure of the novel as he does. Why is it that the novel's preterition converges with the transhistorical movement that also moves through the project of industrialization and cartelization in Western culture (even if the latter cannot see this for itself)? Here the problem of complicity comes to be most disturbingly felt in the text. The reader is in the presence of a double-mindedness more profound and more fundamental, Pynchon suggests, than any denial of complicity can claim. This is why Rathenau's politics, like Leni Pökler's, have a "symbolic" dimension: "These signs are real," he says. "They are also symptoms of a process. The process follows the same form, the same structure. To apprehend it you will follow the signs. All talk of cause and effect is secular history, and secular history is a diversionary tactic" (167). The deliberate echo of the language Leni uses with Franz ("sign" and "symptom") here alerts the reader to that "horizon" within which everything is given in the novel, all its terms, all its binaries, all its meanings—within which, that is, even the novel itself is "framed." As Leni speaks *from* this frame, she speaks *with* Rathenau, and their respective critiques of industrial capitalism are thus homological even though Rathenau's is offered in the spirit of advice: for capitalism to perfect its own form, he says, it must develop for itself a symbolic or "parallel" time, as well as an overlapping (or overmapping) schizophrenizing rationality.

What the precise nature of this frame is becomes even more crucial for an understanding of Pynchon's novel once this complicity is seen to include all political response, either in the novel or to the novel (that is, once the reader experiences the vertiginous way Pynchon's novel interpellates or assimilates him or her into the world it describes). To stop short of such an inquiry is to consign the text to a kind of pessimism from which no redemption is possible, and it is significant that many critics of Pynchon's work do not get much farther than this, which is why Pynchon criticism has always been vexed over the question of his political viability. It does indeed seem that Pynchon totalizes the dominance of industrial capitalism to such a degree that no limit can be ascertained or distinguished from that of nature. It is also true that this reference to a material condition inclusive of the novel itself is just that: a reference, an effect of the text, a representation, given by or within the horizon under discussion here. The theme of complicity demarcates structure in the structure of the novel, which is why Rathenau names it, but it does not tell us much about the novel's specificities as a scene of writing. That is to say, the mark of structure *does* tell us about this scene, but only by exemplifying a technique of fetishization that locates the novel in a symbolic space characterized, as shown, by an arrested temporality, a suspension of the real, a fantasmatic disavowal of the animate or the sensual, and a close connection to the death instinct. These attributes, taken together, establish a range of formal concerns that are intelligible only by referring them to a groundless ground, an abyssal repetition that transforms them into strategies of resistance. This resistance cannot be seen in a reading that stops short at complicity; such a reading, insofar as it makes the relentless intertextuality of Pynchon's novel a figure for that complicity (which it is at one level) without analyzing its formal properties, misses the politics of form that might also be working itself out. For this resistance to be recognized, its context, its formal condition, must also be taken into account.

That this context, or rather this scene of writing, is "masochistic" seems, at least impressionistically, to be the case for episode 19. One does not know how to hear the self-parodic harmonics of Rathenau's speech without some conception of a latent masochism at work in it, a kind of tonal subversion operating on its authoritative utterances. A psychoanalytic interpretation might see Rathenau as a metaphor for the text's aggressive energy "turned around upon itself," its "anti-dynamic," thus a self-torturing based on a feeling of guilt. Rathenau, as a sign for the name of the father, punishes the text for its rivalrous and innately sadistic impulses, its desire not only to destroy but also to replace and be the father in its turn. Complicity in the novel is thus construed as a desire to follow and exemplify the law. But to say that Rathenau is such a representative of the paternal symbolic order, while in its way an admissible reading, nonetheless misapprehends the fantasmatic distortions that govern the scene. Rathenau, after all, is presented as dead, a dead void mediated through another dead voice (Sachsa's) for the auditors at the White Visitation, which suggests that the Rathenau who stands in for the law is doubly negated, a structurally significant absence or hallucinatory presence in the writing. Rathenau's time is preterite, bygone, passed over, vanished. This preterition constitutes both a reversal of causality, doubling the past in an effort not unlike persistence of vision, and a "transfiguration" of death that brings the trace-structure of the novel to a kind of life. Rathenau thus signifies the "double action of repetition," the "abyss of the groundless," and this alters his status as a representative of the law. If he still functions as this representative, it is only in the context of a self-parody that fixes that function in a displacement. For the masochist, says Deleuze, the father is experienced as "already abolished symbolically," and this "experience" determines a peculiar theatricality in which the father becomes precisely that which is humiliated. According to this logic, Rathenau is an image of the father in Pynchon's text that is beaten, ridiculed, tortured—a reading given a strange resonance, I might add, by the fact that the historical Rathenau was Jewish.

Indeed, a bewilderingly complex semantic universe can be glimpsed in this detail. Rathenau's symbolic function takes on another kind of weight with the suggestion that he signifies the novel's hermeneutical (writing and reading) mode: that is, rabbinic or cabbalistic, in which, as Susan Handelman points out, "primary reality was linguistic, true being was a God who *speaks* and creates *texts*, and *imitatio deus* was not silent suffering, but speaking and interpreting" (*The Slayers of Moses*, 4). Pynchon's staging of a search for transcendental signifiers such as the Rocket can be seen in this light to undermine a Western tradition of thought in which language is defined as secondary, fallen, being's accident rather than its essence, and in which the model for interpretation is rather the Incarnation, the word's metamorphosis from a linguistic to a material order (4). The complicity of a strategy based on interpretation and textuality (the world as Book) in the capitalist system described by Pynchon strikes at the heart of a discourse bounded by the opposition between Christian (or Greek) and Jew, along with its analogues: New and Old Testaments, spirit and letter, speech and writing, divinity and perversion. The latter is always the repressed term, the exile, the scapegoat, the outlaw; so when Pynchon, in the figure of Rathenau, condenses the repressed term into that of the law and the father, placing it at the center of his discourse, he in effect displaces the opposition in order to see its (displaced) matrix as inevitably and necessarily his own. The outlaw is the law, Pynchon implies, the perversion is divine, the outside returns on the inside, and this is the structural precondition for meaning in *Gravity's Rainbow*. Put another way, perversion or that libidinal space (of writing) opened to the abyss of repetition is the medium in which the novel unfolds, only perversion here turns against itself, tortures itself in a sort of deconstructive frenzy, *becomes* perverse only in that gesture of deconstruction.

Now it could be argued that this gesture is either reflexive (obsessionally neurotic) or a form of irony, which Deleuze explicitly links with sadism. Ironic decontextualization is of course a central feature of the novel and clearly bears comparison with a sadistic repetition. In stressing the masochist form as I have been doing, my intent is not to foreclose these other readings or apply Pynchon's novel to a particular generic grid to which it can only imperfectly fit; but it does seem that at a fundamental level, the novel has to be read in this "masochistic" light. What is at stake, finally, is the novel's relation to fantasy, the fetish, and the imagination. For Deleuze, the uses of fantasy in sadism and masochism are different: in the former, "a powerful force of paranoid projection transforms the fantasy into the instrument of a fundamental and sudden change in the objective world," and this access to a real situation, an actual pain inflicted by the sadist, entails a destruction of the fetish, a need on the part of the sadist "to believe he is not dreaming even when he is"; in the latter, on the contrary, the maintenance of the fantasy, the dream, the fetish is all-important for the masochist's dramatic or parodic aims—he "needs to believe he is dreaming even when he is not," in order to neutralize the real and contain the ideal in fantasy (*Masochism*, 72–73). This inverse difference is a crucial mark for rendering both sadism and masochism distinct from each other, and it is also this mark that distinguishes the temporal modality of *Gravity's Rainbow* as imaginative and dialectic—that is, as an imaginative parody of the dialectic. The theatricality of Pynchon's style, for all its similarities with sadism, shows a pronounced affinity with the derisive, absurdist, insolent, and "cold" imagination of the masochist.[21]

The essential trope here, then, is not irony but humor. Both are reactions to, and subversions of, a law that has become in its pure form unknowable, indeterminate, an agency making one "guilty in advance" (83), says Deleuze;

but irony is an "upward movement . . . toward a transcendent higher principle," and humor "a downward movement from the law to its consequences" (88). Such a downward movement involves an activity of reiterating and inverting the law in its particulars. "The essence of masochistic humor lies in this, that the very law which forbids the satisfaction of a desire under threat of subsequent punishment is converted into one which demands the punishment first and then orders that the satisfaction of the desire should necessarily follow upon the punishment" (88–89). It is this punishment and its inverted temporality that the reader experiences in Rathenau's speech, the mode of the text's self-torture. It is also why episode 19 ends with a joke (Heinz Rippenstoss, "Nazi wag and gadabout," asks Rathenau, "Is God really Jewish?"), for only with humor can the reader register in Pynchon's prose its complex range of tonalities, ironic, deconstructive, self-parodic, and at the same time rediscover the "downward movement," the low, the preterite, as a value put forth in the novel—a displaced value, to be sure, but one strangely capable of suspension, of buoyancy, in the intertextual abyss. The novel's horizon demarcates a scene of writing in which the fetish plays a constitutive role, and in which the body of the text is a dreaming body, invested in the maintenance of a fantasmatic disavowal of the real. Rathenau's privilege as a spokesman for the novel is thus inflected through this fantasy, this dreaming body, as are all the thematic treatments of the novel's own complicity (as fantasy, as fetish, as sign-object). Even Leni Pökler's symbolic politics must be read through the perverse fantasy, the homological medium of both sign value exchange and symbolic exchange, but in which, nevertheless, an inverse difference (or a "turn") can be glimpsed. Humor is the operator of this difference, the tropological dynamic informing the text's true political desire, which is to identify (in a nonpsychoanalytic sense) with its preterite characters in their fallenness, their determination by a Judeo-Christian culture as textualized beings obsessed with transcendence, caught in the "gravitational" need to signify and represent, to generalize the particular, to form concepts, to narrativize experience.

This desire is linked to an "art of suspense" that, according to Deleuze, "always places us on the side of the victim and forces us to identify with him" (34). Pynchon presents us with a figure for this art at the beginning of *Gravity's Rainbow* in Teddy Bloat, asleep after a night of drink and debauchery, hanging significantly, preposterously, by a single champagne split in his hip pocket, from Pirate Prentice's minstrel's gallery. The thematic of care, of allegiance to the preterite, is here given its first avatar when Prentice, walking sluggishly from the dream with which the novel commences, kicks his cot (equipped with casters) across the floor to catch Bloat as he falls. This gesture assumes its full significance only with the understanding that Prentice thereby allows Bloat to continue sleeping (since he doesn't wake up), and that this continuity through the act of falling, this collusion in the preservation of the dreaming state, constitutes both a complicity *and* a transgression. That is, it opens up the space in which transgression of the kind Pynchon practices is possible, and manifests what may be the only political program the novel can offer, exemplified near the end by Roger Mexico and Pig Bodine, whose activism takes the form of an alliterative trashing of a swank dinner party held by Stefan Utgartholoki, giant and personification of evil in ancient Norse mythology:

>"Oh, I don't know," Roger elaborately casual, "I can't seem to find any *snot soup* on the menu...."
>
>"Yeah, I could've done with some of that *pus pudding,* myself. Think there'll be any of that?"
>
>"No, but there might be a scum souffle!" cries Roger, "with a side of—*menstrual marmalade!*"
>
>"Well, I've got eyes for some of that rich, meaty smegma stew!" suggests Bodine. "Or how about a *clot casserole?*"
>
>"I say," murmurs a voice, indeterminate as to sex, down the table. (715)

This repetition of consonantal sounds as an act of rebellion (with the explicit reference made to eating, to excretion, to flow and the blockage of flow, to the "low" functions of the body) builds in crescendo for another page and a half, infectiously spreading to the more susceptible guests, and ends with the instigators being escorted out by a "black butler [who] opens the last door to the outside, and escape. Escape tonight. 'Pimple pie with filth frosting, gentlemen,' he nods. And just at the other side of dawning, you can see a smile" (717).

The intention behind this scene is not to posit an effective political method at the level of content, since, as many readers have pointed out, the "Counterforce" Mexico and Bodine incarnate never transcends its own implication in the overdetermined networks of power it wants to subvert.[22] What is political about its peculiar line of flight to the outside turns, on the contrary, around this implication. The function of repetition to insert the sonorous cadence of nonsense into semantic structure indicates a move to language, to the level of

131

expression, and as such it symptomatically reproduces the metalinguistic dynamic of social order. The symptom it forms takes on significance not through the attempt to give it the value of practical efficacy but in the way it problematizes that attempt, calling ontology itself into question and compelling the reader to account for his or her own immanent relation to discursive power. If this amounts to little more than a politics of reading, and hence no real politics at all, it does so with a renewed ethical focus on reading the texts of our lives well.

5
DOCILE BODIES AND THE BODY WITHOUT ORGANS: GRAVITY'S *GRAVITY'S RAINBOW*

plas tic: giving form: having power to form or create; CREATIVE, FORMATIVE; capable of being modeled or shaped; susceptible to modification or change: PLIANT, IMPRESSIONABLE; characterized by mobility and flow or the simulation of these qualities; capable of being deformed continuously and permanently in any direction without rupture under a stress exceeding the yield value; having or producing coherency, harmony, and vitality: ORGANIC; capable of growth, repair or differentiation: ADAPTABLE; DUCTILE, MALLEABLE.
plastic: a substance that at some stage in its manufacture or processing can be shaped by flow (as by application of heat or pressure) with or without fillers, plasticizers, reinforcing agents, or other compounding ingredients and that can retain the new solid often rigid shape under conditions of use.—Adapted from *Webster's Third New World International Dictionary*

The previous chapter attempts to locate in Pynchon's text a dimension that could properly be called masochistic, although in doing so what it succeeds in discovering might be proper less to masochism per se than to a particular version of it. Indeed, what it locates in *Gravity's Rainbow* is more a Deleuzian formality, a generic dimension close in its details and aims to what Kaja Silverman calls Deleuze's " 'utopian' rereading of masochism" (*Male Sexuality at the Margins*, 211). This utopianism manifests itself most directly in the refusal by the masochist or in the masochist scenario not only of the father, the law, and a symbolic ordered by the paternal metaphor but of the distinction between symbolic and imaginary, the emphasis on desire as founded on lack, castration, the Oedipus complex, and psychoanalysis itself. As Silverman is quick to point out, Deleuze's "Coldness and Cruelty" does not succeed in freeing its own terms from the density of psychoanalytic theory, in particular where Deleuze uses the category of disavowal. Desire in Deleuze's account remains linked "at the center of its organization" to the very concepts it repudiates (211). "There is an obvious danger," writes Silverman, "that [such a rereading of masochism] be taken literally, as designating the standard form of that perversion, rather than its visionary reconfiguration" (211). Although Silverman acknowledges her sympathy with this "revolutionary" project and astutely isolates what is perhaps its most important contribution (the absence of a homosexual object choice in the Deleuzian masochist implies the constitution of a "feminine yet heterosexual male subject" [212]), she insists on the centrality of the Oedipus complex to masochism and, by extension, the continued relevance of psychoanalysis to cultural critique.[1]

My intention has not been to apply a literal account of Deleuze's rereading to the masochism of *Gravity's Rainbow*. What is germane to the foregoing discussion hinges, rather, on what formally, in the logic of Deleuze's argument (and Pynchon's novel), makes it a "visionary reconfiguration." Freud's death drive inherent to all instincts—energy "bound" or cathected in a return to a prior quiescent state and so given over to the pleasure principle—precludes for Deleuze a *repetition* that focuses the premises of psychoanalytic theory in a critical light. Masochism does not assume the death instinct generated by this theory; it questions that assumption, rewriting the death instinct in terms of a primary negation that unsettles the foundations of theory itself. Here, then, is that visionary element: a shift from what a theory means to how it establishes its meanings, from its content to its expression. Such a dynamic informs the texts under consideration in this book, and even this consideration itself. It invokes the particular historical moment that Pynchon and Deleuze (across the various aporias of culture and language) have in common, which, through an emphasis on the visionary, on utopian revaluation, could be called countercultural in the symptomatic sense developed throughout this study. At stake in Deleuze's critique of psychoanalysis and in the narrative structure of *Gravity's Rainbow* is the cultural possibility of a transformation in the discursive schemata that govern social life in the postwar period. Texts such as these exhibit those schemata and demonstrate their transformation through an implicated practice of writing that makes expression itself a principal object. This can be observed quite clearly in another countercultural tour de force, Deleuze and Guattari's *Anti-Oedipus*.

For that text, psychoanalytic theory forecloses the "visionary" slide from content to expression and as a result denies its own symptomatic status in time. This does not mean it ceases to be a symptom, only that it fails to grasp the peculiar necessity of its own symptomaticity and so degrades its own critical power. It does this through the application of what the authors call an "exclusive disjunctive synthesis." This structuring apprehension of the world, assuming as its principal form a "predicative relation of the One and the many" (42), implies a differentiation in extension of objects and subjects against the backdrop of an "original totality" and in alignment with a final teleological terminus. The multiplicity of things, and the temporal and spatial dimensions for the reality in which they appear, are determined within a linear, biunivocal, and dialectical paradigm. Deleuze and Guattari identify in this synthesis the function of a repression. The unitary ground of being, understood as transcendent, engenders multiplicity only because of its radical alterity to the ontic field of its "figures." As such, it contracts a gravitational pull back to that original oneness that by definition can never be completed (except in a self-extinguishment). This ground exists therefore only as repressed, only as the opposite pole of a force—gravity, if it's a question of placement on the "earth," or desire, if it's a question of situation in the "world"—drawn precisely toward what is not and can never be.

At a psychoanalytic register, this means that a transcendental signifier (phallus, law) orients subjects only in relation to its own absence; it detaches itself from the signifying chain along which, as a transcendent complete object, it distributes "effects of meaning" or exclusive marks of difference (either male or female). "Oedipus," for Deleuze and Guattari, introduces into desire a dual differentiating series that not only generates persons, male and female egos, mommies, daddies, and me's, but in the same gesture projects a prior alterity as the locus of a demand (to accept the categories it imposes), a threat (of dissolution if you don't), and an impossible desire (in the lack of that transcendent object). "The exclusive relation introduced by Oedipus comes into play not only between the various disjunctions conceived as differentiations, but *between the whole of the differentiations that it imposes and an undifferentiated that it presupposes*" (Anti-Oedipus, 78). This exclusive relation not only within the system formed by "Oedipus" but between the system and its ground delivers the subject up to two contradictory yet simultaneous imperatives: erotically invest the "differentiated parental persons" (79) who triangulate his or her desire (as "effects of meaning" or symbols standing in for the law) and renounce any satisfaction with these persons (in conformity with the incest taboo). Desire is in this way consigned to a domain of imaginary substitutions, identifications, and projections, to a "psychic reality" that simultaneously masks and confirms the fact of an original and constitutive repression. For Deleuze and Guattari, this move to extrapolate a "transcendent and common something ... a common-universal for the sole purpose of introducing lack into desire" (72), characterizes the Freudian corpus from beginning to end. The point, for them, is that any accession to the necessity of lack, prohibition, castration, or in other words to the presence of a "common-universal" origin from which all (exclusive) differentiations derive, means that one has already assumed sexual difference, the specification and situation of subjects vis-à-vis an Oedipalized norm, and the primacy of the familial as triangulated scene of desire—in other words, one has already assumed a violence directed at desire that Deleuze and Guattari set out to demonstrate is central to the mechanisms of social power in a late capitalist world.

In contrast to dualistic, either/or, biunivocal order of thought given by the exclusive disjunction, Deleuze and Guattari speak of an "inclusive" use (or transformation) of the synthesis that inverts the predictive relation between the One and the many, positing a primary multiplicity as the ground for a certain unicity in the figures it generates. Instead of a difference (mark or category) in *extension*, articulating subjects and objects in a linear temporal series and a typological space, this synthetic operation yields an *intensive* difference understood as fractal in nature. "*Everything divides*," they write, "*but into itself*" (76). The world of an inclusive disjunctive synthesis appears in the collapse of a determined distinction between ground and figure, at the surface of their condensation where "things" are deprived of an organic outline or volume in depth. They become abstract elements in a foreshortened field of suprasensible or subtle matter, virtual insofar as they evoke a crisis of dimension (one doesn't know "where" they are) or of dialectic actualization (one doesn't know "what" they are). This is why Deleuze and Guattari assert of the subject conceived in this manner that it falls outside the system of "Oedipus," that it does not derive from the differentiating agency of a transcendental signifier and bears no relation to an absent whole object whose lack draws desire into being. "Desire does not lack anything," they write. "It does not lack its object. It is, rather, the *subject* that is missing in desire, or desire that lacks a fixed subject; there is no fixed subject unless there is repression" (26).

To argue for the visionary qualities of a work like *Anti-Oedipus* is not, of course, to refute reservations about its utopian or even idealistic pretensions, and it needs to be said that the issue for this particular utopian text is precisely a kind of idealism. The motile or fluid subject "missing" from itself constitutes a wrench thrown into the conceptual "machine" of an "original totality" and the "exclusive" world that follows from it. This machine provides the model for that idealism: Platonic or Cartesian in provenance, it drives a rationality ramifying itself in space, articulating itself through time, and installing itself in the most categorical modes of perception and common sense. The anti-Oedipal subject is for Deleuze and Guattari no longer a *centered structure* in a rationalized world but a *field of force*, experiencing its own self-identity as a spatial coextension with an intrinsically hallucinatory "outside." It does not lack the objects of its desire because those objects fall within the field it also *is* by virtue of its inclusive unity, which is why the positivity of that desire manifests itself in their terms as "desiring-production," a production of production itself according to the "law" of an identity between production and product. This "partial" subject is a part that replicates the whole *as its own part*, complete in its partiality; it is thus a kind of hologram or virtual avatar playing out a strangely schizophrenic participation in the world and its historical becomings.

Perhaps the most interesting aspect of Deleuze and Guattari's polemic is its performative bravado, its overdetermined compression of discourses yielding that ambiguous tonality of irony and earnestness, the hard-to-gauge weight of the "anti" in *Anti-Oedipus*. Part of the problem is that the text hedges its own literality, fractalizing its assertions and frustrating comprehension to the point that reading and writing itself become the very scene of the polemic, implicating us in the problems it raises. And indeed, Deleuze and Guattari's self-external subject of desire is in the end scarcely intelligible unless it is seen within a larger strategy aimed at discourse, at language, at modes of thought as they are caught up in a process of metalinguistic abstraction, a process apparently hard at work in the impenetrable theoretical labyrinths of *Anti-Oedipus*. As Fredric Jameson has argued in *Postmodernism* and elsewhere, a principal feature of the schizoid time of a late capitalist mode of production is a "spatial turn" signaling an exteriorization of the subjective time-sense, an articulation of subjectivity into a standardized and rationalized object-world where desire finds itself coaptatively engendered within the systems of consumerism and spectacle.[2] *Anti-Oedipus* could be said to constitute an exemplar of this schizoid time precisely in its deployment of the inclusive disjunction to generate the subject who lacks nothing and finds fulfillment everywhere—the subject, therefore, of superfluity itself, the excess and emptiness of consumption. One can, it seems, reconcile the strategy of their book with this appalling suggestion of its complicity only by an appeal to the inclusive or internal difference they themselves elucidate, and which only tenuously—if at all—gets them out of the problem.

But in fact the principal question *Anti-Oedipus* poses is not that of an (exclusive) alternative to "Oedipus" so much as its condition of possibility, that which it has to assume to project itself in its autonomy. Deleuze and Guattari are interested in the inclusive ground against which any system's exclusive "figures" are offset, and which envelops those figures in a virtuality they must deny by way of "grounding" themselves in a stable dimension of reality or meaning. This ground is essentially groundless, they argue, abyssal in nature, an unconditioned condition not given to the systems it makes possible and yet isomorphic with its own foreclosure as an "original totality," a trace of finitude in what cannot be lost (despite the exclusive disjunction), a remainder or reminder of a more primitive multiplicity that the system in toto represses and indeed *has* to repress. Desire for Deleuze and Guattari is only this singular trace of finitude within an Oedipal system, the memento mori of a repetition (Thanatos as a pure or primary negation) that undermines its peculiar retroactive projection of an origin. As such, desire implies a demystifying function within discourse to expose that temporal inversion by which systems arbitrarily produce their own beginnings. And *Anti-Oedipus*, as a performance of the desire it also thematizes, is therefore not a system like "Oedipus," arguing its own exclusive syntheses. Rather, "Oedipus" is *cited* within its more inclusive form, "at the center of its organization," and operates there as the parodied object of systematicity itself.

I have analyzed the "schizoid time" of this citationality in the previous chapter on *Gravity's Rainbow*, notably where an archaeological problematic is linked to figures of reversal and implication, and where inversion characterizes the order of "intermaternal symbolism" in which the masochist disavows "real time" in fantasy. In each instance, what is observable is a meta-parodic mode that is paratactic (it implies a constitutive break within textual machines), serial or accumulative (it implies an "overstuffing" farce or folly), and metonymic (it implies a condensation of part and whole as hologram, fetish, etc.). This mode links the strategies of *Gravity's Rainbow* to those of *Anti-Oedipus*, highlighting in both texts a schizophrenic engagement with the "time" of their own writing. They are, one might say, countercultural autocritiques geared to express how discourse is lived traumatically under late capitalism through an exhaustive *sollicitation* of its excesses, its abstractions, its reifications. But this stake of expression in their work only comes through once the discursive dimension they have in common has been fully elucidated, for only then can the "anti" in "Oedipus," the repetition in return (or reproduction), and (to anticipate my own argument) the "rainbow" in "gravity" appear for what they are: transformations of discourse via the literary construction of inclusive systems incorporating (ingesting, invaginating, citing) the totality of what they disavow.

With this in mind, I would like to look a little more closely at *Anti-Oedipus*, in preparation for a reading of *Gravity's Rainbow* that builds on Deleuze and Guattari's rereading of the death drive as a "deterritorializing" retreat toward the asymptomatic limit of its own text-world. The point of this digression is not to hold up Deleuze and Guattari as authorities supporting my own claims. Their text is an exhibit of the countercultural desire I am thematizing: a performance of the symptom that cannot be thematized without implicating one's discourse in the elliptical and displaced time it evokes.

Anti-Oedipus: A (Countercultural) Theory of Desire

What Deleuze and Guattari formalize in their theory is a perversion of totality, or of the totalizing aims of systematic thought. This is why one cannot see it as an example of such a total system without falling into the discursive habit of totalization they take as their object of analysis. Anti-Oedipus is a system the whole of which, as they write of Proust's In Search of Lost Time, "itself is a product, produced as nothing more than a part alongside other parts . . . though it has an effect on these other parts simply because it establishes aberrant paths of communication between non-communicating vessels, transverse unities between elements that retain all their differences within their own particular boundaries" (43). The production of "non-communicating" parts in a structure of internal differences means for their system as a "whole" that it too is "non-communicating," or rather makes its own strategies of communication hinge on an "aberrant" juxtaposition of elements. As a paratactic collage rather than a syntactic treatise based on logical subordination or consecution, Anti-Oedipus is constructed on a principle of pure addition and contiguity without reference, forming a decentered and "peripheral" system: "We believe only in totalities that are peripheral," they write. "And if we discover such a totality *alongside* various separate parts, it is a whole *of* these particular parts but does not totalize them; it is a unity *of* all of these particular parts but does not unify them; rather, it is *added* to them as a new part fabricated separately" (42, italics mine except for the prepositions).

A principal obstacle to understanding this text that in effect doesn't want to be understood, that expresses only by perverting its meanings in "aberrant" ways, is its ambiguous and troubling emphasis on noncommunication, nonrelation, a catatonic "body" that is "unproductive, sterile, unengendered, unconsumable" (8). This hermetically sealed body, "eyes closed tight, nostrils pinched shut, ears stopped up" (37–38), is the inanimate, nonpersonal heart of their theory, the place in it of refusal and revolt, the body without organs and the body without an image, the groundless ground of a primary death drive understood as the limit of reality itself. As such, it designates the abyss, gap, or break within an inclusive system that renders it hologrammic or virtual, the zero degree of metabolization in the ingested organic (Oedipal) body where a "flow" of amorphous and undifferentiated "matter" is freed.[3] Deleuze and Guattari's noncommunicating text thus argues for the groundlessness of any grounded system—whether that system entails a theory of the body (and desire) or the body of that theory—at two simultaneous registers: that of meaning, or discourse, where a subtle "matter" fluidizes the syntactic architecture of analogy; and that of the subject, where the cathexes of energy that form (or bind) the instincts, condition the experience of pleasure, and organize the sensible world are loosened. In both cases, *Anti-Oedipus* performs the schizophrenia it thematizes in order to highlight the historical schizophrenia it also includes and reiterates.

The nuance of this historical engagement comes through in Deleuze and Guattari's insistence on the "machinic" nature of desire. This terminological choice signifies an investment of desire in the reifying mode of production that governs the processes of desire's subjectivization and, indeed, the terms of intelligibility for material social life in general; but more precisely, it specifies the function of the body without organs (a point of nonproduction) as something produced within the production process. Production, in the widest sense of political economy, also constitutes an inclusive system like that of *Anti-Oedipus*, freeing an undifferentiated flow of subtle matter (in the form of money, goods, or labor) over the surface of the *social* body without organs. Their complex analysis of the abstractions that capitalism introduces into the socius (in the form of "money-capital" and the "free worker" equipped with his or her labor power) makes it clear that the stake of the text's metonymic structure is one of profound implication in the schizoid time of its writing. To say that desire invests the social field, and that because of this investment it eludes repression and appears only in the positivity of production (at all levels), is not to solve the problem of dehumanizing violence embedded in capitalist production. What it does is index the presence in the text, in the time of the text, and in the text of its time, of an ungrounding repetition that "machinic" desire comes to designate. And even though Deleuze and Guattari make a distinction between the machinic and the mechanical, between desiring-machines and "technical" machines, the former always incorporate the latter and assume not an inclusive critique of exclusive systems but two types of inclusive system, one predicated on a primary negation (a groundless ground) and the other on a secondary negation (a grounded groundlessness).

The problem confronted in *Anti-Oedipus*, given that desire is not repressed and the proof for this lies in the vitality of social production itself, is to account for a theory of repression that persuades subjects to an acquiescence in the capitalist machine. Social power works in the seductions of that theory to make subjects desire their own repression (or rather, desire that desire take the form reserved for it in the theory of repression). Deleuze and Guattari do not in their text desire in this way, but they do repeat this desire in order to disturb its deeply mystified function. This is where that historical engagement resolves itself in its greatest cogency, and yet also its greatest paradox: the ungrounding repetitions of *Anti-Oedipus* argue against a capitalist machine compelling subjects to an active investment of its mechanisms only by symptomatically producing the text as an avatar of that machine. Capitalism, in their account, thrives on its own groundlessness; it generates a secondary death drive, or relative limit, to "axiomatize" a primary death drive, or absolute limit, and implicate desire in its systematic articulations (I will return to this "axiomatic" dynamic). *Anti-Oedipus* thus has to turn the screw of its own theoretical articulations, to turn away from historical specificity (at least of a more objectivist variety), and compound the abstractions of its discourse to render the singularity of a subjective experience overdetermined by processes of autonomization in social, psychic, economic, and political life.

This subjective experience exists only in the ambiguation of the category "experience," and its indeterminacy is, according to Deleuze and Guattari, one of "intensive quantities" generated in a "delirium" of pure becoming. "There is a schizophrenic experience of intensive quantities in their pure state, to a point that is almost unbearable—a celibate misery and glory experienced to the fullest, like a cry suspended between life and death, an intense feeling of transition, states of pure, naked intensity stripped of all shape and form" (18). Schizophrenic delirium invests a decomposed space of transition between incommensurable states—invests, that is, transition or becoming in itself. Against the notion of a fixed subject, the subject in delirium experiences only its own transitivity relative to fixed states through which it passes and which define its multiple identities. These states are oriented with respect to the zero intensity that designates the body without organs and are always positive, "never the expression of the final equilibrium of a system" (19), never balanced around a central point or neutral state conceived as the nucleus of an individual "name" or ego. What resides at this center is instead a desiring-machine (a "celibate" machine of desexualized circuitry), producing on its periphery "residual" subjects transected by nonpersonal social and historical flows. The schizophrenic subject is born and dies at each state through which he or she passes, becoming in a literal—and, for Deleuze and Guattari, emphatically not a metaphoric sense—different people, men, women, and children of all races and all places, in all times. "Nothing [in this process] is representative; rather, it is all life and lived experience. . . . Nothing but bands of intensity, potentials, thresholds and gradients. A harrowing, emotionally overwhelming experience, which brings the schizo as close as possible to matter, to a burning, living center of matter" (19).

The "lived experience" adumbrated in passages such as these is clearly not referred to an Oedipal subject marked by sexual difference and endowed with properties of freedom and causality; the phrase falls back on its own body without organs, where its meaning and materiality as language verge on an unbound amorphous state (it is neither "lived" nor an experience). It thereby engenders its own deterritorialization. Such an experience makes sense in its literality only as a textual performance, only as part of a discursive permutation at a foundation level that produces the nondiscursive asymptote of discourse itself. If the implication of this performance is a foreclosure of representation, meaning itself, through the ramification of desire down to something like a "burning, living center of matter," nonetheless the limit-concept that this "matter" signifies manifests itself only in the precise mutations to which they subject their discourse. There is no difference for Deleuze and Guattari between "nature" and "culture" once nature is understood machinically and once the objective being of desire is understood to be reality itself. This is why they distinguish desire from any fantasmatic equivalent rooted in "psychic reality," which is for them not real, imaginary and illusive. But one must hear this kind of assertion in their text through the filter of those mutations before the sophistication of their deterritorializing logic comes through. "If desire produces, its product is real," they write. "If desire is productive, it can be productive only in the real world and can produce only reality" (26). What is real, in other words, is strictly speaking the *production of the real*, the real as a produced process that, while not the production of fantasies or representations, is still a fabrication or artifice of the real insofar as the real is residual and peripheral, and insofar as the subject nomadically "passes" through the series of states that define a potentially infinite range of predicates.

The point of theoretical constructions such as these for Deleuze and Guattari is not to determine what is real but to grasp the real as a function of discursive practices. Their Nietszchean emphasis on the reality of interpretation rather than the interpretation of reality indicates that writing (or reading) is the medium of "real" desire. It is not coincidental that the disjunctive synthesis outlined, for example, is related by Deleuze and Guattari to the second of three stages that compromise desiring-production: that given over to the "recording" of the production process, the differentiation or distribution of its "forces and agents" on the body without organs as a numen or writing surface. Inscription is presented as the act in which a certain abstraction, a certain "divine," "mystic," or mythic appropriation of the real takes place. To write is to write on the body without organs, in (the space of) disjunction, to inscribe repetition on the negative surface of the death instinct. Anti-Oedipus is a desiring-machine; writing is a machine, an alienation felt inclusively or exclusively by the subject of enunciation. It is the divide between exclusive/inclusive, mechanical/machinic, and organic/nonorganic that, as it were, digitizes the Anti-Oedipus machine, although inscription remains what the sides of each dichotomy have in common—they both come under a logic of "miraculation," an "enchantment" of the inscribing surface that obscures or flattens out production (as production of production, the first stage of the schema) so that it appears to originate in the writing (recording) process itself, to derive from it as its effect rather than its cause. This inversion of cause and effect that is writing induces a "false" or "apparent objective movement," "a true perception of movement that is produced on the recording surface," a sort of cinematic image of the real (10).

Deleuze and Guattari's text inverts this inversion, exhibits the apparent nature of the real, its always simulatory essence—which is not to say that in so doing they reestablish a proper causality between desiring-production's first stage, production of production, and its second stage, production of recording. The qualitative difference between the two is given in a simultaneous dimension; production, recording, and consumption (the final stage) occur at the same time, or rather in a time that is simulacral in the special inversely double sense described here. Anti-Oedipus thus calls attention to its own miraculating logic; it simulates simulation, constructs as delirium the exposed delirium of the desiring process itself. If this exposure, this double simulation, is said to be a more fully realized version of that process, that process truer to itself, it does not change the fact that both versions are homologous, that both communicate a certain "divine energy" to each other along "transverse" or "aberrant" lines (13).

Put another way, the exclusive/inclusive distinction passes within the economy of the inclusive disjunction governing their discourse, which is why Anti-Oedipus can be read as a metaparody, citing as parodied texts its objects of critique (most notably psychoanalysis, but also Marxism, ethnography, and history), citing as well citationality itself when it assumes the stability of a centered system. Taken in this light as a kind of travesty of theory and its enchantments, the book appears to theorize its own relation to discourse and to writing as it goes, and this is perhaps its best contribution to discourse in general. Thus a caveat of the kind voiced by Kaja Silverman about "literal" readings of visionary texts becomes in this case much more (but also strangely less) imperative insofar as it is necessary to specify the parodic mode that conditions the presence of psychoanalysis in the language or the machine of its polemic. Without this mode, one cannot see how "real" the deconstruction elaborated in *Anti-Oedipus* is, and why it argues *against* the continued relevance of psychoanalysis to cultural critique. The reading given there starts from the conviction that psychoanalysis is a myth-structure, an "apparent objective movement" on the body without organs, and moreover a lived myth, an unreality lived as real. To this extent, it is no more real (all its empiricities notwithstanding) than its visionary reconfiguration, no *less* visionary in other words, except that it ceases to live its own visionary status parodically and so reifies itself in much the same way that the object of exchange reifies itself for Baudrillard in the sign-value transaction—that is, it hardens into the real, the *hic et nunc*, of capitalist exchange and so "begins to signify the abolition of the [symbolic] relationship" (*For a Critique of the Political Economy of the Sign*, 64).

Deleuze and Guattari's argument against "Oedipus" is most persuasive when it suggests that the practices it underwrites function within a capitalist dispensation to objectify and dehumanize because (or to the extent) of the theory's "miraculated" status. The issue is not that "Oedipus" is a symptom of capitalist production but that it does not live out its own symptomatic relation to a schizoid time in an adequately reflexive fashion. As a result, the theory of psychoanalysis is for them an instrument of psychic repression appropriated by a capitalist socius. How the theory conforms to the requirements of a more generalized *social* repression is what they set out to demonstrate, starting from the central premise that desiring-production and social production are identical (the capitalist machine, that is, also functions with reference to an element of nonproduction, an "immobile motor" [143], a body without organs). The problem for Deleuze and Guattari hinges on the situation of this element of nonproduction within the machine. How does social repression deploy itself when "desire is a part of the infrastructure" (104), unconsciously investing (in delirium) the social field in its entirety?

How can the death drive function *within* desiring-production and also *against* desiring-production? Questions like these refocus the text on the produced nature of the body without organs, since the death drive admits in this instance of regulation or manipulation by social forces. Reality is produced, they maintain, and yet production refers to an absolute limit as a prior condition of the real that as a result does not appear within what it conditions. This reflux on the body without organs toward a primary negation implies a natural determination that contradicts its social production (as secondary negation) within the socius. "We can say that social production, under determinate conditions, derives primarily from desiring-production: which is to say that Homo natura comes first. But we must also say, more accurately, that desiring-production is first and foremost social in nature, and tends to free itself only at the end: which is to say that Homo historia comes first" (33).

In the gyre of these two sentences, a kind of vertigo occurs that envelops a whole theory of universal history. The three avatars of this history, the territorial, despotic, and capitalist machines, all function to regulate, channel, and record flows of undifferentiated energy, to generate grounds on which desire and production are soldered together, to produce a body without organs that appropriates production to itself as its miraculate cause, its "natural or divine precondition" (140). The body of the Earth, the body of the Despot, and the body of Money play in Deleuze and Guattari's system the role of inscriptive surface or text for their respective social forms, each of which writes the reality of that form against the backdrop of its unconditioned condition (on the body without organs). Negation as it relates to textuality (as ground to figure) therefore provides the tension or gravity informing a "contingent, singular, ironic and critical" historical articulation (140). In their terms, the territorial machine "codes" (writes) desire against the "nightmare" of decoded flows, the dread of its own breaking down, and when the codes buckle under the weight of this dread coming both from within and from without, when they begin in fact to break down, the despotic machine appears to "overcode" (or rewrite) its predecessor, to reestablish an illusion of equilibrium in what is always a highly unstable construction. This reflex to balance code and flow, to preserve against a volatile historicity a social and political state in its perfect or ahistorical form, induces a transcendent model or origin, an "Urstaat" against which each successive version of the state measures itself in time, striving to coincide with its ideal structures. But for Deleuze and Guattari, social machines *need* to break down, and because of this they always do, even if they experience this necessity as a death. History is a broken machine, on this account, generating and feeding on disharmony, contradiction, crisis, anxiety, a fear of death that fuels the historical process. The capitalist machine, for its part, must also negotiate the dread of decoded flows, the death drive rising from within and arriving from without, only what it grasps more immediately is that there exists a noncoded and noncodable flow that constitutes desire itself, a radical of disorder in the system that cannot be coded. Decoded flows, according to Deleuze and Guattari, "strike the despotic State with latency; they submerge the tyrant, but they also cause him to return in unexpected forms; they democratize him, oligarchize him, monarchize him, and always internalize and spiritualize him" (223). Desire here invests the latent Urstaat as a kind of death drive, only it also comes to invest the flows that signify the death of the Urstaat: desire wishes for the death of this latency, the death of this death, and realizes itself in a new kind of pleonastic form that heralds a capitalist dispensation of generalized decoding, the production of flows decoded as such.[4]

Social production under capitalism does not work by coding or overcoding, which Deleuze and Guattari associate with the previous stage of historical development. The despotic state institutes itself by establishing "indirect relations between coded flows" and "qualifying" those flows with reference to the "extraeconomic instance" (analogous to a transcendental signifier) from which they seem to emanate (248). But once "money-capital" (decoded flows of production) and the "free worker" (decoded flows of labor) appear in the networks of social organization, an "axiomatic" of "direct relations between decoded flows" takes the place of the code. Instead of an ostensibly noneconomic symbolic exchange between regulated (Oedipalized) subjects, Deleuze and Guattari see an explicitly economic sign-value exchange between depersonalized subjects reduced to "abstract quantities." Money as a generalized equivalent scrambles all coded flows passing through the socius, and all the dominant forms of relation that qualify those flows, by attributing their provenance to the "extraeconomic instance." It decomposes the circuits of exchange grasped in their distribution on the "body of the Despot" and injects into the socius "abstract quantities" (persons and things) that are nevertheless concrete, constituting the substances of the flows in the economic moment of their conjunction.[5] They are decoded flows *because* they are economic, and they acquire substance only in a money-capital that appropriates production by recording it, rewriting society (and history) in the image of its own concrete abstraction and on its own intensive numen. Money then expresses the form of the axiomatic that induces a controlled movement of deterritorialization within the socius, a death drive exorcising (in the more archaic sense of an adjuration) at an exterior limit an absolutely decoded flow and engendering a relatively decoded flow within interior limits that are constantly expanding and reproducing themselves.[6]

The advantage (if there is any) in so drastically simplifying a system as complex as Anti-Oedipus to a summary like this one is that it renders more obvious a certain generality linking it to strategies of narrative and discourse. Its emphasis on the genesis of history, the construction of stages and cycles, the elaboration in detail of a (non)personal and idiosyncratic language, a formal complexity that at its limit threatens to unravel into decomposed intensities, all underscore the degree to which discursive structure is itself the preoccupation of the text.[7] This is one reason why they write in a decoded language of machines and flows: "Nothing is accomplished as long as machines are not touched upon" (112), they assert, and this means their language registers in its theoretical distances or reserves a necessary rupture of "human" systems, an internal dismantling of signification, a practice exemplifying the subversion of meaning they also describe. This practice can be glimpsed, again, in the permutative logic of the system. The three social machines do indeed delineate a historical becoming, a theory of social change, but at the same time they can be (and indeed are) mapped onto the tripartite structures of desiring-production, so that the history they tell is equally the history of desiring-production itself, oscillating from the "molar" to the "molecular," the social to the individual, the past to the present, so rapidly that they appear indistinguishable from one another. They appear as though fused in a moving image, a kind of hallucination (delirium) in which an "apparent objective movement" is produced as a hallucination *within* the hallucination. This double hallucination can be felt clearly in the way the death drive recurs in the theory, repetitiously installing itself in almost every proposition (and even at different junctures within propositions). So conspicuous is this tactic (with its reference or indebtedness to Freud intact, moreover) that it seems what we are actually reading is the story of the death drive as the ground of all discourse, at any rate up to the point a certain controlled eclipse of meaning collapses the story into something like auto-critique or parody. This is not to suggest that the inclusive differences asserted by Deleuze and Guattari are not real (indeed incommensurable) and intended to be taken as such, only that this realism implies within its construction an adaptation that renders it, in a word, schizophrenic, and that only with this understanding can the actual stakes of the theory be grasped.

Of course, it becomes apparent almost from the start of Anti-Oedipus that writing as it is understood even today belongs to a dispensation that is, in their terms, "archaic." It belongs to "imperial despotic representation," to the reference, direct or indirect, to overcoding, to an extraeconomic transcendental signifier. As a result, the text recapitulates (at the level of both content and expression) the history of writing it records.[8] The despotic machine (along with the territorial machine) bears more directly on a moment of historical transition that is our own than on a particular temporal sequencing of the past, a moment passing in the economy of generalized decoding that is capitalism. "Writing has never been capitalism's thing," they write. "Capitalism is profoundly illiterate. The death of writing is like the death of God or the death of the Father: the thing was settled a long time ago, although the news is slow to reach us, and there survives in us the memory of extinct signs with which we still write" (240). The persistence of the "extinct sign" in a system, indeed a language, of decoded flows exemplifies for Deleuze and Guattari a "neoterritoriality" or an "archaism having a perfectly current function" (157), decoded codes like outdated machines encased within the larger axiomatized social machine and subordinated to the entirely different principle of reterritorialization. A language of decoded flows is nonsignifying, indeterminate as regards either its substance (phonic, graphic, etc.) or its support.

> [A] substance is said to be formed when a flow enters into a relationship with another flow, such that the first defines a content and the second, an expression. The deterritorialized flows of content and expression are in a state of conjunction or reciprocal precondition that constitutes figures as the ultimate units of both content and expression. These figures do not derive from a signifier nor are they even signs as minimal elements of the signifier, they are nonsigns, or rather nonsignifying, points-signs having several dimensions, flows-breaks . . . that form images through their coming together in a whole, but that do not maintain any identity when they pass from one whole to another. (241)

It is this writing, this *figure* as "ultimate unit of both content and expression," that Deleuze and Guattari attempt to exemplify in their hologrammic expositions of history and desire. Such an exemplification implies less a simple capitulation to the capitalist system than a rigorously historical determining of the relation between the text and the world it cites or incorporates. That said, it remains the case that *Anti-Oedipus* is still a piece of writing, a textual weave in which the "real" conditions that make desire legible are set forth in opposition to the imaginary equivalents the system so dexterously generates. "Capitalism institutes or restores all sorts of residual and artificial, imaginary, or symbolic territorialities, thereby attempting as best it can, to recode, to rechannel persons who have been defined in terms of abstract quantities.... The real is not impossible, it is simply more and more artificial" (34). If this is true, and if writing per se constitutes such a territoriality (alongside, for example, the state, the nation, the family, the "individual"), then one must grasp this artificiality of the real in a discourse always already implicated in those abstract quantities. "The axiomatic," according to Deleuze and Guattari, "does not need to write in bare flesh, to mark bodies and organs" (250). Bodies, persons, no longer need to be "written" insofar as they have become "private," saturated with an ideology of the individual that conceals the abstract determination or, rather, the marks on the abstract quantities that signify the capitalist recording of production. The ideology of the private person functions as an element in the miraculating process of this decoded writing; it produces a writing that, even (perhaps especially) when it writes bodies, already presupposes another more primary writing *as the real itself*. This discourse is already written without knowing it, and to this extent it *applies* the axiomatic, persuades subjects to an acquiescence in the social requirement of their own repression.

"Oedipus" comes to play this normalizing role for Deleuze and Guattari, not so much out of calculation or intent ("It is not a matter of saying that Oedipus is a false belief, but rather that belief is necessarily something false that diverts and suffocates effective production" [107]), but because as a theory it cannot grasp the historical event (or the temporal dimension in which it occurs) of its own "neoterritorialization," the decoding to which it is subject and which transforms its function into one of psychic repression. "Psychic repression is such that social repression becomes desired; it induces a consequent desire, a faked image of its object, on which it bestows the appearance of independence" (119). This faked image displaces and "disfigures" desiring-production, repressing it by inducing its double, by representing what it represses as "incestuous familial drives" (119). But the incestuous drives, properly speaking, do not exist for Deleuze and Guattari. Those drives are unconscious; they are the unconscious in its "pseudo-expressive form," engendering the Oedipal theater in which desire denies its metonymic relation to production. The idealist conception of desire as founded on lack necessitates for them a division of labor: the object desire feels the lack of becomes the locus of an "extrinsic natural or social production" (25), and desire, intrinsically feeling its insufficiency with respect to this real production, consigns itself to the fabrication of imaginary counterparts to that (lost) object. Now besides the stripping from desire of any other than a negative relation to social production, what Deleuze and Guattari refuse to accept in this notion of fantasy is its determination within a familial context that removes desire from the social field and thus from the libidinal investments (delirium) that, for them, characterize desire in the first place. Because desire is always social in nature, individual fantasy's foreclosure of the social is itself a social act that delivers it to a specific (and reactionary) function: it conducts intact into the subject the "miraculated" forms of social repression and diverts it from the fact of its investment of those forms.

Deleuze and Guattari counterpose to this notion of fantasy a multiple or "group fantasy" that implies a dynamic of radical simulation. They explicitly link this alternative to "a writing that is strangely polyvocal, flush with the real. It carries the real beyond its principle to a point where it is effectively produced by the desiring-machine. The point where the copy [or fantasmatic double] ceases to be a copy in order to become the Real *and its artifice*" (87). The two kinds of fantasy, the two kinds of artifice, and the two kinds of writing here suggested are identical in nature but different in degree, the one exclusive and the other inclusive, related within the inclusive disjunction that governs the text itself. Here the doubling of simulation as a strategy manifests itself, since Deleuze and Guattari in essence simulate psychoanalysis (as simulation in a reductive sense) to underscore the latter's exclusive isolation from the simulacral dimension they elucidate. They do not uphold a distinction between fantasy and production, artifice and the real, but an artifice of the Real, a sort of primary fantasy perfecting itself only in the parodic move to expose as its own interior or inclusive limit the exclusive disjunctions of fantasy in its secondary incarnation.

This is the discourse of *Anti-Oedipus*, its most flexible or plastic feature being its ability to mime or impersonate not only particular discourses but discourse in general, which is one reason it can sustain the desire of what it parodies even "at the center of its organization" and still insist (polemically) on the absolute inadequacy of that parodied object. Parody is therefore essential to grasping this polemic and the way it interpellates its readers, provoking them to a formal or discursive awareness of reading (and writing) as the "real" scene of cultural production.

The Sentence of Death

A distinction is made in *Anti-Oedipus* between perversion and schizophrenia: "The pervert is someone who takes the artifice seriously and plays the game to the hilt: if you want them, you can have them—territorialities infinitely more artificial than the ones that society offers us, totally artificial new families, secret lunar societies" (35). The perverse subject in this regard is intermediate between the neurotic trapped in those territorialities and the schizophrenic in open revolt against them, falling back to the body without organs and refusing his or her reterritorialization by remaining as close to the absolute limit of the socius as possible. This difference implies an incompatibility of technique, genre, and aim that would seem to problematize the use of parody here to describe both masochism and schizophrenic discourse (especially apparent in the divergence between the masochist's disavowal of the real and the schizophrenic's insistence on the reality of desire). It seems to me, however, that this distinction notwithstanding, several points in common can be specified between them that make parody a still compelling designation. The schizophrenic in retreat to the body without organs does not, after all, leave territoriality altogether, since to do so would entail a self-annihilation. The body without organs is still a territoriality (135–36), albeit of a different generic character than its perverse counterpart (a "desert" rather than an aestheticized or artificial society). Both forms of resistance are concerned with the limits of social machines, and in particular with an axiomatics of those limits, their internalization by the desiring subject. Both, moreover, refuse to believe in the displaced or false images projected within the axiomatic, which means they are both critics of images (or "fictions") and of the law those images (and fictions) presuppose.

> Will it ever be suspected that the law discredits—and has an interest in discrediting and disgracing—the person it presumes to be guilty, the person the law wants to be guilty and wants to be made to feel guilty? One acts as if it were possible to conclude directly from psychic repression the nature of the repressed, and from the prohibition the nature of what is prohibited. . . . [But] what really takes place is that the law prohibits something that is perfectly fictitious in the order of desire or of the "instincts," so as to persuade its subjects that they had the intention corresponding to this fiction. This is indeed the only way the law has of getting a grip on intention, of making the unconscious guilty. (Anti-Oedipus, 115)

As Deleuze shows in "Coldness and Cruelty," the masochist acts out this guilt within a territoriality predicated on the absence of the father and parodically inverts the law in its particulars. But the schizophrenic's impersonations of history could as well be seen in this inverse light, this inverted time, insofar as he or she shares with the former a desire to expose as fictitious the machinations of the law (prohibition, repression, the coaptative lure of desire). If the masochist "needs" the law for his or her particular sexualizations and seductions, it is only insofar as the law ceases to be paternal, and this too is true for the schizophrenic. Both create alternative territorialities (of diverse genre), "new alliances," and indeed "new" subjects endowed with a desire that is utopian in a sense that embraces the contradictions and dangers this implies—that could, indeed, just as well be considered dystopian in its negative evaluations of the socius and in its intrinsic relation to the death instinct. Both have a structure in common that enables them to see the law from an outside (a limit) that nonetheless is not exactly outside, and it is this particular place and angle of view that Deleuze and Guattari set out to map. This is why the transition from despotic state to capitalism takes place in a protracted "schizoid time" in which the latter social machine inverts or mirrors the former, and why Deleuze and Guattari refer this tropological time to an oscillation between paranoiac (despotic) and schizophrenic (revolutionary) poles that coexist in schizophrenic delirium: "And if it is true that delirium is coextensive with the social field, these two poles are found to coexist in every case of delirium, and fragments of schizoid revolutionary investment are found to coincide with blocks of paranoiac reactionary investment" (376). This coincidence of the two forms of investment *is* schizophrenia for the writers of *Anti-Oedipus* and thus perfectly coincides in turn with the critique of "Oedipus" they undertake (in all its virulence). It is this oscillation that structures discourse as a rule, they imply, that makes it a desiring-machine and that conditions its potential for a radical break from the capitalist system, notwithstanding the risk it also runs of "turning" reactionary at the same time, as a consequence of this same potential.

In this light, I would like to suggest that the structural matrix for *Gravity's Rainbow* can be found in the inclusive system that conditions both perversion and schizophrenia. The novel, in its encyclopedic scope, its permutative proliferation of detail, knowledges, and discourses, runs along the Möbius strip of a simultaneous time; it attempts to engender in its textual delirium the emergence of a fully capitalist order from the representational meshes of its despotic predecessor, the interface between two epistemes as a kind of crazy manifold of inclusive forms that "shift and slide about" within "what always amounts to the same," desiring-production, the subject who desires.[9] This is the novel's uniquely countercultural wager, that it describes a form of being for late capitalist society; and if the audacity of this claim feels presumptuous, or troubling in the complicities, the encompassments, the abstractions it implies (the "angel stationed very high, watching us at our many perversities, crawling across black satin, gagging on whip-handles, licking the blood from a lover's vein-hit, all of it, every last giggle or sigh, being carried on under a sentence of death whose deep beauty the angel has never been close to" [746]), one must at least acknowledge a certain rigor, a certain "deep beauty" that takes seriously the identity of the human subject (or text) with his or her (its) world (producing and product), and that one can feel the prose of *Gravity's Rainbow* so often trying to approximate. This coextension of text and world, inside and outside, does not go by way of an analogical collapse (a principal tendency of the miraculating process), and parody is the novel's memento mori, its technique of catching (or "tricking") itself out in the gravitational field of Western metaphysics, of "dragging" that angel in Pynchon's prose down into what it has "never been close to," a kind of de-affined affinity with perversity, addiction, and madness ruled over by the *sentence* of death (a death sentence, or *arret de mort*), by a writing that "vibrates" with the schizophrenia of *Anti-Oedipus*.

> The Oedipal situation in the Zone these days is terrible. There is no dignity. The mothers have been masculinized to worn moneybags of no sexual interest to anyone, and yet here are their sons, still trapped inside inertias of lust that are 40 years out of date. The fathers have no power today and never did, but because 40 years ago we could not kill them, we are condemned now to the same passivity, the same masochist fantasies they cherished in secret, and worse, we are condemned in our weakness to impersonate men of power our own infant children must hate, and wish to usurp the place of, and fail. . . . So generation after generation of men in love with pain and passivity serve out their time in the Zone, silent, redolent with faded sperm, terrified of dying, desperately addicted to the comforts others sell them, however useless, ugly or shallow, willing to have life defined for them by men whose only talent is for death. (*Gravity's Rainbow*, 747)

The masochism of this passage is nearer to its standard form than its "visionary reconfiguration" and designates quite distinctly an axiomatized condition of being: caught in the identificatory meshes of a familialized desire, impersonating power and the law in a mode of a perpetual insufficiency (attempting to kill the father who never dies because desire is usurpative in nature), addicted to a commodified exchange that promises "comfort" and delivers the docile subject, the masochist here represents the (male) type of social repression. He is oppressed by the difference between his desire (fantasy, consumption, consummation) and his own production (by men of power who "define" him as self-alienated). This difference conditions the process of social reproduction in the service of power that happens under cover of a growing paralysis, an addictive denial of or escape from the very repression that is experienced as addiction, denial, and escape. The "Oedipal situation" is characterized by its stress under the effects of a social order based on the abstract exchange of money and so signifies what that social order threatens to decode or fragment. But the passage, both in the patness of its analysis and in its ironic undertone, leaves open the question of what role the Oedipal machine plays in the neutralization of agency conceived as a consumptive addiction: that is, does its difference from social repression imply its "dignity" as something desecrated by money, or does it rather imply its status as a kind of drug, the means of a forgetting that lubricates the reproductive (recording) cycle, another comfort to buy and to consume?

This reading raises the question of the novel's relation to the discourses it uses, especially complicated by the sense in which that relation could also be designated "addictive" or consumptive, a sense implied by the function in the passage of the death instinct (an abyssal ungrounding) both at the level of content and at the level of expression, its bearing on the psychoanalytic machine *and* its parodic quotation (a slide to the scene of the text's own production signaled by the use of the present tense and the possessive plural pronoun). "Addiction," as Lacan has famously put it, "opens a field where no single word of the subject is reliable, and where he escapes analysis altogether."[10] The exteriority of psychoanalysis to addiction, its helplessness in the face of the latter's asignifying repetitions, suggests the reduction of psychoanalysis to the status of a commodity, its assimilation within an axiomatic that it doesn't describe so much as apply, an addictive substance or structure expressing the commodity form. If psychoanalysis induces addiction (under the conditions of capitalist production and exchange), it does not necessarily follow that it understands addiction, or that addiction as a radical remainder does not carry with it a schizophrenic charge that, paraphrasing Nietzsche, may not be intelligible but is nonetheless intelligent. It is this sense of addiction (or consumption, a preterite incorporation) as a limit to discourse that Pynchon attempts to outline in or through the formal strategies of the novel.

The foregoing passage occurs late in *Gravity's Rainbow*, after the narrative has begun to fragment and to string itself out in a series of tableaulike passages, each with its own title. The temporal sequencing has also started to slide proleptically to the time of the novel's writing, so that the reference to "40 years ago" could be read in relation either to the end of World War II (thus as a reference to the turn of the century) or to 1970 (thus to approximately 1930). Taken in its ambiguity, the reference roughly delimits the modernist period and the ghostly *analogon* of its postwar aftermath. The text situates modernism within the discursive space of the Zone as the site of a historical event or trauma repressed in the novel and thus symptomatically repeated in order to experience its "omitted anxiety." The postwar period emerges in the wake of this symptomatic repetition, as the inverted double or miraculated cause of its own modernism, caught up in a schizoid time. The flatness or absence of affect in the compulsion to repeat that event of forty years ago, that failure to kill the father, could be likened to a kind of shell shock pervading the novel and underpinning its parodic style. This shell shock, however, is not simply another avatar of a modernist paradigm, expressing an identification with machines (reflected, for instance, in Max Ernst's collages dating from the end of World War I).[11] In the postmodern perspective on modernism established by the novel, what can be seen is a doubling effect, a repetition of the repetition compulsion described by Freud in *Beyond the Pleasure Principle*, an addiction to the addiction described in the quoted passage, a modernism of modernism wherein a certain becoming-machine is linked to a supplemental logic of prosthesis. According to this logic, the body (text) is not only in need of an alien, synthetic, or artificial supplement; this alien substance also invades the body (text), possesses it to such an extent that the body becomes, as it were, prosthetic in relation to it, supplemental in its essence.

What Pynchon explores in *Gravity's Rainbow* is thus something like a machinic addiction or repetition within a specific historical situation. This is why psychoanalysis in the quotation can be said to function like a machine running within the body of the novel, an alien substance, a "nonhumanity," a discourse, a writing. If this particular substance is what Pynchon might characterize as "Bad Shit" (because of its failure to "kill the father," or rather to free us from social repression), it remains the case that the text includes or ingests it, that it "uses" discourse, although this substance abuse (or such will be the argument here) takes as its point of reference the absolute limit, primary negation, the body without organs, and as a result apprehends its own axiomatics, its situation within a logic of decoded flows and desiring-production. In this way, Pynchon's text elucidates the always double implications of its own "deep beauty," its desire for "coincidence" with the world, its constructed delirium of history and the social. This elucidation unfolds through the novel from the first sentence to the last; it creates within the connotative depths and elliptical tonalities of its language a pronounced tension working against any simple judgment or moral positioning. The ironies of this delirium can be felt even when the text's moral stance is most evident. Here Blicero loads Gottfried into the Rocket in preparation for the liftoff, flight, and landing that will in the end explode the novel itself.

> Stuff him in. Not a Procrustean bed, but modified to take him. The two, boy and Rocket, concurrently designed. Its steel hindquarters bent so beautifully . . . he fits well. They are mated to each other, Schwarzgerat and next higher assembly. His bare limbs in their metal bondage writhe among the fuel, oxidizer, live-steam lines, thrust frame, compressed air battery, exhaust elbow, decomposer, tanks, vents, valves . . . and one of these valves, one test-point, one pressure-switch is the right one, the true clitoris, routed directly into the nervous system of the ooooo. She should not be a mystery to you Gottfried. Find the zone of love, lick and kiss . . . you have time—there are still a few minutes. The liquid oxygen runs freezing so close to your cheek, bones of frost to burn you past feeling. Soon there will be fires, too. . . . Get ready, Liebchen. (750–51)

The ironic register here is explicit enough: the sexualization of the Rocket, the mechanization of the human being, the sacrifice of Gottfried (and the innocence he symbolizes) to an erotomaniacal obsession with gravity and transcendence, the sexualization of sacrifice itself, all combine to lace this passage with a sarcasm of absurd reprehension. But its discursive investments set up countertonalities that, especially in the context of the novel as a whole, complicate by redoubling this irony. The Rocket is "not a Procrustean bed, but modified to take him," and this accommodation of the machine to the human signals both a refinement of disciplinary technique and a vicissitude of affect, its swinging over into a more active cathexis of the machine as "mate." The "listing" technical language that resolves the Rocket into its parts, and the way in which the prose feels itself into its interior, come to parallel Blicero's sexualizations, so that Gottfried's "metal bondage" figures the text's own movement inside the machine. The text feels its own desire *as* Blicero's, and this is why Blicero takes over the narrative as he literally does in the quotation. The sexual in general is here another machine: reproductive, repetitive, autoerotic, dehumanizing, it "burn[s] you past feeling" (with fire and ice) in its consummations, travesties a human language of tenderness, love, and care. Indeed, Blicero's sexual perversion is precisely what sacrifices or violates innocence here, which implies that if *Gravity's Rainbow* is itself "perverse," then this sacrifice is also a constituent element of the novel's production.

But if this is the case, the violence in the text that belongs properly to the text implies an identity in nature but also a difference of degree, an implication that indexes a concomitant resistance to the consumerist (Oedipal) model. The power of an "anti-Oedipal" reading is that it can (indeed must) sustain any degree of negativity located in the text (as critique, moral outrage, nihilism, even despair) and still grasp the positivity of its desire, the imaginative principle of its historical analysis. This is one way to understand the fascination *Gravity's Rainbow* exerts, and why its deepest appeal, reaching beyond the moral categories we bring to it, will always be profoundly subversive. Of course this does not (need to) imply that Pynchon's text might not also be the space of a deep-seated ambivalence about its own strategies, agonistic in relation to its own form, or that this agonistic dynamic doesn't in fact produce that form as its result. The process of de-volition that can be traced most clearly in the destiny reserved by Pynchon for Tyrone Slothrop could be said to mirror the text's own de-volition, the movement of its deterritorialization that verges on breakdown, silence, even a kind of autism. Rather, this autism is one limit, one edge, the novel comes more and more to track in itself at the same time that it writes its ending in the negative space of that autism, the highlight-as-shadow that confers on fantasy (and writing) an ethical and political character. In the sections that follow, I set forth that difference between the violence in the text and the violence of the text, the slide from content to expression that in turn produces its abyssal implication in the schizoid time of its postwar moment.

Franz and Ilse Pökler

What I would like to do is to trace this limit, this edge, this track in *Gravity's Rainbow* with more specificity, to open up a metaphoric density or mode of meaning that, within representation and signification, also necessarily eludes them. This elusive hylé is the unreality of the text's own metaparodic strategies, but it is also the reality of this unreality, the turn into its own objecthood signaling through its deterritorializations to the insistence of a certain meaning. My goal in this chapter is to resolve the novel's implicated and inclusive form of expression by demonstrating how it enacts a permutative transformation of discourse along the lines established in the prior reading of *Anti-Oedipus*. The structure of *Gravity's Rainbow*, once again, is hologrammic or metonymic in its attempts to incorporate the Western culture and metaphysics of which it is, albeit strangely, a product. But as a whole-part or infinite set, indexing the groundlessness that its infinitude presupposes, the novel also registers a *desire* that, rooted in expression and (counter)cultural in character, appears only in a complicity that one must always allow to be *dangerous*, marked by its immanence to discourse. This immanence will yield the rhythm of the novel's movement between content and expression and the trace of its deeply preterite nature.

One place a complicit dynamic can be felt is in Pynchon's resumption of the Franz Pökler subplot in the third section (episode 11), where he complicates the network of concepts under discussion here: fantasy, the family, production, reproduction, writing, use and using. Pökler's career as a rocket scientist throughout the 1930s and World War II is catalyzed by Leni's departure. Bereft of the humanizing support of a family (and the mirroring function of his wife), he finds a substitute for that support in the Rocket, and the role of Leni's absence, or more precisely the bitterness or misogyny it induces in Pökler's apostasy to the machine, is carefully tied not only to his own bad faith, the gradual erosion of his freedom and desire under the pressures of war, but to the war itself, to the bureaucracies it generates, finally to the specific crime of genocide that is its result (symbolized in Leni's long internment at camp Dora).

The process whereby Pökler sacrifices his own humanity to the project of the Rocket is explicitly constructed in terms of a schizophrenic fragmentation of the personality. When Leni leaves, Franz falls apart: "Pieces spilled into the Hinterhof, down the drains, away in the wind" (402). At the Peenemunde facility, a generalized decoding of the "individual" scientist signals a "corporate intelligence at work," a mode of production based on the breakdown of the usual divisions of labor (the scientists work in teams or groups, and "no one can really claim credit 100% for any idea" [402]). Where Pökler hesitates in his "embrace" of the Rocket, the choice he faces is articulated between "two desires, personal identity and impersonal salvation" (406), and the former is clearly the site of a freedom opposed by the schizophrenia of the latter, a point of anchorage in an actual social world. Pökler does not, therefore, invest the transcendental abstractions that neutralize or tranquilize his "personal" desire without profound misgivings, which is why Leni is both the origin *and* the destination of his narrative "search" through the episode for a "true" sense of himself and of his relations to others ("his zero signal, his true course," the text tells us on page 406). At the level of content, what Franz undergoes is a tragic metamorphosis as he comes to see the price of his becoming-machine, his fantasmatic orbitalizations, in the wasted figure of a woman who may (or may not) be his wife at Dora in 1945 (the text leaves her identity ambiguous).

This encounter has its implications at the level of expression as well, since references to Franz's "engineering skill" establish him as a sort of Daedalus, a maker of labyrinths to put "between himself and the inconveniences of caring" (428), and also as a figure for writing itself.

> The odors of shit, death, sweat, sickness, mildew, piss, the breathing of Dora, wrapped him as he crept in staring at the naked corpses being carried out now that America was so close, to be stacked in front of the crematoriums, the men's penises hanging, their toes clustering white and round as pearls . . . each face so perfect, so individual, the lips stretched back into death-grins, a whole silent audience caught at the punch line of the joke . . . and the living, stacked ten to a straw mattress, the weakly crying, coughing, losers. . . . All his vacuums, his labyrinths, had been the other side of this, while he lived, and drew marks on paper, this invisible kingdom had kept on, in the darkness outside . . . all this time. (432–33)

This outside, this negative space where the preterite ("loser") body lives its peripherality to the evacuated, machinic center of textual being, and where a certain kind of "individuality" is murdered for an abstract bureaucratic ideal, exists not only for Franz but for *Gravity's Rainbow* to the extent that the Holocaust is never directly submitted to its parodic mutations of form—indeed, its exteriority or muted presence in the background of the novel is quite conspicuous. Dora would seem to be a radical limit to Pynchon's strategies, the arrest or suspension of the joke, the moment before its consummation become the travesty of its own travesty, the text ceasing to be a joke and returning to a seriousness it repeatedly denies itself. Pökler's "writing" is presented as one possible destiny for writing in general, one version of what Derrida, paraphrasing Heidegger's notion of "metalanguage" in his essay "The *Retrait* of Metaphor," calls the temptation "to occupy the place of form, of formal language," an "impossible and monstrous project of the father . . . this

159

mastery of form for form's sake" ("*Retrait*," 18).[12] To attempt to occupy this place of form signals a desire not only to *be* a functionalized language (the Rocket as all metaphoricity) but to reduce everything to such a language, even what Derrida calls the "metaphor of metaphor" or "*quasi*-metaphor" serving as the condition of metaphor in the literal or proper sense and which is not simply metaphoric, not one metaphor among others, since it refers to a Being that "being nothing, not being a being . . . cannot be expressed or named *more metaphorico*" (21). The mode of reference implied in this metaphor of metaphor, referring to the unconditioned condition of reference (the "withdrawal of Being" in Heidegger's sense, analogized in my reading to the abyssal structure of the death instinct as analyzed in *Anti-Oedipus*), using language to speak (or write) about what makes language possible, involves a logic of the supplement, of repetition, of inversion, of doubling that unfolds (folds and refolds) within the language of metaphysics. This inclusive, permutative "turn" in language is not a simple rearrangement of elements within the same rhetorical structure to the extent that it disrupts the movement toward a "proper" sense, defamiliarizes the family, makes *unheimlich* what is *heimlich* in the reference to an absolute limit (to reference).

What this suggests for *Gravity's Rainbow* is that even in the moment of the joke's suspension, even in the collapse of an antiserious tactic deployed throughout the novel, this doubling or permutative recursion turns parody into self-parody, critique into auto-critique. This tension or this turning, moreover, must be recognized to see how formally the novel constructs its "delirium" of history, and why tragedy as the genre (the machine) in which Franz Pökler plays out his "Oedipal" quest for a "true course" is not the ultimate modality of desire for the text. The following quotation, coming immediately after the description of Dora, suggests the degree to which catharsis becomes impossible not only for Pökler but for the reader as well:

> Pökler vomitted. He cried some. The walls did not dissolve—no prison wall ever did, not from tears, not at this finding, on every pallet, in every cell, that the faces are ones he knows after all, and holds dear as himself. . . . But what can he ever do about it? How can he ever keep them? Impotence, mirror-rotation of sorrow, works him terribly as runaway heartbeating, and with hardly any chances left him for good rage, or for turning. (433)

The terse, almost summary, phrasing of this passage is perhaps enough to suggest not only the absence of affect but its diminution and lack of substance before an event of such magnitude as the concentration camp. Although it could be said that Pökler deepens emotionally as a character through the episode, the result is only "impotence," the mirror opposite of a sorrow that takes place only in the imaginary order of wishing, of a desire reduced to mere fantasy, disconnected from a material order of production. What Pökler "finds" is that no redeeming transcendence can result from his recognition of the faces on the pallets, or from the discovery that he "holds them dear as himself," no "turning" can be wrenched from such an event, no signification can survive intact the identity of desire and the world that is legible there. While Franz recognizes at least the preterite type of Leni in the Dora inmates he sees, Leni (or her type) does not or cannot recognize him, and the final moment between them remains one of disjunction, nonrelation, appalling anticlimax (punctuated by his final gesture of giving her [or her type] his wedding ring in the hope that selling it might "be good for a few meals" [433]). And if Franz is like Oedipus at the end of Sophocles' play in this regard, helpless, exiled, and caught in illusion, the reader of the episode cannot be his audience without grasping the novel's insistence on impotence, helplessness, nonrelation, and masochism ("alone with those fantasies that don't look like they'll ever come true") as conditions that strike at the heart of tragedy itself or, more pertinently, call into question the perspective and the agency that tragedy implies (at least for its spectator or reader).

My point here is not to exhaust the possibilities of tragedy (as they are given in Sophocles' play, for example) but rather to highlight how Pynchon "uses" tragedy by way of elaborating a far different textual form. The novel caricatures the tragic quest for meaning to show its metaphysical determination as another search for a "metalanguage." This is the nature of illusion for Pökler, the "impossible and monstrous project" in which he participates; but it is also the project in which the novel participates, albeit as parody, displacing the epistemological desire for totality or unity, exposing in the tragic plot the presupposition of this desire, or rather its "consequence" in a regime of prohibition and law. Tragedy reproduces the imaginary/symbolic binarism that conceals or glosses the unity of desire and production, and it is the text seeing this, reversing the causal inference running from "psychic repression" to the "nature of what is repressed," that constitutes its preterition, which is to say its apprehension of the bodies piled onto pallets at Dora. For if the Holocaust is by and large present in *Gravity's Rainbow* only symptomatically, as its limit, its present absence in the novel is pervasive and indeed formally constitutive, one point of orientation, as it were, for its supplementary articulations. The preterite body/text means only from the limits of meaning, in a seductive mode of acting out (masquerade, impersonation, transvestism, Dora the concentration camp, Dora the hysteric) that eludes discursivity in language according to a logic deeper than that of rationality. This ingested, incorporated, excreted, secreted text of flows that is *Gravity's Rainbow* establishes within the inertias, the perverse territorialities that it sets up, a countermovement in which desiring-production appears, and in which the inclusive relation between desire and history, between desire and the contingency of history, is understood.

This countermovement implies the generalization of the preterite state to all characters in the novel, and correlatively a deconstruction of the distinction between victim and victimizer making visible an economy of social repression in which the locus of that repression has been internalized to the precise degree that history has been externalized from the subject. In this light, Pökler's story in episode 11 can be read within a much different contextualization. The stakes of this deconstruction, the actual victims of repression, are focalized in the figure of Pökler's daughter, Ilse, taken from her mother at Dora and delivered once a year to her father as part of Weissmann/Blicero's plan to ensure Pökler's assistance in the eventual construction of the Schwarzgerat (literally the "accommodation" of the machine to Gottfried's insertion in the 00000). Ilse is what gets lost in the decoded spaces of the Zone, the disjunctive, repetitive, replicative spaces of language and meaning, where metaphor, resemblance, or recognition have eroded before the instrumentalizing forces that overwhelm her father. Pökler lives with/in this language, feeling its discontinuities and its cinematic illusions of movement, its appropriations of desire, its lures and inducements to forget the nature of responsibility or care for others. The problem is that this responsibility itself constitutes another layer of illusion when it predicates itself on its exclusion from, or opposition to, the condition of disjunction that is the Zone, language, the space and time of the novel. The theme of care must be distorted or inverted by this disjunctive language before it can be meaningful again, before even it can grasp the event of its own forgetting, and this entails the necessity of a similarly "inverse" kind of writing and reading.

Episode 11 is remarkable for the stark and uncompromising way it highlights the overdetermination of this theme in the drama of Pökler's paternal love strung through the modes of mechanical reproduction, manipulated by the supervising Weissmann for his intricately sacrificial plots, and confronted by its very identity with those modes and that manipulation, or rather with the historical fact of its own decoding. Franz can literally love his daughter only through that mediation or that decoding, and the resultant distortion of desire induces in him an uncertainty about Ilse's real identity that verges on paranoia. Time decomposes for Pökler in the series of her yearly visits, and any sense of continuity belies a discontinuity running so deep it jeopardizes memory itself, fracturing time into indivisible units whose only principle of succession appears to be either mechanical repetition, pure randomness, or persistence of vision.

> So it has gone for six years since. A daughter a year, each one about a year older, each time taking up nearly from scratch. The only continuity has been her name, and . . . Pökler's love—love something like the persistence of vision. For they have used it to create for him the moving image of a daughter, flashing him only these summertime frames of her, leaving it to him to build the illusion of a single child . . . What would the time scale matter, a 24th of a second or a year (no more, the engineer thought, than a wind-tunnel, or an oscillograph whose turning drum you could speed or slow at will . . .)? (422)

The manipulations of the paranoiac "They" can extend even down to the experience of duration because the "time scale" is relative to an arbitrary unit of measure. This arbitrary quantity determines the synthesis of time that is consciousness itself; it modulates "Pökler's love" to a frequency at which "continuity" can be felt only as "illusion." "They" use Pökler's desire to fabricate "the moving image of a daughter," counting on his susceptibility to believe in the image, to accept it as real because it is what he wants the real to be.[13] This seduction of the image, this modulation of being, this structure of desire, signifies a tactic of control, Franz's oppression by Weissmann, which is why he cannot fully believe that the same daughter appears each year. His paranoia accurately intuits the means of production (the machine, the "oscillograph") that generates the illusory sense of continuity, his experience of the "same" Ilse, but this intuition also reacts on his love for her. Suspicions about her identity lead him to "look for resemblances" (407) to the child he once knew with Leni, then to anatomize and even dissect resemblance in an increasingly obsessive manner. Resemblance, indeed, is elevated into an absolute criterion for belief, so that the illusion of sameness comes to index Ilse's authenticity, and any deviation in her behavior from year to year compounds his suspicion of her imposture. Difference becomes inauthentic, proof of the conspiracy against him, with the result that the "authentic" resides nowhere except in his desire for a "real" daughter (which he can't trust, which he can't believe in). His desire oscillates between a sameness exacerbated to the point of automation and a difference that dissimulates an aleatoric repetition, both of which seem to foreclose the possibility of human love.

The state of mind constructed here is a schizo-paranoiac jamming of the human machine and an incredible evocation of a society, a language, gone mad; but at the same time, Pynchon stages a kind of recursion around or back to that schizoid semiosis as the mode of its diagnosis or critique. When Franz is made to wonder, "one daughter one imposter? same daughter twice? two imposters? Beginning to work out the combinations for a third visit, and a fourth. . . . Weissmann, those behind him, had thousands of these children available" (418), the text is exploring a combinative or permutative facility for nomadic movement that equally governs the breakdown of the human and the germinal possibility of an escape from repression. By turning Pökler always back on himself, on his own desire, his own freedom, no matter how overdetermined these may be, Pynchon stresses the irreducibility of desire to its repressed substitute form, an ontological difference that can be located only within the conditions of its repression as a particular strategy, a particular kind of referentiality, a particular inclusive use of the disjunctive synthesis. Pökler's mistrust of his own desire, conditioned by Weissmann's manipulations, also conditions a potential critique of axiomatized desire. This critique circulates as a kind of "machinic" possibility in the margins of Pökler's delirium, and even though it never exactly manifests itself in the content of his story (Pökler doesn't "find" the ontological difference at Dora or with his daughter), it nonetheless exists in the parodic medium that always characterizes language and form in the novel.

The inclusive structure of *Gravity's Rainbow* creates a strange moire in the flows of meaning it sets in motion, not in order to undermine its own critique, for instance of bureaucracy as a negative schizophrenizing force in Pökler's story (and in capitalist society as a rule), but to uncover the actual method of social repression concealed in that bureaucracy, the violence it directs against desire. In Pökler's case, what this structure clarifies is the oblique dimension in which a desire for the same, for identity or self-identity, for resemblance and unity, appears as one more illusion, one more image or fiction arresting desire in its miraculated simulacrum. As Pökler's paranoia about Ilse accelerates throughout the episode, destabilizing all reference points in the satellitized world of Peenemunde and Zwolfkinder, the children's theme park ("enclave of innocence" in a "corporate State" [428]) that he visits with Ilse each summer, there is a sense in which this paranoia begins to exhaust itself, to detumesce, to collapse in the face of its own bad faith. When Ilse, after many years approaching pubescence, her symbolic function in Weissmann's game changing from substitute daughter to substitute lover or wife, asks her father about sleeping in the same bed at a Zwolfkinder hotel, the issue of desire as rooted in an incestuous drive is explicitly raised. Pökler's response:

> He hit her upside the head with his open hand, a loud and terrible blow. That took care of his anger. Then, before she could cry or speak, he had dragged her up on the bed next to him, her dazed little hands already at the buttons of his trousers, her white frock already pulled above her waist. She had been wearing nothing at all underneath, nothing all day . . . *how I've wanted you*, she whispered as paternal plow found its way into filial furrow . . . and after hours of amazing incest they dressed in silence, and crept out into the leading edge of faintest flesh dawn, everything they would ever need packed inside her flowered bag, past sleeping children doomed to the end of summer, past monitors and railway guards, down at last to the water and the fishing boats, to a fatherly old sea-dog in a braided captain's hat, who welcomed them aboard and stashed them below decks, where she snuggled down in the bunk as they got under way and sucked him for hours while the engine pounded, till the Captain called, "Come on up, and take a look at your new home!" Gray and green, through the mist, it was Denmark. "Yes, they're a free people here. Good luck to both of you!" The three of them, there on deck, stood hugging. (420–21)

Incest catalyzes the euphoric movement of this passage from the initial blow through an extended fantasy of escape. It enacts another "ride" in the theme park, the "escape" ride; indeed, it almost literally drives the boat, Ilse belowdecks "sucking him for hours while the engine pounded." The passage acts out a shrewd denunciation of corporatized desire, its delimitation and co-optation within spaces that dissimulate any relation between desire and power. What it implies in the process, however, is that the notion of an incestuous drive colludes in this dissimulation; power fixes Pökler in the fantasy by seducing him to the desire for incest, by persuading him to its reality in him. But incest is not real *for the text itself*; it belongs wholly to reductive or corporatized fantasy, which is why at the level of plot this passage in effect does not "really" take place. Presented at first as one more moment of narrative articulation, the paragraph ends in a fantasy that retroactively renders even the initial act (the blow) imaginary. The real text, the plot, turns into fantasy and de-realizes the real text, and the reader, lured at first into believing the incestuous relation, gradually comes to acknowledge its unreality. "No," begins the paragraph immediately following, "What Pökler did was choose to believe she wanted comfort that night, wanted not to be alone. Despite Their game, their palpable evil, though he had no more reason to trust 'Ilse' than he trusted Them, by an act not of faith, not of courage but of conservation, he chose to believe that" (421). The "choice" Pökler makes involves a retreat from the fantasy, from a belief in the incestuous drive urged on him from without. His mistrust of Ilse does not disappear, and "They" remain as palpably and malignantly active in his world as ever; but one can still detect a withdrawal from his intense paranoiac investments and from the drive to establish resemblances, continuity, identity.[14] "Even in peacetime," he reasons, "with unlimited resources, he couldn't have proven [Ilse's] identity, not beyond the knife-edge of zero tolerance his precision eye needed. The years Ilse would have spent between Berlin and Peenemunde were so hopelessly tangled, for all of Germany, that no real chain of events could have been established for sure, not even Pökler's hunch that somewhere in the State's oversize paper brain a specific perversity had been assigned him and dutifully stored" (421).

The text relates the discontinuity of time and memory to a historical transformation that is also a transformation of history itself. It both contacts history's "hopeless tangle" and withdraws from history (in the strict sense) inasmuch as the war is no longer seen as a determining cause but itself an effect of some other kind of event, or in another, more catastrophic time than the one Pökler thought he was living. This perception allows Pökler to detach from his own obsessive desire for a "real chain of events," a real time, enough to see that obsession as one more element in "Their game." Even his hunch that the state has determined his fate in an anonymous yet personalized persecutory program stored in its "oversize paper brain" loses its force when Pökler apprehends the historicity of his own and Ilse's decoding. Love and care, he realizes, occur only once this critical deflation of axiomatized desire takes place. Thus Pökler's choice, contextualized as it is by Zwolfkinder, nonetheless constitutes an intuition of the "game" in which he finds himself, and the obligation he still has to his own desire and to Ilse: "Board and pieces and patterns at least all did come clear to him, and Pökler knew that while he played, this would have to be Ilse—truly his child, truly as he could make her. It was the real moment of conception, in which, years too late, he became her father" (421).

Once Pökler sees through a desire for the "same," for an undecoded Ilse conforming to the "knife-edge" of his "zero tolerance," he begins to think of identity inclusively, conceives (of) her in a discontinuous temporal series as a multiple personality, impostor or impersonator, and chooses to love this about her, to see her intrinsically in this plastic or metamorphic sense. The act of "conceiving" a daughter—and conferring on the passage of time an illusory continuity—regains a degree of independence from its determined form in mere fantasy because it conserves difference within its "conception" and grasps the singularities of an other whose subjectivity is "delirious" or nomadic in nature. Only at this point can desire begin to experience its own possibility, its productive power, its critical agency, both for Pökler and for the text itself (and for writing, on which the episode is virtually a sustained meditation). The ability to care appears for Pynchon precisely as a consequence of his decomposing and parodic strategies; these strategies express desire at the level of an intradiscursive resistance to meaning, a repetition that exemplifies a properly preterite mode of being.

Ilse signifies this mode for Pökler in the very elusiveness of her identity. On her first visit, for example, she tells him about wanting to go to the moon (along with the Rocket—"I'd fit inside, wouldn't I?" she asks [410]) and fantasizes about living in "a small pretty crater in the Sea of Tranquillity called Maskelyne B. They would build a house right on the rim, Mutti and she and Pökler..." (410). When on a subsequent visit the scene of Ilse's fantasy shifts to the South Pole, and Pökler reads this shift as another indication of her imposture, the text once again traces in a margin internal to fantasy, evoking in Ilse's "secret lunar society" and "artificial new family" a "double" implication that troubles signification at all levels. The moon is where the Rocket goes, its potential destination, and the Rocket is the novel's central obsession, its organizing fetish, which suggests that the moon, Ilse's moon, is a destination as well for *Gravity's Rainbow*. The moon is a familiar symbol for an escapist territoriality, a place of reflected light where no life is possible, dead and abstract, and Pökler, conscious of his responsibility as a father, considers telling Ilse as much. But to do so widens the gap between them and compounds the decoding of familial desire both are experiencing to the point of absurdity. When Pökler tells Ilse that the Rocket may one day be used to fly to the moon, she assumes he is about to tell her a story, and when Pökler proves incapable of following this up, she fabricates her own. The fantasy is determined as a substitute for the story her father ought to have told her, and thus another instance of the family's decoding. But to deflate the fantasy solves exactly nothing, and this dead end pushes the text in the direction of another truth about the role of such substitutions (and their discontinuities) in the familial relation. Both father and daughter are subject to a desire for continuity that directs them "to the Moon," and there seems to be no escape from this escape, which is to say it also involves a turn or possibility of "real flight" that Pynchon constructs as a remainder of the process of forgetting and the failure to care. The desire for tranquillity, quiescence, or freedom from an instrumentalized life is also a desire for disguise, for the mask in Maskelyne B; and the "lunar society" is also energized by its constitutive "disavowal of the real" that the reader feels precisely in the parodic levity always inherent to Pynchon's prose, the textual displacement toward expression, its peculiar becoming-object.

The Double Light

Here one draws close to the formal center of *Gravity's Rainbow*, which is why Pynchon proliferates associations around the figure of the "innocent," Ilse, Bianca Erdmann, Gottfried, and so on, along a graduated chain of substitutions that include characters like Geli Tripping, Katje Borghesius, Leni, Slothrop, Enzian, Pökler, and even, at the extreme conclusion of the series, Captain Blicero himself. To go to the moon is to escape a certain gravitational pull, to displace meaning from its earthbound determination toward more orbitalized or rhizomatic forms, and this displacement governs the text's deeply interconnected or implicate structure, the way it links its numerous characters, subplots, and themes together in transverse, tangent, or contingent modes. One especially dense point of intersection for Pökler's story and the larger narrative progressions (in particular Slothrop's quest for the Schwarzgerat, the *Anubis* voyage, and Blicero) is the film *Alpdrucken* (the name means "nightmare or incubus" in German, also related to the Greek word *alphos*, "dull-white leprosy," according to Weisenburger [*Companion*, 190]) and its star, Greta Erdmann, the masochistic "Anti-Dietrich" (394) who focalizes Pökler's fantasies and whose image he has in his mind (whose image he fucks) the night Ilse is conceived. The fictional movie, directed by the sinister Gerhardt von Goll (who condenses in one figure the artist, the pornographer, and, as black marketer Der Springer, the capitalist), is presented by Pynchon as politically acceptable fare for the likes of Goebbels, a phantasmagoria of perversion and sadomasochistic clichés centered on the figure of the passive woman. Erdmann in the movie is the object of a male gaze that sustains perversion in the subjective or imaginary domain while exorcising it in the social. She thus functions within an artistic representation that colludes in the historical "nightmares" of Nazism and patriarchy. She is the vehicle for Pynchon of a reflexive critique of male fantasy that works itself out in multiple and overlaid dimensions, as the novel's parodic transgressions of meaning and form. Once again the victim of this specularization is the child, Ilse, who owes her very existence, the text suggests, to this cinematic mediation of the sexual act. But dissimulated in this mediation, this light, this movie *Alpdrucken*, Pynchon writes, is an element of irreducible otherness, a divine light or "Double Light" that persists "beyond film's end" and incarnates an elusive "shadow of shadows" whose implications even the director of the movie fails to understand. In the following passage, Ilse encounters on a Zwolfkinder street a male counterpart who clearly suggests Gottfried:

> Who was that, going by just then—who was the slender boy who flickered across her path, so blond, so white he was nearly invisible in the hot haze that had come to settle over Zwolfkinder? Did she see him, and did she know him for her own second shadow? She was conceived because her father saw a movie called *Alpdrucken* one night and got a hardon. Pökler in his horny staring had missed the Director's clever Gnostic symbolism in the lighting scheme of the two shadows, Cain's and Abel's. But Ilse, some Ilse, has persisted beyond her cinema mother, beyond film's end, and so have the shadows of shadows. In the Zone, all will be moving under the Old Dispensation, inside the Cainists' light and space: not out of any precious Gollerei, but because the Double Light was always there, outside all film, and that shucking and jiving moviemaker was the only one around at the time who happened to notice it and use it, although in deep ignorance, then and now, of what he was showing the nation of starers. . . . So that summer Ilse passed herself by, too fixed at some shadowless interior noon to mark the intersection, or to care. (429)

The intersection of Ilse and Gottfried, both marked and unmarked by the text (it never explicitly says the boy is Gottfried), exemplifies the ligatures that Pynchon uses to structure the novel. Both characters are figured as "white" screens for the projection of transcendental fantasies of escape (with Blicero in fact as the director-manipulator in both cases) who also come from that projection, that whiteness (Weissmann as father). They are cinema children, shadows of a fantasmatic light, its negative space—representations of this negativity become shadows of themselves, double negatives, palimpsests of a "Double Light" that exists "outside all film" (the reference in the text is to lighting a scene or character from both below and above, thus creating two shadows at once). The Double Light signifies the possibility of something beyond the axiomatic lures of the movie, the chance of a critical detachment or perspective from which to glimpse the violence directed at desire. Pynchon links such a perspective to a "Cainists' light" and in so doing again draws a parallel with the preterite not just as an opposing term in a binary structure but as opposed to binarism itself, an outside to the digitization of light waves (sound waves, brain waves) and the co-optation of desire implied in the functions of fantasy. But this preterite exteriority is also inclusive of that co-optation, a condition of its possibility, and the fact is underscored when Ilse literally and figuratively "passes herself by." She too has begun to forget how to care; she too fixes herself at "some shadowless interior noon," in a dream of whiteness numbing pain and feeling to the point of automaton-like insensibility. Grafted onto the critique of male desire implied in her victimization is a further critique of the socioeconomic forces that alienate desire in general (as desiring-production). Ilse, already machinic, becomes a mechanism, fulfills her destiny as one of Weissmann's instruments the same as her father does, by acquiescing to a fantasy that fails to recognize the Double Light, the intersection with Gottfried, and (jumping dimensions) the rhizomatic technique of aleatoric association employed by Pynchon.

At stake in this narrative moment is the deconstruction of dualistic thought, metaphysics, or "phallogocentrism" that occurs in the textual web Pynchon weaves, the eclipse of a "double writing" in the drive for a metalanguage as light without shadow, whiteness without blackness (or inflection of any kind). This steady state of entropic equilibrium envelops the "technical machines" that both Pökler and Ilse become and configures them as machines that no longer work, that are exhausted or used up, archaic. But as encased or neoterritorialized within a capitalist machine that confers on them a "perfectly current function," both characters can also be read as signs for a deterritorialized writing, "broken machines" that are also desiring-machines. Pynchon in this way allows the (digital) binarisms of meaning to return inside his writing while also establishing lines of resistance, internal fronts where textual contestations of an emergent postindustrial order reducing people to machines of a simulacral reproduction can properly take place. Resistance to the decoding (i.e., digitizing) of signification is possible, Pynchon implies, only once the decoding is understood to include even resistance itself, and to mandate as resistance an opening to the Double Light and the possibility it holds out for an autonomous (but hence implicated) desire.

The quoted passage, describing how things "move" in the Zone, the language universe of the novel, refers the reader to this possibility, this "outside all film," by virtue of its doubleness—its deliberate ambiguities, its hybridized and fragmented form (verging on formlessness or pure intensity), its rhizomatic (non)connections, its ekphrastic use of quoted art forms, its polymeric logic. This does not imply a naive projection of redemptive structure onto the novel, nor does it ignore the darkly overdetermined character of the Zone itself. If the shadows of shadows in Pynchon's text are similar to metaphors of metaphor in Derrida's sense, conceived in relation to a complex "withdrawal of Being" (analogous, once again, to an abyssal or groundless ground) that characterizes both metaphysical discourse *and* its undoing, then the Zone could be said to be the site rather of this "withdrawal," of an elusiveness that locates the text's politics in the "turn" to language.[15] Accordingly, what qualifies the Zone as a space of possibility is this reticence, this (dis)appearance of "withdrawal." Of course, the tendency to formalize this double inversion, to transport its insights about language and "Being" back into the realm of the proper and familiar, constitutes a risk any such reflexive turn runs, which is paradoxically why considerations of form are so important, since only at the formal level can one see the decomposition of form that attends the refusal of a text to be one thing or another. *Gravity's Rainbow* traces out a sort of fourth-dimensional line of flight even as it simultaneously grasps its own historical determination and the stakes (world war, genocide, mass exploitation of the earth) that always hang in the balance of this "escape." Thus the essential reticence of "Being" manifests itself in the text's fallenness, in its Cainists' light, in its failures and forgettings, in its worst excesses of absurdity and degradation, in its parallels or convergences with the conditions of its own repression. Listen to this convergence in the following description of Greta Erdmann:

> It was always easy for men to come and tell her who to be. Other girls of her generation grew up asking, "Who am I?" For them it was a question full of pain and struggle. For Gretel it was hardly even a question. She had more identities than she knew what to do with. Some of these Gretels have been only the sketchiest of surfaces—others are deeper.

> Many have incredible gifts, antigravity, dreams of prophecy . . . comatic images surround their faces, glowing in the air: the light itself is actually crying tears, weeping in this stylized way, as she is borne along through the mechanical cities, the meteorite walls draped in midair, every hollow and socket empty as a bone, and the failing shadow that shines black all around it . . . (482)

To hear in these multiple identities a parody of the unitary self without also hearing the coercion and misogynist violence to which this same multiplicity attests is to miss the text's complex ambition to hold together both readings as two sides of the same historical coin. Erdmann's suggestibility or plasticity is a sign of her function as a sex symbol, a specular locus for phallic desire and a tool for the pornographer-capitalist-artist von Goll. Her nomadic subjectivity derives from this capture within the flat, projected space of the movie (as exemplary commodity), and *Gravity's Rainbow* too, at one level, colludes in this appropriation. And yet the novel is also more than the movie it parodies, and this difference confers on its language a kind of rhetorical luminosity, the power of a knowledge that what we are reading amounts to a critique only through its (our) investment in that cinematic space and its desubjectivized representations. Pynchon thus presents Erdmann's nomadisms in such a way that the text's desire confronts itself in its identity with modes of mechanical reproduction that condition the social and historical field in which she moves as a scene of perpetual schizophrenic becoming.

Textual desire here is coded as male, and the figure of the masquerading woman is finally intelligible only in relation to a male norm. If critique (of man's desire) is also self-critique in *Gravity's Rainbow*, a process of self-implication in a social, cultural, and economic order that determines the text as a whole, then even the privilege granted to the multiple subject can be interrogated for its masculinist presuppositions. The very convergence under discussion here as a condition for critique could find itself conditioned by those same presuppositions, with the result that self-reflexivity in a text even vis-à-vis this likelihood cannot guarantee its critical detachment.[16] If this is the case, it may be that Pynchon's text cannot make a guarantee of this kind, and that this complicity marks the text internally as one of its elements or inclusive boundaries. Implication understood this way highlights the simulacral nature of desire and points out the repression (or miraculation) that attends the theoretical or practical shift from desire to agency, desire's instrumentalization in the social domain. Complicity of the "inclusive" kind has therefore the political advantage of exposing in its "exclusive" counterpart a constitutive forgetting of its own conditions and its own limits, and to raise the question of from where, according to what principles, a political act (especially of writing and reading) arises. This is the mode, at any rate, of Pynchon's critique of male desire: to look at the construction of stereotypes in a male imaginary at a place prior to the subject, where this construction effects displacements and repressions that, while they underpin or condition acts of violence and domination directed at subjects, cannot be observed in the same way as those acts. "Fantasy," writes Judith Butler, "is the very scene which *suspends* action and which, in its suspension, provides for a critical investigation of what it is that constitutes action" ("The Force of Fantasy," 112). If this attention to origins, taken far enough, eclipses effective action, it is also true that effective action, taken far enough, eclipses this attention to origins, and the possibility of (at least interpretive) violence works both ways. *Gravity's Rainbow*, for all its brutal linguistic and narrative deterritorializations, is a very delicate text in this regard, since it tries to precipitate in its fantasms the desire of desire, desire in general, or the zero degree of its own origin.

The principal thematic vehicle for this precipitation is the figure of the innocent, of innocence itself not as a simple origin but as always already caught up in its own history, recorded, reproduced, replicated, an innocence of innocence or what Deleuze and Guattari might call the "innocence of madness" (*Anti-Oedipus*, 43). Bianca, Greta Erdmann's twelve-year-old daughter, presents another variation on this theme. Conceived during the shooting of *Alpdrucken* when her mother is collectively raped by the film crew, linked to Ilse and Gottfried as a white screen for the projections of others, she signifies in her manipulated body and eventual death both the desire (turned against itself) of repression as well as its excess, its remainder, that which cannot be reduced to its repressed forms. She condenses in one figure the functions of masquerade (playing out the pornographic stereotypes of a male imaginary) and its stakes, its abusive and finally murderous character. But as much as she is an abused child, she is also active in the stereotypes she recapitulates. Her desire does not appear except through its decoding, as Pynchon implies in the following performance before a captive audience on board the *Anubis*:

> About here they are interrupted by Margherita [Greta] and Bianca, playing stage mother and reluctant child. Whispers to the bandleader, funseekers crowding eagerly around a cleared space where Bianca now stands pouting, her little red frock halfway up her slender thighs, with black lace petticoats peeping from beneath the hem, surely it's going to

be something, sophisticated, big city, and wicked, but what's she doing with her finger posed aside of one dimpled cheek like this—at which point comes the band's intro, and pre-vomit saliva begins to gush into Slothrop's mouth....

Not only is her song "On the Good Ship Lollipop," but she is also now commencing, without a trace of shame, to *grunt* her way through it, in perfect mimickry of young Shirley Temple—each straining baby-pig inflection, each curl-toss, unmotivated smile, and stumbling toe-tap—is somebody fooling with the lights? But the billowings of asexual child-fat have not changed her eyes: they remain as they were, mocking, dark, her own. (465–66)

If Bianca's impersonation of Shirley Temple is degrading in its suggestion of an asexual yet also sexualized innocence, and of her "unmotivated" availability for the spectators, she also reverses the energy of that degradation, turns it inside out in a process of mimicry that makes her performance a parody of innocence in which she remains "mocking, dark, her own." This desire, this agency in the midst of an almost literal metamorphosis of her body, suffuses the theatrical space in which a "real" identity becomes impossible. Her desire is not an essence prefiguring its alienation in that space; it does not exist apart from its performative expression but rather is the desire of that "playing" space understood historically. As an origin, its salient characteristic is its "own-ness," its alterity to any determination of origin, its negative gesture of refusal to be the very forms in which it appears—a formlessness at the heart of form, an approach to states of pure intensity that radically forecloses sense in language, reducing its vocalization in particular to mere "grunts."

To disrupt discourse in this manner, however, does not mean that alienation disappears, only that the object on which it bears is not a self-identical substance. Indeed, the desire of repression, for Pynchon, takes aim precisely at the origin that is not an origin, the (im)propriety in Bianca's eyes, the formless intensity that she incarnates as a dissimulating subject (and a subject dissimulated in fiction). Repression occurs with the refusal of this refusal to be one thing or another even as one passes nomadically through the states of being. The novel's critique of male violence, male rationality, male fantasy, cannot be grasped outside this decisive shift in the economy of repression: what a masculinist, analytic Western culture cannot tolerate is an elusiveness of definition within definition itself. Even Bianca's role as Eurydice for Slothrop, whose sexual relationship both with Greta and her daughter diverts the entire problematic of male violence into the central narrative current, constitutes another avatar of that culture. Bianca as a figure for "withdrawal," for that which withdraws before Slothrop's desire to know, to find his own "true course," calls the very structure of the quest into being, and thus the structure of knowledge that Pynchon decodes. Woman as ontological, one could even say, is the ontic determination of Being and the primary mode of its forgetting, from which it follows that the masquerade to which Greta and Bianca are consigned participates in the violence directed at the origin of the origin. A dissimulating subjectivity dissimulates its own deconstruction, in other words, and proof of this comes even in the extremity of "Ensign Morituri's Story," where Pynchon reveals how Greta entices children (in particular boys) to their death in a black mud pool at the appropriately entitled spa "Bad Karma." Pynchon links this representation of a desire for the murder of "innocence" to anti-Semitism when one of the boys turns out to be Jewish.

> "You know who I am, too," [says Greta]. "My home is the form of light," burlesquing it now, in heavy Yiddish, actressy and false, "I wander all the Diaspora looking for strayed children. I am Israel. I am the Shekhinah, queen, daughter, bride, and mother of God. And I will take you back, you fragment of smashed vessel, even if I must pull you by your nasty little circumcised penis—" (478)

Invocation here of the Kabbalistic Shekhinah, a symbol for "eternal womanhood" and the "feminine element of God" in Gershom Scholem's words (Trends of Jewish Mysticism, 229–30), works ironically to undermine any simple valorization of the feminine. Greta appropriates Jewish mysticism, uses it, quotes it for her own racial hatred, as part of her fatal seduction. Her fallen nature, exiled in matter and sensuality (the "Erd"), separated from the primordial light of the Godhead, manifests itself in the desire for unity, to return the boy as "fragment of smashed vessel" to an unfallen origin at the black pool's "center of gravity." The mystical experience is also a murder of innocence that constitutes a preterite state, Gnostic insofar as the cosmos itself is as a result thoroughly depraved, overdetermined, in quotation marks, "actressy and false." While Greta cannot be the Shekhinah, however, without appropriating a diasporic tradition she wishes to kill, she is the Shekhinah to the extent that the text reconstitutes a Kabbalistic cosmogony for which her depravity is central. The more depraved she becomes, the more in fact she fulfills that tradition.[17] The "eternal feminine" as burlesque colludes in the violence of repression, but it also recuperates something of the repressed in the very foreclosure of its own intelligibility, opening a possibility for "knowledge" that refers to the limits of reference itself.[18]

The *Anubis*

But this double knowledge or Double Light can't be apprehended in a reading confined to the novel's content, however dense and overlaid that content may be. Neither Greta nor Bianca symbolizes an agency of escape, or rather, they compress both this agency and the killing of it (indeed, the text suggests that Greta murders Bianca in the end) into singular figures that signify without externalizing one or the other terms in the binary. This compression as a mode of signification decodes its own meanings by refusing parturition, as it were, holding itself off from the organic cycles of life and death in a suspension that renders its conducting material or its vehicle (language, narrative convention) unreal or simulacral. Thus to see the double possibility held out by the text requires a slide to expression that Pynchon in fact provides by encasing the citation of Kabbalism in a story within the story, highlighting in its intertextuality the text's own preterition, its own mediated form, its own suspension in the place of entropic decomposition. This is also why the story of Ensign Morituri is told on the *Anubis*, and why Slothrop, who meets Greta just before encountering the jackal-headed ship (with Pökler's story intervening), converges with (and diverges from) Bianca at the same juncture it forms in the novel. This white vessel sailing the lowland canals of Northern Europe, drifting with its "screaming Fascist cargo" (491) of orgiastic revelers vaguely toward Peenemunde, the Rocket, and the "white" North, named for the Egyptian god of death and, more pertinently, of burial and embalming as the process of arresting decay in the pharaoh's body—this metaphor for metaphor itself, for the language of the Zone, recapitulates nearly all the themes touched on in this chapter. Its errant course is also the course of the novel.[19] The ship stands in relation to the whole as a "whole-part" or a "production of production" that exemplifies the novel in movement, in progress, in its partiality and its machinic desire. Its voyage down the Spree-Oder Canal in Holland and into the Baltic Sea at the "Oder Haff" simulates sexual penetration; it sails into the body of woman (heard in the pun on "Other Half") as orgasm, death, whiteness, transcendence, as that which withdraws before and interpellates the male quest. The ship orients itself toward the fetish, whether it be the "arrested image" of the woman or the Rocket as the phallus she is said to be but not to have. As a sign for fetishism, it enacts fantasy as a freezing or reifying of movement, as escapism, as sexual perversion, as misogynist and specularized desire, as Oedipalization and commodification. It tracks the becoming other, the becoming-object of the novel, its movement toward or into the inanimate (symbolized by the elemental world of the Baltic Sea and the frozen North). This relay with the inanimate in turn links the *Anubis* to the problematic of addiction, to shooting up the world, to incorporating the nonhuman within a body that, addicted, becomes nonhuman in its turn, assimilated to or coextensive with the world. This "delirium" entails a complicity that Pynchon's play on the word "use" throughout the novel articulates for every character including the novel's innocents, and including both the writer and his readers. Pynchon's critique of Western culture cannot be understood unless this collusion of writing and reading, text and world, language and being, is sustained, for without it, *Gravity's Rainbow* only replicates or reflects the conditions of misery that it dramatizes—*only colludes*, that is, without also presenting itself as a protest and a cultural intervention in history.

To read the novel as a protest is to see how the *Anubis* voyage paradoxically articulates its desire, how it is both fascism and the critique of fascism at the same time, or in the same figure.[20] The movement into the inanimate North, as much as it signifies transcendence, also signifies a deterritorialization, a retreat to the zero degree of the body without organs, a schizophrenic decoding of content and expression registered in the extremity of its absurdism and antiseriousness. It is a writing or a recording on the body without organs that, in calling attention to itself, signals a political consciousness (the novel's actual "counterforce" irreducible to its historical determination, a consciousness that cannot be located within its own locations, a discourse without its own discourse). This elusiveness or imperceptibility is the underlying stake of Pynchon's elliptical, preterite, and parabolic novel. Paradoxically, the discursive mode in which this stake appears is accumulative in nature. It entails a multiplication of meaning insofar as its "point-signs" have "many dimensions" that intersect in it, engendering the intertextual possibility of as many meanings as there are predicative states through which the schizophrenic text passes. This is why networks of symbolism—for example, the reference to Egyptian mythology, or to Kabbalism, or to Shirley Temple—while significant for Pynchon's meticulous construction both of Western culture as a whole and in its late modern phase, have as their cumulative effect to exhaust rather than enrich signification, literally to swamp the connotative depths of the novel to the point where meaning stops or stands still.

The following passage exemplifies this exhaustive dynamic of critical desire in the text. It comes after Bianca's Shirley Temple impersonation, and after she refuses to sing a second song, thereby incurring her mother's punishment in the form of an eroticized spanking that arouses the *Anubis* crowd (including Slothrop). The ensuing orgy is described in extended terms:

> Two of the waiters kneel on deck lapping at the juicy genitals of a blonde in a wine velvet frock, who meantime is licking ardently the tall and shiny French heels of an elderly lady in lemon organza busy fastening felt-lined silver manacles to the wrists of her escort, a major of the Yugoslav artillery in dress uniform, who kneels with nose and tongue well between the bruised buttocks of a long-legged ballerina from Paris, holding her silk skirt for him with docile fingertips while her companion, a tall Swiss divorcee in tight-laced leather corselette and black Russian boots, undoes the top of her friend's gown and skillfully begins to lash at her bared breasts with stems of half a dozen roses, red as the beads of blood which spring up and soon are shaking off the ends of her stiff nipples to splash into the eager mouth of another Wend who's being jerked off by a retired Dutch banker sitting on the deck, shoes and socks just removed by two adorable schoolgirls, twin sisters in fact, in identical dresses of flowered voile, with each of the banker's big toes inserted now into a downy little furrow as they lie forward along his legs kissing his shaggy stomach, pretty twin bottoms arched to receive in their anal openings the cocks of the two waiters who have but lately been, if you recall, eating that juicy blonde in that velvet dress back down the Oder Haff a ways. (467)

Pynchon presents in this passage one of the novel's numerous uroboric figures, a circuit that links the end with the beginning, a circle that becomes a single point, a catastrophic collapse of meaning into tautology and repetition. The time of the *Anubis* "ploughing" the Oder Haff toward the Rocket facility at Peenemunde is discursive in nature, the suspended or fantasmatic time of metaphor and analogy in which discourse is made to vibrate around itself, to intensify its own referentiality to a point of deliberate self-destruction. This gesture to turn language back on itself (or toward its origin) like a snake eating its own tail—or like the benzene ring dreamt of by another character in the novel, the chemist Von Kekulé, that Pynchon seizes on in the Pökler subplot for the connections it implies between organic chemistry, the history of chemical, pharmaceutical, and synthetic dye industries, and world war in the twentieth century—encompasses all of European or capitalist culture:

Ourobouros encloses the world, rendering it "a closed thing, cyclical, resonant, eternally-returning" (412). The foregoing passage's attention to the intermediary role of clothes (and by extension a system of production they presuppose) in the conjoining of clauses and orifices underscores this generalization of the body-text to include its own material bases. Indeed, this inclusive movement underwrites Pynchon's critique of a capitalist system "whose only aim is to *violate* the Cycle. Taking and not giving back, demanding that 'productivity' and 'earnings' keep on increasing with time, the System removing from the rest of the World these vast quantities of energy to keep its own tiny desperate fraction showing a profit" (412).

To grasp this critique of capitalism, one must also grasp the "closed" or self-enclosing system of its language as exemplary of both the Cycle *and* its violation, as a medium (or a delirium) that unites person and world, culture and nature, in a single textual complicity. If the circularity of this passage suggests the idea of a vicious circle and thus Western culture's descent into solipsism, disconnection, and madness, it also plays with and against that circle by ubiquitously highlighting its own connectedness. In a strangely literal fashion, the passage is also about interlocking networks and "closed things." It presents a machinic circuit of flows (semen, the beads of blood) and breaks (the plugging of oral, genital, and anal orifices) that does not simply reflect solipsism, disconnection, and madness; it also exacerbates them, inverts and redoubles them in a process that short-circuits any figurative recuperation of moral perspective. In this way, the passage induces in its midst the preterite body, or what amounts to the same thing, the inversely double circle charged with supplementarity—thus the *two* waiters and the *twin* girls, the double implication in the passage, the reference to a repetition that galvanizes language and transforms it into a performative critique.

The uroboric figure exemplified in the quotation thus deconstructs (in circumscribing) the "World." Nature works like a DNA code, suggests Pynchon, permutatively and genetically, not like an unbounded system with virtually unlimited stores of energy. The irony is that in *Gravity's Rainbow*, the capitalist or technocrat realizes this fact sooner than anybody else. The historical significance of the chemist Von Kekulé's benzene ring, for instance, lies in the consequent discovery that man can synthesize molecules out of the "debris of the given" (413), that is, out of coal tar, the "preterite dung," which leads to the development of artificial chemicals, drugs, plastics, and their markets. The "System" understands the "closed thing" of nature both as an absolute external limit to its own addictive consumption of energy (therefore as something to be exorcised) and as a relative internal limit where fresh possibilities for expansion and exploitation arise. Pynchon constructs this schizophrenic dynamic of exorcism and co-optation, this oscillation between the two limits, to show how decisively it impinges on modern life. The power of synthetic replication and polymerization (which Pynchon implies needed the "energy burst of war" for its development) heralds a properly postindustrial order of production and consumption as well as a new form of social engineering, the creation of a synthetic body, a polymerized subjectivity.[21] The stunning complexity of this argument in the narrative stems from its basic premise that the power of synthesis is in itself a result of nature, even if it means nature's ultimate destruction: antinature and nature, in other words, meet as two ends of a single line bent into a circle. Thus the distinction between nature and artifice ceases to be relevant to Pynchon's text and indeed takes on there the ideologically suspect function of mystifying nature for those subject to the System, obscuring the actual dimension in which social repression takes place. Life in *Gravity's Rainbow* is not "natural" but plastic, ductile, malleable, adaptable, organic but also inorganic, decomposing but also resistant to the cycle of life and death. To say that reduction to a "plastic" life (artificial, abstract, meaningless, repetitious) constitutes social repression in the novel is to miss the degree to which the System in the process of this reduction manipulates the plasticity inherent to life, a polymeric death drive that always turns on or against itself. To turn against this death drive in the name of the liberation of life, energy, or desire is also to turn against nature in its identity with artifice, on behalf of a false or cinematic equivalent whose role is to apply (in its "apparent objective movement") a social axiomatic and persuade one to an active investment in the repressive structure.

Hence the importance for Pynchon of writing as a "double simulacrum" making manifest the miraculation of the capitalist system precisely in its claims on nature and in its comprehension of the "real." He writes the way he does to retrieve from a "plastic" life the plastic power capable of transforming it. He writes to retrieve the capacities of desiring-production from a desire that can only acquiesce to the System, accommodate itself to its insanity, addict itself to its addiction to energy—a desire, in short, that is Oedipal in nature. By recording nature's power of artifice in all its violence, Pynchon renders the "turn" in language whereby plastic becomes "plastic" and sets the docile body flowing. It is therefore never really a question (for parody) of colluding in or celebrating capitalism (complicity in an "exclusive" or, one could say, "elect" sense) so much as indexing in its ductile or docile body the degree of deterritorialization necessary to fissure it, to open in it the inclusive disjunction that makes it a body without organs. Without this fissure and without the parodic deformation of language that Pynchon uses to make the text's relation to discourse double, one could not even read the act of violence perpetrated on that body. Its docility would, in fact, be transparent or coextensive with the real: it would simply be how things are, natural, objectively "given," Oedipalized. This is the principal social fact the novel allegorizes in the *Anubis* voyage, since the characters engaged in the orgy scene collectively exemplify the docile body: decoded, objectified, plugged in to the sexual machine as a parody of nature, they actively invest their own mechanization or polymerization, and they never experience their own inhumanity more than in the moment of orgasm. Sexual desire consummates their repression, completes their metamorphosis into a reified mechanism or plastic (which the passage exemplifies), and displaces them into the co-opting time of a reterritorialization, the seemingly infinite expansion at the capitalist machine's internal limit, which finds its analogue in the endlessness and repetition of the *Anubis* voyage itself. But once again the voyage also enacts a retreat to the body without organs; it orients itself toward the absolute limit and sets the sexual machine, circuit, or circle spinning. Sense and form begin to unravel, decomposing the text. When what transpires on the *Anubis* becomes so improbable as not only to strain belief but to defy it, the text is forcing an impasse or breakdown on the reader that draws him or her close to an "inclusive" complicity, to a limit of discourse that either repulses or fascinates, but never quite leaves one cold.

The Scattering of Tyrone Slothrop

One of the most repulsive absurdities presented in the novel is the romantic relationship between Bianca and Slothrop that develops on the *Anubis* after the orgy. Although hardly on a scale to compete with other showcased perversions (coprophilia with Brigadier Pudding and Katje comes to mind in this regard), its sentimentality cloys all the more in that it sets up one primary motive (Slothrop's "Eurydice-obsession" [472]) for the narrative as a whole, particularly in relation to the "scattering" of the novel and to the theme of care. Bianca as a kind of principle of femininity and innocence interpellates the orgy; her sadistic punishment is its occasion and the cause not only of the text's fascism but of its critique of fascism as well. As a version of Lolita, however, Bianca lacks any realism and appears only as a caricature. When Bianca and Slothrop make love two pages after the orgy in an intricately rendered pornographic scene, the ensuing moment of tenderness between them strikes a decidedly off-key note. Both appear to experience a more authentic emotion in the midst of the *Anubis* madness, and as with all such moments in the novel (Pökler with Ilse at Zwolfkinder, for example), the first impulse is toward escape.

> They have been holding each other. She's been talking about hiding out.
> "Sure [says Slothrop]. But we'll have to get off [the *Anubis*] sometime, Swinemunde, someplace."
> "No. We can get away. I'm a child, I know how to hide. I can hide you too."
> He knows she can. He knows. Right here, right now, under the makeup and the fancy underwear, she *exists*, love, invisibility. . . . For Slothrop this is some discovery. (470)

Slothrop's discovery marks an interface between a fantasmatic desire and a more genuine equivalent defined in terms of its concealment, its refusal of any positive determination in the real. But it is clear by the context that this refusal also envelops the moment of discovery and its determination of love as concealment. The escape entertained at the level of content becomes absurd at the level of expression, a parody reducing escape to an escapism that enmeshes affect in its overdetermined web. The possibility of flight exists not for Bianca or Slothrop but for the text, and for the reader to track this possibility, he or she must read it *through* the absurdity and even depravity of the text's antiseriousness, *through* the feeling of repulsion it induces, without projecting back on the characters and scenarios a narrative coherence they do not possess. Seen in this light, the story of Bianca and Slothrop becomes an obscene fable of the text's abyssal structure that immediately begins to disintegrate, and this disintegration spreads through the networks of the narrative to decode Slothrop's desire for self-knowledge and the ending of the novel as well. Pynchon pushes this obscenity so far it begins to fragment in the movement of auto-critique or self-parody that comes more and more to *nauseate* the novel (like Slothrop at Bianca's rendition of Shirley Temple), to force a vomitory expulsion of (or as) the textual body in an attempt to make the latter as indigestible or unconsumable as possible. The gradual abandonment of temporal continuity that Pynchon stages through the introduction of anachronisms and proleptic references to the time of writing could be said to signal this movement of double fragmentation and disgust. It actualizes the novel's ambition to be a fragmentary whole, to produce and thereby elude its own determination by a capitalist System that works by commodifying everything. This formal preoccupation with escape (as emetic) finds its thematic double in Slothrop, whose slow scattering into textual immanence symbolizes an ambivalence about the text's own schizophrenia, its attempt to "define escape" for itself.

The symptomatic presence of this ambivalence is felt immediately in the text's recoil from its affective display in the previous quote. The moment of discovery passes into self-consciousness and deflects Slothrop into an exaggerated affectation that conceals a restless incapacity for "coming back," staying behind, or taking the time to care. "When he disentangles himself, it is extravagantly. He creates a bureaucracy of departure, inoculations against forgetting, exit visas stamped with love-bites . . . but coming back is something he's already forgotten about" (470–71). The prose modulates noticeably here from the clipped diction of the previous passage to a rhythmic sophistication that again jars with the absurd context, rendering that rhythm affected even as it seduces the reader to its affective sophistication. Pynchon thus performs the moment of loss in order to turn both content and expression into the single movement of disintegration as a forgetting how to love. This movement is construed by the text as a desire for escape that by itself delivers Slothrop and the text to a requisite acquiescence to repressive power. Bianca is the victim of this acquiescence; her invisibility, her ability to hide, her innocence as withdrawal suffers from the schizophrenic decoding of subjectivity that deflects Slothrop and the text into the docile spaces of imaginary escape. The following complexly nostalgic passage sums up this historical consciousness of Slothrop's dehumanization:

> [Bianca's] look now—this deepening arrest—has already broken Slothrop's seeing heart: has broken and broken, that same look swung as he drove by, thrust away into twilights of moss and crumbling colony, of skinny clouded-cylinder gas pumps, of tin Moxie signs gentian and bittersweet as the taste they were there to hustle on the weathered sides of barns, looked for how many Last Times up in the rearview mirror, all of them too far inside metal and combustion, allowing the day's targets more reality than anything that might come up by surprise, by Murphy's Law, where the salvation could be. . . . Lost, again and again, past poor dambusted and drowned Becket, up and down the rut-brown slopes, the hayrakes rusting in the afternoon, the sky purple-gray, dark as chewed gum, the mist starting to make white dashes in the air, aimed earthward

a quarter, a half inch . . . she looked at him once, of course he still remembers, from down at the end of a lunchwagon counter, grill smoke working onto the windows patient as shoe grease against the rain for the plaid, hunched-up leaky handful inside, off the jukebox a quick twinkle in the bleat of a trombone, a reed section, planting swing notes precisely into the groove between silent midpoint and the next beat, jumping it *pah* (hm) *pah* (hm) *pah* so exactly in the groove that you knew it was ahead but *felt* it was behind, both of you, at both ends of the counter, could feel it, feel your age delivered into a new kind of time, that may have allowed you to miss the rest, the graceless expectations of old men who watched, in bifocal and mucus indifference, watched you lindy-hop into the pit by millions, as many millions as necessary. . . . Of course Slothrop lost her, and kept losing her—it was an American requirement—. (471–72)

Pynchon's riff on the loss of innocence experienced by a whole generation of Americans in the wake of world war reads something like a jazz solo or bluegrass breakdown, and its very musicality stresses the way what he writes about bears on how he writes it. The "new kind of time" inaugurated by technological advancement (jukeboxes, automobiles), capitalism ("tin Moxie signs gentian and bittersweet as the taste they were there to hustle"), and war inverts a causal series in the attempt to recollect an event of loss whose temporal dimension cannot be fixed. Nostalgia loses itself in simulacral time, forgets its origin in the retrospective desire to fix an origin, and displaces Slothrop from the historical flow at the same time it pitilessly subjects him to it. But this nostalgia is not simple, at least in relation to the simulacrum of Pynchon's novel, since it dissimulates in its lyricism and detail a feeling not only for a particular past or lost time but for the mutation happening to time itself. *Gravity's Rainbow* feels this mutation musically; it "plays" time in order both to show its production by social forces and to specify in its movement a preterite turn, a desiring-machine (suggested by the contingency of a Murphy's Law, "where the salvation could be"). That this turn has no other "place" than the nostalgia it turns against only signifies the presence of *two texts* and their parodic relation, a detachment or dislocation within language that constitutes its preterition, its "lost time." Music in the passage leads people lindy-hopping into the pit and puts them in contact with a simulacrum; it gives the historical conditions in which escape has to be thought differently, in a different "deconstructive" time, according to principles that Pynchon exemplifies in the novel itself (think in this regard of the novel's propensity for bursting into parodic song). In this way, the critical countermovement of the text becomes clear and provides the register at which, for instance, its analysis of male desire unfolds precisely in Slothrop's incapacity for coming back or caring, an incapacity that both enacts the negation of the feminine and stages a historical "feeling" for the terrible violence it entails for women and for men. This is why both Slothrop and the woman he sees at the lunch counter together experience their "deliverance" into "a new kind of time."

The "American requirement" of a perpetual loss of innocence (or Bianca's sacrifice) can thus be seen through an ironic twist to mandate loss or sacrifice in itself, which is, Pynchon implies, *what one must escape*, the sacrificial core of an axiomatized desire. This is why Slothrop's escapism encodes a repression of Bianca's hiding; it withdraws from this withdrawal, it forgets this forgetting, and as such becomes aware of its own limits, its own affectation, and through this awareness becomes critical or "goes critical," pushing itself into the deterritorializations that make its "real flight" possible. It is not so much a question here of a constituted difference between escapism and escape. The line of flight Pynchon draws between autism on the one hand and radical fantasy or desiring-production on the other forms an inclusive boundary in the text, and its oscillation between "coming back" and drifting off engenders its schizophrenic form.

This oscillation comes to a kind of focus, as already intimated, in Slothrop, whose scattering begins when he loses Bianca on the *Anubis*. Pynchon punctuates this loss by abruptly dumping him into the Baltic Sea. The sudden shift of venue helps to extend the novel's haphazard narrative form. It also catalyzes Slothrop's subsequent progress through the Zone under the alias of Max Schliepzig (Greta Erdmann's leading man in *Alpdrucken*), in the Rocketman getout, as the comic book parody Plasticman, and as the tenth-century Pig-Hero Plechazunga, deepening his historical overdetermination in surprisingly literal fashion. Slothrop's desire to solve the mystery of his sexual connection to the aromatic plastic Imipolex-G, the Schwarzgerat, and the Rocket (his conditioning as an infant by Dr. Jamf permitted by his parents in exchange for his eventual full-ride scholarship to Harvard) loses itself in the bewildering textuality into which he "drifts." Even though the subtext for his journey is the discovery of his actual relation to history (world war, capitalism, industrialization, and the American experience of transplantation from Europe to the New World), the sense of its significance diminishes in the awareness of its infinitely regressing contexts, the counterintuition that the quest structure has been encased in an abyss of vertiginous "conditioning."

The search for the truth of history cannot take place outside the history whose truth one seeks, which is the "truth" Slothrop comes to represent for the novel in general. Not only are his initial escape from the Casino Herman Goering and his later adventures in the Zone staged (by British operatives Sir Marcus Scammony and Clive Mossmoon), but so is his desire in its relation to language: he is "seeker and sought," the text informs us, but also "baited and bait" (490). Slothrop's paranoia consists not only in apprehending his manipulation by Pointsman, Jamf, his parents, and capitalists like Lyle Bland (an American Mason-mystic whose hand can be inferred, if not proven, everywhere in the "plot" against him) but by Pynchon himself as the text's master manipulator. Almost every reference to Slothrop's scattering—to the "flying element" in his character, to his "drifter's spirit" (572), to all his "impersonations of flight" (573)—connotes a textual framework, a "randomness [as] deliberately simulated" as the pinball machines eulogized by Pynchon for the "faith in Malfunction" they inspire (586). The broken machine they indicate in Gravity's Rainbow constitutes one of the novel's first conspicuous subversions of narrative unity: Pynchon places a warehouse full of broken electric pinball machines in Mouthorgan, Missouri, circa 1930, eight years before electric pinball machines were first invented, and makes reference by name to several pinball aficionados in Oyster Bay, Long Island (where Pynchon went to high school), two Seattle suburbs (where he worked for Boeing in the early 1960s), and Inglewood, California (where he was living by 1965).[22]

This intrusion of the author or of the author's time into the narrative underscores the text's consciousness of its own implication in the historical forces it re-creates. Gravity's Rainbow conditions Slothrop to seek the Schwarzgerat (and the consequent incapacity for care or love) by way of trapping an axiomatized desire he both stands for and undermines. His entrapment, his use by Pynchon, has this ulterior motive of trapping the axiomatic trap that links the novel to the problem it also wants to critique. Slothrop's quest for truth becomes a mode of self-parody from the moment one understands the question of structure to be the question of history itself, inaugurating a discursive time that is not causal but simultaneous, overlaid or laminated, schizoid. To designate history as text, as writing, as a broken machine puncturing the illusion of temporal continuity, is to parallel the discontinuous movement of the history Pynchon tries to write: the event of temporal mutation that conceals or seals social repression in an information system capable of modulation in its entropy "indexes," a paranoid structure in which meaning diminishes as correspondences multiply. Slothrop traverses such a paranoid structure and sustains on his person this multiplication and this diminishment of meaning as the mark of his control by forces conducted through characters such as Bland (he submits Slothrop as a child to Laszlo Jamf's behaviorist experiments and so initiates the series of manipulations that will bring him to his vanishing point in the Zone), who has a strange authority to speak for the novel. The plot against Slothrop (or rather the plot in which he finds himself) occurs as a degradation of information that ensures the search for (a particular) truth will be a futile one, and indeed it exacerbates his domination (his emplotment) the more he paranoiacally invests it with meaning. In this way, Pynchon attempts to analyze a mode of social control that consists in a structuration of linguistic spaces (the Zone) that reciprocally structure the structurer. Such reciprocity in turn suggests the structure of *Gravity's Rainbow*, its self-implication in a history that, for example, equates the search for meaning with the extraction of coal from the earth and the synthesizing of molecules to make the plastics that come paradoxically to signify the decoding of truth. Slothrop is, as it were, synthetically produced to represent this preterition both as the substance used or extracted and as the actual extraction of substance from the density of the text. Unlike Bland, who, on dying, ascends to heights of spiritual perspective denied his preterite brethren, Slothrop is condemned to the universal force of a "Gravity" that compels him to search for his own truth while at the same time rendering that search irrelevant.

> The rest of us, not chosen for enlightenment [like Bland], left on the outside of the Earth, at the mercy of a Gravity we have only begun to learn how to detect and measure, must go on blundering inside our front-brain faith in Kute Korrespondences, hoping that for each psisynthetic taken from the Earth's soul there is a molecule, secular, more or less ordinary and named, over here—kicking endlessly among the plastic trivia, finding in each Deeper Significance and trying to string them all together like terms in a power series, to zero in on the tremendous and secret function whose name, like the permuted names of God, cannot be spoken . . . plastic saxophone reeds *sounds of unnatural timber*, shampoo bottle *ego-image*, Cracker Jack prize *fairing for winds of cognition*, baby bottles *tranquillization*, meat packages *disguises of slaughter*, drycleaning bags *infant strangulation*, garden hoses *feeding endlessly the desert* . . . but to bring them together, in their slick persistence and our preterition . . . to make sense out of, to find the meanest sharp sliver of truth in so much replication, so much waste. (590)

To extract a "Deeper Significance" from the consumer objects listed here entails a centripetal pull toward or into the inanimate, a "zeroing in" conditioned by the power of gravity that holds "us" and holds the novel in place. "We" (along with Slothrop) are consigned to an impossible search for truth that yields no result not emptied of substance in the face of "so much replication, so much waste." Pynchon thus constructs desire in relation to a transcendental signifier that expresses the commodity form of subjectivity itself, a desire reified by use, used up as waste, made "preterite" in the hankering after "Kute Korrespondences" that only perfects the mechanisms of social repression. The state of being implied in the term "preterition" thus governs the desire for synthesis, control, and structure; its condition is gravity not only as a physical force but as a death drive that turns against itself in a complex uroboric movement that *Gravity's Rainbow*, through Slothrop as a kind of lightning rod, conducts and channels toward a point of precise detonation in the text, an internal sabotage that becomes its mode of escape.

This is why implication as a theme comes more and more expressly to obsess the novel as it moves toward its conclusion. If gravity is figured as an ultimate constraint or ground for history, as that death or negation against which life struggles but also that suffuses life itself in its material forms, then any possibility of escape, resistance, or counterforce must come to grips with this ultimate ground as a means of ensuring its authenticity. Pynchon poses this problem in his construction of the Counterforce, a political movement galvanized around Slothrop's disappearance in the Zone and composed of characters whose collaboration in Slothrop's emplotment and ambiguous scattering spurs them to a renewed spirit of activism and responsibility. Slothrop becomes a cause, a rallying point, a lightning rod, in fact, the reason and ground for action, and as such he immediately calls into question the forgetting that this reifying use presupposes. Pynchon thematizes the difficulty of protest or social movement in an instrumentalizing world of such complexity that it presents no reference point against which or in the name of which to mobilize. Even the injustices visited on Slothrop are finally insufficient as provocation to hold the movement together; what could hold it together is literally an equal and opposite reaction that comes more and more to look like co-optation by the social order whose transformation it seeks. *Gravity's Rainbow* parodies in the Counterforce a politics that, even when it is self-reflexive about its own principles and clear about the nature of "structure" in a postmodern world, fails to overcome the co-opting forces that beset it, a failure signaled most notably in the way Slothrop is used as a figurehead or symbol (" 'We were never that concerned with Slothrop *qua* Slothrop,' a spokesman for the Counterforce admitted recently in an interview with the Wall Street Journal" [738]). This parody is what troubles and finally undermines any reading that elevates the political program of "creative paranoia" articulated by Counterforce leaders to describe the program of the text itself, which, if it can be called a program at all, appears only in the deployment of that parody. If Pirate Prentice's theory about using "We-structures" against "They-structures" sounds like more of the same to Roger Mexico (638), not a political response so much as a political capitulation, it is less because Prentice is wrong or right and more because the text's politics can be determined not at the level of content, where a radical uncertainty prevails, but at the level of expression, where that uncertainty becomes a political strategy, a form of deconstructive parody in which the novel's preterition perfects itself.

The theme of implication reveals its inclusive or invaginated boundary when the novel is seen as its exemplar. In this light, the failure of *Gravity's Rainbow* to articulate for the Counterforce a coherent politics not co-opted by a capitalist machine becomes symptomatic of a more primary political process at work, a concerted antiseriousness that unfolds in relation to a negativity foreclosing the real itself (herein lies the novel's countercultural desire). Because of this, even Blicero, as the most patently evil character in the whole book, cannot find his judge in another character and signifies no less an object of hate than of desire, a figure of strange destiny for Western humanity. Here Thanatz, present on the Luneberg Heath at the time of the last rocket firing, recalls Blicero as he catches his

> own reflection in the oval mirror, an old face—he is about to don a wig, a Dragon Lady pageboy with bangs, and he pauses, looking in, face asking what? what did you say? wig held to the side and slightly lower so as to be another face in heavy wig-shadows nearly invisible . . . but looking closer you can see bone-ridges and fat-fields begin to emerge now, an ice glaze white bobbing, a mask hand-held, over the shadows in the hollow hoodspace—*two faces* looking back now, and Thanatz, are you going to judge this man? Thanatz, haven't you loved the whip? Haven't you longed for the brush and sigh of ladies' clothes? Haven't you wanted to murder a child you loved, joyfully kill something so helpless and innocent? As he looks up at you, at the last possible minute, trusting you, and smiles, purses his lips to make a kiss just as the blow falls across his skull . . . isn't that best of all? the cry that breaks in your chest then, the sudden, solid arrival of loss, loss forever, the irreversible end of love, of hope . . . no denying what you finally are . . . (670–71)

The common ground that the text finds with Blicero before his mirror, confronted by the brute fact of repetition, fleeing (but also compounding) its suggestion of senselessness in masquerade and transvestic perversion, seems extraordinary given that Blicero is a Nazi, raving paranoiac despot, and child killer all rolled up into one. When the narrator interrogates Thanatz, moreover, and expresses the idea of complicity in such emphatic language (at least to Thanatz), Pynchon seems to warrant a reading of his own novel that leaves no room for "love" or "hope." But as I have tried to show, such a reading makes sense in an Oedipal framework, and *Gravity's Rainbow* presents that framework only via its parodic quotation. The sexualization of the murder of innocence provides the clue to an alternate interpretation by articulating the desire of or for repression in terms that stress its investment in "loss" as a "solid" object or thing, and thus as the fetishizable category of a theory of desire in itself part of the repressive structure. To kill innocence, love, or hope is to reify loss and *require* its appearance in the world. It is thus not the tragedy of loss (with its recuperative possibility) that Pynchon stages in *Gravity's Rainbow* but the loss of loss itself, its parodic duplication in a multileveled or polymeric discursive structure. The version of desire put forth earlier resumes the analysis sustained in the dyads Slothrop-Bianca, Greta-Bianca, Pökler-Ilse, Blicero-Gottfried, recapitulating its themes of ironic reprehension, detumescent incest, Gnostic depravity, and nausea in the process of "making" its escape. This escape dissimulates itself in the text yet also finds itself curiously foregrounded there: it appears in the comic name Thanatz, in Blicero's desire to be a woman, in the trope of doubleness, in the same repetition that Blicero's masquerade attempts to deny. Desire can be said to turn against this constructed escape, this doubleness that exposes as its substrate an origin in which no origin is present, and which constitutes the proper object of the murderous aim. Innocence suffers death in its determination as lost, and it is this suffering that Pynchon feels through the elliptical medium of his novel—this, indeed, that opens the space for love and hope to emerge again, and grounds the novel's abhorrence and condemnation of Blicero as the ultimate annihilator of desire.

In spite of the careful ambiguity that Pynchon fosters to foreclose any recuperation of moral capital (or moral return) by the reader, judgment does take place in *Gravity's Rainbow*. It happens in the dimension of parodic articulation where this foreclosure indexes the possibility of moral critique. Blicero is the Father who carries "the virus of Death" (723) afflicting Western culture, the carrier of the Oedipal law in all its secret insanity and paranoid terror. He signifies its particular form of negation, its intrinsically castrative essence, its vampiric love for the son, Gottfried, whose innocence cannot survive its "beautiful dying." "Fathers are carriers of the virus of Death," says Blicero, "and sons are the infected . . . and, so that the infection may be more certain, Death in its ingenuity has contrived to make the father and son beautiful to each other, as Life has made male and female . . . oh Gottfried of course yes you are beautiful to me but I'm dying . . . I want to get through it as honestly as I can, and your immortality rips at my heart—can't you see why I might want to destroy that, oh that *stupid clarity* in your eyes" (723).

In destroying that "divine light" in Gottfried's eyes, Blicero ensures the redemption of his own mortality. Gottfried must die for death to be "honestly gotten through," and this entails a sublimation of his "immortality," its necessary sacrifice *and* conservation (or apotheosis) within a kind of dialectical sublation. This is what Blicero means by "Modern Analysis," the "special Death the West had invented," which he explicates for Gottfried with a strange cogency and insight. Blicero is the Western mind in its discursivity, its "whitening" desire, indeed its "whitening" of the world, its fascination with edges, with limits (frames and grounds), with frontiers, with the "impulse to empire." (This might be why the woman Blicero wants to impersonate in Thanatz's memory is a "Dragon Lady" with "pageboy bangs," by implication an Orientalist stereotype.) The imperialist drive for conquest at the edge is what Blicero's final madness plays out for the reader. He calls this drive a desire for "return" to "savage innocences" and in fact sees its last chance for satisfaction squandered in the experience of Europe's colonization of America.

> America *was* the edge of the World. A message from Europe, continent-sized, inescapable. Europe had found the site for its Kingdom of Death, that special Death the West had invented. Savages had their waste regions, Kalahari's, lakes so misty they could not see the other side. But Europe had gone deeper—into obsession, addiction, away from all the savage innocences. America was a gift from the invisible powers, a way of returning. But Europe refused it. (722)

The "gift" of America to Europe consists for Blicero not simply of its virgin nature, its whiteness, but of an existence more authentic than "obsession" and "addiction." This critical detachment from European perversion on Blicero's part introduces an imperfection in the pattern, the moire, that Pynchon is trying to sustain through the troubling suggestion that Blicero speaks for the text itself, and even voices, at least in part, its critique of imperialism. This tonal equivocation hinges on the meaning of "return." Blicero's version of colonialism delimits "a way of returning" to the earth *as a* closed system governed by gravity. The "Kingdom of Death" that Europe had the chance to establish in America differs from this version insofar as it refuses "return" and its proper "gravitational" relation to the earth. America becomes the site of an abstraction from the earth that Blicero in effect critiques by arguing *for* a Kingdom of Death that does not go too far or too "deep," a restrained imperialism that stops at the determination of otherness as savage and innocent. The salient irony of Blicero's desire, beyond the fact that it kills its ostensible object, is that this murder happens in the name of a transgression *against* the rationalizing abstractions of European culture, tradition, history, and language. What he wants is escape from the very conditions determining his desire for escape, a territoriality within the medium of culture where he can play out *fantasies* of empire.

This desire, this gravity, this scene of fantasy, finds itself threatened by the new dispensation of an "American Death" where mere "structure" replaces the "great rainbow plumes, [the] fittings of gold, [the] epic marches over alkali seas" that characterized the glory days of imperialism (272). Blicero sets up an opposition between "white" structure and "rainbow-colored" fantasy as though the latter were not derived from the former, as though whiteness did not contain all color. The opposition breaks down, then, when it becomes clear that the "American Death" only represents a logical conclusion to Blicero's desire: less an escape from gravity than a recoil from its "presence" on earth that raises the Kingdom of Death to a new level of technological sophistication. "I dream of a great glass sphere," he tells Gottfried, "hollow and very high and far away . . . the colonists have learned to do without air, it's vacuum inside and out . . . it's understood that man won't ever return . . . they are all men. There are ways for getting back, but so complicated, so at the mercy of language, that presence back on Earth is only temporary and never 'real' . . . passages out there are so dangerous, chances of falling so shining and deep. . . . Gravity rules all the way to the cold sphere, *there is always the danger of falling*" (722–23).

The completely controlled environment of the glass sphere is also the space of a seeming freedom from Blicero's earth, gravity, and time. As such it means *not* intellectual abstractness as the opposite of a grounded "presence" but that (fantasmatic) presence as the deepest tendency of intellectual abstractness, its enabling presumption as the mode of being that understands its dialecticized consciousness to be self-evident, the real and actual copula of experience that needs no theory, only the practice of a "savage innocence." Gravity here is understood as universal, uniting the concept of "return" and the "glass sphere" in the movement of a single death drive that proceeds by uroborically turning back on or against itself. This is why Blicero's condemnation of the "American Death" strikes such a tonally strange, uncanny note in the narrative, ironically foregrounding the formal emptiness of his dissent, or the extent to which the fear of gravity, of "falling," is only the obverse of Blicero's fear of technology (the glass sphere as a sort of space station). The deconstruction of presence undertaken by Pynchon emerges once this emptiness is properly heard, once the text becomes a parody of authorial intention in general, and once its critical countervalence manifests itself in, for instance, the resonance between Blicero's glass sphere and Ilse Pökler's house on the moon. Blicero, now situated in her same perverse territoriality, broaches for the novel once again the issue of fantasy in its double implication, at its internal margin, as the modality of the real that also underwrites its critique. Parody dissimulates in a fantasmatic content a more primary power of fantasy that backs itself up to include or invest the socius itself, a delirium that parallels and envelops Blicero's final madness: the firing of the 00000 on the Luneberg Heath.

The novel's implication in the violence of Western culture thus given appears through the travesty of all Blicero stands for, and it is only in the travesty that Pynchon links him symbolically to Western rationality. Blicero's nostalgia for a "savage," pretechnological time underlies the violent use to which technology is put, its turning back on that very origin as an energy source to be consumed. This circular movement is Pynchon's formula for imperialist and capitalist violence, and *Gravity's Rainbow* is obsessed with its extreme self-destructiveness; at the same time, the novel attempts to stage the moment in which that force of self-destruction turns even on itself, becomes double, consumes consumption, opens up the tautological circle (of presence, of truth) in which the formula makes itself "real." One can observe this peculiar obsession in Slothrop's final scattering, where he "reads paraphrases of himself" in everything he sees and hallucinates the Rocket in every "cross, swastika, Zone-mandala," windmill, or "four-fold structure"—all of which, spun, make a circle (625). Slothrop has reduced the world to a purely solipsistic reflection of his own decoded subjective states. He sees meaning in everything and nothing, spiraling down into complete dislocation and autism. But he also focuses on the same formulaic circle that constitutes the principle of that solipsism, and at some level he tries to grasp the nature of what oppresses him so deeply that it cannot be distinguished from himself: it *is* himself. Slothrop's scattering parallels the novel's withdrawal to the body without organs, its deterritorialization along the inclusive boundary between escapism and escape. This withdrawal, radically indeterminate with respect to either potentiality, registers the oscillation between absolute and relative limits, periphery and center, that characterizes delirium in the strict sense. Slothrop is delirious, apprehending himself within the historical context of manipulation and reification that determines his very being in its intentions, its motives, its objects, and its aims, which is why he finally "becomes a cross himself, a crossroads, a living intersection" (626), passing within the circularity of language, becoming textual, a nodal point in a network that menaces signification with entropy, a broken machine that holds together both his mechanization and his machinic desire. He ceases to "care" about his quest for meaning and becomes so aimless or docile that he loses himself and disappears.

The text could be said to approach here a kind of singularity, to converge toward an infinitely dense vanishing point. The almost pure ambiguity of the moment, anyway, points to a foreclosure of any one determination that signals the text's desire to free itself from the history, the violence, it represents precisely in its structuration of disappearance. The breakdown of narrative unity at the end of the novel could be said to embody this involution as a kind of spinning or cracking up, a stringing out of the addicted text, an emetic production of its internal contents, its discourses, all the things it seems to know (such as what it's like to take off in the nose of a rocket). In this way, Pynchon "breaks" his machine, although in doing so what he establishes is only another mode of production, its deliberate simulation of randomness, a simulation that finds its parodic reflection in the Raketen-Stadt that generates itself at the end of the novel. The escape that the novel seeks occurs in this sabotage that the repressive socius co-opts yet cannot contain. It cannot contain it because escape is here not a thematized movement away from the text but a re-turn to it, an inversely double turn within its hermeneutic circle, a turning against (or an insult to) its own desire for structure that precipitates in its midst a redoubled breakdown prefiguring the "end" of the end (as aim or goal), the "end" of the novel itself (i.e., the explosion of the Rocket and of its structuring function).

Yet another figure for this "turn" is the "stout rainbow cock" that appears over Slothrop at the moment he "becomes a crossroads." As the Rocket in its parabolic trajectory, as the uroboric circle of a self-enclosing earth, as the illusoriness of escapist desire, as the tension between no color (white) and all color (the "rainbow plumes" of Blicero's imperialism), as the perverse territoriality of the preterite who loses loss itself, this rainbow recapitulates the line of flight I have attempted to trace. It is one figural site for the novel's staging of the "struggle" between world and earth as emblematic of the only origin it will recognize: that which apprehends its own nonorigin in the trace that constitutes it. In Heidegger's words, "The earth cannot dispense with the . . . world if it itself is to appear as earth in the liberated surge of its self-seclusion. The world . . . cannot soar out of the earth's sight if, as the governing breadth and path of all essential destiny, it is to ground itself on a resolute foundation" ("Origin of the Work of Art," 49). The foundation of the world, of history, is the "liberated surge" of the earth's "self-seclusion" (or self-enclosedness), its refusal to appear as the mode of its appearance. In this, world and earth "belong" to each other; culture and nature belong to each other in the activity of desiring-production, in a text that presents its own exteriority as its "essence."

Perhaps it is this negative and differential diachrony that gives Slothrop's final disappearance its fullest meaning, particularly in light of the day it takes place: August 6, 1945, when an American plane dropped an atomic bomb on Hiroshima and helped to usher in a properly postwar political and social dispensation. When he "sees a very thick rainbow here, a stout rainbow cock driven down out of pubic clouds into Earth, green wet valleyed Earth . . . his chest fills and he stands crying, not a thing in his head, just feeling natural" (626). The nature, the simplicity that Slothrop feels at the crossroads, the node he forms in the novel and at the origin point of the postwar period, must be understood as a compound of all the historical forces he crystallizes, and so is only as simple as the novel itself is complex. This inverse proportion, however, in the context of a paradoxical dynamic of gravitational pull to the inanimate that approximates the arrested motion or "inner agitation" of the text in "repose," could also exemplify a mode of being, for literature at the very least, capable of achieving some kind of historical freedom. For Deleuze and Guattari, as for Pynchon, such a freedom must extend down to the molecular root or network of instrumentality, mechanism, and finally intention itself. Deleuze and Guattari quote Pierre Klossowski: "The day humans are able to behave as *intentionless phenomena*—for every intention at the level of the human being always obeys the laws of its conservation, its continued existence—on that day a new creature will declare the integrity of existence"

(*Anti-Oedipus*, 368). If it seems too much of a strain to see in Slothrop an avatar of this "new creature," this new "sexless man" reborn in parthenogenesis (to recall Deleuze's discussion of the masochist), it does not strain credulity to understand the novel in its constantly redoubling tropological space as an attempt to formalize the possibility of "intentionless phenomena." Indeed, only with this formalization, I think, can one properly see the analysis of the death instinct that takes place in the novel, without in the process doing violence to the schizophrenic imagination it so clearly manifests.

Slothrop, as the "intersection" of earth and world, matter and form, here comes to stand for the novel itself and its relation to a deterritorializing time. The condition for this postwar historical moment, according to Pynchon, is given by a death instinct that holds one to the earth and draws one toward its inanimate core, and there is no escape from this escape. But there is also more than a mere acquiescence to death (or self-preservation) that the Rocket signifies. If escape is still possible, it must define itself within the implicate orders given by the circle of language and the world, in relation to a horizon that, as much as it arraigns desire, also provokes desire as the capacity to turn the circle differently. Pynchon shows us this capacity in a text that occasions an encounter with the inanimate, the self-enclosing thing, an encounter with which the novel begins and ends. The 00000 Rocket, launched in 1945, falls at the end in some indeterminate future moment (when the novel is written, or when it is read?) on a movie theater whose walls are "hard and glossy as coal," and where those of us "who've always been at the movies" await the resumption of spectral imagery on the screen, in that immobile mobility of the spectator interrupted because "the film has broken, or a projector bulb has burned out" (760). This fantasmatic space, this enclosure in walls of coal, this reliance on broken machines, this descent of the Rocket that detonates us (across the time and space of a spectral postwar period) as it detonates the novel, all together constitute a singularly self-shattering transcendence. Thus *Gravity's Rainbow* is gravity's rainbow.

Singularity, Objective Irony, and *Gestell*

For universal causality, irony substitutes the fatal power of a singular object.
—Jean Baudrillard

Hanjo Berressem sees the novel's "interplay of *writing* and *film* at its most acute" in that last scene (*Pynchon's Poetics*, 198). The narration "includes both the reader and the text (book) itself in a virtual space that is neither textual nor 'real,' " and as such it engenders a specific double articulation that opens over the movie theater a "frightening possibility of 'perceiving perception' " itself, a perception of perception "running *below* experience" (198) or turning around that imperceptible and atemporal *origin of the origin* that I have attempted to track in the previous three chapters. This possibility depends on keeping firm in one's discourse to the virtual nature of any such double perception: no *one* perceives in this way, after all, which is to say its mode is displaced, preterite, machinic, metaparodic. It operates *from* a symbolic ground rather than through a subjective intention. This is why Berressem stresses the *suspension* of the Rocket, the way it does *not* detonate over the movie theater and so ramifies the paradoxical space of a "dispersed" and indeterminate grammatical "play" that always carries with it "threat and menace" (199). But the emphasis on textual play, even when the reticence of its signifying space is invested with absence and death, still risks a sublimation of the essential force that dwells in it and gives it a strange materiality. As scientist/writer Franz Pökler says of the delta t metaphor Pynchon uses to denote the Rocket's suspension, it is "just a convenience, so that [events] can happen" (159). In spite of the manifestly traumatic nature of the repetitions that run through Pynchon's novel, it does insist on the real stakes of technological power, events that *happen* by not happening. Thus my own willingness to detonate the Rocket and the novel underscores its attempt to realize the traumas that virtualize the narration, to evoke the concrete abstraction of its catastrop(h)ic time.[23]

The strangely exacerbated referentiality of the novel's language highlights one prominent and troubling aspect of Pynchon's poetics: his metaphoric use of science and mathematics not only in terms of technology or technical production but as necessity and physical law as well. One conspicuous instance of this is the designation of gravity as a death instinct. The metaphor implied here supposes that the latter borrows from the former its force as a law that cannot be contravened. As a result, Pynchon imports into a cultural space all the solidity and self-evidence of a "natural" fact. He does this, by strange design, as a way of calling into question the nature of "facts" in a spirit similar to Nietzsche's celebrated remark that "facts are stupid." Science in *Gravity's Rainbow* is also stupid, as evidenced in the parodies of the White Visitation, Pointsman, Dr. Jamf, and also Pökler. The scientist in capitalism, according to Deleuze and Guattari, "has no revolutionary potential; he is the first integrated agent of integration, a refuge for bad conscience, and the *forced* destroyer of his own creativity" (*Anti-Oedipus*, 236). The scientist marks in himself or herself the site of the capitalist machine's relative or internal limit, the place of reterritorialized expansion where the element of antiproduction (the body without organs) is "integrated" into its functional role of absorbing surplus value. Deleuze and Guattari's principal model at the level of the socius for this integrated antiproduction is the military-industrial complex, and the scientist used by the military is the symbol Pynchon seizes on to drive home the point that science is first and foremost cultural, subject to a logic not conformable to its causal empiricities.

That said, it is also true for Pynchon that science has presided over a deconstruction of causality that culture (with important exceptions) has been slow to understand, and this deconstruction informs his novel so materially that one cannot read it without also beginning to read this "quantum" shift in the history of science. The failure to read in this way, or the failure to see in science not merely its determination as technē but also how it premises a crisis in the metaphysical understanding of the human (that no mere reassertion of the difference between science and the human sciences can resolve), reproduces a blindness that works in the service of the reactionary capitalist forces outlined by Deleuze and Guattari. "Science," says Klossowski, whom they cite, "demonstrates by its very method that the *means* that it constantly elaborates do no more than reproduce . . . an interplay of forces by themselves *without aim or end* whose combinations obtain such and such a result" (*Anti-Oedipus*, 386). In science, on this account, "intentionless phenomena" are observed to be "natural" (for instance, at the quantum level, nonlocality or inseparability implies a noncausal connection between objects) and even immanent in its own method. They precipitate in its instrumentalized midst a limit to its own predictive powers of control, a frame within which science presents its objects, an "enframing" essence that "sets up" and "sets upon" a nonhuman reality that confirms and legitimates its own objectivity.[24] Especially for the hardest of sciences, modern physics, the object, and by extension matter itself, takes on an implicit or implicate nature with respect to the observer and registers within its very structure the synthesizing or informing activity of the scientist.[25] This theoretical activity, this physis as poiesis, exemplifies nature in its quiddity and makes man as scientist "natural" in the unexpected way intuited, for instance, by Spinoza, when he ventured the idea that consciousness might be a quality inherent to all matter.[26] What is real is the production of the real, an assertion the validity of which Deleuze and Guattari, at any rate, can extend down even to the networks of living tissue (conceived, it will be recalled, as interconnected machinic flows).

The proposition that science, the scientific method, even causality itself, might find its ground in a more primary "revealing," is symptomatic of a much more general crisis concerning the relation or distinction between science and the human sciences.[27] The problem of how to understand cultural or human activity without reference to an objective truth that hierarchically delimits and privileges the scientific relation to reality, or that, to paraphrase the philosopher Richard Rorty, holds out the possibility of a "non-perspectival" theory about the universe, arises only when science conceives of itself in mechanistic terms, or with respect only to the results that it is able to achieve. Indeed, the emphasis put here on making, on production, must be tempered by the distinction Heidegger draws between manufacture or "the using of means" (*The Question concerning Technology*, 13) and a "bringing-forth" that happens neither "beyond all human doing" nor in or through "man" (24). The constructivist fallacy, which consists in reducing all things to a measure of "man" itself determined by a technological or utilitarian order, conceals a dimension of historical implication (a "destining") that "claims" man by obscuring his relation to truth as "unconcealment."[28] That is, Heidegger articulates in his essay on technology two modes of poetic revealing, one of which, linked to causality and production, conceals its own essence as a revealing and cuts itself off from its origin in the other, more authentic "bringing-forth." This latter, more authentic activity cannot be viewed as production unless that category comes to register the peculiar historicity or temporality Heidegger associates with poiesis. "All coming to presence [or bringing-forth]," he writes, "keeps itself everywhere concealed to the last. Nevertheless, it remains . . . that which precedes all the earliest. . . . That which is primally early shows itself only ultimately to men" (22). This reversal of first and last things entails an inverse logic that informs every revealing (of the real): the product (which is brought forth, presented) also produces (brings forth, presences) itself, establishes itself as that *ek-sistent* condition in which the maker ("man") comes to understand himself as "man" (and as maker).

Deleuze and Guattari's notion of desiring-production, it is clear, bears the mark or mutation of this inverse time, and most pertinently in its emphasis on inscription, on a writing of the real that brings to the fore a primary fictiveness generating the subjects who generate it. *The fiction of desiring-production is precisely its genius*, and this does not change when Deleuze and Guattari make of it a theory of matter, couching it in a vocabulary borrowed from physics or biology. A similar textual dynamic governs Pynchon's metaphoric use of the scientific in *Gravity's Rainbow*. This is why the association of a death drive with the law of gravity says more about the pseudoscientific nature of the former than anything else, and also suggests how the troping of science can be seen strategically to play out the novel's critique of technology. When the death drive becomes for Pynchon as necessary as gravity, a deterritorialization not only of language but of necessity is set in motion, not by way of reducing one to the other so much as fracturing the code that differentiates science from nonscience, undoing both signifiers, breaking down and through the discursive or symbolic structure that defines things as pure presences that can be ordered, measured, organized, and substituted. To say that gravity is a death drive is *not* a metaphor any more than it is a fact, not this discursive structure reconstituted, but another structure whose constituent element is its own discontinuity, its own fissuring productions of the real and of the discursive. The novel's "intentionless" process functions to make its figures "real" in the sense of being "point-signs," "ultimate units of content and expression" that break down the ends and means of meaning. Gravity is a death drive (just as, for Deleuze and Guattari, desiring-production is a "real" activity) because only when the "reality" of this broken language is acknowledged can the deconstruction of technology (and discourse) properly take place.

Thus when Pynchon puts art and science together in *Gravity's Rainbow*, the result is a deterritorialization of a technological paradigm that amounts in effect to its disappearance (so Slothrop is able to feel "natural" at the moment of *his* disappearance, marking the ironic moment at which freedom from the technological becomes possible). Another analogue for this movement (Slothrop's disappearance *as* the disappearance of technology) is a singularity at the center of a gravitational field, a point of infinite density and curvature in space and time within the event horizon of which nothing is observable. The Rocket, or the tip of the Rocket, is the most obvious singularity for the novel, the "point" at which technological annihilation arrives, but also the "no-point" at which technology annihilates itself or exposes its own limit and frame. This double implication that the Rocket signifies also informs the novel's representations of pornographic sexuality:

> All Margherita's [Greta's] chains and fetters are chiming, black skirt furled back to her waist, stockings pulled up tight in classic cusps by the suspenders of the boned black rig she's wearing underneath. How the penises of Western man have leapt, for a century, to the sight of this singular point at the top of a lady's stocking, this transition from silk to

bare skin and suspender. It's easy for non-fetishists to sneer about Pavlovian conditioning and let it go at that, but any underwear enthusiast worth his unwholesome giggle can tell you there is much more here—there is a cosmology: of nodes and cusps and points of osculation, mathematical kisses . . . *singularities!* (396)

The use of a mathematical concept to describe the fetishist's experience of a woman's body here has the virtue of linking fetishism to a certain rationality and scientistic objectification. At the same time, the passage, by referring as it does to "Pavlovian conditioning," makes it clear that the metaphor of singularities cannot be thought in the same mechanistic way as Pavlov's stimulus-response experiments. The fetishist's singularity enfolds other and richer dimensions of significance and desire than the nonfetishist realizes. The figure opens up for the reader an "uncertainty" still linked to the scientistic and still given within a necessary and objective horizon. Indeed, the ambiguity of this particular kind of metaphor appeals to Pynchon more than any other. To resume the passage:

> Consider cathedral spires, holy minarets, the crunch of train wheels over the points as you watch peeling away the track you didn't take . . . mountain peaks rising sharply to heaven . . . the edges of steel razors, always holding potent mystery . . . rose thorns that prick us by surprise . . . even, according to the Russian mathematician Friedmann, the infinitely dense point from which the present universe expanded. . . . In each case, the change from point to no-point carries a luminosity and enigma at which something in us must leap and sing, or withdraw in fright. Watching the A-4 pointed at the sky—just before the last firing switch closes—watching that singular point at the very top of the Rocket, where the fuze is. . . . Do all these points imply, like the Rocket's, an annihilation? what is that, detonating in the sky above the cathedral? beneath the edge of the razor, under the rose? (396)

What the metaphor of singularity specifies in this series of examples is "mystery" or "enigma" in general: the impossibility of any ultimate answers or ends; and the presence of an absolute resistance to appearance or production (or presentation) that also makes production possible, that grounds it in a process of revealing the unrevealable (or that it is unrevealable). This truth as "unconcealment" governs the novel's linguistic universe, structuring its paradoxes and driving its broken machines, which is why the tip of the Rocket, "where the fuze is" (where the plastic Imipolex-G and the fairing for

Gottfried are as well), must also be a singularity, a point of such density and implication that it explodes (into) (as) the novel. The answer to the question whether "all these points imply . . . an annihilation" is that they do, only not every annihilation is the same or implies the same kind of destructiveness. Like the difference between escape and escapism elaborated earlier, or like the difference between schizophrenia at the absolute limit and at the relative limit of the capitalist machine, two orders of annihilation can be inferred "under the rose," two modes of "revealing" can be glimpsed in the Rocket's aleph. This doubleness is what Heidegger means by *danger*, the forgetting that threatens all revealing and that, in the case of technology, leaves man with no other recourse than to imagine himself in the orders of instrumentality that precede and surround him, *as an instrument in his essence*.

At stake in the figure of the Rocket is a subjectivity risking the loss of its connection to "revealing," which is to say to history or to the production of the real. Deleuze and Guattari's notion of desiring-production attempts to describe this endangered historical subjectivity, and to do this, they must displace (or parody) both desire and production (i.e., place them *beside* each other). Because the activity of making cannot be understood as constructivist without forgetting the very historical relation at issue, Deleuze and Guattari posit a subject who appears as a *residuum* or consummative "reward" (remainder, excess, jouissance) of the tripartite production process, however overlaid or implicate that process may in fact be. The production of recording, itself produced by the production of production, in turn engenders (on the recording or inscriptive surface) a kind of subject who only retroactively "consummates" desiring-production and only initiates this consummation to the extent that his or her subjectivity takes a fluid or nomadic form. It is a "strange subject" that appears in the production of consumption, they write, "with no fixed identity, wandering about over the body without organs, but always remaining peripheral to the desiring-machines, being defined by the share of the product it takes for itself, garnering here, there, and everywhere a reward in the form of a becoming or an avatar, being born of the states that it consumes and being reborn with each new state" (*Anti-Oedipus*, 16). The subject's peripherality to the desiring-machines (which occupy the center or nucleus of the self) guarantees a desire capable of modification through a limitless range of predicates. To pass through the series of metastable states is to affirm the becoming of desire at the expense of any consistent person or ego. The disjunctive or differential positions that the subject traverses are inclusive, related across a "distance" or abyss that ensures the *singularity of* each state and underscores the degree to which "passage" between them entails an alteration of the real itself. Thus the subject "is not simply bisexual, or between the two, or intersexual. He is transsexual. He is trans-alivedead, trans-parentchild. . . . He does not confine himself inside contradictions; on the contrary, he opens out and, like a spore case inflated with spores, releases them as so many singularities that . . . now become points-signs, all affirmed by their new distance" (77). The subject acts out a poiesis that defines being as singular points or points-signs, in the textual warp and woof of a writing that short-circuits signification (thus it is always "affirmative," not vacuolized by lack or "exclusive" in its differentiations).

This particular strategy for articulating the alternative to being's objectification is suggestive for *Gravity's Rainbow* as well. The Rocket is also a desiring-machine, a singular point at the center of consciousness that ensures the subject's singularity with respect to the symbolic structures that objectify him. The subject (of writing) in Pynchon's novel is this "stencilized" or "enframing" negative space around the Rocket, a point-sign to which the subject relates as that *danger* holding in it a "saving power" that, for Heidegger, presents itself as an unmasking not of technology but of the humanist subject that supports and legitimates it. "Technology," he writes, "makes the demand on us to think in another way what is usually understood by 'essence'" (*The Question concerning Technology*, 31). The essence of technology, Gestell, the forgetting of its own provenance in poiesis, undoes the fiction of a fixed and enduring self predicated on concepts of *essentia*, substance, and *eidos*. The Rocket stands for this undoing, and what's more, *without it this undoing could not happen*. As a made thing, a product, a machine, a figure, a fetish, it delivers man to "that which, of himself, he can neither invent nor in any way make" (31), even as he makes it. This "residual" truth that the Rocket secretes is, you might say, what every Rocket-obsessed character in *Gravity's Rainbow* is looking for or desires, one more dimension, context, or frame within which to situate the Rocket's attraction for Slothrop, for Pökler, for Enzian Oberst and the Zone-Hereros, and also for the novel itself with its flight-obsessed language.

The Rocket must be read not simply as a sign of alienation or dehumanization but also as deeply material to desire itself, the object of a cathexis that "saves" desire from its determination in a metaphysical order of the human, an order predicated on the forgetting of a primary poetic ground and thus on the *separation* of desire from any relation to history or to making.[29] By "human" what is meant here is the "individual" who causes or wills, and the individual's failure to recognize him- or herself in the machine as a mode of self-extension backed up to include the world or include Marx's "species-life." The Rocket is a sign for a creativity or imagination that is "inseparable" from a nonhuman reality, a reading that should in no way mitigate the equally valid claim that the Rocket figures our isolation from that species-life, our objectification by the symbolic structures of a late capitalist economic and social formation. It signifies a creative principle or a freedom in desire that is grounded in the approach to its own negation or limit (the body without organs), insisting through our actions and our productions as that which commits us to the world we make even as it makes us. This peculiar commitment informs Pynchon's novel from beginning to end; it is the sadness of a responsibility accented in his prose much like Enzian's detached and almost wistful feeling for the Zone and its transformations:

> Separations are proceeding. Each alternative Zone speeds away from all the others, in fated acceleration, red-shifting, fleeing the Center. Each day the mythical return Enzian dreamed of seems less possible. Once it was necessary to . . . observe boundaries. But by now too many choices have been made. The single root lost, way back there in the May desolation. Each bird has his branch now, and each one is the Zone. (519)

The evacuated "Center" of the Zone, the space or singular point from which a subversion of the possibility of "return" proceeds, is literally (for the Schwarzkommandos and the Zone-Hereros) occupied by the Rocket (as Real Text, as mystical fetish, as "orunene," a symbol of self-negation and suicide). It inaugurates a movement to the periphery that the text experiences as an atomization of the Zone into purely solipsistic entities or presences. But as much as this movement to the margin parallels a negative fragmentation of the social body, it also parallels an entropic movement that describes the universe and thus expresses a necessity that cannot be reversed. The second law of thermodynamics countermands Enzian's desire for a "single root" or secured Center to which the Zone-Hereros might return, and at the same time it registers the possibility of a nomadic subjectivity. His diagnosis of the solipsistic Zone is correct (hence the tone of tragic resignation that Enzian so often strikes), but the text also implicates Enzian in the condition diagnosed or, rather, diagnoses his desire for a Center as the innermost tendency of that solipsism, with the result that Enzian appears "out of touch" (519), disconnected from what goes on around him. Of course what also becomes clear is that this disconnection (this lack of "touch") privileges Enzian in a way different from the scientist or "master" who diagnoses. A transformation of that solipsism occurs from the moment the text's irony is registered, and opens the way for Enzian to rediscover "re-turn" (or eternal return) in the very "red-shifting" peripherality that he observes, in the fact of that separation metamorphosed into an ontological ground.

This metamorphosis therefore occurs not for Enzian but for the reader of *Gravity's Rainbow* in the mode of its broken machines. One index for this occurrence, again, is Pynchon's quotation of science (entropy) as a kind of textual leverage into uncertainty or the limits of causality, precipitating language into a new relation to the object world, bringing it "close to matter" or close to an object-being occulted in subjectivity. For Heidegger, the determination of a thing as a tool or as an object of research (as standing-reserve) strips it of its singular object-ness, makes it disappear as an object (*Technology*, 19). To recover this objectivity of the object (or rather, to recover an objective relation to the mode of revealing that conditions the presentation of objects), requires that the (humanist) subject disappear in its turn, yielding to a version of subjectivity with, at its heart, not a rational being or essence but the object reconstituted as such, calling into question the subject as master or, in Baudrillard's words, "universal causality." "The possibility, the will of the subject to situate itself at the transcendental heart of the world and to think of itself as universal causality, under the sign of a law of which it remains master, this will does not prevent the subject from invoking the object secretly, like a fetish, like a talisman, like a figure of the reversal of causality, like the locus of a violent hemorrhage of subjectivity" (*Fatal Strategies*, 114).

In *Gravity's Rainbow*, the Rocket standing at the Center of textual subjectivity becomes in the play of its fetishizations the agent of this subjective wound—which is why Pökler's first encounter with a rocket involved, it will be recalled, an experience of anomalous duration (the firing of the rocket and its explosion "where he'd stood" seem simultaneous and suggest an uncertainty as to whether the rocket *causes* a disappearance of Pökler's body, or whether the disappearance of Pökler's body causes the production of the rocket), and why Slothrop's sexual link to the V-2 seems to Pointsman like a similar "reversal" (he does not know whether the falling of the rocket causes Slothrop's erections, or vice versa). The irony employed in these instances implies that the Rocket is an "object" as well as an instrument, cut off from its own ends and made the ground of an objective form of being. This objective irony, which is for Baudrillard "readable at the very heart of information and science, at the very heart of the system and its laws, at the heart of desire and of all psychology" (72), functions in *Gravity's Rainbow* to signal its "fatal" strategy of foreclosing the centered subject from the text. The novel's multileveled, multidimensional, latticed emulation of a crystal could be said to have this trope as its structural principle, a principle not causal in nature, but fatal: "In fatality . . . the linkage [between objects or events], far from being causal, is rather this: the sign of the apparition of things is also the sign of their disappearance. The sign of their birth will be the sign of their death" (157). Singularity replaces causality, and the singular object passes to the center of subjectivity. This strategy that Baudrillard calls "catastrophic" everywhere marks *Gravity's Rainbow*, not only in its simulations of randomness but in its intricately patterned, implicate organization. It is the "soul" in Pynchon's "stone," and the seduction of his monumental book.

6

TOTALITY AND THE REPETITION OF DIFFERENCE: REREADING THE 1960S IN *VINELAND*

One's mind and the earth are in a constant state of erosion, mental rivers wear away abstract banks, brain waves undermine cliffs of thought, ideas decompose into stones of unknowing, and conceptual crystallizations break apart into deposits of gritty reason. Vast moving faculties occur in this geological miasma, and they move in the most physical way. This movement seems motionless, yet it crushes the landscape of logic under glacial reveries.—Robert Smithson, "A Sedimentation of the Mind"

Robert Smithson, the environmental artist who died in the same year that *Gravity's Rainbow* first appeared (1973), refers in the epigraph to the earth's coextension with the mind, to a reason so deeply embedded in the entropic processes of nature that it assumes a geological form. In chapter 3 of this book, I introduced Heidegger's distinction between the "world" and the "earth," seeing in their interplay a relation between appearance and withdrawal, an opening out and a self-enclosing that mimic an ontic/ontological tension. By the end of chapter 5, I circled back to the chiasmus at the heart of that relation's arrested movement, the double and inverse repetition that precipitates in the novel a breakdown of narrative coherence. The interpretation of this self-shattering textual desire resonates at social and subjective registers as well. This is the principal reason why the violation of temporal unity in *Gravity's Rainbow* takes the form of references to the late 1960s, to the *time of writing* understood in its two distinct yet overlapping senses: that projected by the act of writing, and that in which its writing transpires. Slothrop's 1945 scattering, its singular evocation of the virtual ground on which the novel rests, presents itself in this double light as the delirium of one born (or thrown) into the postwar period. Slothrop's children (dreaming about their father) face a world in which subjectivity sustains the shock of a biopolitical penetration so internally fractalizing that ordinary sensation and cognition feel like addiction—governed, that is, by a compulsion that has its source outside the individualized self. Psychic identity unfolds in a discursive medium only to cancel itself out, to evanesce in semiotic equivalences that condemn one to a desire for lost substance and the emptiness of a fantasmatic substitution. Metalanguage—the linguistic production of social reality—is not unlike an experience of nodding or (gaily) tripping because it makes transcendence the reflex of power, innocence its coaptative lure, exception the deepest tendency of its rule. Hallucination passes to the center of normative life and entails for each species of deviation or dissent that it grasp its own essence in a preobjective and anoedipal existential space.

As with many other countercultural productions, *Gravity's Rainbow* exploits a hallucinatory excess to uncover the collective hallucination of the normal. Strung out or "spacey," it performs the double binds at the heart of those discursive neutralizations that made the counterculture an experiment in complicity. The novel found its escape in (rather than from) its time, via the empty form the latter assumes in society and in the self as a certain incorporation of totality. Slothrop's becoming a "cross" mirrors, you might say, the cross Tommy—that deaf, dumb, and blind kid who also discovered the body without organs of his time—becomes in Pete Townsend's rock opera: a Christlike figure who takes on and reiterates the sins of a late capitalist world figured (in Ken Russell's film) by ball bearings and pinballs, theme parks, and junkyards of smashed machinery. If the analogy between these two contemporary examples is suggestive, the counterculture can be said to disclose a profoundly negative eschatological structure. The reveries present in the experiences of rock music, sexual liberation, communal living, and acid trips eroded the consistency of the representations on which social order relies for its force and legitimacy, only to express, through a turn to language, the schizoid logic of that order all over again. Such experiences engendered the strange necessity of an implicated salvation, a symptomatic time wherein power reproduces itself in bodies and minds, at the ground of being, the source of life, and the frame of nature. Thus Tommy, no less than Slothrop in *Gravity's Rainbow* annihilated by the end of his film, gives himself over (as a cross) on that mountaintop to a sun that symbolizes rebirth only by first recalling us to the entropy it also signifies, the light and heat of a rationalized universe. Life does not live, but in a peculiar death-in-life or burning out that the counterculture stages so cannily in artifacts such as these, we rediscover, as a consequence of perceiving the immanence of power (and the finitude of this perception), a possibility of desire and imaginative freedom.

One darker implication of Smithson's "glacial reveries" is a potential cancellation of the ontological difference, since his ironic figure determines the "earth" that eludes determination, locating rationality in the place of its other. The 1960s, one could say, is a moment in the postwar period when it becomes clear that such a determination has taken place; this is what Heidegger in fact calls metalanguage. What remains interesting about cultural production during this moment is that starting from this perception, it attempts to understand difference, singularity, supplementarity, the reserve or remainder where the "human" resides in necessary contortions of discourse. To respect this trace element is no longer simply to valorize escape or elusiveness, the "earth" as last refuge of authenticity, for here too discourse prevails. The strategy adopted by artists like Smithson and Pynchon is instead to posit a discursive time in which existence itself becomes a function of how it is read, at stake in the choices made to wrest it from unconsciousness and render it sensible and intelligible. In this chapter, I will once again focus on grounds, foundations, absent causes, history, and totality as these concepts relate to a problematic of reading raised by Pynchon's rereading of the 1960s in *Vineland*. I will show how its reassessment of the decade (and, it can be inferred, of Pynchon's previous work) mirrors a more general cultural shift away from abyssal constructions of social life and the sublimating desire elucidated throughout *Lines of Flight*. This shift manifests itself in critical circles as a reaction against "language" and "theory" in practice, and before turning directly to *Vineland*, I would like to characterize this reaction in more detail as it helps to place the novel in the context of the late 1980s and 1990s.

The Turn against Theory

The most significant theoretical substratum of the readings given in previous chapters emphasizes the indissociability of content and form in expression. An ethical claim is made for a performative approach to cultural labor and in particular to acts of reading that index a problem of reference that is historical in nature, indelibly marking a postwar period and therefore informing cultural perceptions in ways that can be analyzed only by virtue of one's own implication in that period. The pertinent historical attribute is a metalinguistic tendency to fix experience in a symbolic solution from which precipitates of "reality" are derived. The mediated nature of the real comes more and more into focus as a displacement of the distinction between theory and practice, language and being. This displacement is *felt* in the anomie to which a rationalized and privatized modern life reduces subjects, a hollowness in the forms of freedom legitimated by consumerism, a self-alienation that constantly renews one's complicity in social order. Pynchon provides in his notion of a "preterite" tense or state of textual being an apt metaphor for this elliptical, digressive, or virtual feeling inside a late capitalist mode of production. A preterite person finds himself or herself subsumed in language, trapped in discourses that dictate conditions of possibility, shape perceptions, experiences, modes of identity, deep structures of belief. One contention here has been that the 1960s were a preterite time during which politics was conceived in terms of discursive projects, reorganizations of those deep structures, "cultural" revolutions, struggles not only over causes but over what counts as real and what doesn't. The first principle of this politics was that the nondiscursive takes the form of a limit-concept; it eludes discourse so radically that only discourses reflexive about the intrinsic nature of their own grounds, boundaries, or difference prove capable of apprehending it. In other words, and once again, *expression matters*.

In recent years (since at least the early 1980s), a resistance to this discursive politics has led to more or less allergic reactions to theory in progressive circles both inside the academy and out. The arguments are directed especially against forms of expression that maintain levels of abstraction too remote from life or common sense to be meaningful to any but an "elect" few (usually situated in an ivory tower and, as with the women in Remedios Varo's tower, hard at work on their own foundations). Theory is seen to be a symptom of the political reaction that set in with the election of Ronald Reagan in 1980 (if not before), and hence to exemplify an appropriately apolitical criticism for an apathetic and authoritarian time. Such a reading of theory (again, expression as an ethical or metaethical imperative for the critic and cultural producer to perform their own implication in a catastrophic time) is only possible, however, if its "elect" autonomy in the 1980s and 1990s is divorced from its "preterite" symptomaticity in the 1960s and 1970s, which is to say only once the latter has been either carefully distinguished from what theory evolves into or rejected outright as merely collusive, merely the expression of social power. This means that the debate over the value of theory conducted most recently in venues such as *Social Text*, *Lingua Franca*, or *The Nation* or in colloquiums across the country (such as the "Left Conservatism Conference" held at the University of California–Santa Cruz, in April 1998, which included input by such thinkers as Judith Butler, Paul Bové, Wendy Brown, Barbara Epstein, Donna Haraway, and others) has for a subtext a deeper struggle over the legacy of the 1960s. Laid over the rejection of theory in the present is a rereading of the recent past that attempts to stabilize a political tradition based not on modalities of discursive transformation or symptomatic iteration but on nonironic social movements rooted in an older populism and galvanized, substantialized, by their continuity with an active political life in need today of revitalization. Implied in this rereading is a call to return to history, to a sense of value, meaning, and consequence, or what amounts to the same thing, to a "time" when the discursive framework of social life was intact and our actions could once again speak louder than words.

In part, this call or this need to sum up the countercultural 1960s stems from a perception that its postwar "period" is ending or has ended, and that as a result it can be comprehended from a vantage point outside the period itself. A revisionist urge proves especially irresistible given that the period in question so resolutely presents itself in a traumatic mode, as a kind of antiperiod defined as a structure of differences and founded on a temporal discontinuity. As might be expected, my view is that such an extrinsic vantage point can as a result only be a fiction, subsumed within the time it presumes to categorize. To project back into the counterculture a continuity that it either could have achieved but did not, or did achieve but could not thematize, is to miss the way in which it focuses this projection in a critical light. One could say that a crisis in foundation or origin lay behind the disorders of the time, its inability to be the coherent scene of a political event, tradition, or narrative. This crisis redirected political energy to the desire for order itself at a discursive level as it sought to render experience intelligible and stable. It exposed in what Foucault calls an "essentially reticent clarity" a "certain stratum of the original in which no origin was in fact present" (*The Order of Things*, 333) and where an abyssal ground strains out of social and political life a feeling of substantiality. This is why the time retroactively projected on the 1960s by progressives and conservatives alike today has to be a function of how it is read, since in our time, time is a function of language, not a linear and represented series of self-present moments but a catastrophic (or catastropic) and heterological displacement requiring of historical consciousness that it grasp its own symptomaticity in the act of constituting its object.

Such an implicated logic has at least governed the generalizations made about the 1960s and the readings of Pynchon's corpus presented in this book, and not simply because I think the "turn" against theory implies a misreading but, more subtly, because misreading is strangely a necessity of the time, the symptom of what Fredric Jameson calls a "totality [that] affirms in the very movement whereby it denies" (*The Political Unconscious*, 55), the sign of a general preterition the historical force of which has to be sustained before transformation becomes possible. The stake in reading Pynchon's works from the 1960s has always been this possibility, with the crucial proviso that it exist not as the projection of a social and symbolic unity but as the modification of this unity in a hologrammic "part-whole," an open or infinite set, a "partial" totality that his texts can be seen to model. This is why progressive (or reactionary) criticisms of "elect" theory today carry with them so unmistakable an odor of bad faith: if the Pynchon of *Gravity's Rainbow* is right, then such criticisms themselves signify gestures of "election" or exemption insofar as they repress the nondistinction of language and being (or rather the internal nature of their difference) that conditions the possibility of political transformation today.

Vineland is a strategic retreat from the excesses of Pynchon's previous fiction, and as such it constitutes an anomaly in his corpus and an exception to the hermeneutic argument offered here. As a story about the counterculture's escape from technocratic society, *Vineland* evokes the lines of flight I trace through *V.*, *The Crying of Lot 49*, and *Gravity's Rainbow* in a soberer, more reflective light, but as such it lacks the ambition to reconstitute its own discourse that, in my account, sutures the earlier work to its (untimely) time. Ironically this suggests that *Vineland* is not *of* its time (understood more broadly as the postwar period), that it digresses from its time precisely in the move to thematize it, to make itself timely. Unlike *Gravity's Rainbow*, where the 1960s appears only as prolepsis and displacement, in *Vineland* it appears analeptically, as a series of reminiscences no less mediated and no less *about* mediation, but nonetheless without the displacement toward expression that made the earlier novel so singular in all the senses of this word. *Vineland* does not perform its own content, and hence it presupposes the categorical stability of that content (the 1960s, the counterculture) in isolation from the process of its production. The novel is about preterite characters dealing with their own desires for order, their complicities in power, their human weakness, but it is not itself preterite. This is why its style is mannered (i.e., it lacks an "expressive" dimension) and why its tone is essentially moralistic, that of a literary master nudging his characters (and readers) toward the right thing to do, which in this case is to reread the 1960s in the light of older traditions of political action and commitment.[1]

I would like to analyze here the strategy of rereading implicit in Pynchon's 1990 novel within the same metahistorical context adopted in previous chapters. The recent turn against theory to which *Vineland*, in its own way, belongs is not without a symptomatic cogency to the extent that it underscores the problem of cultural autonomization that now more than ever engenders inertia, entropy, or "missing matter" in a contemporary social universe. Theory constitutes for many an avatar of this problem because it assumes this entropy to be a kind of incontrovertible thermodynamic law, a process according to which resistance of a political or critical kind can no longer be defined as its *reversal*. To put up resistance, as I have argued can be inferred from Pynchon's texts, is to exacerbate, repeat, or overstuff to the point of farce. As a strategy, this leaves many without a clear sense of direction, disoriented, swamped, and finally immobilized in an *aporia*. The tenuousness of any claim that theory is political in its reiterations of discourse stems from what Jameson calls its antinomic formalism. Unlike the material and historical contradiction that Jameson argues has to be the zero degree of any political praxis, the *antinomy* signifies a purely logical paradox open only to contemplation and thus immunized against its context. The antinomy as a ground or "subtext" of criticism, he maintains in *The Political Unconscious*, is the "place of ideology" where contradiction in effect cannot come, and thus it catches up those forms that it predicates in an infinite regress of pure thought. The critique implied in Jameson's distinction reserves for theory of the antinomic kind a negative or "second-degree" status, since no matter how reflexive about ideology it may be, it cannot escape ideology itself and so confines itself to a symptomatic relation to a late capitalist mode of production.

In a sense Jameson's work could be taken as exemplary of the antitheoretical "movement" legible in American culture today, certainly of its best and least xenophobic elements. His attempts to situate the practice of thought on the ground of "History" and in orientation with an ultimate moment of "collective unity" work from within aporetic tendencies to establish limits, zones of alterity, singularities where the "pain" of history resides. As a critic who does not do theory in the restricted sense intended here, Jameson has the virtue of conserving in his work what I have taken to be the fundamental stake of theory itself: the nondiscursive limit or ground of the "real" internal to discourse that incites the latter to progressively more paradoxical stagings of its own finitude. But Jameson's disavowal of antinomy does not go quite so far in this literary direction. The price of having it both ways, of that peculiar distance so proper to disavowal, is that the performativity on which the nondiscursive limit depends finds itself confined to a dialectic and Marxist form carefully differentiated from "second-degree" equivalents of an overly aestheticizing kind. As a result, criticism, exposing unconscious historical contradictions within or behind the aesthetic drive itself, has also to recover the "unity of a great collective story" or "uninterrupted narrative" (*The Political Unconscious*, 20) that informs a "fundamental history" of class struggle and emancipation (from, in Hegelian terms, a potential or "oppressed" state of being "in itself" to an actual and free state of being "for itself"). To write political criticism is for Jameson to enter discourse by setting his method off from its antidialectic competitors and claiming a more privileged relation to the (Lacanian) "Real" ground in the very act of this exclusion. But as Deleuze and Guattari might put it, the difference between the two types of method is inclusive to a partial and virtual totality. It appears in a metonymic process of traumatic fracture in the ground of history that implicates one in its irreality at the moment it is repressed. The internal difference between the two methods, then, reopens the question of theory and of the value placed on expression, for Jameson's way out of the problem only folds him back into it, only catches him up in the rhythm of a rereading or rewriting that continually repeats the metalinguistic symptom. This is in fact the proper dynamic of a "necessary totalization" that Jameson reserves for his method, except that it displaces him back into the very aporetic mode he disavows. Jameson might be wrong, in other words, when he argues that behind every antinomy lies a contradiction. In fact it may be just the opposite: behind every contradiction one finds a prior antinomy, an abyss of discourse precisely where one thinks to fix its other, an immersion in an intrinsically rationalized history.

Jameson's decision to arrest the abyssal ground of discourse in "contradiction" is interesting because he does so with a complete awareness of its theoretical indefensibility. The kind of critique advanced here is fully and preemptively understood in his work as a limit to be exorcised, a reduction and even trivialization of discourse to an almost classical rationalism. But the price (deliberately incurred) of that exorcism is a misreading of theory itself, since its aporias are not avatars of pure thought divorced from context but symptoms of a mode of production that generates a context of absence. What gets misread is this symptomaticity, or more specifically the repetition that drive it; repetition becomes rationalism, pure thought, antinomy or ideology, when in fact it here solicits them, cites or encases them within a form of thought dedicated to its own heterological determination and so situated in a world where antinomy has become its very condition of possibility. What's interesting is not that theory must be exorcised in order to resist a metalinguistic domination felt, say, in a privatized and standardized socius but that it is constructed as a demon or ghost to be exorcised in order to legitimate a type of politics. An inversion is involved here, the same inversion isolated as the "turn" in Pynchon's work and in the theoretical models brought to bear on that work in previous chapters—a temporal "de-miraculation" that is precisely *the exorcisable substance*, what must be removed from the political body for it to exist in its self-identity.

Jameson affords a good rhetorical example of the reaction against theory, then, to the extent that he requires the fiction of antinomy to generate resistance in his text. This requirement informs the more general call to revitalize political life in America today, whether it is done with Jameson's careful sophistication and eye for the constraints of one's time or with blind ideological desperation in the face of what may be the death throes of democracy in the Clinton/Bush America. With his exemplarity in mind, I would like to analyze a little more closely how Jameson constructs the ground of his discourse, by way of fleshing out my own Deleuzian repetition of that ground in a reading of Vineland.

Totality and the Repetition of Difference

The fundamental concept of the fundament in The Political Unconscious is an "absent cause" analogous in most respects to what Deleuze calls an "unconditioned condition" in the essay "Coldness and Cruelty," analyzed in chapter 4 of this book. Jameson tracks this notion of effectivity through a number of other concepts, notably expressive causality, totality, mediation, his own political unconscious, and finally "History" and a nonsymbolizable "Real." In each he specifies the virtual function of a ground that passes away in that which it grounds, a nondiscursive "subtext" linked to the text it predicates by virtue of a constitutive alterity. This allows him to set at a distance those "second-degree" theories suggesting that "history is a text [and] the referent does not exist" (35), since history and the referent are, properly speaking, connotative dimensions of texts and thus figural offspring of a reading practice. Jameson's critical method rests on the assumption that history is "not a text, not a narrative, master or otherwise, but that, as an absent cause, it is inaccessible to us except in textual form, and that our approach to it and to the Real itself necessarily passes through its prior textualization, its narrativization in the political unconscious" (35). Interpretation takes on its importance for Jameson as the privileged activity of rendering that unconscious of the text intelligible. To read is to grasp the absent cause in (or as) a political act of expression that honors its otherness but also at the same time authorizes a gesture of exclusion. To read in Jameson's way signifies a reticence with respect to the paralogistic collapse of text and subtext, a need to maintain figure and ground in an extrinsic relation that insures the reader against an ideological closure.

But it could also be said, within the terms of Jameson's political hermeneutic, that history is a text because it (dis)appears only in the moment of ideological closure, and the referent does not exist because it lacks the criteria for existence itself as an absent cause. This internal situation of the method's other (an antinomic collapse of subtext and text) finds its more theoretical articulation with Jameson's discussion of Althusser's structural causality, a concept of effectivity according to which the figure/ground distinction is more forcefully displaced and the cause (ground) is seen to be coextensive with its effects (figures). The structure that results from this indicates a connotation flush with its denotative surface, an unconscious lifted into consciousness and lived as the (internal) breach in the contour of an ontic self-identity. With this notion of a "Real" structure, the thingness of things is called into question, or rather the discursive preconditions for their appearance and intelligibility as objects are themselves objectified. It is in this prior discursive sense that the real can be understood as a text, albeit a virtual one, opened on the inside to what it is not, the world or history modeled on an "absent" totality that cannot remain closed even as it confers on each totalization the irreality of an arbitrary and self-originating act of power.

Jameson does not reject a principle of structural causality for his own discourse, although he prefers an "expressive" variant critiqued by Althusser for its dialectical underpinnings and allegorical articulation of whole and part. For Jameson, this sort of critique falls prey to an error of the "second-degree" type: it denies existence to the referent that remains active and palpable in (perhaps only in) the dialectic and so aestheticizes the real by denying it a historical determination. Conventional historicism as a practice rooted in allegory's discovery in texts of a "master code" or underlying "uninterrupted narrative" (20) yields, despite its relative uselessness for structuralist and poststructuralist practitioners, a "fundamental dimension of our collective thinking and our collective fantasy about history and reality" (34). It is sometimes unclear in Jameson's rhetoric whether this "fundamental dimension" is that of an absent cause or of allegory's master code (hence the suggestion that he locates in the political unconscious or absent cause a *particular* Marxist narrative where he elsewhere maintains no narrative exists), but what is clear is that its renunciation by those practitioners entails a repression and a willingness to be ahistorical. His method sets out to conserve what is fundamental in historicism: a ground construed as absent, subtextual, but also immunized against a certain excess, a delirium of history that passes over into ideology. Of course he is not advocating mere historicism, either, given its ideological saturation in common sense, empirical experience, and objectivity. Instead Jameson's project is to balance excesses and elude ideological closure, to steer a median course between a secured ground and that abyssal whirlpool into which the referent vanishes altogether. This is why a structural causality turns out to encompass Jameson's dialectic variant such that the "symbolic act" he advocates must generate its own world as immanent and intrinsic, the groundless ground of a fundamental narrativity rather than the ground of a particular narrative.[2] "The symbolic act begins by generating and producing its own content in the same moment of emergence in which it steps back from it. . . . [It] brings into being that very situation to which it is also, at one and the same time, a reaction. It articulates its own situation and textualizes it, thereby encouraging and perpetuating the illusion that the situation itself did not exist before it, that there is nothing but a text, that there never was any extra- or contextual reality before the text itself generated it in the form of a mirage" (81–82).

What interests me in this formulation of the symbolic act is the necessity it implies to generate this mirage, or rather the indispensability of the mirage to the process of which it is the result. An absence of context is an effect of the text, and its derived or prior discursive status must always be understood by the method; but Jameson also sets the method off from this discursive abyss, and in the process it ceases to understand (about itself, anyway) that the real it projects, distinct from its decontextualizing mirage, is also a decontextualizing mirage, that it "exists" only as a derivation of the symbolic act. The precession of the effect toward the cause or origin of Jameson's discourse marks its implication in a context of absence I have been designating the postwar period, and does so precisely when he stigmatizes theory or makes it the other of his own practice.

That other returns as an internal difference within one's attempts to stabilize a discourse, and it is this repetition that constitutes a "fundamental dimension" of collective cultural life—not the "master code" of allegorical desire, not that ultimate resolution of the order behind appearances that every discourse seeks to establish, but the impossibility and in fact embarrassment of this desire itself, its groundless and insubstantial simulacrum. For Deleuze, another desire overlays this cited equivalent, a desire of repetition that very routinely satisfies its aim of undermining order, since for him it signifies a kind of libidinal entropy. Jameson has a conceptual formulation of this desire in what he calls an "imperative to totalize," which could be extended to mean an imperative to misread that symptomatically commits one (him) to history; but he means by history a dialectic that underwrites an externalization of the mirage of theory and so, one could say, a misreading of misreading itself, a totalization attempting to close off the irreversible effects of entropy and therefore deny the intrinsically breached or broken totality that such an attempt presupposes. The problematic crux of Jameson's discourse can be found here in this doubling dynamic that seeks in effect its own exorcism, its own ghostly investiture, and the limit of its own assertions.

Jameson, once again, is well aware of this limit and of the arbitrary arrest of an abyssal ground that attends the production of discourse. What needs to be assessed is whether his attempt to remain reflexive about discourse and adhere to a dialectical definition of the political amounts to an adequately *historical* position, given the nature of the symptomal time that we have lived since at least the end of World War II. Or put in a different register, does Jameson's working idea about implication in history sufficiently implicate his readers in the postwar period, or is it assuming a perspective that forecloses viable counterhegemonic critical possibilities? Answers to such questions will help to contextualize the problem of theory's (relative) relevance in intellectual life today. It will help to clarify the kinds of rereadings of the recent past that can yield a sufficient *cultural* commitment in the present, and those that, by contrast, implicitly or explicitly demand a historical amnesia. Does one have to work within Jameson's dialectical framework to be political today? Is social or personal resistance to abstraction in a "language of pure signifiers" made possible by the decision to externalize that abstraction, or does it on the contrary depend on the internalization (citation, incorporation) of that abstraction and hence a more active implication, a taking of "reality and history" as texts after all, even though this involves us in antinomy, assuming experience into a preterite texture of existence? Two politics, and two desires of cultural production, are implied here: one that construes resistance in history as the return of a continuous narrative (for Jameson the Marxist story of the "collective struggle to wrest a realm of Freedom from a realm of Necessity" [19] that both performs and thematizes its own absent cause) that the critic will support through his or her objectification of the political unconscious; and another that sees resistance in a destabilizing repetition that grounds a far different social and political life, one for which Freedom would consist in controlling the unity of language and being, gaining power over the discourses that govern power itself, and realizing in oneself, one's actions, and one's world a fully temporal implication.

A quote from Deleuze's *Nietzsche and Philosophy* pertinently evokes the degree to which, in the final analysis, the tension here is not, as Jameson's construction of antinomic theory can sometimes imply, between progressive (i.e., committed to the symbolic actualization of a social unity) and regressive (negative, critical) political modalities but between two versions of what Jameson calls the "utopian vocation" of combining ideological demystification with the progressive unfolding of a collective impulse. Deleuze is here referring to the "eternal return" in its two variants:

> We misinterpret the expression "eternal return" if we understand it as "return of the same." It is not being that returns but rather the returning itself that constitutes being insofar as it is affirmed of becoming and of that which passes. It is not some one thing which returns but rather returning itself is the one thing which is affirmed of diversity and multiplicity. In other words, identity in the eternal return does not describe the nature of that which returns but, on the contrary, the fact of returning for that which differs. (48)

The *unicity* implied in this repetition of difference signifies the ground of a politics (on whatever level) that does not work within the dialectic framework of a unifying narrative; rather, that narrative is cited within a totality that vitiates closure and undermines the "real" unities of time, space, and action, a totality conceived as the infinite set of a world always in excess of any comprehension. Deleuze's shift in this passage from a repetition of constituted things or subjects to one that constitutes them in their non-self-identity entails an existential dimension that is intrinsically possible, open or anticipatory, and positive in the structure of internal differences it projects. His theory of pure becoming or of "passage" passes itself off as practice, and this "passing" indicates a suspension, a simulacral indeterminacy that, for all it looks like the "mirage" of history's repression, convokes the gravity of a history itself in danger of repression whenever this "difference" is not grasped. Here, then, is a utopian project of a type not quite isomorphic with Jameson's in The Political Unconscious, since it stipulates as the internal coherence (or tendency) of history a repetition that grasps "Freedom" less as a transcendence of "Necessity" than as a coming to grips with its own implicate orders of discourse and power. But neither is it far apart from Jameson insofar as it retains in a sort of mirror relation the narrative of narrativity and, within that, the pulsions and resistances of material life.

Rereading the 1960s in *Vineland*

The two senses outlined of what it means to be utopian inform very different versions of the 1960s: on the one hand, a political effervescence inspired by Jameson's narrative of collective unity, which fails because of an insufficient political will; on the other, a breakdown of this narrative concomitant with a shift in the mode of production into a late capitalist phase that necessitates micropolitical strategies. Adherence to the former tends to presuppose a reading of the latter as a euphemization of a fragmenting political field; adherence to the latter takes this fragmentation as a fractalization making possible a range of politico-discursive forms repressed by the implied totalization of the former. The cultural counterpoint of these (re)readings can be seen in the narrative structures of Pynchon's texts. The emphasis on discontinuity, entropy, and virtuality in the novels from the 1960s clearly indicates an exploration of the totality of postwar social life in terms of a "repetition of difference." But *Vineland*, not from the 1960s but about them, just as clearly drives its stakes into the ground of a "repetition of the same."

This decision stems from a need to read the manifest failure of the time either to sustain a progressive trajectory or forestall the subsequent "Nixonian Reaction" (*Vineland*, 239) and, later, "Reagan Revolution" in all their intimately terrorizing zeal. *Vineland* is a rereading of the 1960s in the light of the 1970s and 1980s that adopts the position that "implication" as a strategy cannot produce its own grounding in history and that this failure to do so can be situated in relation to a discrete period. The 1960s are definitely *over* in the novel, and if they were over before they even began, caught up in the gyre of discursive inversion and repressive desublimation that gave the time its peculiar feeling of euphoria, *then this too is over*. What remains in the aftermath of a preterite orbitalization, suggests Pynchon, is not a textual subject but the fleshly human being, "an animal after all, with a full set of pain receptors," charged with the responsibilities of care, stewardship, and concerted resistance to inertial force (physical, social, or political). This shift of emphasis is not registered in the text at the level of content, nor does it suggest that somehow the *body* is more at stake in *Vineland* than it is in the earlier, more textually reflexive novels. In many respects, *Vineland* presents its readers with a familiar literary world: preterite figures in an overdetermined landscape attempting to cope with the forces of entropy both within themselves and without. But these preterite and entropic elements do not function in the same way at the level of expression, where the ground of Pynchon's discourse has shifted, and what is meant by a "world" is now a nondiscursive element in an extrinsic or exclusive relation to the text. The body, social order, "reality and history" exist not as limits invaginated in language but as previously constituted entities and concepts *outside* language, and therefore as discourses given the distinction of a nondiscursive being.

The "sixties" as a period is the novel's first example of this *discursive out-*

side, since rather than designating a temporal mode of heterological breach that catches up its historian, sociologist, artist, writer, or critic in the time of his or her own epistemological desire, it finds itself reduced to a content or attribute without a performative dimension. The nuance here is that performativity itself constitutes the reduced content; in being about the 1960s as a discursive time, Pynchon's text excludes in the act of thematizing a form of expression that presumes an intrinsic or internal relation to its own ground, a "history" grasped *as* that form and in the act of writing. This is why *Vineland* seems like the earlier novels in its subject matter and style and yet clearly strikes so different a note. It thematizes the mediated nature of the 1960s by filtering it through stories and anecdotes told by its middle-aged "veterans" to teenage interlocutors, and indeed it (literally) appropriates their narrative reconstructions, takes over their nostalgic voices, and becomes another veteran of the time; but in this appropriation, the novel itself ceases to subsume its own perspective in the distorting element of story and discourse, linking the latter instead to an autonomizing repetition compulsion that it historicizes. The "real" period of the 1960s then begins to emerge in a light that, however filtered, can nonetheless reveal the filters themselves, expose their effects in a nontextualized social field, and indicate a possible transcendence not actualized in the period itself.

That repetition is a "subtext" of *Vineland* can be inferred from the novel's epigraph, a message *outside* the text that comes in the form of a quotation from a song by the rhythm-and-blues singer Johnny Copeland: "Every dog has his day, / and a good dog / just might have *two* days." The doubleness adverted to here resonates forward into the kaleidoscopic story of Zoyd Wheeler, his daughter Prairie, her mother Frenesi, her mother's friend DL, and their complicated relations to that avatar of an invested social repression, the federal prosecutor Brock Vond. But the resonance is doubly complicated by a further connotative question: what does it mean to be a "good" dog, to live in an ethical manner such that one's repetitions bear on a community in fruitful and caring ways? This question has perhaps been present in all of Pynchon's novels, but the answer given here, once again, is qualitatively different. The implication of the text in an objectifying and dehumanizing violence, like the complicities of the characters, unfolds through a rereading of implication and complicity, an encasement of parodic strategies within a heightened realism. Repetition is still at work, but it now clearly understands its utopian project in terms of a responsibility to an underlying narrative of political continuity.

The action of this rereading is felt most distinctly in the exclusive difference between abstraction on the one hand ("Tubal" distraction by the mesmerizing media of television and computers, the "wide invincible gaze practiced by many sixties children, meaning nearly anything at all, useful in a lot of situations, including ignorance" [214], the musical reveries, surfer's raptures, and various "mind hard-ons" cataloged in the novel) and on the other a "cause-and-effect" history in which the apparatuses of social control articulate their simulacral structures. This historical ground, while in most ways the same reifying array of bureaucracies, military or national security institutions, industrial installations, and spectral marketplaces dramatized in *Gravity's Rainbow*, differs to the degree that its historicity in *Vineland* is assumed within the causal terms it projects and establishes for itself. A reification of time is thus legible in Pynchon's construction of a reifying social and political power. Human beings in the novel are dehumanized in causal time; the "human" is not already a dehumanization in the establishment of time as causal. They are not caricatures but characters, despite the intertextuality of their funny names and the improbability of the things that happen to them, and as such they instantiate nondiscursive singularities in his discourse. One can hear this instantiation, for instance, in the story of Frenesi's mother, Sasha, a longtime political activist capable of grasping the novel's fundamental issue of how proactively and progressively to enter history. Here the narrator recounts the emergence in her youth (circa 1930s) of her practical political philosophy from an overly "theoretical" version of Marxism:

> The injustices she had seen in the streets and fields, so many, too many times gone unanswered—she began to see them more directly, not as world history or anything too theoretical, but as humans, usually male, living here on the planet, often well within reach, committing these crimes, major and petty, one by one against other living humans. Maybe we all had to submit to History, she figured, maybe not—but refusing to take shit from some named and specified source—well, that might be a different story. (80)

One senses in the prose of this passage a humanist desire to capture the "living present" in which Sasha's perceptions make sense. Pynchon's rendering of Sasha's capacity for concrete intervention in a "named and specified" world implies its own distance from a "world history" in which the naming and specifying act implicates one in the order of causality. The possibility of refusal and protest that Sasha comes to symbolize for the novel hinges on the necessity to act in spite of that implication, without knowing whether it means "submission" to or in "History." By the end of the novel, where a family reunion presided over by Sasha reads like an orchestral celebration of the tradition more or less inaugurated by her "refusal to take shit," it becomes clear that its peculiar suspension of knowledge signifies a displacement in the ground of history itself toward a dialectic similar to that designated in Jameson's work. The novel sustains the critique of a "theoretical" implication and therefore the requirement for political agency of a divestment from abstraction. It narrates the story of its characters' difficult acceptance of this requirement against the backdrop of a period, the 1960s, where a certain contamination by theory obscured the links with older forms of activism and solidarity.

This reading of the 1960s as too hieratic, too discontinuous and hence dehistoricized, underlies an analysis of American society in the novel that remains crystal clear about the interpellative nature of power. Its new discursive ground does not in any way diminish an ability to read the ambiguation of identity and place wrought by a metalinguistic rationalization of experience. Even Sasha, a blacklisted Hollywood script reader during the McCarthyist 1950s, understands the simulacral modality of order in a postwar dispensation, and how fraught with contradiction it leaves anyone's "different story."

> To Sasha the blacklist period, with its complex court dances of fuckers and fuckees, thick with betrayal, destructiveness, cowardice, and lying, seemed only a continuation of the picture business as it had always been carried on, only now in political form. Everyone they knew had made up a different story, to make each of them come out looking better and others worse. "History in this town," Sasha muttered, "is no more worthy of respect than the average movie script, and it comes about in the same way—as soon as there's one version of a story, suddenly it's anybody's pigeon. Parties you never heard of get to come in and change it. Characters and deeds get shifted around, heartfelt language gets pounded flat when it isn't just removed forever. By now the Hollywood fifties is this way-over-length, multitude-of-hands rewrite—except there's no sound, of course, nobody talks. It's a silent movie." (81)

The narrator here identifies a reifying force of social power in Hollywood with a "rewriting" autonomization of the political field. Ideologically saturated, the cinematic and deterritorialized nature of this field entails a repressive arraignment of desire in the Chinese box of an endless narrativity, and in particular, narratives about the past, retrospective stories that take advantage of history's strange existence in the present to dishonor the "truth" of so much "lying." This is the paradoxical space of the novel with its own spectral rewritings of the 1960s, only the question of its implication in a generalized narrativizing drive now implies a *particular* narrative, a dishonored history beyond its scripted and spectral analogons. The novel's perspective, like Sasha's on the 1950s, depends on an extrinsic reference point, on reference itself as the compass on which one can take one's "true" bearings.

What these examples from the text suggest is a kind of orienting function in Pynchon's prose that operates even where it anarchizes syntax, modulates into farce, or exacerbates the nonsensical. The novel exercises control over its narrative limits, specifying them in the period of the 1960s where an abyssal metalinguistic excess obscured the referent and delivered culture to the political morass of the 1980s. The counterculture that *Vineland*'s middle-aged characters recall is then read as a symptom of this excess and complicity, a dilation of the pseudofreedom available to consumers that vitiates the political commitments of revolutionaries like Frenesi and DL no less than the voidlike reveries of surfer dudes like Zoyd. Pynchon narrates the symptomaticity of the counterculture most forcefully in Frenesi's slow metamorphosis from activist to snitch and FBI flunky, catalyzed by a sexual attraction for Brock Vond that becomes more and more impossible for her to repress. As Sasha's daughter, raised on movies and on repeated distortions of history in her "real" life, Frenesi crystallizes for Pynchon a subjective entrapment in the shadow boxes of narrative and consumption. Her inability to overcome a specular desire for "make-believe" informs her political activities as a student at Berkeley and then her betrayal of fellow activists at the (apocryphal) College of the Surf. Frenesi evokes for the novel a more general dynamic of the counterculture to refuse and avoid "history" that mysteriously transforms commitments into evasions. Politics is for her also an escape from politics, and her escape (with Brock Vond, who manipulates her into causing the death of her lover Weed Atman, a prominent professor halfway between Norman O. Brown and Herbert Marcuse) in turn delivers her to the political structures of social control (Brock Vond, knowing her complicity in the murder, uses the information to keep her working for the FBI). The circularity of her desire becomes emblematic of a growing isolation within the privatized and autonomous cultural nonspace of America itself, a passive implication in power that envelops Frenesi as it does the 1960s as a whole. Here Pynchon, narrating Frenesi's confusion before the forces slowly subsuming her in the plots of Brock Vond and alienating her from her friend DL and her mother, touches on the figure of nonrelation that governs his analysis.

> How was she going to sit down and talk any of it over? Who with, anyway? She'd have to tell it, silently, to DL who would miraculously forgive her, to the Sasha whom years ago it had been possible to tell anything. Make-believe interlocutors, dolls in a dollhouse. Frenesi had thought for a while that her need to talk would build out of control, till she was helpless to hold it in and she ended up as a crazy woman on a bus bench, along an endless flatland boulevard, talking out loud without rest, like an astronomer seeking life out in space. (236)

This crazy astronomer on the bus bench (recalling other orbitalized figures in *Gravity's Rainbow*, like Blicero in his space station or Ilse Pökler on the moon) exemplifies a desire to establish continuity with the progressive commitments Sasha represents. Its mode is that of projection, since the events in which Frenesi gets caught up make its fulfillment impossible and thus constrain it within a pure virtuality. This desire conceals another and contrary, masochistic desire that effectively denies itself, refuses actualization, actual community, and invests a fantasy of its own emptiness. Pynchon is interested here in the function of this fantasy within a larger cultural capitulation to authority, its status as an avatar of the desire for order that he dramatizes in Frenesi's almost insensible metamorphosis into spy, snitch, and ultimately professional underminer of community. For all the anguish she feels in this role, and that she expresses as a longing to talk over her misdeeds with her friend and her mother,

> in practice she'd only kept getting up one morning after another till at some point she found she'd adapted well enough to what she was becoming. The house in Culito Canyon she was crashing at had a redwood deck with a table and chairs where she could sit out in the early mornings, drink herb tea and make believe—her dangerous vice—that she was on her own, with no legal history, no politics, only an average California chick, invisible, poised at life's city limits, for whom anything was possible. (236)

The act of "make believe" is an embrace of possibility or potentiality in itself, hence an "averaging" entropic disappearance from, or ghostly haunting of, the social field that strategically enables Frenesi to "adapt" to her new life as an FBI agent. Her fantasy of pure freedom as an escape from the compulsions she experiences paradoxically comes to be the form of compulsion itself, since she is forced later on to repeat the fantasy in her underground life as a paid criminal for the FBI, deprived of a name and an identity, used by shadowy superiors for reasons she does not comprehend, free-floating inside the orbits of social power, at once free and the very essence of unfreedom. "Poised at life's city limits," Frenesi sees her fantasmatic desire literalized in ironies that Pynchon deploys as part of a more comprehensive reassessment of Frenesi's entropic, virtual, superfluous, oddly returning time.

That part of Pynchon's intent in *Vineland* is to reread his earlier work as examples of the countercultural moment can be inferred from the novel's allegorical dimension, the way that "master narratives" become a subtext of stories like Frenesi's, in which the desire for mastery or the master (Brock Vond) plays itself out in a text conspicuously preoccupied with mediation, with telling stories about the past, and with the question of what stories best represent a community to itself. The use of parody and farce in the novels from the 1960s, their metonymic substitutions whereby each text becomes a preterite character alongside its preterite characters, the subversions of analogy, signification, communication—all these elements point to repetitions of a metalinguistic world that make of their own complicity the ground of a critical apprehension. Pynchon in *Vineland* could be said to stage the limits of these paratactic strategies, to implicate them in the satellitized orbit of that crazy astronomer and so in the functions of an authoritarianism that ripens through the following decades. When Frenesi agrees to help Brock Vond undermine the movement that she, along with DL, her lover Weed Atman, and others created at the College of the Surf, she

> understood that she had taken at least one irreversible step *to the side of her life*, and that now, as if on some unfamiliar drug, she was walking around *next to herself*, haunting herself, attending a movie of it all. If the step was irreversible, then she ought to be all right now, safe in a *world-next-to-the-world* that not many would know how to get to, where she could kick back and watch the unfolding drama. No problem anymore with talk of "taking out" Weed Atman, as he'd gone turning into a character in a movie, one who as a bonus happened to fuck like a porno star . . . but even sex was mediated for her now—she did not enter in. (237; italics mine)

Frenesi's double sense of juxtaposition *beside* herself constitutes a figure for the metalinguistic enforcement of a detached self-reflexivity extended to the very grounds of being. At the same time, it marks an iterative strategy of exposing, as a result of that metalinguistic domination, the catastrophe *for* being that attends its displacement toward expression. Frenesi signifies this displacement at the level of content; she signifies a preterite confusion of language and being that *Vineland* quotes by way of establishing a distance from its own preterition and stabilizing a period, the 1960s, characterized by a highly ambivalent desire for (escape from) social order.

The repetition of repetition legible in *Vineland* therefore implies a detachment of its own; only by the end, where a certain peace is made with the past, Brock Vond is literally if not altogether symbolically killed, and characters such as Frenesi are allowed to speak the words denied them for so long in the (non)space of their countercultural voids, it appears that the novel, at its second remove from the 1960s, does not in fact repeat the metalinguistic symptom so much as the moment of emergence from its "dollhouse" world of make-believe. "Vineland" becomes at the Traverse-Becker family reunion the scene of a restoration, a healing of the wound of abstraction, immunity, spectacle, self-enclosure. The novel declares its allegiance to its preterite characters not by an act of masochistic identification (or incorporation) but by forgiving them their finitude, by a solidarity predicated on a principle of divine justice that allows for a (retributive) "return" on one's painful investments in the "world-next-to-the-world." Pynchon fittingly recounts this compensation between Frenesi and Sasha in an allegorical story:

> Early in the morning Sasha dreamed that Frenesi, perhaps under a sorcerer's spell, was living in a melon patch, as a melon, a smooth golden ellipsoid, on which images of her eyes, dimly, could just be made out. At a certain time each month, just at the full moon, she would be able, by the terms of the spell, to open her eyes and see the moon, the light, the world . . . but each time, in some unexplained despair, would only cast her gaze down and to the side, away, and close her eyes again, and for another cycle she could not be rescued. Her only hope was for Sasha to find her at the exact moment she opened her eyes, and kiss her, and so, after a wait in the fragrant moonlight, it came about, a long, passionate kiss of freedom, a grandmother on her knees in a melon patch, kissing a young pale melon, under a golden pregnant lollapalooza of a moon. (362)

Once again the connotations of Frenesi's predicament in this dream conjure the "master code" of Pynchon's reading of the 1960s. Her enclosure in an object suggests a withheld or potential state, a ghostly incapacity to appear, to be actual, that, despite a desire to be "rescued" and to "see the moon, the light, the world," repeats itself on the principle of "some unexplained despair." The sorcerer's spell, one could say, is the antidialectic spirit of the time, its embrace of the hermetic, its rejection of the organic or the generative (the melon remains in the melon patch month after month, neither growing nor rotting—a condition meant to echo Frenesi's abandonment of her baby, Prairie, on running off with the immaculate Brock Vond), its "smooth" (pure), "golden" (unblemished, perfect), and "ellipsoidal" (elliptic, deviating) escape from history and reality. Sasha's role is to reconnect her ensorcelled child—and her generation—to the narrative of social unity represented by the family reunion and its promise of "freedom" in history. The moon, an object of escapist desire, the site of incident light, of life at a "second degree"—this moon continues to preside over the moment of reconciliation, active in the allegory as a reminder that the "world" is intrinsically dreamlike, intrinsically mediated, but that nonetheless it can be seen for what it is and thus admit of change and passional transfiguration, a "real" freedom in the "golden" simulations of an ideologically overdetermined time.

But a question remains in Pynchon's allegory: What is the nature of the "despair" that resists reconciliation? Does it conceal a desire, and if so, what kind of desire? Is it the desire of allegory itself, oriented toward the reconstitution of a master code, or is it a wrench in the allegorical machinery that precipitates a malfunction, revealing its broken nature? Pynchon is careful to leave this question "unexplained," but an approximate answer does emerge in the text. It signifies a kind of death wish, a return to inanimate or inertial origins, Thanatos as the ground on which the Freudian pleasure principle rests—desire, then, understood on a material model, as an attribute of an Oedipal subject. The counterculture, refusing the pain of history and keeping to lines of least resistance, thus becomes a symptom of normative social order in the very trajectory of its line of flight to Vineland. The story of this line of flight, the story of *Vineland*, unfolds as a dialectic between a despair (Frenesi, the 1960s) capable only of reproducing power and a freedom (Sasha, the 1930s) that offers a practical means of resistance. What the 1960s understood as politics (counterhegemonic strategy, micropolitics, cultural revolution) turns out to be anomie and fragmentation, an ideological disjunction from the "fundamental narrative dimension" that enables community. Pynchon clearly tilts in this Jamesonian direction, projecting the "ghost" of theory, metalanguage, or antinomy in a narrative of exorcism that never forgets the danger posed by abstraction inside its own haunted repetitions.

The other version of the 1960s mentioned at the beginning of this section cuts through and across the story, granting the 1960s' "despair" the coherence of an anti-Oedipal desire that surprises the effect of ghostliness at the origin of (its own) narrative movement. The desire of theory, on this account, shatters redemptive structures, challenges the recuperations of unity on an ontological level, and asserts a difference that opens the discursive field of the real. In this light, Pynchon's characterization of Frenesi (and her time) can seem reductive, denying her (it) a certain cogency of resistance to normative discourses (say, in her case, discourses of reproduction, motherhood, and femininity that condition the narrative of redemption). The dramatic universe projected in the more narrowly allegorical version of the 1960s here collapses; its pulsions, its urgencies, dematerialize, become weightless, invested with the strange levity of a simulacrum. Repetition implies a constitutive groundlessness, a being haunted not by the ghost of theory but by its own theoretical determinations. The more intimate understanding of the rationality that seizes identity, perception, and experience *escapes* by its very nature. It depends therefore on its expression, on reflexive forms that index its possibility by performing their own implicated relation to a differential and catastrophic time. Here, indeed, one has a way of reading cultural productions from the 1960s not as abstractions but as complex interventions in history, a way of grasping the intelligence of the time's antinomic excesses in their symptomaticity, or rather as articulations of a symptomatic modality of cultural participation. The political effect of this modality is to gauge the depth of metalinguistic force in the social field, and not only at cultural registers but extending into the most quotidian experiences of self, place, and community. Pynchon's earlier fiction attempts to give an imaginative shape to this quotidian dimension of a postwar world, to narrate the vacuolized body of the time in artifacts that inscribe within themselves a "double" consciousness of history. *Vineland* offers a different kind of inscription, a different narrative means of working through the paradoxes of everyday life. But to do so, it has to blind itself to the relentless intimacy of metalanguage, its presence at the very ground of the text's *own* being and its phantom habit of coming back whenever its foreclosure has been assumed and some "real" otherness projected.

The novel doesn't take this haunting repetition lightly—as one sees in the persistent temptation to order in Frenesi's daughter Prairie, who is visited in her sleeping bag the night of the reunion by a rapturous Brock Vond—but it does convert that repetition into a meaning it "names and specifies" rather than a process of becoming or self-metabolization that it performs. Entropy here indicates a force to resist in the stabilization of a viable cultural form (the novel as a representation of social unity) and not the force of resistance itself (fracturing representation because it supports social order). As I have tried to suggest, this shift mirrors a changing time and a sense that the type of resistance generated in the 1960s does not amount to a genuine politics. This more contemporary perception, born out of a frustration with entrenched authoritarian investments in American social life, relies for its cogency on (re)readings of the 1960s that either sanitize the entropic social and cultural forms apparent in it or dismiss them as frivolous and apolitical. As a result, it is difficult today to understand the recent past with much clarity, or to scan the entropy it discloses in any kind of impartial light. But a starting point for more objective assessments can be to focus on this difficulty, or rather on its historical specificity, the 1960s as a moment in the evolution of a more nuanced criticism demanding of its practitioners (and readers) a stamina in the element of narrativity that needs neither to sanitize nor to dismiss.

Ironically this stamina depends on its *perception* in the social field, the telling of its story through time in forms of expression too often rejected as overly theoretical. The 1960s that emerges from this narrative can be defined as the moment of a cultural "reverie" working on different levels to short-circuit discourse from within, to crystallize inside its iterations an imaginative apprehension of the ground on which a political desire can be based. Certainly the counterculture conjured in *Vineland* does not succeed in being more than a symptom of its time or in forestalling the forces of co-optation that render it inert. But expecting such success might not be the point of rereading the 1960s today, if the goal is to trace in that decade the beginnings of a revitalized political life rooted in an imagination *for* immanence, for the implicate orders of social life at the turn of the century. In this light, one might wonder if *Vineland* in its realism is any more appropriate a narrative form for the task of representing a community's political desire and obligation than, say, *The Crying of Lot 49* or *Gravity's Rainbow*, where this peculiar imaginative poeisis, antirealist and antitraditional, is so much more clearly in evidence.

7
A VIGILANT FOLLY: LINES OF FLIGHT IN *MASON & DIXON*

Against such helpless Exposure as this, a vigilant Folly must be the only Defense . . .

Any Argument from Design . . . must include a yearning for Flight . . .
—Mason & Dixon

With the publication of *Mason & Dixon* in 1997, Pynchon returns to the reflexive and self-implicating narrative modes of his earlier work. Where *Vineland*, as I argued in the previous chapter, was *about* preterite characters without being itself preterite, *Mason & Dixon* firmly lodges its own preterition in its structure and at the level of expression. The novel focuses on a situation that is incidental to the world historical events happening more or less concurrently (most notably the birth of the American republic). The situation it narrates, the running of the Mason-Dixon Line westward through the American continent, ends on an inconclusive note in the wilderness somewhere east of the Ohio River. The Line becomes what the Reverend Wicks Cherrycoke calls "Some great linear summing up of Human Incompletion" (692). One senses, reading this novel, that much has been written about very little, and that as detailed and carefully constructed as the text is, in the end not much happens to its two protagonists but the usual (albeit dream-distorted) ontic trivia of eighteenth-century surveyors in the New World. Pynchon's prose is throughout a maniacally sustained parody of English diction at the time, and so persuasive that even scholars have felt compelled to classify it as an eighteenth-century novel (a panel devoted to just this topic took place at the 1998 Modern Language Association conference). But it is precisely its parodic and displaced character that, on the contrary, makes it a late-twentieth-century work, speaking to its time in its untimeliness, evoking through its elliptical and symptomatic fabulations very contemporary concerns about the legacies of the Enlightenment. The numerous proleptic references in the novel to such things as surf music, eighty-mile-long malls, real estate developers, billable hours, katsup, and "Bad Energy" all serve to remind us of the stakes it has driven into the ground of an everyday life characterized by acontextual desire and the technological drive to master the processes of life. *Mason & Dixon* is a narrative analysis of this desire, this drive, and correlative concepts of transparency, truth, reason, synthesis, and control.

Pynchon begins by making a consistent link between technocratic society and writing, what Michel de Certeau calls a "scriptural apparatus of modern 'discipline' . . . inseparable from the 'reproduction' made possible by the development of printing" (*Practice*, 131–32). The result of this process has been the mediation of orality, voice, the resonating human body by a "scriptural economy" so totalizing that the former only exist implicated in its system, intextuated in its networks and historical mappings.[1] The story of Mason and Dixon's inscriptive desire returns us to an archaeological moment in the construction of that scriptural economy, binding together the projects of modernity (colonialism, scientific progress, democracy, and capitalism) with the law of metalanguage—conspicuous in the various field-books, almanacks, day-journals, and minute-books into which they record their work and their lives, or are recorded by the bureaucrats who oversee them. Thus the practice of writing takes on for Pynchon a symptomatic, even a metonymic, relation to the history of metalinguistic conquest, one episode of which he tells in *Mason & Dixon*. De Certeau defines writing as "the concrete activity that consists in constructing, on its own, blank space—the page—a text that has power over the exteriority from which it has been isolated" (134). Such a definition applies equally well to the imperialism implicit in Mason and Dixon's Line, since "Detachment," writes Pynchon, is "the beginning of the West" (445). The analogy between writing and colonizing rests on an act of defection that, as it writes *over* the blank space, also articulates it as blank—it both detaches the space and detaches itself from it in a dual movement of projection and capture that catches up the "West" in a specular autonomy.

To tell the story of the West as the "non-place" implied by this detachment, *Mason & Dixon* does what Mason and Dixon do, and the performative intertwining of content and expression attends in it the tracking of the heterological "power over exteriority" that Pynchon seeks to unmask. To follow that track necessitates a reading able to sustain that intertwining in its own "body," and it is with this ethical caveat in mind that I will explore the novel's unusual contemporaneity.

The tactics of parody and fabulation deployed by Pynchon support a thematic focus on abstraction in the work of "Star-gazing" that Mason and Dixon do for a living (Mason is an astronomer, Dixon a surveyor; both use the positions of the stars to locate themselves literally and figuratively on the earth).

The character Maskelyne, another astronomer better connected to the shadowy East India Company that underwrites their first expedition and then to the Royal Society that funds the Line, exemplifies this abstract rationality and its temptations for Mason:

> Maskelyne is the pure type of one who would transcend the Earth,— making him, for Mason, a walking cautionary Tale. For years now, after midnight Culminations, has he himself lain and listen'd to the Sky-Temptress, whispering, Forget the Boys, forget your loyalties to your Dead, first of all Rebekah, for she, they, are but distractions, temporal, flesh, ever attempting to drag the Uranian Devotee back down out of his realm of pure Mathesis, of that which abides. (134)

Transcendence in a "pure Mathesis" is here counterposed to an affinity with the earth, with the organic world where life and death maintain their gravity, and with the human world of fraternal fellowship. This distinction between the universality of reason and the finitude of the body structures the narrative at many levels, magnetizing the needle in its moral compass. At the same time, Pynchon complicates the distinction by grasping in his story the fundamentally chiasmic relation between the opposed terms. Mason's attraction to the stars involves him with other "Lens-men" like the sensualist Dixon, and their stormy friendship both derives and suffers from their common susceptibility to the seductions of what the narrator later terms "Sky-Structure." If obsessiveness in their vocation threatens worldly concerns and pleasures, it also dovetails with them in the contrapuntal rhythm between work on the Line and the various furloughs back down and above it. Temporal "flesh" in its subjection to earthly gravity does not for Pynchon preexist the rational inscription of the earthly space in which flesh lives out its destiny, except as a matter requiring a form or shape to be intelligible.[2] Like Jacques Vaucanson's "Mechanickal Duck that shits" (372), Pynchon's novel implicates the organic as a structural principle and a human value in the mechanism of an emerging cybernetic order.[3]

That "flesh" and its transcendence coexist and mutually determine each other in the act of running the Line can be inferred in the above passage from a second distinction between Maskelyne's Mathesis and Mason's dead wife Rebekah, a ghost whose haunting reminds him of the way, caught up in his sky-structuralism, he neglected her when she was alive. If Mason is not the pure type of the rationalist scientist, he nonetheless experiences a complicity that weighs him down with guilt. His guilt ironically links him to the living world in the form of her visitations, when she dispenses advice like the following: " 'Look to the Earth,' she instructs him. 'Belonging to her as I do, I know she lives, and that . . . even you, Mopery, may learn of her, Tellurick Secrets you could never guess" (172). Rebekah symbolizes an irrational and invisible element in the earthly that Mason abstracts in his obsession with astronomy. But as such she is not a *body* and therefore not subject to the gravity that holds a body in its place. The opposite of pure Mathesis is not simply an empirically given earth on which human bodies live but something less tangible, more secret, which shares with transcendental things the quality of insubstantiality. Mason's haunted relationship to Rebekah indeed takes on the appearance of an obsession not unlike the obsession with stars, an analogy driven home by the narrator in one of Mason's worrying moments:

> [Rebekah] assum'd that he well understood her obligations among the Dead, and would respond ever as she wish'd. Yet how would he? being allow'd no access to any of those million'd dramas among the Dead. They were like Stars to him,—unable to project himself among their enigmatic Gatherings, he could but observe thro' a mediating Instrument. The many-Lens'd Rebekah. (195)

Mason's metaphoric conflation of his telescope and his dead wife comically indicates his fantasmatic sexual predilections as an inveterate man of science, but it also points to the mirror relation at the heart of the novel between reason and unreason, the universal and the particular, technology and organicity. Across this series of implicated opposites, both body and earth (explicitly analogized in the text) assume a ghostly and negative form that prevents Mason, whose most salient trait is a lingering melancholy, from fully living in the present.

Pynchon thus makes clear through the figure of "many-Lens'd Rebekah" that the empirical domain comes into being with its rational organization, and that the precondition for an ethically grounded temporal existence is not in fact a "living present" but an absence that haunts it from within. Dixon's childhood teacher Emerson gives this absence its precise formulation for the novel when he says, "Time is the Space that may not be seen" (326), and it is this invisible space that Mason and Dixon penetrate by way of marking a boundary and defining an orientation (a westward "Vector of Desire," as Wicks Cherrycoke puts it). Although Pynchon portrays Dixon as the more earthbound of the two surveyors, his desire to map is also rational insofar as it seeks to conform territory to a mental image whose psychological function is that of stabilization and control. The consequence of this control is not simply to organize the territory for various affective investments but simultaneously to reduce it in its "reality" to a fantasy world. Here the narrator tells us about Dixon's earliest motivations for running the Line:

> He must, if one day call'd upon, produce an overhead view of a World that never was, in truth-like detail, one he'd begin in silence to contrive,—a Map entirely within his mind, of a World he could escape to, if he had to. If he had to, he would enter it entirely but never get lost, for he would have this Map, and in it, spread below, would lie ev'rything,—Mountains of Glass, Sea of Sand, Serpent's Cave, endless Prairie. . . . another Chapbook-Fancy with each Deviation and Dip of the [Compass] Needle. (242)

The metaphors of duplication and verisimilitude in this passage suggest in Dixon's desire an escapist drive that renders his eventual life work a Line of flight into a real virtuality ("a Map entirely within his mind, of a World he could escape to"). This paradoxical figure clearly underpins the metalinguistic violence that the Line entails (note how it implies the conversion of the world into a "Chapbook-Fancy"), but on two levels: it signifies (1) the unreal colonization of an invisible space that (2) is itself unreal. One can refer this figure to an "areality" that converts organic matter into a legible (or classifiable) thing via the imposition of an "aerial" or transcendent form, and at the same time hear in it an "aeration" or breath that maintains a continuity with organic cycles. Here the complexity of Pynchon's narrative comes to the fore: Mason and Dixon's work (and the work of *Mason & Dixon*) symptomatically reiterates the project of conquest that modernity engenders, and this project appears in its double status not simply as a repression of the "Space that cannot be seen" but as its avatar, the institution of a virtual order that one will henceforth have to accept as real.

The dynamic of Pynchon's novel, in other words, is not dialectical conflict between opposites (earth and sky, wilderness and civilization, superstition and reason, or speech and writing) but a repetition that encloses terms in a single complicity—or, to shift the register to that of spatiality, not an isotropic clash between constituted objects but a preobjective flow of amorphous and undifferentiated matter. The America that Mason and Dixon encounter is no ordinary "place" in the sense that this means delimited or enclosed, ordered according to principles of extension and causality—in a word, Newtonian space. Pynchon proceeds not from a notion of coexistence (where each object, point, or locus in space is externalized with respect to every other) but rather from ideas of palimpsests and Möbius strips, invisible Ley-lines and parallel universes. Pynchon offers perhaps his most ingenious metaphor for this America in the quartz prisms that Mason and Dixon place on the marker stones along the Line. These crystals disclose "a fine structure of tiny cells, each a Sphere with another nested concentrickally within, much like Fish Roe in appearance" (547). Nested inside such nested structures is what the expedition's "Quartz-scryer" Mr. Everybeet calls a " 'Ghost,' another Crystal inside the ostensible one, more or less clearly form'd" (547). Mr. Everybeet explains:

> " 'Tis there the Pictures appear . . . tho' it varies from one Operator to the next,—some need a perfect deep Blank, and cannot scry in Ghost-Quartz. Others, before too much Clarity, become blind to the other World . . . my own Crystal,"—he searches his Pockets and produces a Hand-siz'd Specimen with a faint Violent tinge,—"the Symmetries are not always easy to see . . . here, these twin Heptagons . . . centering your Vision upon their Common side, gaze straight in,—"
> "Aahhrrhh!" Mason recoiling and nearly casting away the crystal.
> "Huge, dark Eyes?" the Scryer wishes to know.
> "Aye.—Who is it?" Mason knows. (442)

The *face* that Mason sees in the crystal inside the crystal "varies from one Operator to the next" according to who it is he or she wishes to see or is haunted by (in Mason's case, this will again be Rebekah, whose eyes he recognizes in the crystal). The doubly crystalline prisms that mark the Mason-Dixon Line, and that also mark boundary and location in *Mason & Dixon*, contain representations of "other Worlds" than the "ostensible one." This spectral investiture of desire in the objects by which "place" is established clearly exhibits a fundamental strategy of the novel to fold desire and the object, the time that desire actualizes and the space that the object defines, into one telluric (and also textual) surface. Space is the invisible world that dwells in matter (quite literally, it turns out later in the novel, invaginated into the earth) and *can* be seen after all (for Mason in fact sees it), so long as perception finds the right balance between opacity (the "deep Blank") and transparency ("too much Clarity"), the variable point of visual acuity that can never be fixed.

Pynchon is conceptually close in anecdotal narrative details such as these to what Maurice Merleau-Ponty calls a "human" or "anthropological space."

Distinguished from a "geometrical" system of objective relationships between determined points that is experienced as perspective, convergence, depth, and position by a synthesizing eye/I, "anthropological space" designates a spatial condition or frame that cannot be "put into perspective by consciousness" (The Phenomenology of Perception, 256). Unlocatable and ungraspable, this "more primordial" dimension forms an infinite set around the objective world that is not itself objectivizable, an "outside" in which Merleau-Ponty finds the "essential structure of our being [as a] being situated in relation to an environment" (284). This "relation" is one of implication in a totality, an envelopment of the subject in a prepersonal "depth" that, beneath or coterminous with geometric space, commits that subject to an existential immediacy irreducible to acts of comprehension. Anthropological space has the "thickness of a medium devoid of any thing" and indicates a "depth which does not yet operate between objects, which . . . does not yet assess the distance between them, and which is simply the opening of perception upon some ghost thing as yet scarcely qualified" (266). Such an experience of ghosts (and such a ghostly experience) precedes the differentiation of perception and dream, and as such it constitutes what Merleau-Ponty calls a "direction of existence," an intention immanent to the world in which it orients itself, a desire that is not the property of a constituted subject but a direction taken, a velocity or rate of change in a fluctuating and multiple space. The way Mason looks into the piece of quartz and sees the "huge, dark Eyes" of a ghost is a pure perception that does not presuppose an act of consciousness within an objective or even an ontological order.[4] It cannot be that Mason sees a ghost in the crystal anymore than he can see the crystal without the ghost orienting his gaze or quickening his desire in it. This gyrelike implication of Mason in his world comes through most distinctly in the "recoil" that it produces in him, the terror that almost causes him to drop the crystal and signifies that death, that nothingness, that infinite regress at the heart of time as it reduces "Mason" to no one and his world to a "non-place" of ghostly "pictures." This is why Wicks Cherrycoke, commenting on Emerson's homily about time as invisible space, adds "that out of Mercy, we are blind as to Time,—for we could not bear to contemplate what lies at its heart" (326).

But Mason & Dixon does contemplate what lies at the heart of time, albeit in modes of attenuated catastrophe, and its conjurations of that "non-place" unfold in the way that Emerson, his student Dixon, Mason, and the narrator Wicks Cherrycoke all cease to be "characters" in a realist novel. They are "selves entirely word-made" as the foppish Son of Liberty Philip Dimdown puts it, woven into the texture of a massive pastiche that performs the spatial laminations it also thematizes in sly metaphysical exchanges like this one:

> "Lo, Lamination abounding," contributes Squire Haligast, momentarily visible, "its purposes how dark, yet have we ever sought to produce these thin Sheets innumerable, to spread a given Volume as close to pure Surface as possible, whilst on route discovering various new forms, the Leyden Pile, decks of Playing-Cards, contrivances which, like the Lever or Pulley, quite multiply the apparent forces, often unto disproportionate results...."
>
> "The printed Book," suggest the Rev'd [Cherrycoke], "—thin layers of pattern'd Ink, alternating with other thin layers of compress'd Paper, stack'd often by the Hundreds." (389–90)

The Pynchon whose "dark" tactics stand revealed here at the "pure Surface" of writing opens the "space" of encounter with the American wilderness by locating it at the level of a language that is flush with its own specifically temporal ground. At stake is a kind of *duration* that refers "America" to an anterior plane of undifferentiated "pictures" or images on which perception becomes a function of pure transition, of a "lived present" defined always in terms of its own disappearance.[5] *Mason & Dixon* is a "travel" story in the sense that de Certeau maintains "all stories are travel stories" (*Practice*, 115), tissues of metaphors that move, *metaphorai*, "spatial trajectories" that make the "places" they traverse textual nonplaces in which the act of delimitation meets its own internal limit, the "ghost" of a figural or semiotic motility that haunts the geometrical structures it founds.

De Certeau, building on Merleau-Ponty's ideas on spatiality in *The Practice of Everyday Life*, constructs an opposition between place (*lieu*) and a space (*espace*) linked to narrative tactics of inversion, quotation or doubling, ellipsis, metaphor, and metonymy. The ruses of rhetoric "describe" ("as a mobile point 'describes' a curve" [116], he writes) an element of almost Brownian motion that depends on its "operation" in a multidimensional present that is always other to itself, furrowed internally by the specters of its own singularity. Space for de Certeau is "like the word when it is spoken, that is, when it is caught in the ambiguity of an actualization, transformed into a term dependent upon many different conventions, situated as the act of a present (or a time), and modified by the transformations caused by successive contexts" (117). Space is a practice of place, a putting into motion of one's own time and contingency. Only in the grip of such a practice, in fact, does "time" come to quicken in us a historical sense, a feeling for the historicity of our actions as they play out symptomatically the displacement of time (or, to be more precise, the displacement of this sense for the displacement of time, usually in the name of history or of some more objective relation to the past, to a tradition, to a place). De Certeau makes this coimplication of time and practice explicit by asserting a certain nondistinction between spaces and places. The former (spaces) is the play in structures (places) that marks not an external but an internal difference, a non-self-identical "labor" at the heart of place (placement, position, positionality) that constantly transforms it into its opposite and vice versa.

This is why the turn to language and narrative is important to de Certeau: the "story," he writes, incisively highlights the overlapping of space and place, their coextension in a practice of "moving" or ever-shifting signification. Under the pressure of a history consisting in the progressive technicization of space (and the strict regulation of time), "spatial practices"—those concerned with the remainders of a process of rationalization and colonization undergone since the Enlightenment—pass into the domain of literature, where they take the form of "everyday virtuosities that science doesn't know what to do with and which become the signatures, easily recognized by readers, of everyone's micro-stories" (70). The story, in other words, dissimulates the "invisible Space" or temporal nun that paradoxically dies beneath the instruments of its own delimitation and designation. This sacrifice underlies the "primary function" of the story to "authorize the establishment, displacement or transcendence of limits, and as a consequence, to set in opposition, within the closed field of discourse, two movements that intersect (setting and transgressing limits) in such a way as to make the story a sort of 'crossword' decoding stencil . . . [or] dynamic partitioning of space" (123). Only through this "stencilization" does space come into being at all, and this is why it remains constitutively tied to a practice (of writing) that "nests" another practice "Concentrickally within" its own demarcative procedures.

With this we are clearly in the topography of *Mason & Dixon*, a novel about its own narrativity and, precisely through this reflexive turning around on itself, about America too, about its delimitation and colonization, about the enclosure of space in proper places (or properties), and about its own (and our) complicity in that enclosure—a complicity that in turn conditions the possibility of *seeing* the imperialist history it reproduces within the ever-shifting boundaries of "anthropological space." Pynchon hints at this textual overdetermination in the previously quoted passage on lamination, where the printed book becomes one more device (like the lever or the pulley) to extend our powers of control. *Mason & Dixon* is about a technological society only by first being technological, sustaining its own narrative desire to found, to originate, to *be* a world in its "disproportionate" multiplication of forces and effects. To use and be used is one obvious subtext of a literary practice as wedded to citation, parody, and encyclopedic "overstuffing" farce as Pynchon's, and his novel clearly reflects this problem back on its readers. The ingenuity of *Mason & Dixon* is that to read it well is almost necessarily to provoke the "ghost" of a spatiality that disappears beneath our interpretive tools, to involve us in a "Destiny . . . to inscribe the Earth" (221). But such an involvement in the story of Mason and Dixon must also entail an involvement in *Mason & Dixon*, its linguistic involutions, its opacities and transparencies, its reflexivity defined not as abstraction but as the carefully constructed limit to the abstraction that governs the resistance to reading (or seeing). What gets lost in this resistance is a time deeper than memory and thus an immemorial space (Pynchon calls it "America") that does not ever appear except insofar as it alters reading (perception) toward a commitment to the polyvalences of language.

This "space" is the stake in Pynchon's mode of writing and in any reading of it, a history, a continuing legacy, a haunting, a repetition on which no reflection is possible except by way of acknowledging its precessionary grip on every act of writing and reading. Pynchon understands this as a logic of implication, of texts that are "general" in a Derridean sense and that form vortexes into which the reader is plunged. *Mason & Dixon* is an attempt to bring this logic into a clear literary focus, telling a story about founding acts that takes as its own foundation a kind of textual vortex. Pynchon affords a glimpse of this vortical structure in passages like the following, an extended riff on the specific inscriptive desire that both Mason and Dixon and *Mason & Dixon* act out:

> Does Britannia, when she sleeps, dream? Is America her dream?—in which all that cannot pass in the metropolitan Wakefulness is allow'd Expression away in the restless Slumber of these Provinces, and on West-ward, wherever 'tis not yet mapp'd, nor written down, nor ever, by the majority of Mankind, seen,—serving as a very Rubbish-Tip for subjunctive Hopes, for all that *may yet be true*,—Earthly Paradise, Fountain of Youth, Realms of Prester John, Christ's Kingdom, ever behind the sunset, safe till the next Territory to the West be seen and recorded, mea-

sur'd and tied in, back into the Net-Work of Points already known, that slowly triangulates its Way into the Continent, changing all from subjunctive to declarative, reducing Possibilities to Simplicities that serve the ends of Government,—winning away from the realm of the Sacred, its Borderlands one by one, and assuming them unto the bare mortal World that is our home, and our Despair. (345)

The almost vertiginous experience of this sentence suggests (phenomenologically, as it were) the movement of the text as a whole, orthogonal and yet at the same time devious, swerving through qualifications, meandering to its final resting place in the word "Despair." Pynchon, that is, works here at two levels: semantic, where Mason and Dixon's "West-ward" momentum is glossed in terms of a "declarative" desire for the "subjunctive" space of America; and syntactic, where that desire is made to circulate through an essentially sinuous writing. The transformation of the subjunctive into the declarative on the first level is inverted on the second level: Pynchon's diction takes the reader back to a state of "unmapped" disorientation and ambiguity, back to the overdetermined realm of dream. The dreamer, Britannia, moves toward the dream of America as the dream returns to the dreamer, agitating at the center of the latter's intention to "see," "record," and "measure." This double and deviating movement organizes the entire novel: Mason and Dixon penetrate the wilderness and then withdraw into already penetrated zones of civilization (they construct the Line in spring and summer, then wait out the winter in Philadelphia), and in addition they make brief excursions above and below the Line (north to New York, south to Maryland and Virginia). *Mason & Dixon* "triangulates its Way into the Continent" in spiderlike fashion, assimilating invisible spaces into the ordered places of empire to evoke the *space of rationality itself*, the scene of empire as it materializes in the practice of language.

De Certeau has written elegantly about this rhythm of departure and return in discourse. The sleight of hand by which discourse about the other becomes a discourse authorized by the other has for its basic structure the travel story: narrative's constituent relation to limits, to what de Certeau calls "frontiers" and the "bridges" that mark their co-optation (127), underscores its function in the process of legitimating a disciplinary organization of knowledge. The urge to delimit is also an urge to narrate; the urge to narrate, in turn, cannot be differentiated from a de-temporalizing rationalization of space. "Normative discourse," writes de Certeau, "operates only if it has already become a story, a text articulated on something real and speaking in its name" (*Practice*,

149). This articulation on (or of) the real is why Pynchon writes as he does, short-circuiting the normativity of narrative discourse through the fabrication of "Net-works" and rhizomatic surfaces that flatten the depth-effects of meaning. That the quoted passage is in fact elaborate parody, not meant to be taken as exemplary of any hidden intent except insofar as it exemplifies precisely the nothingness that adheres in levity, indicates the method of the text's metacommentary on American colonialism. The latter in its fundamental scriptural mode envelops the text and the text of its reception (our reading) as well. It happens in the most basic assumptions of representation and truth, transforming "Borderlands one by one" into interiorized limits, internal differences that open the inside to its "Sacred" other.[6]

Mason & Dixon is thus a profoundly heterological novel concerned with the strangeness of its own authority in a world founded on the displacement of limits. Pynchon's is a discourse *without its own discourse* because even this registration of the arbitrariness of authority resonates with the violence it finds so strange. It specifies in its untimely representations how present practices don't simply thematize the past but perform and reproduce it. History lives in the present through the methodological choices we make for its representation (and precisely because those choices are themselves historically determined). Pynchon drives this point home by magnifying his own choices and narrative modes to the point of overwhelming history in the ambiguities of fiction. This comes through perhaps most tellingly in the mediated status of the narration, which fluctuates between Pynchon's omniscient third person and the unreliable Wicks Cherrycoke, who recounts the story to his sister's family in 1786, some eighteen years after the fact. Cherrycoke was a witness to the running of the Line, but he freely embroiders and invents scenarios he knows only secondhand or through patchy textual records. He functions to mark a fluctuation in the text between a sonorous voice and its transcription that frustrates the reader's discursive work of settling the novel's time and place, its meanings, even its values. The abandonment of the Line before its completion ensures for the novel a subjunctive open-endedness that deflates the reader's desire for closure. Obsession and dream take over where "reality" leaves off, fable substitutes for history, but in this way Pynchon narrates not the transgression of a rationalizing metalinguistic power but the much more troubling story of an affective investment in structure, the semiotic libido circulating in the interstices of discourse.

The novel's homage to the subjunctive should therefore be read not as the triumph of dream over reason but as the latter's intrinsic oneirism, the madness of reason that can produce only avatars of itself, Lines of flight that symptomatically play out the fundamental abstraction of a modernity predicated on a generalized writing. This is why *Mason & Dixon* is such a contemporary novel, for it speaks to the distinctly modern problem of an extrinsic social power inseparable from intrinsic processes of subject formation, from the sense of "you" or "I" that puts that power into some kind of perspective. Analytic discourses on consumerism, law, the role of the state in a global economy, the virtuality of electoral politics, the privatization of public space, the impact of information technologies, and the possibilities for art and culture in a late capitalist mode of production all turn around the Möbius strip of a power inscribing itself in bodies. Put in question is desire's investment of that power. "The act of suffering oneself to be written by the group's law is oddly accompanied by a pleasure," writes de Certeau, "that of being recognized (but one does not know by whom), of becoming an identifiable and legible word in a social language, of being changed into a fragment within an anonymous text, of being inscribed in a symbolic order that has neither owner nor author" (*Practice*, 140).

The anomie of everyday life today derives from this pleasure taken in intextuated being, the absence of an overtly repressive force that this complicity entails, and a nonseparability that makes of the spaces we live in not containers but fields, habituses that we *are* more than inhabit. *Mason & Dixon* dramatizes this "helpless Exposure" to the outside by giving its implicate order a cultural form, albeit the displaced form of the "nowhere" implicit in the novel's "vigilant Folly," its parodic transvestisms of the real. Dixon reminds us of this peculiar drama with his espousal of the "inner-surface Philosophy," which argues for the presence of another world inside the earth. As the narrator puts it, this philosophy is less "studied" than "endur'd," which is to say it unfolds in the space of hesitation between mind and body, essence and existence:

> The Interior had remain'd less studied philosophickally, than endur'd anxiously, by those who might choose to travel Diametrickally across it,—means of Flight having been develop'd early in the History of the Inner Surface. "Their God [says Dixon of the people who live in the Interior], like that of the Iroquois, lives at their Horizon,—here 'tis their North or South Horizon, each a more and less dim Ellipse of Sky-light. The Curve of the Rim is illuminated, depending on the position of the Sun, in greater or lesser Relievo,—chains of mountains, thin strokes of towers, the eternally spilling lives of thousands dwelling in the long

Estuarial Towns wrapping from Outside to Inside as the water rushes away in uncommonly long waterfalls, downward for hours, unbrak'd, till at last debouching into an interior Lake of great size, upside-down but perfectly secured to its Lake-bed by Gravity as well as Centrifugal Force, and in which upside-down swimmers glide at perfect ease, hanging over an Abyss thousands of miles deep. From wherever one is, to raise one's Eyes is to see the land and Water rise ahead of one and behind as well, higher and higher till lost in the Thickening of the Atmosphere. . . . In the larger sense, then, to journey anywhere, in this *Terra Concava*, is ever to ascend. With its Corollary,—Outside, here upon the Convexity,—to go anywhere is ever to descend." (739–40)

This passage recapitulates many of the tropes at work in the novel. It literalizes the collapse of opposites such as outside and inside, real and imaginary, descent (subjection to gravity) and ascent (release from gravity), place and nonplace. The lack of a threshold between these binominal terms produces a specific kind of disorientation that disturbs the stability of Newtonian space. It suggests a seamless continuity between dimensions that both subjectivizes the world and objectifies the subject. The active metaphor here is philosophy's *mirror of the mind* in which things appear doubled and inverted, transposed into upside-down images that function to (re)produce symbolic order. The context for the foregoing citation is an argument with Mason, who strenuously asserts the impossibility of an inner surface on scientific grounds. But it's important to grasp that Mason's skepticism is not trivialized, and Dixon's espousal of indeterminacy is no less complicit in the rationalism that Pynchon seeks to analyze. The kleinbottle of the earth is not simply the figure of a tautological reasoning rejected by science; it parodies the (mechanical) repetitions at work in the technological (pragmatic and utilitarian) paradigm created by science. Gravity remains a law for Mason's skepticism and Dixon's belief, for the outer as well as the inner surface, and also for the pure surface of writing where Pynchon inscribes his implicate order.

As a parody, then, the inner-surface Philosophy is the inverted double of inversion, discourse catching itself out in its specular nature—a self-parody or metaparody that indexes its own ideological appurtenance.[7] The text neither mystifies (with Dixon's fanciful imagination) nor demystifies (with Mason's objectivity). It questions the assumptions common to both operations; it indicates the presence in them of a modern sensibility for unveiling, making true, rendering transparent. This sensibility is also inverted because it projects its own cause or origin (as an effect) to legitimate its desire and eclipse it in reason (via the function of disavowal). The perversity of reason is the theme that emerges in the passage, and what gives its upside-down nature the force of critique. Here one can begin to place in a proper context Pynchon's narrative techniques: the deliberately archaic diction and punctuation; the long sentences verging on incoherence through the use of dashes and the heaping on of present participles ("dwelling . . . wrapping . . . debouching . . . hanging . . ." in the previous passage); the deliberate warping of dimension that makes it difficult for the reader to imagine just what kind of space has been constructed; and, most significantly, the reader's consequent uncertainty about how to place himself or herself in the novel's world, how to "identify" with or in it given the estranging effects of its language. Syntactic disorientation works for Pynchon to problematize the "Eyes" or "I's" that "see the land and Water rise ahead of one and behind as well," in that heterological precession that sweeps the subject up in its vortices. Perception is once again brought into an anthropological space and confronted by ethical imperatives to look at and through the discursive mechanisms of looking itself.[8]

These imperatives are met (if they are) in a distinctly textual and textural domain that it is the virtue of Mason & Dixon to have given a literary form. One recognizes this domain in the foregoing quotation's references to travel, journeys, "Flights" that aren't extensive movements between a here and a there so much as intensive transformations, rhetorical reversals, strange figural trajectories. Pynchon is telling a story about stories through "spatial practices" that put in motion his own time, and this then situates it in its time (the time of a turn to language). The novel's reflexivity is a shrewd and resonant commentary on how contemporary life came to assume its present dimensions. It also suggests tactics for writing, reading, and living more humanely in a technocratic order that has grown so complex that our humanity now requires this heterological reflection on its own limits in order to exist at all. Pynchon models this kind of reflection in his difficult work, and he demands it of his readers as well. For the line of Flight into the inner surface of Mason & Dixon is also Mason and Dixon's Line of flight, which in turn exemplifies those lines of flight Pynchon writes on the (blank) page.

CONCLUSION: TOWARD A THEORY OF THE COUNTERCULTURE

The exception . . . thinks the general with intense passion.—Kierkegaard

The focus of this book has been to evoke a symptom, to trace its displaced contours and identify its iterative principle in the act of interpretation itself. The time of Pynchon's work and the time in which that work inscribes a place (or nonplace) demand an intensely reflexive analysis that calls into question its own grounds. In this demand one can recognize that symptom as a preoccupation with origin, with beginning, with production across all its conceptual registers. The heightening of this metaphysical concern today comes at least in part as a reaction to a radical devaluation of one's sovereignty, the vanishing substance of one's actions in a cultural sphere dominated by consumerism; a political arena where, as Baudrillard drily puts it, "one never feels more powerless than when one goes to vote"; and global economic marketplaces rapidly revising one's relationships to national and democratic social structures. The difference one makes in the world, the mark of difference itself, tends to disappear with a late modern mode of production, leaving only the torsions of a remorseless identity caught in the compulsion to repeat.

One consequence of this (our) paradoxical time is an abstraction that seizes one even in the singularities of commitment. Involvement and detachment become more and more indistinguishable from each other. This is not only true for the specialist whose field or subfield has grown so complex that only a total commitment to a small set of problems ensures any possibility of either a practical or a theoretical result (whether you're a physicist or a lawyer, an economist or a political activist, a novelist or a critic). It's also true for anyone met with the demand to participate in a life-world so specular and autonomous that involvement can only mean detachment—even if it doesn't at all follow from this that detachment therefore becomes a kind of involvement. Our time has so incorporated the acontextual values of scientific investigation, and so extended the techniques of social power into the most intimate spaces of everyday life, that it is difficult to know what opposition might consist in because it seems as if what needs to be opposed is precisely one's self as the carrier of that power. So disorienting has this biopolitical implication become that it's not entirely fanciful to think of ordinary life as having gone through the looking glass—or on an acid trip. What's up is down, what's left is right, what's public is private, what's progressive is reactionary, what looks like care is contempt, the best lack all conviction and the worst are full of passionate intensity.

What is taken for a rational world, the product of a modernity that has so successfully realized its visions of property, propriety, progress, and contractual obligation, seems in any honest phenomenological description to be crazy. But its madness is not the other of reason so much as reason itself, or reason on the heterological track of its own limit or unconscious . . . once again its ground, principle, or origin. There, in the condition of possibility for the sovereign subject, lies the germ of the differences one makes, the source of the singular value they have lost in the modern world.

The time of this obsession with origins is close to what Emmanuel Levinas calls an "immemorial" and "unrepresentable" past "before my freedom—before my beginning, before any present" and outside a "rigorously ontological order" of objective causality and being" ("Ethics," 84). This preoriginal or an-archic time grounds a subject in history, but it is not as such historical and indeed falls outside of being's purview altogether. Nonphenomenal, it does not "show" itself or let itself be "named" except at the price of its inscription in an "already said" symbolic regime that governs the constitution of consciousness. For Levinas, the lived historical time of identity, will, and experience—the world given to perception and that happens *for someone*—unfolds in the medium of a thematized language or metalinguistic writing. As such, what one feels as movement and becoming, action and history, dissimulate their synchronic fixity in an essentially discursive domain of generality and particularity, rule and exception (*Otherwise than Being*, 35–37).

Diachronic time for Levinas, paradoxically, happens (by not happening) at the origin that was never an origin, in a certain "questioning" after the priority and self-identity of an intrinsically rational consciousness dedicated to mastery of the object-world.[1] "It is in the passivity of the non-intentional . . . that the very justice of the position within being is questioned, a position which asserts itself with intentional thought, knowledge and a grasp of the here and now. What one sees in this questioning is being as *mauvaise conscience*; to be open to question, but also to questioning, to have to respond. Language is born in responsibility" ("Ethics," 82). Levinas counterposes to thematized language (the "said") another mode of language ("saying") that "scintillates in the said" and links a hermeneutic respect for the ambiguities of figural being to this ethical responsibility (*Otherwise than Being*, 36). This other mode corresponds to diachrony and the preorigin, but in its "non-intentional passivity," it does not signify *another* language so much as a potentiality of the said, that condition of its possibility that it virtualizes in order to exist. This is why Levinas can write: "The saying extended toward the said and absorbed in it, correlative with it, names an entity, in the light or resonance of lived time which allows a *phenomenon* to appear" (*Otherwise than Being*, 37). The an-archic "saying" articulates with this entity the "said" world in which it assumes a displaced or differential (non)being. In its very elusiveness it *expresses* the position within being, which it then also questions. "Bad conscience" indicates this complicity of saying and said, diachrony and synchrony, time and history, for a subjectivity that "appears" in a similar process of nomination and inscription.

One tendency of the recursion around the origin that characterizes this (our) time is to idealize the an-archic, to invert its diachronic status and bring it into the light of synchronic day. Multiple examples of terms used to describe this preorigin exist in the world of theoretical investigation: "saying," the preobjective, the absent cause, structural causality, *différance* or the trace, the nonsymbolizable Real, the "immonde," the figural or rhetorical ambiguities of language, the semiotic *chora*, the body without organs, et cetera. Each of these terms works by betraying the groundless ground to which they refer, and each term grasps this betrayal as intrinsic to its meaning. So implicating does such "bad conscience" become that some writers now designate the preoriginal space by its opposite: thematized language, symbolic order, or, for Judith Butler, power itself. She writes, "Power acts on the subject in at least two ways: first, as what makes the subject possible, the condition of its possibility and its formative occasion, and second, as what is taken up and reiterated in the subject's 'own' acting. As a subject *of* power (where 'of' connotes both 'belonging to' and 'wielding'), the subject eclipses the conditions of its own emergence; it eclipses power with power" (*Psychic Life of Power*, 14).

The precession at work in this move to situate the effect of power (or agency) at its cause deserves considerable reflection. To suggest the saying is said, the real is symbolic, ambiguity is literality, an-archy is law, *différance* works, or power is power is to carry complicity in the symptom of metaphysical thought to a limit where its nondistinctions and tautologies threaten to collapse these concepts into useless analytic tools.[2] What in fact preserves their efficacy is only the symptomaticity that they make necessary and that precipitates a differential but material *force* in language or structure that quite literally gains its force from the self-producing character of the origin. If power is that which properly speaking *founds itself*, then the political effect of repetition can be to highlight the arbitrary nature of that act. Giorgio Agamben crystallizes this effect in what he paradoxically calls the "sovereign exception" (*Homo Sacer*, 19). Counterposing rule (law or *nomos*, juridical order) to exception (an an-archic excess or state of nature) in a discussion of constituting acts, Agamben writes: "The rule applies to the exception in no longer applying, in withdrawing from it. The state of exception is thus not the chaos that precedes order but rather the situation that results from its suspension. In this sense, the exception is truly, according to its etymological root, *taken outside (ex-capere)*, and not simply excluded" (18). By this "taking outside" at the heart of the state of exception, Agamben does not mean a movement in extension or an exclusive difference between a here and a there, a before and an after. Just like Pynchon in *Mason & Dixon*, Agamben subtracts from his discourse the causal time or objective space (the "here and now") of Newtonian physics. To be taken outside is to be incorporated inside along the surface of (yet another) Möbius strip.[3] The function of this inside/outside nondistinction is to reveal the complicity of the exception in the rule, the anarchy of order itself. "In its archetypal form," writes Agamben, "the state of exception is therefore the *principle* of every juridical localization, since only the state of exception *opens the space* in which the determination of a certain juridical order and a particular territory first becomes possible" (19, italics mine).

Pynchon makes use of this complex topographical figure Agamben calls the exception by way of a shrewd assessment of the implicate space and inverted causality of late-twentieth-century life. The postwar period becomes the scene of an exceptional sovereignty, which in turn permeates that scene with its displacements, constituting the virtual reality of its discursive time. "What happened and is still happening before our eyes," writes Agamben, "is that the 'juridically empty' space of the state of exception (in which law is in force in the figure—that is, etymologically, in the *fiction*—of its own dissolution . . .) . . . is starting to coincide with the normal order, in which everything again becomes possible" (38). This coincidence of "normal order" with the state of exception engenders a figural space much like the Zone in *Gravity's Rainbow*: an evacuated and depolarized textual/textural field where the secret link between an-archy and law appears. This indeed might explain the peculiar historical vertigo that the novel can inspire in its readers, for Agamben's implication is that we are witness now to the emergence of a "new nomos," a "coming to light of the state of exception as the permanent structure of juridico-political de-localization and dis-location" (38). It is the presence of this structure in the indeterminacies of *Gravity's Rainbow* that makes any affirmative reading of its counterforces, creative paranoias, or humanist redemptions so difficult to sustain. The novel's preterition, like the sub-rosa worlds of V. or the WASTE underground in *The Crying of Lot 49*, expresses the unconscious logic at the heart of that structure and not the alternative to it.

In this, Pynchon's work is truly the symptom of its postwar moment, defined by that exceptional sovereignty whose models we begin to find less in politicians than in cultural figures whose embodiments of rebellion converge bizarrely with "normal order." Without unduly eliding the differences between Allen Ginsberg, Jackson Pollock, Thelonius Monk, Marlon Brando, Elvis Presley, James Dean, Bob Dylan, Joni Mitchell, James Brown, Andy Warhol, the Velvet Underground, Iggy Pop, and many others, one can still discern in them, beyond the possibilities of genuine culture they may continue to represent, the charismatic an-archy of a world where "everything is possible."[4] This does not mean one stops liking them, or their newer avatars, but it does require a reflexive approach to the last fifty years of cultural history that grasps that reflexivity in the process of its formation. As Pynchon's work indisputably demonstrates, the postwar period marks the emergence of necessarily symptomatic cultural forms that evolve new strategies for understanding their acontextual situations. If those strategies have as yet been only imperfectly analyzed, it may be because recent critical culture has not fully plumbed the depth of its own exceptionality in all the senses of that word. It has not learned to take its simulacra seriously and so realize their *dangerous* possibilities for insight into the nature of social order.

The same cannot be said for the countercultural artifacts themselves, or at least those (like Pynchon's novel) that achieve a high degree of reflexivity. Take, as another example, Nicholas Roeg and Donald Cammell's 1974 film *Performance*, a relentless (auto)critique of the relation between power and art. James Fox, the henchman of a gangster he has alienated and exemplar of the smooth, manipulative, but well-adjusted "Organization Man" of 1950s social criticism, hides out in rock star Mick Jagger's labyrinthine house and even more labyrinthine "new" androgynous masculinity. Doppelgängers of each other, Fox and Jagger are caught in a mirror relation that the film literalizes by dressing Jagger up as a gangster while he sings a song that ends, "I am the boss." Both are performers, creators of simulacra that express social power in and from their very exceptionality vis-à-vis the codes of normal life. The insular space of that exception—the rambling, rundown crash pad/recording studio overstuffed with the gaudy detritus of Western culture—and its recursive time, embodied in the film's acausal editing as well as the hallucinogenic trip on which the principal characters go after ingesting mushrooms, become dimensions of the very outside world from which the two protagonists withdraw. The counterculture is here a richly specular *imago mundi* predicated on a continuity between outside and inside. The film indelibly inscribes this metonymy in its ending, where the two protagonists merge so completely into each other that we no longer know who is who, or what is what. James Fox appears to shoot Jagger in the head just before his enemies take him away to be killed. In a brief animated sequence, we follow the bullet into and out the other side of Jagger's brain, where we discover Jagger, dressed in the costume Fox had been wearing (and Jagger had chosen for him), driving away in a Rolls Royce with the real gangster Fox had crossed. The trajectory of this bullet inside (Jagger's brain) out (to the world of real gangsters) leaves us perfectly uncertain whether either man is alive or dead, or whether this dead-alive state signifies any sort of escape from the hothouse of their self-identity. Indeed, any sense of an escape seems mitigated by the fantasmatic manner in which the real effect of the bullet is sublimated and the (realist) order of its force rendered imaginary.

Nonetheless, along the Möbius strip of the film, one can trace a line of flight that consists in a movement from the level of content, where a total disorientation sweeps away the markers of subjectivity, to that of expression, where a hallucinatory form reveals the hallucinatory structure of social order. The escape happens (by not happening) as the question, in bad conscience, of a being that asserts itself in the intentionality of the question. This is not a trippy countercultural aestheticization of anarchy for its own sake but a smart interrogation of that new *nomos* emerging into the light of day. Or rather, the counterculture is *both*, and only as such does the political character of its singular, contingent, ironic critical energies become clear. That this unusual politics has not been clear to commentators on the 1960s derives from their need to project back into the counterculture the mark of difference it so resolutely excludes. This projection comes from a variety of cultural quarters: from the conservative who deplores the loss of moral values and tradition in 1960s rebellion (George Will, Dinesh de Souza), to the ex-radical who highlights the "New Left" elements of that rebellion to impose on the period as a whole an oppositional dialectic through which political change is normatively understood (Todd Gitlin), to the cultural fetishist of retro 1970s styles lost in a fantasy of the period where "authenticity" remains alive (the plethora of androgynous rockers or singer-songwriters who still listen to Buffalo Springfield and Stevie Wonder).

One detects in these various manifestations of metaphysical desire a reluctance, if not outright refusal, to consider the doubleness that emerges during the period as the principal trait of an expressly political formalism. Where irony disappears in subsequent accounts, the counterculture becomes either a destroyer of value or the relay point for new values tied to "normalizations" of hitherto disenfranchised groups (women, African Americans, homosexuals). Where irony remains, it becomes "kynicism," the "bad" equivalent of an incorporated consumerism that anesthetizes people to the anomie around them. But in few instances is the relation at the heart of the exception between power and fiction so specified that irony becomes itself a mode of self-implicating political discourse. The various avatars of counterculture, punk rock in the 1970s, identity politics in the 1980s, club culture in the 1990s, all established themselves on commitments to performative tactics of local sociopolitical intervention. At their best they precipitated in the social field a crisis around representation and normative discourse, but they also did little more than that, disclosing in themselves the metalinguistic tendencies of the society they challenged and leaving entrenched structures of power and status intact.[5]

It may therefore also be the case that the price of these commitments becomes increasingly a mystification of the symptom they reiterate, the ethical stake that symptom drives into displaced time and intentionless phenomena. To ground one's actions and will in the certainty of principles is different from letting the ground unground one's position within being, even if the latter operation does not differ from the former at the same time. What this latter *Abgrund* reveals about the subject in history (or "in act") is its investment in an exclusive or represented difference that, in making, it also masters. This mastery thrives perhaps nowhere better than in the person (of whatever persuasion) who today believes in the consequentiality of his or her choices. I do not mean to disparage this belief or the mastery that comes with it, only to highlight in the self-identity it projects a potential for the mystification of a deeply fragmented social experience. The postwar society of the spectacle witnesses an unprecedented stripping away of substance from that person, but it also allows for a glimpse of the domination that insists in the demand *for* substance. The various countercultural movements of the 1960s made this insistence visible in failures that were not entirely without intention, and their legacy has been to open in the wake of their dissolution a new question of power that traverses the social field from its molecular units to its molar aggregates.

This question takes place as the displacement of being in language, and it potentializes that field to the point of rendering it virtual. Thus one enters the bewildering acid trip of a life-world in which it becomes difficult to know where one is, what one is doing, whether one's decisions really matter, or what the prospects are for community and care. At the same time, one grasps the strange complicity of (op)position that conditions a progressive political desire adequate to the globally metastasized late capitalism we inhabit. If counterculture takes the form of exception I have attempted to outline here, then perhaps it is in the embrace of its impossibility that one discovers today the chance at transformation it always hopes for. This is why fictions like Pynchon's play such an important cultural role, for they instruct one in the responsive and responsible nature of a language that serves as the medium of transmission for power itself, and in the most immediate undergrounds of one's being.

NOTES

Introduction

1 Quoted in Jonah Raskin's biography of Hoffman, *For the Hell of It*, 194.
2 One can see in the sense of "infinitude" and inclusion that characterized the counterculture (or to the extent that it did) an ideological accommodation to the imperatives and requirements of a capitalist order; in particular, reading with Bercovitch, this accommodation manifests itself as an autonomization of language and culture analogous to the conflation of "history" and "rhetoric" he analyzes in Puritan texts as a discursive mode of American capitalism. See *The American Jeremiad* and, for a reading of this particular thematic in *Gravity's Rainbow*, chapter 3 of this volume.
3 In his essay "The Antinomies of Postmodernity," Jameson contrasts the purely formal and logical *antinomy* to a more dialectic *contradiction*, arguing that the former indelibly stamps contemporary thought at the price of an abstraction from context (or situation) and content (or reference). He accordingly analyzes the antinomies of postmodernism (identity/difference, space/time, change/permanence, utopia/dystopia) for how they collapse back into one another, and thereby as symptoms of a deeper social contradiction imbedded in a simulacral mode of production (*The Seeds of Time*, 4). I rely in this book on the antinomies he specifies and the property of reversibility they disclose, always with an eye to the deep symptomaticity of my own discourse, but also with the additional understanding that in a "preterite" tense, one can find—or rediscover—those forces, flows, and blockages of the material situation presumably euphemized in the turn to language. My tendency here is to extend Jameson's general argument into poststructuralist fields that he is careful to differentiate from his own chosen identification with Marxism. In chapter 6, I argue in more depth for a closer convergence between Jameson's dialectic mode and Deleuze's "second-order" theoretical articulations. In particular, I suggest that when Jameson too vociferously insists on a distinction between a dialectical approach and a performative iteration of that approach, he is missing the point—or the profoundest implication—of his own work, which, indeed, I take to be implication itself in the specific sense I am using it here.
4 The phrase is Michel de Certeau's (*The Writing of History*, 37), whose notion of writing as an "operation" very much informs the method employed here: "The fragile boundary between a past object and a current praxis begins to waver," he writes, "as soon as the fictive postulate of a *given* that is to be understood is replaced by the study of an *operation* always affected by determinisms, always having to be taken up, always depending on the place where it occurs in society, and specified, however, by a problem, methods, and a function which are its own" (37).
5 Pynchon's disparagement of *The Crying of Lot 49* in the introduction to that book makes no reference to explicit flaws, but it does find it lacking in "positive and professional" qualities of

good writing. In the context of the introduction as a whole, which can be read as a rather alarming apostasy of the surreal, discursive, and farcical strategies that make Pynchon's work so interesting, one may infer that the absence of these qualities signifies its lack of competence as a *realist* work, since that appears to be the criterion of judgment he employs.

1 Imperium, Misogyny, and Postmodern Parody in *V.*

1 I think it's true, however, that de Lauretis and Pynchon might differ over the nature of one's complicity in signifying systems. Where de Lauretis's critic uses discourses that are inherently phallocentric for the purposes of her own appropriation, Pynchon parodies those discourses from a peculiarly decentered place—appropriates them, indeed, not so much to use them critically, as descriptions of, or solutions to, a particular material condition, but to expose them as symptoms and to reject their versions of experience, however caught up in them one might be. This difference has much to do with the different genres in which they work.

2 Psychoanalysis functions to lock desire into a "pseudo-expressive form of the unconscious" and cover over a process by which desire "unconsciously invests the social field" (*Anti-Oedipus*, 167). What gets lost always, they say, is the relation of social repression to desire, or the mechanism by which social machines involve desire in a repulsion-attraction network. Once this relation is recognized, they say, one can begin to answer the question "Why do we desire our own domination?"

3 That process unfolds as a series of linkages between the body without organs and desiring-machines (their "relationship") that creates at the interface they form points of disjunction where new connections are made. Deleuze and Guattari give a clear example of this in their discussion of kinship structures among primitive societies: "Through women, men establish their own *connections*; through the man-woman *disjunction*, which is always the outcome of filiation, alliance places in *connection* men from different filiations" (*Anti-Oedipus*, 165; italics mine). Networks are woven on the recording surface, marking it off into coordinates like a grid, and the ensuing formations, having passed through a "repulsion" stage to an "attraction" stage (where intensive flows invest the networks), pass themselves off as real or natural (a "person").

4 Giorgio Agamben understands this destructive element in Baudelaire's "shock" not as the simple nihilation of meaning, value, and the past but as the attempt to make of that nihilism the "last possible source" of connection (*Man without Content*, 107). The paradox of a (dis)continuity with the past and a (non)meaning for the artist very much governs the narrative logic of *V.* and situates it in an explicitly modernist context. The novel, one might say, turns the screw of that modernism to the point where even the figure of paradox loses its stability, and we are faced squarely by the prospect that even (non)meaning loses its meaning. It is Pynchon's willingness to push this possibility in his own work that gives it a peculiarly postmodern diabolism.

2 Ekphrasis, Escape, and Countercultural Desire in *The Crying of Lot 49*

1 For a succinct rehearsal of theoretical trajectories on the relation of consumption to signification, see Jean Baudrillard's "Sign-Function and Class Logic" and "The Ideological Genesis of

Needs" in the volume *For a Critique of the Political Economy of the Sign*. Stuart Ewen's *Captains of Consciousness* and *All Consuming Images* remain canonical starting points for understanding the historical relations between markets, spectacle, and the capture of desire by advertising. For a more recent and accessible account of sociological perspectives, see also Celia Lury's *Consumer Culture*.

2 Vitiation describes for Marx the inverse relation under capitalism between the worker and his labor power (expressed both in the product and in the activity of production). "The *alienation of the worker in his product* means not only that his labor becomes an object, assumes an *external* existence, but that it exists independently, *outside himself*, and alien to him, and that it stands opposed to him as an autonomous power. The life which he has given to the object sets itself against him as an alien and hostile force" ("Alienated Labor," 134). To the alienation of the thing is added the alienation of the worker *from himself* or from his "species life," conceived as his implicated relation to the "inorganic" world. Ideally, "the object of labor is . . . the *objectification of man's species life*; for he no longer reproduces himself merely intellectually, as in consciousness, but actively and in a real sense, and he sees his own reflection in a world which he has constructed" (140). Work within a capitalist order, however, "vitiates" this self-reflection in the constructed world by taking away the worker's species life, his real objectivity as a species-being, his produced and producing relation to an inorganic body, to his "belonging" within an inclusive and interdependent nature.

3 Critic Hanjo Berressem, writing an Oedipa's encounter with the Varo painting in a Lacanian vein, sees it as "a perfect allegory of the reflexive space and the 'symbolic matrix' in which Lacan describes the construction of the ego," a space structured like a language and yielding as a result "no objective reality" (*Pynchon's Poetics*, 92). The specular character of Oedipa's consciousness is what I am trying to establish in my own reading, on a theoretical register different from, but nonetheless indebted to, the work of Lacan. The difference, as will become apparent, consists in a critique of the duality in language that divides the fantasmatic projection from a nonsymbolizable real (on the model of the difference between the signifier and the signified), thus reserving for the projection an overly "psychic" reality. In what follows, I attempt (using Deleuze and Guattari) to fuse the specular and the real in a "delirium" that allows one to speak again of an objective reality, but one in which, as Berressem astutely points out, Oedipa's "perceptions are her own only to the extent to which they are ultimately not her own" (92). Berressem's reading of a subjectivity drifting through the "oscillating" text-world of the novel is uniformly subtle and allusive.

4 The problem of coral reef formation confronted by biologists up to Charles Darwin centered on the fact that corals, in Darwin's terms, "require for their growth a solid foundation within a few fathoms of the surface" of the sea (*Coral Reefs*, 128). Because the likelihood of geological foundations as uniformly present at or near the ocean's surface (as the global distribution of reefs would indicate) is scant, Darwin proposed a correlation between reef growth and a rising sea level, arguing that coral grows at a limited depth, dies as the sea rises, and so provides its own foundation. This coral-like production of the foundation at the surface is suggestive for the kind of structure legible in Pynchon's novel, a structure that supposes a nondistinction between ground and figure, inside and outside, as its basis. Deleuze refers this figure internal to its own ground to the concept of "difference in itself," a difference grasped not as a displacement in space (i.e., external or extensive in nature) but inclusively as an intensive field

of variable and differential relations that is isomorphic to its own limit (*Difference and Repetition*, 21–22). Deleuze and Guattari's work on acentered or rhizomatic systems not defined "by a set of points and positions, with binary relations between the points and bi-univocal relations between the positions" (*A Thousand Plateaus*, 21), rests on this concept of an intensive field that renders a system simultaneous with each of its parts (like a hologram), multileveled or multi-dimensional, and expressed in the singular movement of an absolute or "free" difference.

5 See Janet Kaplan, *Unexpected Journeys*, 20–23, for an account of the triptych in relation to Varo's life as an artist.

6 This is quoted in the book *Remedios Varo*, by Octavio Paz; cited in Kaplan, 21.

7 This vehicle is one of many fascinating machines that recur in Varo's work, and that conspicuously offer a means of conveyance that leaves its passengers in a state of suspension (they are often standing or sitting as they move, float, or hover through a painting), and sometimes even include towers or (usually circular) domiciles in their construction.

8 I am attempting here an economic formulation of Kant's paradox of internal sense, inflected through Deleuze's reading of difference in itself. For him, difference as such can be understood as a form differentiated from a ground that does not in turn differentiate itself from the form, with the result that the ground "rises" to the surface and "dissolves" the form's empirical and symbolic content, rendering it empty. Difference is grasped not "between" two things in a classificatory manner but in the "autonomous existence" of the rising ground that comprehends its own limit (*Difference and Repetition*, 21–22). With this displacement, forms (whether of matters, substances, subjects, or objects, of meanings in the broadest sense) assume a certain concrete abstraction or intensive nature apprehensible only as an internal difference that articulates into the structure of being an originary otherness or alterity. An "abstract line" (referred to by Deleuze in conjunction with a brief discussion of Odilon Redon, whose work intersects Varo's in thematic as well as technical ways) would be the contour of this singular form or of the intensive trait that it becomes once it is no longer opposable to other forms. The object so defined, whether it be of thought, of desire, or of labor—the materiality of things in themselves—assumes a virtual or subtle being that Deleuze, and Deleuze and Guattari, conceptualize in terms of differential forces, intensive fields, and bodies without organs.

9 Varo evokes this singular experience or "abstract line" through techniques, first innovated by surrealist artists such as Max Ernst and Varo's friend Oscar Dominguez, of decalcomania, which entails blowing and blotting paint on the canvas in such a way that color intensifies and contours assume an ambiguous definition (Kaplan, *Unexpected Journeys*, 122). This effect is prominent in the texture of yellow, foliage-like fog on which the lovers rise in "The Escape."

10 In Deleuze and Guattari's words, "The social character of enunciation is intrinsically founded only if one succeeds in demonstrating how enunciation in itself implies *collective assemblages*. It then becomes clear that the statement is individuated, and enunciation subjectified, only to the extent that an impersonal collective assemblage requires it and determines it to be so. It is for this reason that indirect discourse, *especially 'free' indirect discourse*, is of exemplary value; there are no clear, distinctive contours; what comes first is not an insertion of variously individuated statements, or an interlocking of different subjects of enunciation, but a collective assemblage resulting in the determination of relative subjectification proceedings, or assignations of individuality and their shifting distributions within discourse. Indirect dis-

course is not explained by the distinction between subjects; rather, it is the assemblage, as it freely appears in this discourse, that explains all the voices present within a single voice" (*A Thousand Plateaus*, 80). This formulation of an enunciative "assemblage" resonates in *The Crying of Lot 49* with Mucho Maas's LSD-inspired "spectrum" (or immanent plane of movement) on which being becomes a matter of multiplicities (or "whole roomfuls of people" [143]). More formally, it works itself out in the novel's intertextual excesses, exemplified by Oedipa's reading excursions through "The Courier's Tragedy," the text's propensity for breaking into parodic song, or its punning wordplay around names like "Oedipa Maas," "Dr. Fallopian," "Pierce Inverarity," et cetera.

11 The difference between the book and the assemblage-as-book is analogous to that more celebrated difference between arborescent and rhizomatic systems. For Deleuze and Guattari, "The first type of book is the root-book: the tree is already the image of the world, or the root the image of the world-tree. This is the classical book, as noble, as signifying and subjective organic interiority" (*A Thousand Plateaus*, 5). The "fascicular root" proceeds, by contrast, to "abort" the "principal root" and graft onto it an "indefinite multiplicity of secondary roots" that grow rhizomorphically, and support a "modern" text that is asignifying, asubjective, and anorganic (5).

12 For Deleuze and Guattari, this process entails a "transparency" in the world that makes being a matter of *passing* or impersonation. "Animal elegance, the camouflage fish, the clandestine: this fish is crisscrossed by abstract lines that resemble nothing, that do not even follow its organic divisions; but thus disorganized, disarticulated, it worlds with the lines of a rock, sand, and plants, becoming imperceptible" (*A Thousand Plateaus*, 280).

13 This is a restatement in other terms of the Deleuzian paradox of a rising ground. A subject experiences the uniqueness of its "essence" only in terms of an existence that is that essence, or only in the empty form of an indifferent existence that invades the autonomy of the "I" and articulates it through time. This point is made forcefully by Jean-Luc Nancy in *The Experience of Freedom*. Man's egocentrism, Nancy maintains, entails a "concentration in itself" of being and a setting apart of the subject's essence in what Hegel calls "a hatred of existence" (14). This unfreedom or "evil," however, is the "first discernible positivity" of freedom and can be understood only in a coimplicated or "masochistic" relation that renders the "experience" of freedom singular or imperceptible, not a constituted difference, attribute, or mode but an internal difference calling forth a particular kind of deconstructive apprehension. Experience for Nancy, indeed, needs to be defined in its "nomadic" singularity or imperceptibility, not in extension but intensively and according to a differential logic (145).

14 For Deleuze, "Death does not appear in the objective model of an indifferent matter to which the living would 'return'; it is present in the living in the form of a subjective and differential experience endowed with its prototype. It is not a material state; on the contrary, having renounced all matter, it corresponds to a pure form: the empty form of time" (*Difference and Repetition*, 113). The theoretical matrix touched on here will be developed in greater detail in the following three chapters. What is important to grasp, and what will become increasingly central to my analysis of the death instinct's function in Pynchon's work, is that the difference between the two models (Freud's and Deleuze's) is internal, *not external*. Deleuze's model does not yield *another* determined or represented modality of "life-death" than that given by Freud. Rather, they relate to each other across an iterative or citational gap. The time that

invests the subject for Deleuze is an implicated one in the precise sense I attempt to elaborate throughout this work.

15 I have shifted theoretical registers from Deleuze to Deleuze and Guattari. The analogy between them is as follows: the repetition of the same is to the relative limit what the repetition of difference is to the absolute limit. Deleuze and Guattari speak in *Anti-Oedipus* of two types of reflux toward the body without organs (understood as that limit): one, relative, presents itself to be reterritorialized in turn by the capitalist machine; the other, absolute, entails remaining at the limit and living it in a schizophrenic mode of "pure intensities." This theoretical matrix will be developed in subsequent chapters, particularly chapter 5.

16 See Peter Euben's analysis of *The Crying of Lot 49* in *The Tragedy of Political Theory* for an example of the recuperative reading I have in mind. Euben compares Oedipa's story to Oedipus's "search for meaning and identity" (284) and claims for her a power of mediation between opposites (male and female, difference and sameness, low and high cultures, "exile" and "incest") that signify the two limit-cases between which a political identity and community can be founded. She functions as a kind of Hermes-like messenger and so as a figure for analogy itself, for the linking or structural principle of an alternative social and political system symbolized by the Tristero. But for Oedipa to be the "founding mother who can save America" (303), for her to be the linchpin of an alternative social, political, sexual, and psychological structure not undone by the simulacra of contemporary society, she must be "real," just as the Tristero and the WASTEful system it signifies must be a "genuine society of communicants in which real information is exchanged and real diversity sustained" (303). That is, the kind of alternative system Euben has in mind cannot tolerate the ambivalence that nonetheless marks the novel throughout and *expresses* its economy of waste (which is precisely suspended between the real and the unreal, between fact and fiction, between presence and spectrality). As a result, the only way he can locate political agency in the text is by negating the implicated structure I have been attempting to analyze here—and therefore canceling, in the name of a political freedom, the very possibility of freedom held out by the novel.

17 For two interesting accounts of the fundamental negativity that circulated in two specific subcultures of the late 1960s, see Robert Morris's essay "Three Folds in the Fabric and Four Autobiographical Asides as Allegories (or Interruptions)" (*Art in America*, November 1989) on the "philalias-like" motivations behind minimalist art; and Mary Woronov's autobiography *Swimming Underground*, for her lively portrait of life in Warhol's Factory, as inflected through the experience of a deteriorating drug addiction. Gitlin's account of the New Left also dwells with considerable thoughtfulness, if not much theoretical depth, on the strange fatalism that seemed to hang over the unraveling of events, coalitions, and even friendships through the last years of the decade. Numerous cultural representations of that fatal quality in the times could also be cited here (think, for instance, of the gradual and creeping rhythm with which *Easy Rider* moves toward its eventual bloody denouement).

18 See Gitlin's book *The Sixties* for an account of the New Left that identifies the causes of its eventual breakdown with the anarchic tendencies of the counterculture.

19 For an account of the complex and fraught history of the art world's relation to politics throughout the 1960s and early 1970s, see Tony Godfrey's *Conceptual Art*.

20 The "inherited disposition" (39) of this masochism, according to Bersani, allows for the human organism in its psychosexual development, through an "identification with the suf-

fering object" (41), to survive onslaughts of "shattering stimuli" before it has developed the ego structure it needs to resist them. The subject then incorporates and becomes in its libidinal being that very shattering onslaught as the condition of its stability. The important point here is that this masochism grounds the normative subject in a disavowing oscillation between fear and reassurance. In the terms of my earlier argument pace Deleuze, masochism names the material or relative death instinct. Its *absolute* variant occurs only with its displacement in a sublimation that focuses the relative death instinct in the light of a theoretical reflection. Derrida, in his reading of *Beyond the Pleasure Principle*, also formulates a drive or "force" of "disappropriation" (*The Postcard*, 352) at work in and on Freud's argument that cannot be defined (as self-identical or present to itself) and that therefore manifests itself in an always interpretive textual mode. See "To Speculate—on Freud" in *The Postcard* and chapter 4 in this volume for more elaboration of this performative dimension both in Freud's text and in Pynchon's (through the Deleuze of *Masochism*).

21 Bersani uses the distinction between sexuality (as self-shattering aggression) and sex (as organ- and object-specific genital constitution) to underscore the "abstract" but not necessarily "desexualized" nature of this nonreferential libidinal energy. He is speaking in particular of the process of sublimation. See the chapter "Sexuality and Esthetics," in particular pages 34–50, in *The Freudian Body*.

22 This dynamic becomes especially obvious when one tries to incorporate theory as complex as that of Deleuze and Guattari into one's own exposition, as I have been doing throughout. For a rendition fuller than I can give here of the relationships between "assemblages," "multiplicities," "anomalies," desire as a line of flight run to the edge of deterritorialization, and so on, see the chapter "1730: Becoming-Intense, Becoming-Animal . . ." in *A Thousand Plateaus*. One suspects that the point of their densely involuted work (however contrary to stated intentions this may seem) was to thwart one's ability to apply it and, in consequence, to performatively underscore the aleatoric politics of expression they advocate, and that makes them (as perhaps we all are) avatars of the counterculture I am attempting to describe.

23 Hardt and Negri write, "Mechanisms of command [in 'Empire'] become ever more 'democratic,' ever more immanent to the social field, distributed throughout the brains and bodies of its citizens. The behaviors of social integration and exclusion proper to rule are thus increasingly interiorized within subjects themselves. Power is now exercised through machines that directly organize the brains (in communication systems, information networks, etc.) and bodies (in welfare systems, information networks, etc.) toward a state of autonomous alienation from the sense of life and the desire for creativity" (*Empire*, 23). A little further along in their exposition, they are even blunter: "The political synthesis of social space is fixed in the space of communication" (33). This space, by their account, relates to language and discourse specifically through its function to legitimate social authority (in the minds and bodies of people). In line with Deleuze and Guattari, they refer to biopower as a "production of production" or of the producer who grasps his or her own domination through the overdetermination of agency. The trope of inverse and double time lurks here: the sovereign subject comes only at the end of a process that determines him or her as metonymies (or holograms) of the system itself. The end precedes the origin, the origin discloses its an-archic ground of arbitrary force. In "Empire," they maintain, "we are dealing with a special kind of sovereignty—a discontinuous form of sovereignty that should be

considered liminal or marginal insofar as it acts 'in the final instance,' a sovereignty that locates its only point of reference in the definitive absoluteness of the power it can exercise" (39).

24 For Hardt and Negri's "deconstructive politics," see page 47 of *Empire*. The possibility of liberation hinges for them on a true apprehension of the global biopolitical context. The latter's virtuality contains the possibility for a new citizenship that transcends the identitarian and localized models of political life given by the state. Hardt and Negri embrace in globalism asubjective multiplicities and assemblages that prefigure a "new terrain of humanity" (47) and a genuine advance from the violence of the past. But this liberation hinges on a nondialectical and immanent *repetition* of the deepest tendencies within the global system. The "ontological drama" of liberation begins, they maintain, when "the development of Empire becomes its own critique and its process of construction becomes the process of its overturning" (47). Their utopian project comes through precisely in the ontological privilege they grant this repetition. My sense here is that the desire this repetition drives tends toward theoretical autonomy—tends toward philosophy, just what Hardt and Negri are doing even if their model for philosophy is material, "subjective proposition, desire, and praxis . . . applied to the event" (49). When philosophy intervenes in worldly praxis, it produces texts; that is, it produces itself as symptom of the metalinguistic biopower they elucidate so well. My argument in the present work stresses the necessity of that symptom as a sort of memento mori within the utopian project.

3 Turning Around the Origin in *Gravity's Rainbow*

1 The closely interrelated concepts of production, origin (origination), and time combine here around a fundamental critique of will, or creative impulse, what I will call (pace Baudrillard) "universal causality." My argument is that *Gravity's Rainbow* parodies the intentional structure of a Cartesian subjectivity dedicated to mastery and control of the earth through its encasement in a reflective (and closed) system. Giorgio Agamben, in his book *The Man without Content*, analyzes modern subjectivity in terms of its principal attribute, originality. He argues that this attribute comes into being at the same time as the producer or artisan loses his embedded relation to (or in) a traditional society. As the producer loses his bearings in modernity, one sees the paradoxical overvaluation of his "genius" (which functions in an aesthetic economy much like labor power did for the worker in a political economy). The quality of originality comes to express the alienation of the artist, which for Agamben then produces the phenomena of modern art, right down to the antiart of the readymade and pop art. For Pynchon to tell this story of the mystifying character of originality (or production), he must do so in a self-implicating mode that links its originality inversely to its degree of alienation. "What does *originality* mean?" asks Agamben. "When we say that the work of art has the character of originality (or authenticity), we do not simply mean by this that this work is unique, that is, different from any other. Originality means proximity to the origin" (*Man without Content*, 61). Such proximity, however, in a modern society, entails proximity to an *abyssal* origin, hence to the problem of an origin that cannot be original so much as arbitrarily fixed and naturalized as such. *Gravity's Rainbow* is original to the degree that it lacks originality (i.e., opens into a discursive or typological dimension where things become intelligible in their simultaneous

generality and uniqueness), or to the degree it maintains proximity to questions of (arbitrary, an-archic) power embedded in acts of origination.

2   Heidegger contends that this structure determines the object in terms of its "equipmentality," and that it "readily presents itself as the immediately intelligible constitution of every entity," comprehending all things through the "being of equipment." The form-matter distinction thus presides over a totalization that we nonetheless experience only in its self-evidence (Poetry, Language, Thought, 29). Although the "product" is determined by Heidegger as intermediate to the "naked" thing and the "work," his essay attempts to understand the being of the product without recourse to the form-matter distinction as the mode of its inquiry into the being of the work. That is, as Derrida argues in his commentary on the essay, the three determinations of the thing are less differentiated than "interlaced" in such a way that the work is also a product, useful insofar as its very uselessness gives the self-evidence of the form-matter distinction in the product to be thought (The Truth in Painting, 299). The work or oeuvre (ergon) for Derrida is also an "hors d'oeuvre" (parergon), a supplemental structure linked in its essence to its limit, frame, or edge. The work has no being apart from its contexts and as such is not so much a work as it is a text in the strict sense.

3   I agree with Berressem that there are not "decisive differences" between the three novels. Each unfolds in a "fully cybernetic universe" of metalinguistic domination that Pynchon "singles out . . . for investigation" (Pynchon's Poetics, 120). Berressem sees parallels in (1) the search for identity undertaken by Stencil, Oedipa, and Slothrop; (2) mystery signifiers like V., the Tristero, and the V-2 rocket; and (3) the investigation of counterculture or counterforce "caught in a mirror structure" with social power (120). For arguments that stress differences between the three novels see Edward Mendelson's introduction to the volume of critical essays entitled Pynchon, McHoul and Wills's Writing Pynchon, and Brian McHale's Postmodernism.

4   Steven Weisenburger traces "Blicero," a Germanic nickname for death, to Grimm's Teutonic Mythology. The word derives etymologically from bleich (pale) and blechend (grinning) and connotes a whitening or "bleaching" effect as on the bones of a dead body. See A Gravity's Rainbow Companion, 31.

5   "Fashion continually fabricates the 'beautiful' on the basis of a radical denial of beauty, by reducing beauty to the logical equivalent of ugliness. It can impose the most eccentric, dysfunctional, ridiculous traits as eminently distinctive. This is where it triumphs—imposing and legitimizing the irrational according to a logic deeper than that of rationality" (Baudrillard, For a Critique of the Political Economy of the Sign, 79). The social logic of the sign system, centered on the signifying nature of the commodity divorced from any determination as symbol, instrument, or product, is for Baudrillard "differential" and "hierarchical," dislodged from the economic rationality of "need," free-floating or orbital. See the essay "The Ideological Genesis of Needs," in For Critique of the Political Economy of the Sign.

6   In symbolic exchange, the object exists only as the medium of a concrete relation or "transferential pact" and as such is not, strictly speaking, an object at all, since it does not matter which object is exchanged except insofar as it symbolizes that particular exchange. It is arbitrary and singular, says Baudrillard, and as such "not autonomous, hence not codifiable as [a] sign," that is, not economic because it is incapable of bearing an exchange value. The relation it seals is "ambivalent" and libidinal, based on a mutual presence and absence that the individuals in the exchange continually ratify. In sign value exchange, on the other hand,

the object is reduced to a "coded difference," that is, reified into a sign-object that signifies the reification of the symbolic relationship. "Instead of [the object] abolishing itself in the relation that it establishes, and thus assuming symbolic value . . . the object becomes autonomous, intransitive, opaque, and so begins to signify the abolition of the relationship." The sign object (as commodity) is *also* independent of particular objects, but it is not *singular*, it does not name a relationship. It is abstracted from its determination not only as a *symbol* but as a product and instrument as well, says Baudrillard, and thus becomes an object of consumption "recaptured by a formal logic of fashion, i.e., by the logic of differentiation." For Baudrillard, this development renders political economy (by itself) obsolete as a tool for the analysis of capitalism because it cannot account for the political economy of the sign, without which the emphasis on production and exchange value would only confirm the deepest ideological tendencies of the system and not challenge them. See "The ideological Genesis of Needs," in *For a Critique of the Political Economy of the Sign*, 64–67. For a critique of the notion of symbolic exchange, see Lyotard's *Libidinal Economy*, 104. For Lyotard, the distinction between an economic and an extraeconomic domain (i.e., between value and libidinal intensity, sign and symbol) must presuppose an "external referent" and a theory of alienation. Even symbolic exchange is a form of political economy, in other words, and Baudrillard, in losing sight of this, therefore cannot understand clearly how "libidinalized" political economy always already is. It is this kind of insight, more than a critique of signification from the point of view of an alternative symbolic exchange, that will govern the readings given hereafter.

7 "The transpolitical is the transparency and obscenity of all structures in a destructured universe, the transparency and obscenity of change in a de-historicized universe, the transparency and obscenity of information in a universe emptied of event. . . . The end of the scene of the historical, the end of the scene of the political, the end of the scene of fantasy, the end of the scene of the body—the irruption of the obscene. The end of the secret—the irruption of transparency" (Baudrillard, *Fatal Strategies*, 25).

8 See also D. Bennett's "Parody, Postmodernism, and the Politics of Reading," in *Critical Quarterly*, which McHoul and Wills quote in support of their argument for the inadequacy of parodic interpretations of *Gravity's Rainbow*.

9 Hence I am less interested than McHoul and Wills in differentiating my approach from a "transcendent" equivalent, and more interested in the iterations of transcendence that underline the symptomatic nature of the postwar "time" to which our readings belong (and which is marked by precisely this symptomatic belonging). Clearly this self-implication is also one subtext of their own nested readings of Pynchon, but the particular distinction they make between parody and the postrhetorical operation sutures a slightly more dogmatic (or exclusively differentiated) moment in their argument. On whether this dogmatism signifies in their work the same (naive) embrace of indeterminacy and free play (on the level of intertextual relations) that reinscribes a bourgeois individualist ideology, see Michael Berubé's careful critique of their deconstructive approach in chapters 4 and 5 of his *Marginal Forces/Cultural Centers*.

10 I am indebted to Steven Weisenburger's *A Gravity's Rainbow Companion* for this reference.

11 See pages 53–54 of *Writing Pynchon* for the details of this argument. They never (and probably never would) use the word "existential" here, but the peculiar postrhetorical space they attempt to open out in *Gravity's Rainbow* does bear significant similarities to, for instance,

Merleau-Ponty's preobjective and nongeometric "anthropological space" (see *The Phenomenology of Perception*, 256, as well as chapter 7 of this volume for my own bearings in Merleau-Ponty). The "single dimension" to which McHoul and Will refer, it should be noted, is linguistic in nature, related to the arbitrariness of the signifier and falling above the "bar" separating it from the signified. This prompts them to equivocal statements about this dimension's ontological status (they tend to privilege textuality over and above the "world" outside the text), which Berubé sees as a reduction of their discourse to the mere "free play" of a fictive language severed not so much from its referential functions as from its peculiar existential commitment to its sociopolitical contexts (228–34). A category of "anthropological space" that holds together discourse and being would, it seems to me, provide a common ground for McHoul and Wills's deconstructive interest in reading strategies and Berubé's critique in terms of reception, both of which imply an implicated textual/textural *field* where writing eclipses its various aesthetic ideologies and takes on material and ethical force. For a perceptive analysis of the field metaphor in *Gravity's Rainbow*, see also N. Katherine Hayles's "Caught in the Web: Cosmology and the Point of (No) Return in Pynchon's *Gravity's Rainbow*."

12 This dichotomy structures much of the criticism written to the present day. See Josephine Hendin's "What Is Thomas Pynchon Telling Us?" (in Harold Bloom's *Thomas Pynchon's "Gravity's Rainbow"*) and Craig Hansen Werner's "Recognizing Reality/Realizing Responsibility" (in *Thomas Pynchon*, also edited by Harold Bloom) for early examples of work that seeks to foreground humanist values and referential naturalism in his fiction. In *The Self-Apparent Word* (1984), Jerome Klinkowitz argues that Pynchon writes "dramas of the signified rather than self-referential performances of the signifier" (59)(!). Even with more theoretically sophisticated work, one discerns the rhetorical habit of qualifying "poststructuralist" types of assertion with acknowledgments of the "reality" Pynchon never gives up on. Thus Thomas Schaub, in *Pynchon: The Voice of Ambiguity* (1981), can move from perceptive readings of entropy and information theory, spectral consumer culture, and mathematical singularities that intextuate Pynchon's characters (and readers) in densely metaphoric fields, to statements like the following: "Pynchon's books are not self-reflexive because they reveal and document the reality of history. He acknowledges the paradoxes of language but retains the social power of the naturalistic novel. In Pynchon's writing language succeeds in binding people together" (150–51). Very similar moves to assert "possibilities" seemingly closed down in the fiction can be tracked through Peter Cooper's *Signs and Symptoms* (1983) and Molly Hite's *Ideas of Order* (1983). What one notices in criticism like this (especially in light of Pynchon's dogged self-reflexivity) is the critic's need to find the value of *connection* (whether this is understood socially as community or semantically as meaning, analogy's "coming together") in what he or she is reading. The assumption appears to be that this is a prerequisite for an artifact's cultural value. Berressem, one of the best critics of Pynchon we have, tries to mediate between the two poles by integrating them in a single analytic focus on subjectivity. His *Pynchon's Poetics* synthesizes self-reflexivity and realism in Pynchon's work by "interfacing" various theories on the subject in culture (most notably Lacan's). While his work is sophisticated and interesting, it remains essentially reactive to the "problem" of Pynchon's (post)humanist status. My own sense is that the polarities of this debate need to be questioned in and of themselves, even transcended in order to read Pynchon's work in new ways. McHoul and Wills suggest how this might be done in their advocacy of a reading that,

accepting the "postrhetorical" nature of truth in *Gravity's Rainbow*, divests the whole humanist question of its urgency or "angst" (51).

13. Many of Pynchon's critics, having misheard the displaced tonalities of parody in his work, assume a referentiality for concepts that are functioning within a far different economy. Thus Maureen Quilligan, distinguishing Pynchon's self-reflexivity from that privileged by poststructuralist critics, argues that "Derrida is . . . trying to find a rhetoric of writing which will allow him to go beyond the epistemology of Presence, while Pynchon is firmly mired in the problems of Presence" (117). My sense of this miring implication in Presence is that a parodic irony erodes the difference Quilligan insists on here. Molly Hite, discussing the logocentric "Holy Center Approaching" of *Gravity's Rainbow*, maintaining that "in Pynchon's novels human beings try to construct meanings because the premise that the center did not hold constitutes an original loss" (32). This loss names a tragic "Fall" in Pynchon's narrative and structures the desire of his characters in terms of a primordial nostalgia for unity. Hite then sees hope in Pynchon's pluralist embrace of multiplicity over and against this totalizing nostalgia (which he parodies), but significantly, that pluralism (and that parody) must presuppose the reality of an original unity to be active in the text. In my argument, nostalgia does not denote the same postlapsarian economy of loss and original unity: nostalgia exists in the novel, but as the catalyst for a movement of repetition that discloses in its parodies the specular nature of that economy and a different desire for the loss of that loss (which, in its double negation, assumes a strange positivity).

14. I am quoting Robert Bernasconi's reading of Heidegger in *The Question of Language in Heidegger's History of Being* (68).

15. Thus, although explicit reference to Heidegger is not in evidence in this passage, the mode by which Heidegger compounds the forms and conventions of philosophical discourse with "ordinary" (and excluded) language becomes one (modernist) rubric for grasping Pynchon's admixture of high and low literary languages. For a critical analysis of this effect in Heidegger, see Pierre Bourdieu's *The Political Ontology of Martin Heidegger*.

16. See Louis Mackey's "Paranoia, Pynchon, and Preterition," in *Thomas Pynchon's "Gravity's Rainbow,"* ed. Harold Bloom, for a rehearsal of the numerous connotations the preterite has for Pynchon. The novel "displays on its rhetorical surface a linguistic paranoia which answers to the 'deep' paranoia of its plots and personae. That is, by preterition (passing over) it constructs them as preterite (past). What is conspicuously omitted is perspicaciously obscured" (58).

17. Berubé understands the novel's deconstruction of the "preterite/elect" distinction as one registration of its own complexly relative position in a literary and cultural field polarized by high/low or center/margin concepts. Rather than fixing the novel as a "preterite" voice from/of the oppressed (as numerous critics have done), Berubé sees it as fluctuating between the various poles according to its use and operation by readers. (See chapter 4 of his *Marginal Forces/Cultural Centers* for more on this argument.) But preterition does not work simply at the level of content in *Gravity's Rainbow*. Instead, it marks the fluctuation of content and expression that engenders its singular textual/textural or existential status *and* its political force. The whole notion of a "field," so crucial to Berubé's argument for the political nature of Pynchon's work, hinges on the very implicated relations between spatiality, discourse, and embodied subjects that fall under the rubric of preterition for Pynchon.

18 The *axiomatic* stands opposed to the *code* in Deleuze and Guattari's account. The latter establishes "indirect relations between coded flows" and "qualifies" those flows with reference to an "extra-economic instance" (or transcendent signifier) from which they appear to emanate. But once money is used as a substitute for the code, it becomes apparent that as "a general equivalent [money] represents an abstract quantity that is indifferent to the qualified nature of the flows" (*Anti-Oedipus*, 248). Money is an "unlimited abstract quantity" of intensive or subtle, deterritorializing matter that decodes the qualified flows. The "axiomatic" is a "direct [i.e., economic] relation between decoded flows"; it establishes their qualities only within a "differential relation" not linked to any extraeconomic instance. "The quality of the flows results solely from their conjunction as decoded flows; outside this conjunction they would remain purely virtual." It is in the axiomatic, or in a qualitative abstraction, that paradoxically the flows appear or become visible (that is, no longer virtual). In effect the flows are abstract and concrete at the same time. The axiomatic "holds" decoded flows in a bound state on the deterritorialized body of capital, says Deleuze and Guattari, but only by way of reterritorializing those flows in a socius "more pitiless than any other" (245). Modern societies negotiate two distinct limits: one, absolute and exterior, represents the purely decoded or schizophrenic flows, and must be constantly pushed back and exorcised; the other, relative and immanent, represents the axiomatized flows that capitalism must constantly reproduce on an ever-widening scale. The axiomatic, in short, is their word for the manner in which capitalist society harnesses the decoded flows while nonetheless maintaining them in a state of strict control.

19 Deleuze and Guattari, describing the functions of the modern (capitalist) state, write, "Civilized modern societies are defined by processes of decoding and deterritorialization. But *what they deterritorialize with one hand, they reterritorialize with the other*. These neoterritorialities are often artificial, residual, archaic; but they are archaisms having a perfectly current function, our modern way of 'imbricating,' of sectioning off, of reintroducing code fragments, resuscitating old codes, inventing pseudo codes and jargons" (*Anti-Oedipus*, 257). In their account, the capitalist state operates first by decoding (or scrambling) the older "despotic state" to axiomatize the liberated flows. The neoterritoriality is a fragment of code "lodged" within the applied axiomatic, archaic in the sense that it functions according to principles of the older despotic dispensation, but only "encased" within another social system operating on profoundly different principles. Deleuze and Guattari cite writing in general as an example of such a neoterritoriality (240). Enzian's intuition about the displaced or secondary status of the war taking place around him (that it isn't "real") could be read as an apprehension of the "real" war (i.e., the power struggle between nations), as an "archaism" given a "current function" within a larger late capitalist system he has as yet no experience or precedent for deciphering.

20 Leo Bersani, writing on this moment in the novel, underscores the fundamental ambiguity of any "Real Text" constituting the allegorical key by which a truth might be deciphered. The novel's truth is that there is no "real" distinction between truth and delusion, a feature, Bersani notes, of the paranoid sensibility in general (geared to find meaning in "orders beyond the visible," where no truth apparently exists). Freud's uneasy relationship to paranoia (seen most directly in his study of Daniel Schreber) derives from a resemblance between his own theory and the paranoid symptom. The "truth" Freud finds in paranoia is a "theoriz-

ing activity" uncomfortably like his own search for truth (in paranoia). Bersani sees in the way this devaluation of truth into paranoid theory encircles Freud a dynamic of Pynchon's text, which "mak[es] us move on the same field of paranoid anxiety as his characters" (188). It is what Bersani calls this "unavoidable complicity" of writer and reader, and also of content and expression, that I want to specify in the infinite regress of Enzian's "break" and the space of the Zone. Berubé, commenting on Bersani's essay, sees in this paranoid complicity the necessarily uncertain mode of investigation for the "postmodernist" critic in general, over and against a tendency in Pynchon criticism to understand paranoia as a hedge *against* uncertainty (*Marginal Forces*, 220–21).

4 A Close Reading of Part 1, Episode 19, of *Gravity's Rainbow*

1   Other registers at which the problematic of time, connection, use, and control will be worked through in the episode include that of the connection between parents and children, between sexual partners, between revolutionary conspirators, between corporate and industrial cartels, and between molecules in an industrial process. Pynchon saturates his text with this thematic of "touch" (and, of course, not touching) across the various aporias.

2   Criticism that has focused on pornography in *Gravity's Rainbow* has tended to understand it as a form of abstraction that falsifies a "real" world of experience (see, for example, Steven Weisenburger's "The End of History?" and Dwight Eddins's "Paradigms Reclaimed," as well as Hite's *Ideas of Order*). Berubé provides a clear corrective for this tendency, grasping the "real" it projects as already an abstraction that envelops the reader in a pornographic desire for the "lost unity" of one's own ego. He defines pornographic desire rather as a fetishization of a unity that is fundamentally imaginary (*Marginal Forces/Cultural Centers*, 246) and operates both within the text and on the text, in the world of its reception. This definition modulates the text of *Gravity's Rainbow* to a register of implication similar to that I am attempting to understand here.

3   If the reader can't grasp this sabotage, then nothing prevents him or her from seeing the anti-Semitic stereotype Rebecca exemplifies—elaborated in more detail over the next two pages—as anything more than consciously or unconsciously perpetrated by Pynchon on his readers. The reader will miss the extent to which the text interrogates its own nature as a sign system, as well as the relation between a capitalist society that produces such sign systems (through the process of commodification) and racism.

4   This flat or neutral "difference" is, in my reading, another formulation of the levity inherent to Pynchon's language, its "antiserious" or its "abyssal" character. This is why the moment described is followed immediately by Franz's discovery that his old friend Kurt Mondaugen (our old friend from V.) is one of the scientists present at the test. In the next paragraph, in fact, Pynchon briefly rehearses the story of the "Siege Party" in South-West Africa narrated in the earlier novel, linking Franz (and his epiphany) to the narrative strategies employed there (and analyzed in chapter 1). This intertextual link (which functions as well to introduce Major Weissmann into Franz's story) itself constitutes a decontextualization, an echo or reminder of absurdity undermining the illusion of dramatic unity that galvanizes the text precisely where Franz and the rocket "meet." Into this "galvanic" mode, as it were, Pynchon imports the vertigo of a schizophrenic language.

5. The difference between them is made explicit when Leni fantasizes about making love to her friend: "What would it be like, to be taken to bed by her? To do it not just with another woman, but *with a Jewess*. . . . Their animal darkness . . . sweating hindquarters, pushing aggressively toward her face, black hairs darkening in fine crescent around each buttock from the crevice . . . the face turned over a shoulder smiling in coarse delight. . . . Leni's fair skin, her look of innocence, and the Jewess's darker coloring, her rawness, contrasting with Leni's delicacy of structure and skin, pelvic bones stretching cobwebs smoothly down groins and around belly, the two women sliding, snarling, gasping . . . *I know there's coming together* . . ." (156). The contrast of innocence and animal darkness once again invokes implicitly an anti-Semitic stereotype that Leni, in her fantasy, duplicates and, indeed, sexualizes. The Jew is figured as libidinality itself, the bestial id, what Lyotard in *Libidinal Economy* calls an "unnatural nature" that, according to Hegel, represents a failure of the dialectic insofar as it refuses to submit to the necessary death out of nature that (through the *Aufhebung*) reconciles man to nature once again at the level of the Idea. "The Jews could not . . . abandon themselves to disintegration or death . . . because they were attached not to an Idea, but an animal existence; and they believed in their god because, completely separate from nature, they found reunion with this latter by virtue of a domination" (Hegel, *Hegels theologische Judenschriften*; quoted by Lyotard in *Libidinal Economy*, 126). Lyotard interprets this fixation in an unnatural animal existence that the dialectic must transcend to entail a breakdown in the master/slave relationship. The Jewish god is a false master whose domination is predicated on an absence of dialogue. No *symbolic exchange* in Hegel's sense is possible for the Jew, who comes to signify lack of relation, an impenetrable body or unconscious that refuses its dialectical assimilation in an explicitly Christian discourse. Lyotard's critique of symbolic exchange (precisely in its Baudrillardian form) presupposes the Hegelian antecedent that places the desire for such exchange within the economy of the dialectic. Pynchon likewise implicates Leni's desire (for symbolic exchange) in an intellectualized or analytic need for sameness, agreement, conformity. Even though she desires the difference that makes symbolic exchange possible (in desiring Rebecca), and even though her inability to accept Rebecca's *Zusammentreffen* is coded as a critique of the latter's complicity (Leni sees through the discourse of the liberatory body to its own dialectical underpinnings), that desire and that critique are nonetheless similarly grounded in the dialectic. This complicity holds true for every character in the novel. The impossibility of any exteriority to this space or structure, however, does not in any way invalidate desire; rather, it expresses desire (in all its ambivalences) as a movement *within* or *through* the discursive matrices that produce and perpetuate violence in Western culture. Cf. Lyotard's discussion of symbolic exchange in *Libidinal Economy*, in particular pp. 124–27.

6. This is one way to understand *Gravity's Rainbow* as a historical novel: historical fact or detail is always precise but presented in the mode of a dream, distorted according to principles of displacement and condensation. In Leni's fantasy you can detect in her attitude to Von Hindenburg a trace of the dilemma radical Germans found themselves in around 1930. The militarist president represented bourgeois democracy against the radical extremes of Nazism and Communism, and indeed only so long as he lived would the Weimar Republic survive, his death in 1933 removed the last obstacle in Hitler's rise to power. This made him an unlikely symbol of hope against the Nazi threat and highlighted the uneasy position of a Left forced to choose between the virtual despotism of Von Hindenburg and the overt totalitarianism of

Hitler. The precise references to Von Hindenburg's nasal voice, the concern (shared by most Germans as Hitler became more belligerent) that he might die, and also Leni's particular faith (even distorted or dreamlike) in Von Hindenburg's basic humanity (which, in its paternalistic undertones, exposes her own middle-class reflexes exactly in the midst of her radical beliefs) do suggest the actual historical moment of the episode with considerable clarity.

7 "Latex" is defined as the white fluid produced by various seed plants and the source of rubber, but also "a water emulsion of a synthetic rubber or plastic obtained by polymerization" (Webster's Collegiate).

8 Franz contrasts to Leni's primitive calculus an ethic of production: "The important thing is taking a function to its limit," he says. "Delta t is just a convenience, so that it can happen." The event itself is what matters to the engineer in Franz, although the fantasmatic dynamic of his "death-wishes" suggests suspense, the arrest or neutralization of the real. In this sense *both* Franz and Leni participate in approaches to zero, the movement of desire toward self-extinguishment or "into" the inanimate.

9 "The pleasure principle," writes Freud, "is a tendency operating in the service of a function whose business it is to free the mental apparatus entirely from excitation or to keep the amount of excitation in it constant or to keep it as low as possible" (76). Pleasure occurs only once the excitation, conceived as mobile and undifferentiated, is bound or differentiated by another libidinal, "cathectic" energy. This binding process resolves the excitation into an experience of pleasure.

10 The sexual instincts prolong or attenuate the desire to die by themselves returning to an earlier state of development. This is why Freud insists on a distinction between the ego instincts and the sexual instincts: both involve regressions, but the first "arise from the coming to life of inanimate matter and seek to restore the inanimate state" (52), whereas the second "reproduce primitive states" to effect a "coalescence" that leads to reproduction and thus persistence in the face of death or "the appearance of immortality."

11 Eros, that is, underwritten by the death instinct, emerges as the constitutive foundation of the pleasure principle; and the binding function of Eros, for Deleuze, is characterized as "repetition" (*Masochism*, 113).

12 Defusion is a displacement of cathectic energy that renders it undifferentiated, thus incapable of binding excitations and producing pleasure.

13 The principle of the unity of opposites is crucial for Freud's conception of the sexual instincts, which, by seeking to reunite or integrate fragmented components in the reproductive acts, take on at least the semblance of a progressive, developmental character.

14 This international symbolic order sets itself up as an alternative not only to the paternal and psychoanalytic equivalent but to what Deleuze calls the "singularly unanalytical conception of the mother as representative of nature and the father as sole principle and representative of culture and law" (*Masochism*, 63). The thrust of his argument is clear: a critique of the concept of symbolic order when it founds itself on the displacement of the real from a desire that can then only repeat its powerlessness vis-à-vis a paternal metaphor or transcendental signifier. This concept colludes in the abstraction that order instantiates rather than analyzes it.

15 Actually this form is articulated by Deleuze in a slightly more complicated manner. He divides the state of waiting into "two simultaneous currents," one of waiting for a deferred pleasure, the other of expectation for a pain that ensures the satisfaction of that pleasure: "The mas-

ochist waits for pleasure as something that is bound to be late, and expects pain as the condition that will finally ensure . . . the advent of pleasure. He therefore postpones pleasure in expectation of the pain which will make gratification possible" (71). This is how Deleuze underscores the resexualization that occurs in masochism: sexual pleasure is experienced in the empirical domain, although it seems to proceed from pain. This appearance is not "real," however, and pain (like guilt) has a theatrical being for the masochist, it plays a role, it appears only as an "effect," always subsumed in the masochist fantasy. Put another way, the masochist's pleasure proceeds not from pain but from repetition, which is independent of both pleasure and pain.

16 Pleasure attends the binding of excitation, so a pleasure in unbound, mobile energy flows can only be another kind of pleasure than that yielded by Freud's definition, even though, as Deleuze emphatically asserts, the masochist's pleasure in no way contradicts the pleasure principle. Desire in "Coldness and Cruelty" is independent of pleasure, *expressive* in the sense this means bound up with textual forms and discursive formulations. Deleuze is interested not in the elaboration of a descriptive theory yielding what desire "is" but in the way that desire appears as a nondiscursive limit of discourse and in discourses that achieve an adequate reflexivity about this limit. It should be noted that Deleuze's discursive shifting in "Coldness and Cruelty" between a psychoanalytic language invested in the truth of its claims about the subject and a more metadiscursive language of expression has not persuaded many critics, either when it seems as if he is making claims of an empirical kind or, conversely, when he is privileging cultural production in the more reflexive fashion I focus on here. My own sense is that Deleuze here is quite close to the "aesthetic of masochism" adumbrated by Leo Bersani in *The Freudian Body*, and in particular to that aesthetic's relation to the necessity of "theoretical fictions" that Bersani sees both in Freud's work and in his own reading of it.

17 I return in more detail to this anti-Oedipal problematic in chapter 5, but the basic contention is that repetition configures a ground, origin, unconscious, or real *immonde* (to use Lacan's phrase) that doubles itself, creates the unconscious of the unconscious, the origin of the origin, the reality of the real, which makes possible an apprehension of the social power encrypted in language and naturalized in psychoanalytic discourse. I should underscore that the terminological shift away from the register of lack in desire is not so much a criticism of Lacan—for whom not only unity but its loss is a retroactive illusion given by language to the subject—or of Berressem when he uses him, since the results of the latter's analyses lead in quite similar directions to my own. Still, the rhetorical emphasis on lack does slip easily enough from a description of distorted desire to the distortion of desire (a desire that in Deleuze's account tends precisely toward such a description).

18 Hayden White, in his essay "Writing in the Middle Voice," suggests (following Barthes) that all modernist writing is obsessional in the strict psychoanalytic sense: that is, characterized by a reflexive self-torture that is neither active nor passive. "So, in the case of obsessional neurosis," writes White, "neither the aim nor the content of a drive undergoes change. The *content* of the drive (hate) undergoes no change; the *aim* (to torture) remains active. The *object* of the drive is changed from something external to the subject to the subject's own ego, but without any payoff in pleasure of the kind that might be felt by either the masochist or the sadist" (184). The "middle voice," which Freud links to obsessional neurosis in "The Instincts and Their Vicissitudes," expresses a kind of transitivity in which the subject/object

distinction is negated. To write in the middle voice is to "place the writer-agent *within* the writing process and reveal the constitution of the subject-of-writing as the latent principle, aim, and purpose of all writing" (187). This concept suggests a provocative approach to understanding Pynchon's work in general, although unlike Deleuze's account of the perversions, White's essay refrains from a direct critique of the psychoanalytic "symmetries" that govern the theory (184), focusing instead on a moment of flexibility in Freud's own corpus.

19 Information is understood here in a more technical sense as it relates to entropy. Information is what can be known about a particular system, and the degree of possible information is measured by the degree of entropy in that system. The greater its complexity, the more possibilities (of arrangement, function, or structure) it has, the more entropic it can become. Maximum entropy is maximum possibility, but as a result any *one* form becomes more improbable, and the possibility of knowledge about the system thus diminishes. In information theory, the message restricts the number of possibilities within a range outside of which no information at all could be conveyed. The receiver must not know in advance what the content of the message is in order to receive it, but also must not be so saturated with possible choices (of content) that no probability of knowledge obtains. Entropy, then, in information theorist Claude Shannon's words, is "a probability distribution, assigning various probabilities to a set of possible messages . . . a measure of what the person receiving a message does *not* know about it before it arrives [and] an index of his uncertainty as to what to expect" (cited in Jeremy Campbell, *Grammatical Man*, 63). In the complex system of *Gravity's Rainbow*, you could say a degree of entropy obtains that both (1) maximizes possibility and minimizes communication and (2) underscores the structural necessity of entropy in meaning systems generally, exemplifying the constant negotiation or balance between absolute constraint (no information, no possibility, total certainty) and absolute freedom (all information, all possibility, total uncertainty). The "net of information" in the foregoing quotation signifies a modulation in the entropy index that ensures a level of uncertainty effectively rendering characters like Sachsa docile, and thus works in the service of social control. The complicity of the "medium" of expression in this docility is a subtext here, insofar as the episode exacerbates that modulation. At stake is a masochist strategy risking its co-optation by the forces of power in order to destabilize the myth of a transparent communication on which these same forces rely for ideological cover. Pynchon can thus be said to parody the intersection of information and capitalism precisely in this risk of complicity.

20 The cartel, being a conglomeration of different corporate entities under a single organization, is thus a whole to which all its subsidiaries are parts. It is this whole that Rathenau urges his auditors to "schizophrenize" or wrest from an explicitly nationalist form, in a premonition, perhaps, of the multinational corporate structure based, for instance, on "foreign direct investment" wherein, according to James Taggart in *The Pharmaceutical Industry*, "by locating in a foreign country, the multinational corporation extends itself to the new location in ways which go well beyond the mere transfer of capital. . . . technological and managerial skills are transferred to the host country and integrated with local factors of production. This often produces international trade flows *within* the corporate structure" (47, italics mine).

21 Deleuze: "The irony of sadism lies in the twofold operation whereby he necessarily projects his dissolved ego outward and as a result experiences what is outside him as his only ego. . . .

Irony is in fact the operation of an overbearing superego, the art of expelling or negating the ego, with all its sadistic consequences" (125). This projective evacuation of the ego outward is a good way of understanding the function of paranoia in the novel. In my reading, however, it seems less useful to focus on paranoia as the novel's predominant trope, attempting to radicalize its functions and render it "creative," for the reason that such a focus cannot account for the particular attributes of Pynchon's world. In the sadistic vortex of Pynchon's irony, no political will, hope, or redemption may indeed be possible, but in the suspended textual atmospheres of masochism, I think strategies of resistance can (and do) exist.

22 Most critics agree that the options of "creative paranoia," militant irony, or countercultural pranksterism associated with the Counterforce in the novel do not amount to anything like a political movement capable of overcoming the co-opting social power of "Them." Still, critics have taken pains to underscore an optimism in Pynchon linked to contingency, accident, randomness, Murphy's Law, or Godel's theorem. See Peter Cooper's *Signs and Symptoms* (especially the chapter "Pynchon's Solutions") and Molly Hite's *Ideas of Order* (her argument rests on the renovative possibilities of multiplicity and pluralism). Gabriele Schwab sees in the Counterforce's failure a "transcendence downward into a world of farcical insignificance" and "designifying potential" that she links to dadaist strategies of resistance to symbolic orders ("Creative Paranoia," in *Thomas Pynchon's "Gravity's Rainbow,"* 108). My own argument tends more in this semiotic direction, since it shies away from the kind of naturalist reading that looks in characters for models of behavior to be emulated in some extratextual world. Pynchon is thinking of countercultural resistance only in a mode of deviation and displacement, and it is this mode that instantiates its politics, or that *makes it countercultural*.

5 Docile Bodies and the Body without Organs

1 For Silverman, the masochist subversively "acts out" the process whereby subjects are constituted or "spoken" by the cultural symbolic, but this subversive acting out nonetheless occurs within the Oedipal matrix that expresses the cultural law. "Until our dominant fiction undergoes a radical metamorphosis, however, subjectivity will always carry the imprint of the family. And even in the event of such a metamorphosis, the subject will still be defined by lack and alterity. We can not, then, start from zero with subjectivity; we can only hope to negotiate a different psychic relation to the Laws of Language and Kinship Structure than that dictated by the dominant fiction" (213). This negotiation is a way to understand how a relation of "complicity" with dominant social forms might be relevant to cultural critique, although for Deleuze (and Deleuze and Guattari), it effectively closes down the possibility of subversion, since it expresses the subject's desire within the fiction or myth-structure that *itself* constitutes repression (this would be the register at which I attempt to use the word *complicity* or *implication*).

2 See the chapter of *Postmodernism* entitled "Space." Jameson links the subjective time-sense to a high modernist existentialism largely absent from later cultural artifacts, prompting him to posit a dissymetrical reversion of time into space as a feature of "postmodern" societies. This "antinomy" clearly informs a spatialized subject like Deleuze and Guattari's "schizo," as well as the various metaphors that cluster around it, such as that of a field, a multiplicity, the "law" of the identity of production and product, or, recalling the reading of *The Crying of Lot 49* in chapter 2, *nomadism* with its implication of an inclusive movement through uniform space. For

other examples of texts interested in this paradox of time as space see also Maurice Blanchot's *The Writing of the Disaster*, Guy Debord's *The Society of the Spectacle*, and Georges Bataille's *Accursed Share, Volume 1* (in particular the essay on general economy).

3. The language of "flows" in *Anti-Oedipus* is partly rooted in Freud's model of undifferentiated energy and the cathexes that form the instincts. But it may also be useful to think of this "matter" by analogy to a Kantian ideal or idea of reason, thus as unalloyed by any interest, end, or finality: that is, as suprasensible. For Deleuze and Guattari, I think, the virtue of such an analogy consists solely in the way it stresses the foundational nature of the flow as an "unconditioned condition" not given in experience, not organized or sexualized in any one particular form. Another correlate, then, would be the Deleuzian masochist's "realized ideal," or repetition in its relation to absolute negation, an "independent force" conditioning the pleasure principle, sexual difference, the subject's relation to the law, and so forth. What defines this suprasensible domain is the death drive not as a transcendental law but as its perversion. This perversion, you might say, *is the law* for desiring-production and the schizoid subject.

4. The temporal dynamic of the shift from feudalism to capitalism, unlike the sudden and synchronic reappearance of the despotic state, is diachronic for Deleuze and Guattari. Because the despotic machine actively repels the possibility of decoded flows, capitalism could only appear with the contingent event of a generalized decoding that combined decoded flows with a *desire for* decoding freed from its enmeshment in the "nets of the despotic State" (*Anti-Oedipus*, 224). This conjunction is contingent and implies a period of time in which to establish the "break" between the two social forms (a period of time, moreover, that capitalist culture continues more or less to live even today).

5. This conjunction represents a "schizoid time" insofar as it entails a mirroring relation between the despotic state and capitalism (*Anti-Oedipus*, 223). Where the *code* is central for the former, establishing between coded flows an "indirect" relation routed through the function of a transcendental signifier, the *axiomatic* of the latter establishes "direct" or economic relations between decoded flows. This inversion of the despotic code in the axiomatic inaugurates a diachronic time in which the former has a kind of reflective or simulacral being for the latter; the difference between them is only given in the operation of a "turn" where the simulacrum (of substance, meaning, desire, exchange) can properly appear. Time is schizoid because it is uniquely tropological, uniquely the time of a discursive or epistemic shift.

6. "Concerning capitalism, we maintain that it both does and does not have an exterior limit: it has an exterior limit that is schizophrenia, that is, the absolute decoding of flows, but it functions only by pushing and exorcising this limit. And it also has, yet does not have, interior limits: it has interior limits under the specific conditions of capitalist production and circulation, that is, in capital itself, but it functions only by reproducing and widening these limits on an always vaster scale" (*Anti-Oedipus*, 250).

7. I do not mean to suggest that this generality reflects on Deleuze and Guattari's scholarship or on the accuracy of their generalizations. They make their case in extraordinary detail, but even the use of detail is subordinate to what feels to me like a parodic quotation of myth, genesis stories, the poetic elaboration of an idiosyncratic language, syntax, form, and even the creation of a historical or cultural memory.

8. This history is elaborated in terms of different systems of representation proper to each social machine. In territorial representation, "graphism" is a generalized writing that "leaves the

voice dominant by being independent of [it]" (*Anti-Oedipus*, 203), marking signs on the body (of the earth) that "respond to the voice" but "do not align themselves on it" (202). Both the designating word and the designated thing are signs in a disequilibrium that a third element, the eye, the visual, resolves by "seeing" the sign "without reading it" (204). Writing has a purely designating function without containing the sign within an order of meaning—a function, it should be emphasized, in the service of "germinal intense repression" on which the primitive socius is based. With imperial or despotic representation, this graphism becomes writing in a narrower sense, aligned on the voice as a transcendent or fictitious substance that expresses itself only through a linearized writing (in books, for instance). The sign becomes a signifier and subordinates writing to a detached voice by way of establishing the priority of signification. This writing deterritorializes writing in general, rerouting a primitive desire through the desire of the despot (the transcendental signifier).

9 Berressem hinges his critical approach on a "topography" in *Gravity's Rainbow* of "'one-sided,' convoluted space" that is explicitly represented as a Möbius strip (*Pynchon's Poetics*, 121). This space internalizes the difference between inside and outside, but it also unfolds simultaneously in time, giving Berressem a means of writing simultaneously about subjectivity and textuality, culture and writing. His theoretical registers are numerous, but his focus is mostly on Lacanian models of the subject in relation to language and digitality, which he expertly deploys in his readings.

10 *Ecrits*, 534; quoted in Avital Ronell's *Crack Wars*.

11 For an analysis of shell shock, repetition compulsion, and the machinic dimensions of modernism, see Hal Foster's "Armor Fou," *October* 56, 65–97.

12 This project of the father to reduce everything to language—or rather to a single language—is what, for Derrida, Heidegger means by "metaphysics." Heidegger insists on it: 'metalinguistics' ... is the metaphysics of the 'technicalization integral to all languages'; it is intended to produced a 'single, both functional and interplanetary instrument of information.' 'Metasprache and Sputnik ... are the same.' " See also Heidegger's essay "The Nature of Language" in *On the Way to Language*, from which Derrida quotes.

13 Many critics have commented on the use of cinematic metaphors in Pynchon's work. Some, like David Marriott (see his article "Moviegoing"), rely on a distinction between the film image and a "reality" in which its ideological nature becomes clear. Others, like McHoul and Wills, collapse this distinction and see the filmic in specifically structural and textual terms. Berressem attempts to mediate between these two extremes in his work on the relations between language and culture in *Gravity's Rainbow*. Reviewing a tendency in film theory to distinguish the "analog" naturalism of film from the "digital" mediation of language, Berressem stresses the embedded relation of film in symbolic structure. "In language, the subject sinks into the voids between the signifiers; in film, it falls into the void between the single images on a reel" (*Pynchon's Poetics*, 156). The effect of persistence of vision is analogous to a "persistence of thought" that displaces both subjectivity and meaning onto a single and continuous plane of implication. Berressem then traces out this Möbius strip in the ways that Pynchon deploys cinematic metaphors and practices in *Gravity's Rainbow*. See the chapter "Text as Film—Film as Text" in *Pynchon's Poetics*. For an exhaustive analysis of these deployments in the novel, see also Charles Clerc's "Film in *Gravity's Rainbow*."

14 See Berubé's *Marginal Forces/Cultural Centers* for a cognate reading of the Franz/Ilse sequence

that grasps its critique of semantic or analogic structure. He reads the Franz/Ilse sequence for a "form of representation . . . which reassembles illusory lost (maternal, cultural) unities as a means to control and domination" (256). The suggestion is that Berubé finds in the text support for a reading of reading itself, which reveals in representation the deployments of social power. This comes through when he maintains that the price of Franz's believing Ilse to be the "same" girl from year to year was his inscription "within the structure of pornographic representation" (252), where representation *tout court* becomes pornographic.

15   For Derrida, paraphrasing Heidegger, the history of metaphysics corresponds to a forgetting of the question of Being, a "withdrawal" that also conditions concepts and metaphors in the literal and proper sense. The metaphysical concept of metaphor, that is, also constitutes or replicates a withdrawal of Being, which means that metaphysics as the ground or limit of metaphor are *also* a metaphor of metaphor. The narrow concept of metaphor must itself withdraw or become elusive to apprehend the quasi-metaphoric nature of what conditions it. "The so-called metaphysical discourse can only be exceeded (*dé bordé*), insofar as it corresponds to a withdrawal of Being, according to a withdrawal of metaphor as a metaphysical concept, according to a withdrawal of metaphysics, a withdrawal of the withdrawal of Being" ("The *Retrait* of Metaphor," 22). This doubling of "withdrawal" has the effect of underscoring its own metaphoricity in the mode of a "turn" that is, for Derrida, also a "re-turn." "If one wished that *withdrawal-of* be understood as a metaphor, this would be a curious inverting— one would say almost *catastrophic*, catastropical—metaphor: its end would be to state something new, something unheard of about the vehicle and not about the apparent subject of the trope. *Withdrawal-of-Being-or-of-metaphor* would be by way less of leading us to think Being or metaphor than the Being of the metaphor of *withdrawal*" (23). Such a catastrophic inverse doubling of the metaphor of withdrawal suggests its undesignatable or indeterminate being as a kind of shadow metaphysical language always brings with it, which "appears" only in the repetition here exemplified. "But as this withdrawal of the metaphoric leaves no place free for a discourse of the proper or the literal, it will have . . . the sense of a re-fold (*re-pli*), of what retreats like a wave on the shoreline, and of a re-turn (*re-tour*) of an overcharging repetition of a supplementary trait, of yet another metaphor, of a double trait (*re-trait*) of metaphor" (22). By redoubling metaphor, accelerating the supplementarity of language, the essential reticence of Being is respected, and it is this reticence that the Zone in *Gravity's Rainbow*, in my reading, comes to symbolize and enact.

16   Teresa de Lauretis persuasively argues for the limitations of a postmodern feminist discourse (in particular on cinema and spectatorship) that rests on the "optimistically silly notion of an unbounded mobility of identities" (*The Practice of Love*, 140). Such a notion presumes a universal, ungendered, and deracialized subject and equivocates the distinction between a private fantasizing subject and the historical or "technosocial" situation of that subject vis-à-vis cultural representations. Taking Judith Butler as one spokesperson for this approach, de Lauretis tracks in Butler's argument for pornography (against Andrew Dworkin in particular) an elision of the difference between pornography and fantasy. "In equating the pornographic text with the pornographic fantasy . . . [Butler] conflates fantasy with representation and disregards the different relations of production of fantasy that obtain for the subject in a private or analytic situation, on the one hand, and for the subject in a public context of representation, on the other" (146). Butler's interest in fantasy as providing the basis for a

critical and interpretive subjectivity capable of disrupting identity in the social domain assumes a single (textual) medium for fantasy, representation, and action that forecloses effective political identification. What makes de Lauretis's argument so compelling is her attempt to wrest fantasy from its private and imaginary delimitation in the analytic scene and open it to the social and historical "public" forces that always traverse it. The subject's oscillation "back and forth from the subjective dimension to the social" (125) gives de Lauretis a way of thinking about sexuality and gender that pays attention to the subject's disruptive but also disrupted relations to actual material conditions of production. It is significant, however, that she needs to retain the distinction not only between subjective and social but between imaginary and symbolic as well, to have this category of public fantasy work for her. She conceives of the social agent (lesbian, gay, or straight) in Oedipal terms, in other words, and thus accedes to the functions of castration and lack in the subject's constitution. The collapse of the social into the subjective that she calls "silly" entails a dehistoricization of the subject, and yet her critique needs to sustain the imaginary/symbolic split that, in Deleuze and Guattari's account for example, *itself dehistoricizes the subject*. De Lauretis's critique of the theoretical emphasis on multiple identities provides an important check on the tendency to valorize desire as polymorphously perverse or pre-Oedipal, but in so reading what theorists like Butler are doing, she also projects on them the very (psychoanalytic) distinction they are attempting to do without and presumes any such attempt to be fundamentally apolitical or universalist (this is, at any rate, an unfair reading of Butler's work). At issue in this debate is perhaps less the usefulness of psychoanalytic theory per se as how to use it, with what degree of (non)seriousness one suspends its scientific or descriptive claims and allows it to be what Leo Bersani (whom she quotes) calls a "passionate fiction." But it seems to me, following Deleuze and Guattari anyway, that this suspension and permission are what the emphasis on multiple identities can make possible, always understanding this emphasis within the discursive dispensation that makes it always a function of how one theorizes.

17 This dimension of the complex symbolism surrounding the Shekhinah in the Kabbalah links the figure to the feminine Sophia (or "Wisdom") in various Gnostic sects, a personification of the "fallible aspect of God" (Jonas, *The Gnostic Religion*, 176) whose passion or fall plunges her into an abyss of "divine degradation" (178). Scholem discusses this analogy in *Origins of the Kabbalah* in particular as it relates to what he calls the "double Shekhinah," which incarnates "God's presence" both "above and below," both as the uncreated primordial light and as its created counterpart filling the earth (179–80). This fission of the Shekhinah into (creating) mother and (created) daughter marks for Scholem a "fluctuation of terminology" in Kabbalist texts that bears on the situation of the primordial light in the cosmos: sometimes the Shekhinah stands for the primordial light itself, and sometimes for its "emanation" exiled in the lower world, or for its "reflection." As such, she is both visible and invisible, dwelling in the "form of light," associated with the moon and its phases. Sophia is also linked to the "moon-, mother-, and love-goddess of Near Eastern religion," according to Jonas, and forms an "ambiguous figure encompassing the whole scale from the . . . most spiritual to the utterly sensual" (177). She too divides into an unfallen form and its fallen emanation, often referred to by the appellation "Prunikos," or "Whore." The relation between upper and lower worlds is in both Jewish and Gnostic texts ultimately a problem of origins, and in particular of an origin that cannot be stipulated or determined rationally.

18 For a discussion of *gnosis* as an antirational and purely formal knowledge opposed to Greek conceptions of *theoria*, see Hans Jonas's *The Gnostic Religion*, 33.

19 The word "Anubis" derives from the ancient Egyptian verb "putrefy" and thus linked the god to the decomposing process. But in particular, Anubis presided over the ritual of mummification: by preserving the dead body, it was thought, the deceased spirit could be assured of rebirth in the Afterlife, which is one reason the jackal-headed god was often represented in black as a symbol not only for death but also for fertility, since in the ancient Egyptian's mind it suggested the silt of the Nile. See Hart, *A Dictionary of Egyptian Gods and Goddesses*, 20–25.

20 It is interesting to note that one of the roles fulfilled by Anubis was to preside over the Egyptian "weighing of the heart" ceremony. According to Hart, "He stands by the scales, sometimes adjusting the plumb of the balance, and is described as 'he who counts the hearts' . . . [and] as 'claimer of hearts' [he] frees the king from restrictions on earth in order for him to join the gods of the sky. Anubis guides those who have passed the rigorous test and whose hearts have been vindicated as honest toward the throne of Osiris" (25). His association with the "good heart" and with the scales of justice complicates Pynchon's use of Anubis in the novel in ways that parallel the "turn" I am attempting to describe here.

21 Pynchon literalizes this cybernetic possibility for control in the aromatic hetercyclic polymer Imipolex G, the substance that mysteriously stimulates Slothrop's sexual drive and that is *itself* susceptible to sexual stimulus (it has erectile tissue). As Berressem notes, this substance combines synthesized material with more natural benzene or aromatic rings and so "marks exactly the threshold between nature and simulation, by way of that between skin and plastics" (137). See "The Real Text" in *Pynchon's Poetics* for a strong reading of the metaphoric (and not so metaphoric) relation between plastics and interpellative social power in the novel.

22 These details were ferreted out by Weisenburger in *A Gravity's Rainbow Companion* (250–51).

23 Berressem's reading is considerably overdetermined by Lacanian, Derridean, Baudrillardian, and also de Manian theoretical categories that I have not touched on, and it must be said that its complexity clearly points to a similar kind of insight about the (ir)reality of language in Pynchon's text as I am suggesting here. In particular, his structuration of the unbreachable gap between language and a fundamentally nonsymbolizable "real" (held open in Pynchon's text by the asymptote of Zeno's Paradox) allows for an insistence of the real in the text that must nonetheless always be "interrupted" or absent (24). To encounter the (impossible) real would be, in Berressem's words, the "end of desire, the text, and, ironically, writing itself" (24) My own sense of the novel's end, however, is that in fact it marks the end of these things (desire, text, writing), which is to say it detonates what Berressem calls the "incessant desire to bridge th[e] void—the delta t—[that] defines the subject's fundamental relation to language" (24). If desire is as real as this detonation, it doesn't *seek* to achieve the closure of that void (absence or lack); it *is* this closure. It does not "lack its object," as Deleuze and Guattari put it. This, it seems to me, is the most uneasy *implication* of *Gravity's Rainbow* at its end.

24 My language here refers to Heidegger's essay "The Question Concerning Technology" in the volume of the same title.

25 See David Bohm's *Wholeness and the Implicate Order* for his notion of an "enfolded" and hologrammatic universe that presupposes an undifferentiated flow of energy as the ground for order in general. This underlying "undivided wholeness" implies "a *new order of fact*, i.e., the fact about the way in which modes of theoretical understanding and of observation and

instrumentation are related to each other" as different "phases of unfoldment" in an implicate order that also includes (as another phase) the object itself (144). These phases are holograms of the entire process, "projections of a common ground" conceived as a multidimensional reality (212). Bohm, needless to say, only presents *one* theory (popularized for the layperson) attempting to explain the physical world in terms that correspond to quantum mechanics, and he can hardly be said to "represent" modern physics as a whole. However, Bohm also factors this "partiality" into the account and indeed makes it emblematic of the theory itself: "Is this [implicate] ground the absolute end of everything? In our proposed views concerning the general nature of 'the totality of what is' we regard even this ground as a mere stage, in the sense that there could in principle be an infinity of further development beyond it. At any particular moment in this development each such set of views that may arise will constitute at most a *proposal*. It is not to be taken as an *assumption* about what the final truth is supposed to be, and still less as a *conclusion* concerning the nature of such truth. Rather, this proposal becomes itself an *active factor* in the totality of existence which includes ourselves as well as the objects of our thoughts and experimental investigations" (213). What is interesting about Bohm's stance here is that with it, one thing is indeed put forth as *conclusive*: the necessarily propositional nature of scientific research. That Bohm's pragmatism might actually be a model for scientific endeavor becomes clear once an exclusively mechanistic view of the universe is abandoned.

26 Cited in S. R. Hameroff's "Quantum Coherence in Microtubules" (99). This essay presents a summary of the work done in physics that suggests the presence of cognition in living cells—a proposition, it should be noted, that is according to Hameroff still largely speculative.

27 For an overview of the philosophical debate between a representationalist or realist understanding of science, on the one hand, and an antirepresentationalist, pragmatic understanding, on the other, see Richard Rorty's *Objectivity, Relativism, and Truth*. For a "Continental" view on the same debate that factors in what Rorty's liberalism cannot or will not address—a critique of postindustrial capitalism in an era of generalized communication—see Gianni Vattimo's *The Transparent Society*.

28 Heidegger is interested in how the "real" gets "set up" as "ready to hand," as material to be manipulated, as objectified and separable matter or energy to be used (and used up). "Man," he argues, accomplishes this "revealing" of the real but also "does not have control over unconcealment itself, in which at any given time the real shows itself or withdraws" (18). "Man" is always already "challenged to exploit the energies of nature," and only insofar as he is so challenged or so caught up in the very determination he also "accomplishes" can he experience his own freedom, his participation in history. This "complicity" in history needs to be grasped as that which premises both a forgetting of "man's" active "belonging" to the production of the real (as poiesis) and the recovery of this belonging in the "demiraculation" of a utilitarian world. The poetic capacity for "man," according to Heidegger, manifests itself most distinctly in this deconstructive operation.

29 Berressem, making a similar argument, points out how germane the V-2 is to any desire for escape from the death-in-life of the capitalist socius that the novel so relentlessly narrates. Its "speed brings about the destruction of the space in which operational control and power operate. By reversing cause and effect [i.e., in breaking the sound barrier], it renders the system's rational modes of protection useless" (*Pynchon's Poetics*, 193). But significantly,

Berressem sees this intrinsic relation between the Rocket and desire as negative, a "fatal choice" (195) between death-in-life and "real death." A basically tragic sense of that choice then grounds a discussion of utopian values ("love," "togetherness," connection) in the novel that index a humanist Pynchon at work even behind his relentless subversions of utopia (for Berressem, Pynchon is "both a fantastic and a humanist writer" [198]). My own reading brushes against the grain of this tragic sensibility (for absence and lack) in the novel to open out its commitment to a poeisis rigorously maintaining the social character of the subject, its hologrammic (or metonymic) relation to its world. The Rocket then signifies not a (passive) real death but an (active) mode of production, not the repression of desire by social forces but its capacity and strange positivity in the axiomatics of late capitalism.

6 Totality and the Repetition of Difference

1 See Edward Mendelson's review of *Vineland* in *The New Republic* for a ringing endorsement of this moralism in the novel.
2 Of course, the narrative of narrativity itself could be what Jameson means by the fundamental narrative dimension of human experience, only if that's the case, I see no (exclusive) difference between his dialectic and the "second-degree" theories that he distinguishes from it. This once again foregrounds the problematic nature of his construction of theory.

7 A Vigilant Folly

1 The term "scriptural economy" belongs to de Certeau, whose work on everyday life and its relation to writing I will be following here. I do not mean to reproduce a metaphysical distinction between speech and writing that presupposes for the former term an original value that has been lost in the process of intextuation. The problem, once a scriptural economy has been established, is that the orality that precedes it can only have the status of a meaning, can only be mediated through cognitive or semantic structures that manifest themselves in fact as idealizations of that sonority lost to writing. To "hear" what de Certeau calls the "sounds of the body" (*Practice*, 162) in a modern context means to recover their semiotic indeterminacy *within* texts, and this, I will argue, is what *Mason & Dixon* sets out to do.
2 The principal point in referring to a "form-matter" distinction at this juncture is not to underscore an *idealism* in Pynchon's text that subsumes ontology under the rubric of a fundamentally psychological perception (along the lines of Berkeley's *esse est percipi*). To say that the body in its materiality comes into "being" alongside its in-forming categorization signifies rather a *critique* of the rationalism that secures the body in a naturalized symbolic regime—it (or one) "is" a body only by first being intelligible as such, that is, determined, delimited, classified, categorized (as a species, a gender, a class, a racial identity, a worker, a father or mother, etc.). As I argue in chapter 3 with respect to *Gravity's Rainbow*, it is the self-evidence of this identification that demands to be thought in the text with respect to the body's reduction as thing (or what Heidegger calls "equipment," something available to be used and used up). To be a body, in other words, is to *have* a body, and it is the relay run from "being" through reason to a "having" that remains unanalyzed (as possession, as property, as the propriety of the self-identical subject endowed with volition) that Pynchon seeks quite literally to "un-earth."

3. By this designation is meant a society in which systems of control, be they technological, economic, political, or otherwise, take on a life of their own (become self-moving) and transform the subjects who manipulate them into manipulated "operators" in a fully functional technocratic order. As that order erodes the efficacy and meaning of the subject's will, one sees paradoxically its overvaluation in the concept of production itself. To grasp what a technocratic order means, one must therefore track this concept's transformation from an act of poeisis that embeds the producer (or artist/artisan) in a human context to a *labor* that on the contrary excises the producer from that context and isolates him or her in the mode (or monad) of an autonomous creative will. I follow here de Certeau's discussion of this transformation from the eighteenth century to the present. As artistic or artisanal *techniques* became detached from art itself in the form of *machines* that "do the work for you," he maintains, producers lost the objective determination of a *practice* and withdrew into a purely subjective knowledge or "*savoir-faire*." This intuitive know-how became the domain of a new kind of producer to whom *practice* reverted in newly technologized forms. The subject became an "engineer" equipped with a "taste," "tact," or "genius" that was simultaneously unconscious and "logical," original and automatic. Judgment in the Kantian sense (mediating a practical *art* that knows but does not reflect on what it does and a theoretical *science* that provides this obscure knowledge with a reflective language, however supplemental it might be) was the skill this new "engineer" had to offer, but at the cost of internalizing a technological relation to the means of production. The creative impulse (originality, genius) that inheres as a property of the subject presupposes this technicization even (perhaps especially) when it implies a denigration of knowledge that is self-conscious. This denigration paradoxically indexes the privilege of consciousness by founding the modern distinction between practice (art) and theory (science). De Certeau sees this practice/theory distinction as *heterological* in nature: know-how signifies the incorporated (and idealized) "other" of theory, that object of the "engineer's" theoretical knowledge that supports and authorizes it. See *The Practice of Everyday Life*, 61–76, for a fuller discussion of the relation between technology and practice since the eighteenth century. See also Giorgio Agamben's discussion of the priority a notion of will and creative impulse has maintained in Western culture since the Renaissance in chapter 7 of *The Man without Content*. Agamben points out that the concept of originality occurs historically at the same time as the artist/producer loses his or her embedded social role in traditional societies. The more displaced and irrelevant the artist becomes in modern societies, the more paradoxically his or her "genius" comes to be valued, leading to the kinds of stark contradictions we see today in art (for instance, a Campbell's soup can signed by Andy Warhol can be worth thousands of dollars).

4. By pure perception I mean to echo Merleau-Ponty's emphasis on a nonthetic or "pure description of phenomena prior to the objective world . . . giving us a glimpse of 'lived' depth, independently of any kind of geometry" (258). The anterior "depth" at which neither objects nor the I/eye has been posited becomes the enveloping or engrossing "situation" of the existential subject, who is grasped in terms of implication and motivation rather than production or causality. Phenomenal space for this subject "is neither an object, nor an act of unification on the subject's part; it can neither be observed, since it is presupposed in every observation, nor seen to emerge from a constituting operation, since it is of its essence that it already be constituted" (254). Even though phenomenal space, preobjective and prelogical, is

distinguished for Merleau-Ponty from being (nothing in it *is* or exists as determined), phenomena do have a "significance" that can be "recognized" if not "thematized." This nonthematic recognition—or a version of it linking its independence from a thetic order to the "being" of language—is what the designation "pure" perception is meant to convey here.

5   When Merleau-Ponty maintains that "geometrical space" is "temporal before being spatial," he means that its necessary precondition is the (no)thingness of an always passing present (or *nun*). "Things coexist in space because they are *present* to the same perceiving subject and enveloped in one and the same temporal wave. But the unity and individuality of each temporal wave is possible only if it is wedged in between the preceding and the following one, and if the same temporal pulsation which produced it still retains its predecessor and anticipates its successor. It is objective time which is made up of successive moments. The lived present holds a past and a future within its thickness. . . . We know of movement and a moving entity without being in any way aware of objective positions, as we know of an object at a distance and of its true size without any interpretation, and as we know every moment the place of an event in the thickness of our past without any express recollection" (275). What Merleau-Ponty calls a "lived present" in which knowledge happens without a rational knower (i.e., "only *with the help of* time," he writes) is understood here in a distinctly *catastrophic* or "catastropic" register: the lived present is never self-present or proper to itself and cannot secure even a phenomenological description from the slippages of meaning that index themselves in the *language* of its expression.

6   Apropos of the functions of the "frontier" and the "bridge" in the "story," de Certeau maintains that the "bewildering exteriority" accessed via the "bridging" of the frontier *causes* its conversion into an "alien element" previously arraigned (by this very process) in the interior. By virtue of a coming into contact with the outside, that is, the subject of narrative (the "traveler") "gives ob-jectivity . . . expression and re-presentation . . . to the alterity which was hidden inside the limits." As a result, his or her *departure* from the fold of the familiar ends with a *return* experienced as a discovery, in objectivized form, of the very exteriority sought beyond the frontier. "Within the frontiers, the alien is already there, an exoticism or sabbath of the memory, a disquieting familiarity. It is as though delimitation itself were the bridge that opens the inside to its other" (*Practice*, 128–29). By internal difference, then, I mean the incorporated "other" or limit that conditions this repetition and that constitutes the text's implicated relation to a colonialist history.

7   Marx identifies inversion as the principle mechanism of ideology, by which the latter represses materiality (in exchange value) and autonomizes things (commodities) in a naturalized imaginary field. Sarah Kofman analyzes the metaphoric instability of the terms Marx uses to elucidate this mechanism in her book *Camera Obscura*. Marx's desire to counterpose real social contradiction to its fantasmatic mythologization reveals its own ideological character in optical metaphors (ideology is a camera obscura, Plato's cave, a simulacrum) that presuppose a value in "clarity, light, transparency, truth, rationality" (14). For Kofman, the notion of inversion (or the inverted image on the camera obscura's screen) is the ideology of modernity itself, the means by which it legitimates its project to enlighten (or reinvert) the world by preemptively projecting that world as a dark or obscure place. In the process, she argues, modern humanity "forgets that transparency is itself a product of history" (18). Her deconstructive unveiling of the assumption that behind the veils of illusion and error lies the truth and not the

infinitely regressing veils of the unconscious mirrors the metaparodic dynamic I am attempting to substantiate in Pynchon's text. In both cases, the deployment of an infinite regress serves to historicize the epoch of modernity.

8 Both Descartes and Locke use the metaphor of a camera obscura to understand the mind's relation to the eye. If, as Kofman argues, the metaphor contains its own mystification, then it also structures perception in such a manner that the mystification itself cannot be seen. To look at looking is therefore to read the metaphor symptomatically and in the context of the modern sensibility these philosophers helped to inaugurate.

Conclusion

1 The an-archic origin of the origin constitutes the object of a repression by which, for Levinas, the subject—which he takes to be founded in the specific form of a phenomenological reduction—reproduces social power and abrogates an ethical relation to the other. The value placed in that reduction on an unmediated perception, and on a subjectivity transparent to itself as a *Cogito* or a transcendental ego—the value of our objective relation to the other—breaks down under the pressure of a history that now takes as its proper object the subject of history itself. Although the phenomenological notion of an intentional ego involves a further conception of nonintentional and nonobjectivizing states of duration, and thus bears within itself a pre-reflective or nonreflective consciousness irreducible to the will of the subject, Levinas insists that nonetheless, this immediate consciousness still presupposes a *representation* capable of "conversion" into "clear and distinct data" ("Ethics," 80). According to Levinas, anterior time or duration for the phenomenological subject is subordinated to the basically empirical act of perception rendering the object (and the object-world) *masterable*.

2 The best rubric for understanding this problem is the by now canonical Foucault-Habermas debate in the 1970s and 1980s. Habermas's reproach of Foucault (and poststructuralism generally) that he engages in a "totalizing" critique of modernity exposes the potential weakness of such concepts as, for example, a "biopower" so saturating and dispersed that it becomes invisible, incalculable, and hence nonexistent (if power is everywhere, then power is nowhere at the same time). The radicality of the concept then folds back into the very modernity it rejects, leaving one without either a clear critique or alternative. All that it manages to endorse is the various identity politics or weak countercultures that construe resistance in terms that focus on discursive rather than structural transformations of social order. The counterargument against Habermas's qualified embrace of modernity, that he assumes in the norms of dialectic critique the very problems he would redress, seems equally persuasive on the grounds that, with Habermas as well, one sees a folding back into modernity rather than a genuine contestation of its grievous excesses. My argument here has attempted to balance itself between the cogency of both sides to see the double bind or impasse the debate as a whole manifests. But I swerve rather decisively toward the poststructuralist camp with the considered sense that the symptomaticity of this double bind has in fact always been its point. Habermas's failure not only to see the necessary implication of his own discourse in the normativity Foucault excavated so beautifully but also to grasp the metadiscursive argument that accompanies this excavation seems to me a grievous limitation indeed. See Nancy Fraser's essay "Michel Foucault: A 'Young Conservative'?" for a good overview of the debate.

3 Agamben adverts explicitly to the metaphor in *Homo Sacer*, as here when he defines the relation between the exception and a state of nature: "The state of nature and the state of exception are nothing but two sides of a single topological process in which what was presupposed as external (the state of nature) now reappears, as in a Möbius strip or a Leyden jar, in the inside (as state of exception), and the sovereign power is this very impossibility of distinguishing between outside and inside, nature and exception, *physis* and *nomos*" (37).

4 For Agamben, this phrase echoes in a European context back through the two world wars to Nietzschean and Dostoyevskean evocations of a fundamentally arbitrary universe (Ivan Karamazov's "everything is permitted"). The phrase also had currency for the counterculture in America, signifying the optimism and transformative potential of the times. Todd Gitlin refers in *The Sixties* to the "divine premise that everything was possible" as the legitimating matrix of radical thought and action, an "unravelling, rethinking, refusing to take for granted, [and] thinking without limits" that informed the various movements he chronicles (7). Gitlin, at least in retrospect, also understands the darker implications on the freedom this phrase names, although not to the degree that those implications penetrate precisely what was most "divine" about it. The anarchic elements of the 1960s he analyzes tend always to be polarized over and against simultaneous but qualitatively distinct elements that instantiate the "good" version of events (the New Left over the counterculture, for example, or the New Left in touch with earlier populist traditions of political culture over the more nervy and doctrinaire factions that eventually did it in).

5 It is not my intention here to reach conclusions about the lasting practical consequences of micropolitics in America over the last half century—a topic that deserves careful investigation and debate. See Jameson's "Periodizing the Sixties" in his *Ideologies of Theory*, vol. 2, for a critical perspective that situates antihegemonic practices in relation to broader historical contexts. Michael Hardt and Antonio Negri speak to the limitations of localized struggle and identity politics in their book *Empire* (see particularly the chapter "Alternatives within Empire"). For an anecdotal indication of the tensions and paradoxes that shape identity politics today, see Jesse Jackson's book *It's about the Money*. It details the "Fourth Movement" of his Freedom Symphony, a historico-musical riff on the phases of the civil rights struggle. They are (1) emancipation from slavery; (2) movement to end legal apartheid; (3) the right to vote; and (4) the struggle for economic security and equal opportunity, glossed by Jackson in an *L.A. Times* article as "access to capital" (*L.A. Times*, 31 January 1999). For a suggestive (though again anecdotal) analysis of the complicated legacy left by the feminist movement, see Jane Gallop's *Feminist Accused of Sexual Harassment*. In her autobiographical account of sex harassment complaints filed against her at the University of Wisconsin, she argues that antidiscrimination laws passed in the late 1970s and early 1980s—arguably the most enduring legislative legacy of the feminist movement—have in their broadness (Gallop was eventually found guilty of "consensual amorous relations with a student" by university officials) become divorced from contexts of discrimination and applied on behalf of conservative social agendas to censor and police the open and free pursuit of knowledge, which she sees as necessarily traversed by transferential relations between students and teachers.

WORKS CITED

Agamben, Giorgio. *Homo Sacer.* Trans. Daniel Heller-Roazen. Stanford: Stanford University Press, 1998.
———. *The Man without Content.* Trans. Georgia Albert. Palo Alto: Stanford University Press, 1999.
Bachelard, Gaston. *The Poetics of Reverie.* Trans. Daniel Russell. Boston: Beacon Press, 1969.
Barthes, Roland. "The Discourse of History." In *Comparative Criticism: A Year Book,* ed. E. S. Schaffer, trans. S. Bann. Cambridge: Cambridge University Press, 1981.
Bataille, Georges. *Accursed Share,* Volume 1. Trans. R. Hurley. New York: Zone Books, 1988.
Baudrillard, Jean. *Fatal Strategies.* Trans. P. Beitchman and W. G. J. Niesluchowski. New York: Semiotext(e), 1990.
———. *For a Critique of the Political Economy of the Sign.* Trans. C. Levin. New York: Telos Press, 1981.
———. *Simulations.* Trans. P. Foss, P. Patton, and P. Beitchman. New York: Semiotext(e), 1983.
Bennett, David. "Parody, Postmodernism, and the Politics of Reading." *Critical Quarterly* 27, no. 4 (1985): 27–43.
Bercovitch, Sacvan. *The American Jeremiad.* Madison: University of Wisconsin Press, 1978.
Bernasconi, Robert. *The Question of Language in Heidegger's History of Being.* London: Macmillan, 1985.
Berressem, Hanjo. *Pynchon's Poetics.* Chicago: University of Illinois Press, 1993.
Bersani, Leo. *The Culture of Redemption.* Cambridge: Harvard University Press, 1990.
———. *The Freudian Body: Psychoanalysis and Art.* New York: Columbia University Press, 1986.
Berubé, Michael. *Marginal Forces/Cultural Centers.* Ithaca: Cornell University Press, 1992.
Blanchot, Maurice. *The Writing of the Disaster.* Trans. Ann Smock. Lincoln: University of Nebraska Press, 1995.
Bloom, Harold. *Kabbalah and Criticism.* Seabury Press: New York, 1975.
Bohm, David. *Wholeness and the Implicate Order.* London: Routledge, 1980.
Bourdieu, Pierre. *Language and Symbolic Power.* Trans. G. Raymond and M. Adamson. Cambridge: Harvard University Press, 1982.
———. *Pascalian Meditations.* Trans. Richard Nice. Stanford: Stanford University Press, 1999.
———. *The Political Ontology of Martin Heidegger.* Trans. P. Collier. Cambridge: Polity Press, 1991.
Butler, Judith. "The Force of Fantasy: Feminism, Mapplethorpe, and Discursive Excess." *Differences: A Journal of Feminist Cultural Studies* 2, no. 2 (1990): 105–25.
———. *The Psychic Life of Power.* Stanford: Stanford University Press, 1997.
Campbell, Jeremy. *Grammatical Man.* New York: Simon and Schuster, 1982.
Clerc, Charles. "Film in *Gravity's Rainbow.*" In *Approaches to "Gravity's Rainbow."* Columbus: Ohio State University Press, 1983.

Cooper, Peter L. *Signs and Symptoms: Thomas Pynchon and the Contemporary World*. Berkeley: University of California Press, 1983.
Darwin, Charles. *The Structure and Distribution of Coral Reefs*. New York: D. Appleton, 1889.
Debord, Guy. *The Society of Spectacle*. New York: Zone Books, 1994.
de Certeau, Michel. *The Practice of Everyday Life*. Trans. Steven Randall. Berkeley: University of California Press, 1984.
———. *The Writing of History*. Trans. Tom Conley. New York: Columbia University Press, 1988.
de Lauretis, Teresa. *Alice Doesn't*. Bloomington: Indiana University Press, 1984.
———. *The Practice of Love*. Bloomington: Indiana University Press, 1994.
Deleuze, Gilles. *Difference and Repetition*. Trans. P. Patton. New York: Columbia University Press, 1994.
———. *Masochism*. Trans. J. MacNeil. New York: Zone Books, 1991.
———. *Negotiations*. Trans. M. Joughin. New York: Columbia University Press, 1995.
———. *Nietzsche and Philosophy*. Trans. H. Tomlinson. New York: Columbia University Press, 1983.
Deleuze, Gilles, and Félix Guattari. *Anti-Oedipus*. Trans. R. Hurley, M. Seem, and H. Lane. Minneapolis: University of Minnesota Press, 1983.
———. *Kafka: Toward a Minor Literature*. Trans. D. Polan. Minneapolis: University of Minnesota Press, 1986.
———. *A Thousand Plateaus*. Trans. B. Massumi. Minneapolis: University of Minnesota Press, 1987.
de Man, Paul. *Blindness and Insight*. Minneapolis: University of Minnesota Press, 1971, 1983.
Derrida, Jacques. *Of Grammatology*. Trans. G. Spivak. Baltimore: Johns Hopkins University Press, 1974.
———. *The Postcard*. Trans. A. Bass. Chicago: University of Chicago Press, 1987.
———. "The Retrait of Metaphor." *Enclitic*, fall 1978.
———. *The Specters of Marx*. Trans. P. Kamuf. New York: Routledge, 1994.
———. *The Truth in Painting*. Trans. G. Bennington and I. McLeod. Chicago: University of Chicago Press, 1987.
Eddins, Dwight. "Paradigms Reclaimed: The Language of Silence in *Gravity's Rainbow*." *Markham Review* 12, no. 72 (1983).
Euben, Peter. *The Tragedy of Political Theory*. Princeton: Princeton University Press, 1990.
Ewen, Stuart. *All Consuming Images*. New York: Basic Books, 1988.
———. *Captains of Consciousness*. New York: McGraw, 1976.
Foster, Hal. "Armor Fou." *October* 56.
Foucault, Michel. *The Order of Things*. New York: Random House, 1970.
Fraser, Nancy. "Michel Foucault: A 'Young Conservative?'" In *Feminist Interpretations of Michel Foucault*, ed. Susan J. Hekman. New York: Routledge, 1996.
Freud, Sigmund. *Beyond the Pleasure Principle*. Trans. J. Strachey. New York: W. W. Norton, 1961.
Gallop, Jane. *Feminist Accused of Sexual Harassment*. Durham, N.C.: Duke University Press, 1997.
Gitlin, Todd. *The Sixties: Years of Hope, Days of Rage*. New York: Bantam, 1993.
Godfrey, Tony. *Conceptual Art*. London: Phaidon, 1998.
Hameroff, S. R. "Quantum Coherence in Microtubules." *Journal of Consciousness Studies* 1, no. 1 (1994).
Handelman, Susan. *The Slayers of Moses*. Albany: SUNY Press, 1982.
Hardt, Michael, and Antonio Negri. *Empire*. Boston: Harvard University Press, 2000.

Hart, George. *A Dictionary of Egyptian Gods and Goddesses*. Boston: Routledge, 1986.
Hayles, N. Katherine. "Caught in the Web: Cosmology and the Point of (No) Return in Pynchon's *Gravity's Rainbow*." In *The Cosmic Web: Scientific Field Models and Literary Strategies in the Twentieth Century*. Ithaca: Cornell University Press, 1984.
Heidegger, Martin. *The End of Philosophy*. Trans. J. Stambaugh. New York: Harper and Row, 1973.
——. *On the Way to Language*. Trans. P. Hertz. New York: Harper and Row, 1971.
——. "On the Origin of the Work of Art." In *Poetry, Language, Thought*. Trans. A. Hofstadter. San Francisco: Harper and Row, 1971.
——. *The Question concerning Technology*. Trans. William Lovitt. New York: Harper and Row, 1977.
Hendin, Josephine. "What Is Thomas Pynchon Telling Us?" In *Thomas Pynchon*, ed. Harold Bloom, 37–46. New York: Chelsea House Publications, 1986.
Hite, Molly. *Ideas of Order in the Novels of Thomas Pynchon*. Columbus: Ohio State University Press, 1983.
Jackson, Jesse, Sr., and Jesse Jackson Jr. *It's about the Money*. New York: Crown Books, 2002.
Jameson, Fredric. *Ideologies of Theory: Essays 1971–1986*, Vol. 2. Minneapolis: University of Minnesota Press, 1988.
——. *The Political Unconscious*. Cornell: Cornell University Press, 1981.
——. *Postmodernism*. Durham: Duke University Press, 1991.
——. *The Seeds of Time*. New York: Columbia University Press, 1994.
Jonas, Hans. *The Gnostic Religion*. Boston: Beacon Press, 1963.
Kaplan, Janet. *Unexpected Journeys: The Art and Life of Remedios Varo*. New York: Abbeville Press, 1988.
Klinkowitz, Jerome. *The Self-Apparent Word: Fiction as Language/Language as Fiction*. Carbondale: Southern Illinois University Press, 1984.
Kofman, Sarah. *Camera Obscura*. Trans. Will Straw. Ithaca: Cornell University Press, 1999.
Lane, Anthony. "Then, Voyager." *New Yorker*, 12 May 1997, 97–100.
Lefebvre, Henri. *Everyday Life in the Modern World*. Trans. S. Rabinovitch. London: Penguin Press, 1971.
——. *The Production of Space*. Trans. D. Nicholson-Smith. Oxford: Blackwell, 1991.
Levinas, Emmanuel. "Ethics as First Philosophy." In *The Levinas Reader*, ed. S. Hand. Oxford: Blackwell, 1989.
——. *Otherwise than Being*. Trans. Alphonso Lingis. Pittsburgh: Duquesne University Press, 1998.
Lury, Celia. *Consumer Culture*. New Brunswick, N.J.: Rutgers University Press, 1996.
Lyotard, Jean-François. *Libidinal Economy*. Trans. I. H. Grant. Bloomington: Indiana University Press, 1993.
Mackey, Louis. "Paranoia, Pynchon, and Preterition." In *Thomas Pynchon's "Gravity's Rainbow,"* ed. Harold Bloom, 53–68. New York: Chelsea House Publications, 1986.
Marriott, David. "Moviegoing." *Pynchon Notes* 16 (1985): 46–77.
Marx, Karl. "Alienated Labor." In *The Portable Marx*, ed. E. Kamenka. New York: Penguin, 1983.
McHale, Brian. *Postmodernism*. New York: Methuen, 1987.
McHoul, Alec, and Wills, David. *Writing Pynchon*. Urbana: University of Illinois Press, 1993.
Mendelson, Edward. Introduction to *Pynchon: A Collection of Critical Essays*, ed. E. Mendelson. New York: Prentice-Hall, 1978.
——. "Levity's Rainbow." Review of *Vineland*. *New Republic*, 6 July 1990.

Merleau-Ponty, Maurice. *The Phenomenology of Perception*. Trans. Colin Smith. New York: Routledge, 1962.

Michaux, Henri. *The Major Ordeals of the Mind*. Trans. R. Howard. New York: Harcourt, Brace, Jovanovich, 1974.

Morris, Robert. "Three Folds in the Fabric and Four Autobiographical Asides as Allegories (or Interruptions)." *Art in America*, November 1989.

Nancy, Jean-Luc. *The Experience of Freedom*. Trans. B. McDonald. Stanford: Stanford University Press, 1993.

Pynchon, Thomas. *The Crying of Lot 49*. New York: Perennial Fiction, 1966.

———. *Gravity's Rainbow*. New York: Penguin Books, 1973.

———. *Slow Learner*. Boston: Little, Brown, 1984.

———. *V*. New York: Bantam Books, 1963.

Quilligan, Maureen. "Thomas Pynchon and the Language of Allegory." In *Thomas Pynchon*, ed. Harold Bloom, 111–17. New York: Chelsea House Publications, 1986.

Raskin, Jonah. *For the Hell of It: The Life and Times of Abbie Hoffman*. Berkeley: University of California Press, 1996.

Ronell, Avital. *Crack Wars*. Lincoln: University of Nebraska Press, 1991.

Rorty, Richard. *Objectivity, Relativism, and Truth*. Cambridge: Cambridge University Press, 1991.

Roszak, Theodore. *The Making of a Counterculture*. Berkeley: University of California Press, 1968.

Schaub, Thomas. *Pynchon: The Voice of Ambiguity*. Chicago: University of Illinois Press, 1981.

Scholem, Gershom. *Origins of the Kabbalah*. Princeton: Princeton University Press, 1962.

———. *Trends in Jewish Mysticism*. New York: Beacon Press, 1958.

Schwab, Gabriele. "Creative Paranoia and Frost Patterns of White Words." In *Thomas Pynchon's "Gravity's Rainbow,"* ed. Harold Bloom, 97–112. New York: Chelsea House Publications, 1986.

Silverman, Kaja. *Male Subjectivity at the Margins*. New York: Routledge, 1992.

Smithson, Robert. *The Collected Writings*. Ed. Jack Flam. Berkeley: University of California Press, 1996.

Taggart, James. *The Pharmaceutical Industry*. London: Routledge, 1993.

Vattimo, Gianni. *The Transparent Society*. Baltimore: Johns Hopkins University.

Weisenburger, Steven. "The End of History? Thomas Pynchon and the Uses of the Past." *Twentieth Century Literature* 25, no. 54 (1979).

———. *A Gravity's Rainbow Companion*. Athens: University of Georgia Press, 1988.

Werner, Craig Hansen. "Recognizing Reality/Realizing Responsibility." In *Thomas Pynchon's "Gravity's Rainbow,"* ed. Harold Bloom, 85–96. New York: Chelsea House Publications, 1986.

White, Hayden. "Writing in the Middle Voice." *Stanford Literature Review*, fall 1992.

Woolf, Virginia. *A Room of One's Own*. New York: Harcourt, Brace, 1957.

Woronov, Mary. *Swimming Underground*. Boston: Journey Editions, 1994.

INDEX

Abstract Line, 54, 57, 79, 258 nn.8, 9
Addiction, 107, 154–55, 177, 179, 191, 207
Agamben, Giorgio, 249–50, 256 n.4, 262 n.1
Althusser, Louis, 216

Bachelard, Gaston, 5–7, 9
Barthes, Roland, 30–31
Baudelaire, Charles, 41
Baudrillard, Jean, 15, 23–24, 75–77, 102, 144, 196, 205–6, 246
Bercovitch, Sacvan, 8, 86–87
Berressem, Hanjo, 121, 196–97, 257 n.3, 275 n.13, 278 n.23, 279 n.29
Bersani, Leo, 66, 68, 267 n.20
Berubé, Michael, 264 n.9, 266 n.17, 268 n.2, 275 n.14
Blake, William, 2
Bloom, Harold, 122
Body without Organs, 9, 13, 36–37, 45, 139–46, 177, 181, 194
Bohm, David, 278 n.25
Bourdieu, Pierre, 7–8, 68–69
Broken Machines, 13, 19, 37–38, 45, 49, 62, 67, 72, 146, 170, 184, 186, 196, 204
Brown, Norman O., 45, 73, 224
Butler, Judith, 173, 210, 248, 276 n.16

Copeland, Johnny, 221
Counterculture, 1–11, 14, 16, 45, 64–69, 77, 139, 208, 211, 220–21, 226–30, 250–53

Darwin, Charles, 257 n.4
De Certeau, Michel, 21, 232, 238–39, 241, 243, 255 n.13
De Lauretis, Teresa, 33–35, 276 n.16

Deleuze, Gilles, 11, 16, 58, 66, 116–22, 129–30, 133–34, 151–52, 218–19
Delirium, 1–2, 9, 69, 121, 141, 143–44, 150, 152, 156, 160, 164, 177, 179, 193–94, 207, 216
Derrida, Jacques, 78, 83–84, 159–60, 171, 262 n.2
Desiring Machines, 10, 13, 36–37, 49, 140, 144
Desiring-Production, 10, 13, 36–37, 72, 143–47, 199, 202
Deterritorialization, 37, 123, 138, 142, 146, 181, 194, 196
Dickinson, Emily, 70, 79

Ekphrasis, 13, 45–46, 50, 62, 92
Empty Form, 5, 11–12, 20, 58, 60, 62–64, 66, 208
Entropy, 13, 19, 45, 49, 72, 90–91, 186, 204–5, 208, 212–13, 217, 220, 225, 229–30
Escape, 1–2, 4–5, 13, 18, 44–45, 47, 50–58, 60–63, 105–6, 182–83, 185, 188, 194, 225, 251
Euben, Peter, 260 n.16
Exception (State of), 249–51

Foucault, Michel, 10–11, 211, 283 n.2
Fox, James, 250–51
Frankenheimer, John, 44
Freud, Sigmund, 16, 113–21, 155

Gallop, Jane, 284 n.5
Gitlin, Todd, 65, 252
Gravity, 8, 19, 49, 60, 70–72, 135, 192–93, 197, 200
Guattari, Félix, 9–10, 16–17, 36–38, 45, 49, 55–56, 67, 71–72, 134–51, 173, 195, 197–99, 202–3

Habermas, Jürgen, 283 n.2
Hardt, Michael, 69, 284 n.5
Hegel, G. W. F., 269 n.6
Heidegger, Martin, 4, 19, 71, 84, 195, 199, 203, 207, 209
Heller, Joseph, 44
Helmslev, Louis, 12
Hite, Molly, 266 n.13
Hoffman, Abbie, 6–7
Hologram, 17, 19, 44, 47, 52, 69, 95, 98
Hysteron proteron, 83

Implication, 4, 10, 12–14, 17, 18–19, 21, 41, 43, 58, 68–69, 81, 89, 172, 179, 189, 196, 208–11, 214, 217–22, 224, 226, 229–33, 237, 239–40, 243–44, 248; as implicate order, 278 n.25; as involution, 67–68
Innocence, 3, 18, 168, 173–75, 185, 190–91
Internal Difference, 18, 55–57, 137, 139, 214, 217, 219

Jackson, Jesse, 284 n.5
Jagger, Mick, 250–51
Jameson, Fredric, 3–4, 20, 39–40, 137, 211, 213–19, 255 n.3
Jardine, Alice, 33

Kafka, Franz, 71–72
Kant, Immanuel, 258 n.8
Kierkegaard, Søren, 246
Kleinbottle, 244
Klossowski, Pierre, 121, 195–96, 198
Kofman, Sarah, 282 n.7, 283 n.8
"Kynicism," 252

Lacan, Jacques, 154, 257 n.3
Lefebvre, Henri, 4
Lennon, John, 95
Levinas, Emmanuel, 247–48
Lyotard, Jean-Francois, 264 n.6, 269 n.5

Mackey, Louis, 266 n.16
Marx, Karl, 257 n.2
Masochism, 8, 45, 64, 113, 116–22, 127–30, 133–34, 151–53

McHoul, Alec, 24, 33–34, 78, 81, 275 n.13
Merleau-Ponty, Maurice, 21, 236–37
Metalanguage, 4–5, 18–19, 137, 159, 161, 170, 208–9, 223, 226, 232, 235, 247
Michaux, Henri, 29
Miraculation, 37, 143, 150
Möbius strip, 81, 152, 236, 249, 251

Nabokov, Vladimir, 44
Nancy, Jean-Luc, 259 n.13
Negri, Antonio, 69, 284 n.5
Nietzsche, Friedrich, 40, 142
Nomadism, 37, 55–56, 71
Nostalgia, 74, 96, 83, 184

Parody, 12, 15, 20, 24, 26, 28–31, 34–35, 37–38, 61, 64, 72–73, 76–78, 85–86, 88, 91, 101–3, 138, 143–44, 150–51, 160, 186, 190, 232, 240, 242; as metaparody, 12, 16, 39–40, 43, 78, 81, 84, 101–3, 244
Performance (film), 250–51
Poeisis, 7, 9, 198–99, 203, 230
Pop Art, 43
Preterition, 2–3, 10–11, 14, 17–19, 63, 81, 86, 90, 97, 124–25, 162, 175, 187–89, 211, 220, 231, 250

Quilligan, Maureen, 266 n.13

Repetition, 1, 11, 44, 50–53, 58, 60–62, 115–21, 127–31, 134, 138, 155, 164, 179, 207, 219, 221, 227, 229
Reverie, 5–7, 9–10, 45, 77, 208, 230
Roeg, Nicholas, 250–51
Rorty, Richard, 199
Roszak, Theodore, 3, 5
Russell, Ken, 208

Sacher-Masoch, Leopold von, 118
Schizophrenia, 10, 18, 29, 37, 39, 48, 52, 63, 67–69, 79, 98, 126, 137–38, 140–42, 147, 150–53, 172, 180
Scholem, Gershom, 174, 277 n.12
Seconds (film), 44
Silverman, Kaja, 133–34

Index

Singularity, 11, 16, 19, 45, 56, 194, 200–203, 206, 259 n.13
Smithson, Robert, 207–9
Symbolic Exchange, 76, 102, 111, 144, 146, 269 n.5

Theory, 13, 20, 68–69, 142, 144–45, 209–15, 218, 223, 228, 229
Tommy (film), 208
Townsend, Pete, 208
Trace, 83–84
Turn (Linguistic), 10–11, 15, 71, 84–85, 88, 130, 145, 160, 171, 211, 239

Utopia, 7–8, 20, 219

Varo, Remedios, 13, 46, 48, 50–56

Weisenburger, Steven, 168
White, Hayden, 271 n.17
Wills, David, 24, 33–34, 78, 81, 275 n.13
Woolf, Virginia, 26
Writing, 1, 5, 10, 12, 16–17, 19, 26, 56, 70–72, 76–79, 83–84, 91, 97–98, 121–23, 127–29, 134, 138, 142–43, 147–48, 170, 177, 196, 223, 235, 243, 247

Stefan Mattessich is Professor of English at Santa Monica College.

Library of Congress Cataloging-in-Publication Data
Mattessich, Stefan.
Lines of flight : discursive time and countercultural desire
in the work of Thomas Pynchon / Stefan Mattessich.
p. cm. — (Post-contemporary interventions)
Includes bibliographical references and index.
ISBN 0-8223-2979-4 (cloth   )
— ISBN 0-8223-2994-8 (pbk.   )
1. Pynchon, Thomas—Criticism and interpretation.
2. Counterculture—United States. 3. Desire in literature. 4. Escape
in literature. 5. Time in literature. I. Title. II. Series.
PS3566.Y55 Z698 2002   813'.54—dc21   2002006330

www.ingramcontent.com/pod-product-compliance
Lightning Source LLC
Chambersburg PA
CBHW070754230426
43665CB00017B/2358